Selected Letters of John Jay
and Sarah Livingston Jay

Calais 12 Octr. 1783

Dear Sally

I arrived here between eleven and twelve last night without being at all the worse for the Journey, tho travelling at night diminishd. my usual Quantity of Sleep, or rather of Lying a Bed; for I have long been a Stranger to what is called a nights Sleep.

The Inns on this Road are bad, and yet I have not been plagued with Bugs – I was told by two or three Landladies that there were no Bugs in this part of France, and my Man says it may very well be, for that there are none in Flanders, which is not far off – This is a singular Fact, and I wish to ascertain it –

The Weather is fine, and I shall probably have an agreable Passage to Dover, from whence I shall again write to you, unless I should arrive in Time to set out for London before tomorrow. — My Compts. to the Houshold of Passy – Kiss our sweet little Girls for me, and continue assured of the affection of your faithful

John Jay —

Mrs. S. Jay —

Selected Letters of John Jay and Sarah Livingston Jay

Correspondence by or to the First Chief Justice of the United States and His Wife

JOHN JAY AND SARAH LIVINGSTON JAY

Compiled and edited by Landa M. Freeman, Louise V. North *and* Janet M. Wedge

McFarland & Company, Inc., Publishers
Jefferson, North Carolina, and London

Frontispiece: A letter from John Jay to Sarah Jay, 12 October 1783 (John Jay Homestead State Historic Site, New York State Office of Parks, Recreation and Historic Preservation, JJ.1986.23)

The present work is a reprint of the illustrated case bound edition of Selected Letters of John Jay and Sarah Livingston Jay: Correspondence by or to the First Chief Justice of the United States and His Wife, *first published in 2005 by McFarland.*

LIBRARY OF CONGRESS CATALOGUING-IN-PUBLICATION DATA

Jay, John, 1745–1829.
[Correspondence. Selections]
Selected letters of John Jay and Sarah Livingston Jay : correspondence by or to the first chief justice of the United States and his wife / John Jay and Sarah Livingston Jay / compiled and edited by Landa M. Freeman, Louise V. North and Janet M. Wedge.
p. cm.
Includes bibliographical references and index.

ISBN 978-0-7864-4504-2 (softcover : 50# alkaline paper) 

1. Jay, John, 1745–1829 — Correspondence. 2. Jay, Sarah Livingston — Correspondence. 3. Statesmen — United States— Correspondence. 4. Judges— United States— Correspondence. 5. Statesmen's spouses— United States— Correspondence. I. Freeman, Landa M., 1937– II. Jay, Sarah Livingston. III. North, Louise V. IV. Wedge, Janet M. V. Title.
E302.6.J4A4 2010 973.3'092 — dc22 2004020167

British Library cataloguing data are available

©2005 Landa M. Freeman, Louise V. North and Janet M. Wedge.
All rights reserved

No part of this book may be reproduced or transmitted in any form or by any means, electronic or mechanical, including photocopying or recording, or by any information storage and retrieval system, without permission in writing from the publisher.

Front cover: Portrait of John Jay (Gilbert Stuart c. 1784), JJ.1999.2; portrait of Sarah Livingston Jay (Daniel Huntington, after Alexandre Roslin miniature of 1783) JJ.1983.7; both courtesy John Jay Homestead State Historic Site, New York State Office of Parks, Recreation and Historic Preservation.
Back cover: Wax seal with the Jay motto, *Deo Duce Perseverandum* ("God leading we must persevere")

Manufactured in the United States of America

McFarland & Company, Inc., Publishers
Box 611, Jefferson, North Carolina 28640
www.mcfarlandpub.com

For Julia Warger ...
who started us on our journey. It was her vision to explore
the Jay Papers at Columbia University for the purpose of
enriching the interpretation of Jay family life at the
John Jay Homestead State Historic Site in Katonah, New York.
Once embarked upon that task, we became so
enchanted with the Jays we conceived of this book.

Contents

Acknowledgments

Our encounters with John and Sarah Livingston Jay, their families, and their friends over the last five years have been an exhilarating adventure. Along the way, we have been encouraged and supported by many people. We are deeply grateful to them all.

We greatly appreciate the friendly and professional guidance from the staff of the Rare Book and Manuscript Library, Columbia University: Director Jean Ashton, Curators Bernard Crystal, Tanya Chebotarev, and Jane Siegel, and Jennifer B. Lee, Public Services and Programs. Our heartfelt thanks are especially extended to Kevin Connell and the late Henry Rowen, whose expertise and friendly advice have been invaluable. While at Columbia, where we were known as "the Jay Ladies," we were privileged to meet other Jay scholars: Frank W. Brecher, Professor David Gellman, and Walter B. Stahr. In their willingness to share their knowledge and enthusiasms with us, we were very fortunate.

We also were happy in the kind assistance we received from Jennifer Plick and the loyal volunteers at the John Jay Homestead in Katonah, New York; Jan Horton, independent researcher; Erica Schilling Hunningher, editor in London, England; Alison Beall of the Marshlands Conservancy in Rye, New York; Susan and Henry H. Livingston III at Oak Hill; Arthur W. Schwartz at Sedgwick House; Laura Levine at Liberty Hall; Virginia B. Bowers, historian of Albany, New York; Marjorie B. Burress, historian of North Bend, Ohio; Virginia T. Mosley, historian of Tenafly, New Jersey; Barbara Allen, curator of the Massachusetts Historical Collection at Stockbridge, Massachusetts; Bruce Fullem, site manager, Steven Oakes and Allan Weinreb at the John Jay Homestead; Dr. Janet Asteroff, independent scholar and photographer; Rachel Onuf, archivist of the Historical Society of Pennsylvania MSS. Collection; and Angela A. Mattia, former collections access assistant at the Museum of the City of New York.

Many thanks go to the New-York Historical Society; the Gilder Lehrman Collection, the Gilder Lehrman Institute of American History, New York; the Pierpont Morgan Library; the Huntington Library, San Marino, California; the Massachusetts Historical Society; the Museum of the City of New York; the New York Public Library; the New York State Library/Manuscripts and Special Collections at Albany; the New York State Office of Parks, Recreation and Historic Preservation; Kenneth W. Rendell Inc.; the Westchester Historical Society; and the Wisconsin Historical Society for their help and permission to use letters in their collections.

We are grateful to our husbands— Jefferson Freeman, James H. North, and Nicholas Wedge — who encouraged us to persevere. We would not have succeeded without their advice, assistance, and support.

Preface

Who was John Jay? Some may recall that he was the first chief justice of the United States; others may remember him as the diplomat responsible for the treaty with Britain in 1794 that bears his name. But he was much more important than these two facts indicate. Quite simply he was one of the central figures in winning independence for his country and establishing it as a nation.

John Jay, of French Huguenot and Dutch ancestry, was born in New York City in 1745, the eighth child of Peter Jay and Mary Van Cortlandt. He grew up on a farm in Rye, New York, to which his father moved the family to escape the epidemics that periodically ravaged the city. John was educated at home, for a time attended a Huguenot school in New Rochelle, and then was tutored to prepare him for entrance to King's College, now Columbia. After graduation he clerked in Benjamin Kissam's law office and prepared for the bar. Upon becoming a lawyer he established a practice with his classmate and friend Robert R. Livingston, Jr., and set about making a name for himself. He married Sarah Van Brugh Livingston in 1774.

Jay's life, like those of thousands of other Americans, was radically changed by events presaging the American Revolution. Deeply concerned on a moral and legal level by Britain's abuses of power and by what Jay perceived as an attempt to deprive Americans of their rights, he became involved in politics. As a delegate to the First Continental Congress he was a leader of the group that protested British policy by petitioning for redress of grievances, all the while hoping for reconciliation. When the Declaration of Independence was adopted, however, he cast his lot with the Patriots.

Thereafter he was unwavering in his support for the American cause. He helped craft a constitution for New York and was designated its chief justice. A delegate to the Second Continental Congress, he also served as its president. In 1779 he was sent by Congress to Spain to secure aid for the United States and then to Paris, where as a peace commissioner he played an important role, perhaps the most important one, in negotiating the treaty that brought an end to the Revolution in 1783. On his return to the United States he served as secretary for foreign affairs, arguably the most influential position in the government under the Articles of Confederation.

When a new federal constitution was proposed, Jay worked tirelessly for its ratification; he was an author of the *Federalist Papers*, along with Alexander Hamilton and James Madison. Once the Constitution took effect and a government was formed, President George Washington appointed John Jay chief justice of the United States Supreme Court. His service in this position was interrupted in 1794 when the president asked him to go to England to seek resolution of issues that threatened to precipitate another war. Jay reached an agreement with Britain — known as the Jay Treaty — that generated enormous controversy in the United States, although it accomplished the directive that he had been given by Washington: to prevent a war which America was not prepared to fight.

Returning to the United States in 1795, John Jay resigned from the Supreme Court when he found he had been elected governor of New York State, a position he filled for two three-year terms. When Jay retired in 1801 to his Bedford farm in Westchester County, he was only 56 years old. Sadly, his beloved wife died the next year, leaving her husband to raise their two youngest children. John Jay lived quietly in retirement for 28 years, supervising the farm and continuing, if only from a distance, to support the causes that interested him: the manumission of slaves, the improvement of agriculture and the missionary work of the American Bible Society.

John Jay's contribution to the establishment of the United States warrants his being called a Founding Father. He has, however, yet to be acknowledged as such. There have been relatively few books about him: the most recent scholarly biography was published in 1935 by Yale historian Frank Monaghan. The acknowledged expert on John Jay was Columbia University's Richard B. Morris, who wrote books and articles on aspects of Jay's career and, most importantly, edited and published two volumes of a projected multi-volume series of selected Jay correspondence. Unfortunately, Morris died before he could complete this work. Recent renewed interest in the revolutionary generation will certainly result in new works about Jay and a reassessment of his significance.

If John Jay the public man has received too little attention, the private man has received even less. This book, *Selected Letters of John Jay and Sarah Livingston Jay*, specifically addresses this problem. It breaks new ground by focusing on the flesh-and-blood man: John Jay as son, brother, friend, and father, and as husband to the love of his life, Sarah Van Brugh Livingston.

Sarah was the daughter of William Livingston and Susannah French. Born in New York City in 1756, she grew up in a politically charged household. Her father was a member of the prominent New York Livingston family and a leader of the New York bar. In the 1770s he moved his large family to Elizabeth Town, New Jersey. A staunch supporter of the Patriot cause during the Revolution, Livingston served in the Continental Congresses, was elected the first governor of the state of New Jersey — a position he retained until his death in 1790 — and was a delegate to the Constitutional Convention.

Educated at home, Sarah learned French and studied the classics as well as the Bible. Petite, attractive, accomplished, she was a welcome addition to the New York social scene and much sought after by eligible young men. It is not clear where or under what circumstances John Jay met her; what is certain is that he was smitten. He wooed and won her. The couple was married in April of 1774 in the parlor of Liberty Hall, the Livingston home. He was 28 and she 17.

Letters in this book, several published here for the first time, have been carefully selected to chronicle the personal lives of John and Sarah Jay in the tumultuous times during and after the American Revolution. The correspondence reveals the deep and abiding love of husband and wife, their strong religious faith, their concern for their children, their aging parents and sometimes-difficult siblings. Readers will share the couple's joys and mourn their losses, appreciate the dangers and difficulties of travel, enjoy descriptions of the lands they visited and events they witnessed, and gain a real sense of the effort required for even the wealthy to survive in their era.

Importantly, the letters showcase the woman at John Jay's side: his beloved Sally (as Sarah was known), who not only bore his children and tended to his comfort and well-being, but also lightened him up, entertained his friends as well as government officials, and in general furthered his political career. Sarah's lively intelligence, powers of observation, social skills, political savvy and more than competent management of family affairs, including finances, during John Jay's frequent absences are clearly reflected in her letters and make reading them not only informative but also a delight. For far too long the woman of the period on whom historians focused, and who charmed readers, has been Abigail Adams. It is time Abigail moved over and shared the spotlight with Sarah Jay.

Finally, this collection of letters provides information about and insight into the radical changes wrought by the swirl of events surrounding the American Revolution. It catalogs their impact on a family that lived through and participated in them, revealing the adjustments and sacrifices they were forced to make in order to survive and serve.

Most of all, this is a book to be enjoyed. Readers of these "little fugitives" and "messengers of love" will come to know and care about this couple as we have: John Jay who has "twenty little things to say" to his beloved helpmeet and Sarah who promises her husband to be "your wife 'till death, & after that a ministring spirit."

Editorial Method

If only everyone could have the experience of reading eighteenth century letters in manuscript form! It is difficult to convey the excitement and pleasure that comes from handling sheets of paper that were actually touched by the writer, someone who lived during the creation of the nation, who played a part in its shaping. Such letters convey the reality of life as it was lived, of events as experienced and interpreted by participants. Reading them evokes a sense of immediacy that is almost impossible to achieve in any other way, short of time travel. Then, too, something of the person, other than what is actually expressed in writing, is conveyed by the physical letter itself. The handwriting soon becomes familiar, recognized as belonging to a particular individual. Images materialize: Sarah Jay wrestling with a quill pen while a small child wriggles on her lap; John Jay pondering what to say to his wife, scratching out mistakes, penning lines in haste as official business presses; little Peter Augustus struggling to write a letter to his distant parents, his aunt guiding his hand. And it is easy to succumb to the charms of the language of that earlier age. The letterwriting conventions are engaging, the formality and courtesy at their core contrasting with the lack of these qualities today.

The goal of this book is to provide transcriptions of selected manuscript letters of John and Sarah Jay — to each other and to members of their family and to friends— in the hope that, even in print form, they will work some of the same magic for readers that they have for the authors.

Care has been taken not to compromise historical accuracy and authenticity by the desire to attract and inform. Letters have been presented in their entirety whenever possible, with judicious editing of material which would tend to confuse rather than enlighten. Explanatory notes have been kept to a minimum so as not to be intrusive. Family members and others mentioned in the correspondence have been identified in the introduction, appendix, footnotes or index. For unfamiliar persons referred to only by surnames in the letters, first names have been added in brackets. The location of datelines, salutations and closings has been regularized, appearing in the same place regardless of where they are in the various manuscripts. In the interest of brevity, these shorthand notations for the main characters have been used: JJ for John Jay, SLJ for Sarah Livingston Jay, and PAJ for Peter Augustus Jay.

To understand and enjoy the letters to the fullest degree, readers are strongly advised to read the material that precedes them — biographical and chronological in nature — as well as the contextual essays in the back of the book, whose topics relate to the period and to particulars of the correspondence. To assist readers further, an introduction to each part is included as well as "bridges" between certain letters to provide continuity and background information.

Since part of the attraction of letters of the period lies in their tone and style, most of the prevailing conventions of letter writing have been retained except for those which interfere with ease of reading or comprehension. Common expressions, perhaps mystifying at first, become clear in context: "I find no occasion to enlarge on these Heads," the word "Heads" here means *matters*. Important nouns are capitalized, as was the custom. The ubiquitous ampersand has been kept, used not only in place of "and" but also in *&c.* for "et cetera." Writers, John Jay in particular, often used "y" to represent the runic letter called thorn, which stands for "th." *Ye* therefore equals *the*. This usage has been retained as it is rather charming and adds to the pleasure of reading the letters.

Letter writers of the time used abbreviations and contractions freely—for assorted words as well as the names of persons, places and months— and not just in drafts. These have been transcribed as they were written when readers are likely to be able to decipher them easily; when the meaning is not clear, missing letters have been supplied in brackets. For example, the word *received* often occurs as *rec'd*, with or without apostrophe or period. Since the intended word is apparent, especially in the context, it appears as written. In the case of *wh*, if it is not immediately clear whether *with* or *which* is meant, the missing letters have been included in brackets: w[hic]h. Letter writers not only used many abbreviations and contractions but they also usually wrote their endings in superscript — letters appearing above the line of writing. For example, Philadelphia often appears as "Ph^{a}." and "affectionate," in a closing, as aff^{e}. The decision was made *not* to use superscript in the book, as it does not make for ease of reading.

Readers will soon discover that almost every letter begins with a recitation of letters received or written, a desirable practice given the vagaries of the mail. Two abbreviations are commonly used to indicate the month if it is not named. If the date of the letter mentioned occurred during the current month, the abbreviation *Inst.* (Instant) is used; the previous month is referred to as *Ult.* (Ultimo).

That punctuation during this period was minimal will soon become evident to readers. This custom has been respected, except in a few instances. Periods have been added where thoughts clearly end, or to break up run-on sentences. And much-overused dashes have, for the most part, been replaced by periods or semicolons. Sentences thus created begin with capital letters. Sequences of words without the addition of commas have been retained because they are understandable, though they may be a bit confusing at first glance.

In a few letters, words are unclear or the paper has been torn. In these cases, an educated guess has been made as to what word or words might have been intended, with these appearing in brackets. If no guess was possible, an underlined blank is inserted for the missing word(s). Some letters, particularly drafts, contain crossed-out sections. These have, on occasion, been included if the content is revealing or particularly interesting.

With regard to spelling, the use of *sic* to indicate a misspelling has generally been avoided. Readers should assume that the words they are reading have been transcribed as written. English spellings were still in use for the most part: "favor" appears as *favour*, "neighbor" as *neighbour*. One quickly becomes accustomed to arcane forms: *shew* for show and *chuse* for choose, for example. Many words, by today's standards at any rate, are frequently misspelled, even by the well educated. John Jay always wrote *recieve* for "receive;" indeed he always reversed the *i* and *e* following a *c*. The truth is that spelling tended to be idiosyncratic and arbitrary.

Because the letters are not in manuscript form readers will miss at least one interesting though hard-to-read element of handwriting. The double "ss" as in "happiness" was handwritten as a kind of ligature in which two letters run together: something resembling a lowercase *f* followed by an *s*. Print has eliminated these often difficult-to-decipher letters. Another quaint convention that is lost in the present format is the use of "catchwords." The last word on a page in a multi-page letter was placed in the lower right corner and repeated in the first line of writing on the following page as a cue to readers.

There is no question but that handwriting is expressive and has the ability to convey emotion. While this quality is lacking in a print edition, the conventions, styles and usages that have been retained, along with the content, enable readers to become acquainted with the correspondents in a truly personal way and to appreciate the quality and character of their lives.

Introduction

The Livingston Family

The marriage of Sarah Van Brugh Livingston and John Jay united two prominent New York families. She was a great-granddaughter of the founder of Livingston Manor; he was the grandson of a Huguenot émigré merchant. Sarah's father, William Livingston, was a well-educated New York lawyer, writer, aspiring artist, and political figure who became the first elected governor of New Jersey. William married Susannah French in 1747; they had thirteen children, four of whom died in infancy. One son, Philip, died at age 8 in a boating accident and another, John Lawrence, was lost at sea aboard the *Saratoga* in 1781.

In 1760, William began buying property on the outskirts of Elizabeth, New Jersey, with the intention of retiring as a gentleman farmer. A decade later, owning more than 120 acres, he began construction on a two-story, fourteen-room house that he called Liberty Hall. The family lived nearby until it was ready.

The couple supervised the education of their children; during William's frequent absences, the task fell mostly to Susannah. His intelligence and keen powers of observation were nicely balanced by her even temperament and calm resignation in the face of adversity. The family was a lively one, and the bonds of affection between its members were strong. William tried to maintain tight control over their lives, but his patience would be sorely tried by the behavior of several of his children.

Hopeful suitors beat a path to the Livingston door. The first to be wed was Mary, to a young lawyer, James Linn, on May 27, 1771. This turned out to be a disastrous marriage and ended in divorce. Judith married a Continental Army soldier and New York merchant, John W. Watkins, in 1780. This too proved an unhappy alliance. The oldest Livingston son, William Jr., so angered his father by neglecting his studies and by his dissolute behavior that he was frequently threatened with disinheritance. These three siblings would live their lives dependent on trusts set up in their father's will. Their sister Sarah, and after her death her daughters, attempted to ease their woes with financial assistance.

Another son, Henry Brockholst, unwilling to study law, served as aide-de-camp to General Philip Schuyler as well as briefly to General Benedict Arnold before becoming private secretary to John Jay (December 1778). Brockholst sailed with the Jays for Europe. Though he wrote to his sisters on February 3, 1781, that John Jay was

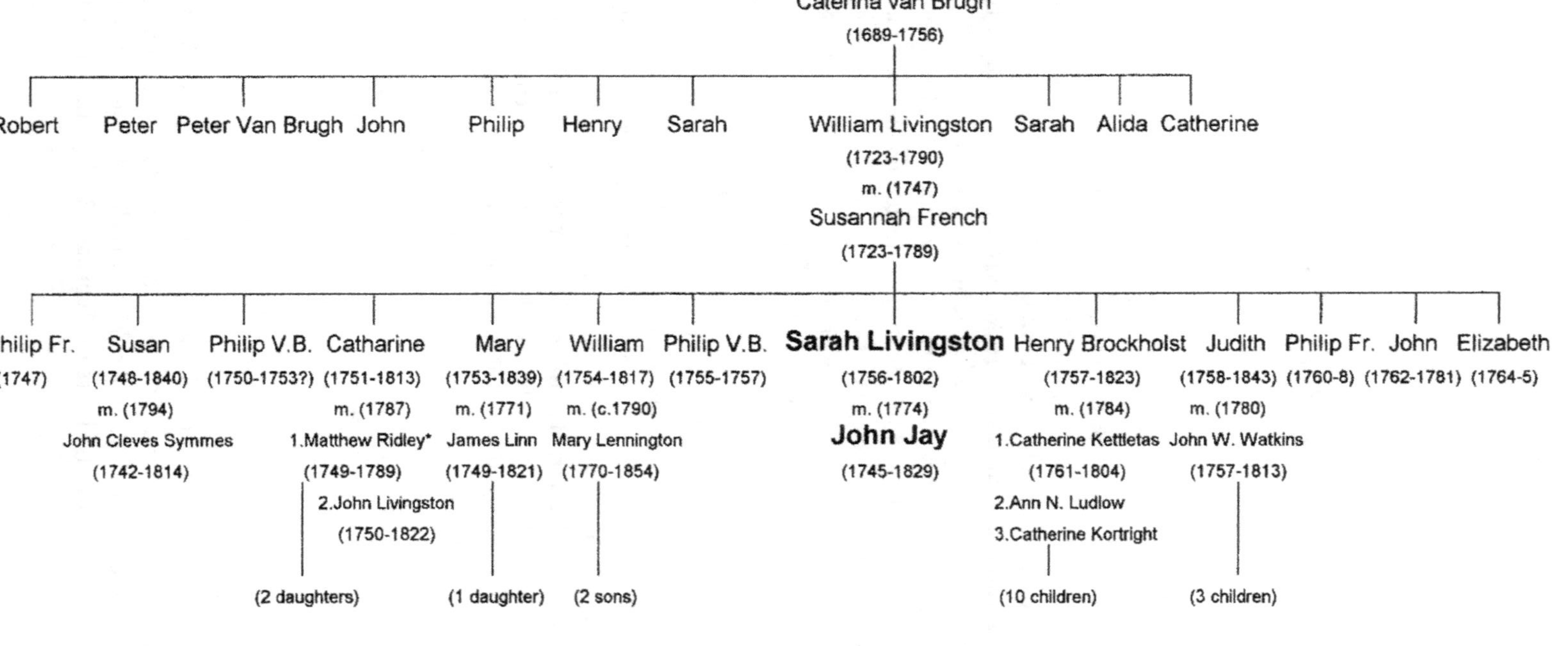

* Matthew Ridley, a widower, had a son, Essex, from his marriage to Anne Richardson.

"the best of men" and on December 3, 1781, that "Mrs. Jay looks charmingly, & as all married Ladies ought to do," his troublesome behavior soured the once affectionate relationship between himself and the Jays. Brockholst left Spain and returned home on March 11, 1782, carrying dispatches for Congress and seeds for his father. The British captured the ship as it approached America and Brockholst was confined to the Provost Gaol in New York City. After his release, he dutifully began his law studies and then outraged his father by suddenly marrying his landlady's daughter (1784). Nonetheless, father and son were soon reconciled. Sarah, after the unpleasantness in Spain, treated her brother with caution. Brockholst's ill feelings toward John Jay did not abate and he frequently involved himself in issues opposing Jay. He did write Jay a letter in March 1801 asking for a reconciliatory meeting, but whether it was ever held is not known. Brockholst, a capable lawyer, was appointed an associate justice of the U.S. Supreme Court by President Thomas Jefferson in 1807.

Three of the Livingston daughters did not disappoint. Nicknamed "the Three Graces," Susan, Catharine (known as Kitty), and Sarah were intelligent, courageous, witty, capable, and politically astute. William must have been very pleased when Sarah married John Jay. He had come to know Jay at meetings of "the Moot," the debating society for lawyers in New York City, and looked upon John with warm affection. He and his wife delighted in their grandson, Peter Augustus Jay, whose company assuaged the distress they felt when Sarah and John left for Europe.

Though she had a reputation of being quite the flirt, Catharine was a careful observer of the political scene and a respected reporter to the Jays in Europe about the tumultuous events occurring in America. On April 14, 1787, she married Matthew Ridley, a widower with a son, Essex. William Livingston was delighted with his new son-in-law, writing to John Jay that not only were he and Matthew similar but so were Essex and Peter Augustus Jay. Indeed, the two boys established a close bond. Matthew and Kitty had two daughters, Susan and Matilda. Unfortunately, Ridley died in 1789, six days before Matilda's birth. Kitty, so lively and vibrant in her youth, had difficulty coping after her husband's death. The death of her parents shortly thereafter was another blow. Sarah urged Kitty to come from Baltimore to New York, but she sent Essex and the girls to stay instead. On November 3, 1796, Kitty married her cousin, John Livingston, and moved to Oak Hill, his new home overlooking the Hudson River and Catskill Mountains. Sarah was delighted to have her sister closer by.

Susan, the teacher and caregiver in the family, was the last of Sarah's sisters to marry. Affectionate and levelheaded, she taught her nephew Peter Augustus Jay to read and write, as she had her younger siblings. It was she who took care of her parents at the end of their lives and then moved to Baltimore to support the widowed Kitty. In 1794, Susan was married to Judge John Cleves Symmes, a widower with two daughters, Maria and Anna, known as Nancy. They moved to North Bend, Ohio. With the newlyweds came Nancy Symmes and Kitty's older daughter, Susan, now about six. Aunt Symmes would oversee her niece's education and upbringing. At first, all seemed well. Susan in her long letters to Sarah described the house she and

Opposite: **Sarah Livingston's family tree.**

Symmes designed and were building on the Miami River. She also wrote about her participation in the wedding of Nancy Symmes to Captain William Henry Harrison on November 25, 1795. The judge did not approve of Harrison "being bred to no business," so the young lovers "made a kind of run-away match altho it was at home, her Papa being absent." Had the judge only known that Harrison's "no business" would turn out to be the presidency!

Susan left Ohio and her husband in 1808, never to return. She maintained friendly relations with all her relatives and visited the Bedford farm several times during John Jay's lifetime. After her niece Susan married Theodore Sedgwick, Jr., in 1810, Susan Symmes lived with his family in Stockbridge, Massachusetts, until her death.

The Jay Family

John Jay's siblings are no less interesting than Sarah's. John's father, Peter, a successful New York City merchant and entrepreneur, wed Mary Van Cortlandt, a member of the large landowning family, in 1728. The couple had ten children, seven of whom reached maturity. The family moved to Rye, New York, shortly after John Jay was born in 1745, partly out of concerns for the children's health. The property overlooked Long Island Sound, and Peter Jay worked hard to make it a profitable farm. During the Revolutionary War, the Jays moved to Fishkill, New York.

Their first-born, Eve, was 38 years old when she married the Reverend Henry Munro in 1766. Born in Scotland, a widower twice over with a daughter from his first marriage, he had served as a missionary in Yonkers, New York, where Col. Frederick Philipse (a Jay cousin) had built a church. In 1767 Peter Jay Munro was born, and a year later Reverend Munro was named rector at St. Peter's in Albany, New York. Imprisoned as a Loyalist, he fled America in October 1777. He never saw his wife and children again.

Eve was a worry for her father and her brothers. All her life she had been in poor health and prone to "hystericks." Now, abandoned and impoverished in the turmoil of war, she was totally dependent on her family. She was unable to take care of her son, who was then raised by John and Sarah Jay. At age 13, Peter Jay Munro accompanied them to Europe, eventually serving as Jay's unofficial private secretary in Paris. Returning to America in 1784, young Munro began his law studies in the office of Aaron Burr and was later admitted to the bar. On January 1, 1790, he married his cousin Margaret White. The Jays looked upon Peter Munro as a son; he was an integral part of their family. As an adult, he was a helpful friend to Sarah while John was away and a compassionate provider for his mother in her declining years.

Peter and Mary Jay's first son was Augustus, known as Gussie or Gustey. An amiable soul, Gussie learned to read and write despite having a learning disability. In later life, he lived independently in lodgings with help from his brothers.

Life was also difficult for two other children: Peter and Anna Maricka, called Nancy. They contracted smallpox during the epidemic of 1739 and were left blind. It seems that young Peter may have had some vision, as he became a proficient farmer and manager of the Rye property after the War. Nancy was totally blind and never learned to read or write, signing her will with an X. Despite their afflictions, they seem to have been cheerful people. Both John and Sarah enjoyed staying with them at Rye; they were also very fond of Peter's wife, Polly.

The second son, James, was arguably John's intellectual equal but was enormously ambitious and egotistical. He received his medical degree in Edinburgh in 1753 and after continuing his studies in France returned in 1756 to New York, where he had a successful practice. In June 1762, he traveled to England to collect funds for King's College and was knighted by King George III on March 25, 1763, for his successful endeavors. Questions about the funds raised resulted in a morass of lawsuits and counter suits which were not settled until 1773. This episode was a great embarrassment to the Jay family. During this time, James was practicing medicine in London and Bath; he also wrote a book, *Reflections and Observations on the Gout*. By 1776, he was offering his help to the British, trying to effect a peaceful solution to the British-American conflict. He also invented an invisible ink, which was used by his brother John, Silas Deane, and George Washington.

In 1778 James returned to America, loaned $20,000 in colonial currency to James Mease, the clothier general of the Continental Army, and served as a member of the New York State Senate. He clearly hoped to make a major contribution toward ending the war but seemed to complicate matters instead. Both John and his youngest brother, Frederick, looked askance at the comings and goings of their older sibling. George Clinton vouched for his loyalty but, after the British captured James in New Jersey (April 1782), wrote, "He is no great loss to us & the Enemy will gain as little by him if he should be disposed to serve them." James returned to England and, traveling to Holland and then to France, tried to meddle in the peace process. John Jay, hard at work with the preliminary negotiations, did not appreciate the machinations of his older brother. Was James a double agent? It's unlikely, as he was interested only in pursuing his own glory.

Before the end of 1784, James returned to America. His marriage to Anne Erwin produced two children. James continued to practice medicine and attended William Livingston in his final illness. He ran for the New Jersey Assembly in 1800 but was defeated. In 1808 and 1813, he petitioned Congress for repayment of the loan he had made during the Revolutionary War, but without success. The estrangement between the brothers was never bridged; John's attitude is reflected in a letter to his son, Peter Augustus (1811): "Few of Sir James's Measures correspond with the Rules of Prudence, and therefore those Rules seldom enable us to account for them."

The last son born to the Jays was Frederick, known as Fady. Father Peter described him as "a merry diverting Fellow" but not as interested in learning as John or James. In 1765, Frederick was placed as an apprentice for five years to his cousin James DePeyster, a merchant and trader. He married Margaret Barclay (known as Peggy) on November 17, 1773. When the Revolutionary War disrupted his mercantile business, Frederick joined the militia and served in the New York Assembly. Most importantly, the care of his elderly parents and his afflicted siblings fell upon his shoulders; he helped them move from Rye to Fishkill in the hope of finding them a safe haven. He also had occasional care of his nephew, Peter Augustus, when John and Sarah were

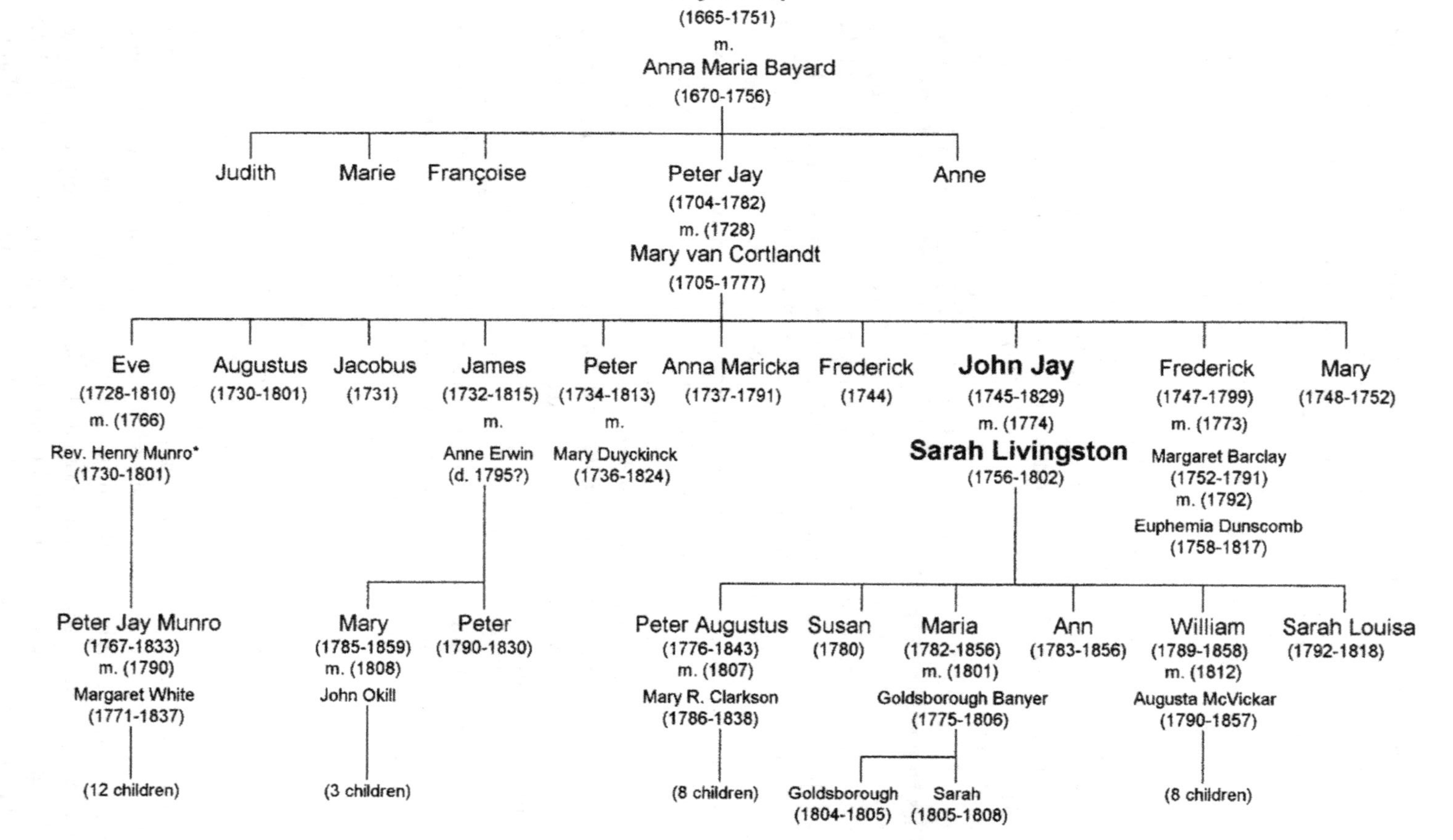

* Rev. Munro, a widower twice over, had a daughter, Elizabeth, from his first marriage.

abroad. No wonder Frederick felt very much put upon and ill used by his family. After the War, he was unable to find his niche and never attained the success he so fervently craved.

Portraits of John and Sarah Jay

Several portraits of John Jay and only a few of Sarah were painted over the years, and of course, they were painted in the style that was fashionable at that period. While these pictures are both handsome and interesting, it is very difficult to tell from looking at them what the Jays were really like.

Of the existing portraits of Sarah Jay some show her as a young matron, in elegant and formal dress, with her hair stylishly arranged. In one, however, she is pictured informally, as a mother with her two youngest children, sitting in a garden during an intimate family moment. Appealing as these images are, what do they really tell us about her? Was she a fashionable grande dame or a sweet and loving mother and wife—or both?

In two nineteenth-century books, *The Queens of American Society* by Mrs. Ellet and *John Jay* by George Pellew, there are "written portraits" of Sarah Jay which provide additional clues about her personality, character and appearance. She is said to have inherited some of her father's finest traits, both intellectual and moral. These were further developed by the education she and her sisters received at home. Sarah was the embodiment of gentleness and grace and she possessed a delicate sensibility, along with the keen powers of observation revealed in so many of her letters.

Courageous and hard working, Sarah was a definite social asset to her husband. She devoted her life to sustaining, supporting, and assisting him in his career. During John Jay's many and lengthy absences, she managed their household, their several properties, and their investments with competence and intelligence. She was a good diplomat and filled her own public roles with grace and dignity. Her cousin Janet Livingston Montgomery, writing to Mercy Otis Warren shortly before the Jays sailed for Europe, predicted that Sarah would be a hit there:

> You speak of my dear friend, Mrs. Jay.... She is one of the most worthy women I know; has a great fund of knowledge, and makes use of most charming language; added to this, she is very handsome, which will secure her a welcome with the unthinking, whilst her understanding will gain her the hearts of the most worthy. Her manners will do honor to our countrywomen, and I really believe will please, even at the Court in Madrid [Ellet 53].

Physically Sarah was quite the beauty: petite, with a brilliant complexion, fine teeth and bright eyes. In Paris, during the Jays' two-year residence there, she was known as "la belle Américaine." Fashion conscious and knowledgeable about current styles, she wrote to family and friends in America describing the latest designs and sent packages of fabric along with matching laces and ribbons.

Opposite: **John Jay's family tree.**

John Jay in his portraits appears serious, upright, and dignified, always wearing formal attire: stylish court dress, a dark suit, or his Supreme Court robes. But from looking at these portraits, can we tell what he was like? Was he as stiff and proud as he seems?

The letters and various written descriptions of John Jay reveal a complex man. Without a doubt, he was intelligent, hard working, loyal, ambitious, and devoted to his country. As a lawyer and diplomat, he was both eloquent and persuasive. He could be affectionate, compassionate, and fun loving when it was appropriate. On rare occasions he was even ribald. He was a loyal friend. Admired by some colleagues, he was highly respected by most and heartily disliked by a few. To those across the negotiating table from him, he could be "irritable, obstinate, and a stickler for the letter of the law."

As a husband, John was completely and totally devoted to Sarah. A loving but stern father, he exhorted his children not only to have faith in Providence but also to improve themselves and rise to each challenge in life. Extremely prudent, he believed that nothing should be written in a letter that might be held against him or his kin, as he valued his family's good name above all else.

Regarding his personal appearance, John Jay was tall, slender, and graceful, with a refined, rather handsome face. An eyewitness in Boston gave the following description of Jay riding circuit:

> His height was a little less than six feet; his person rather thin, but well formed. His complexion was without color, his eyes black [they were really blue] and penetrating, his nose aquiline, and his chin pointed. His hair came over his forehead, was tied behind. When standing, he was a little inclined forward, as is not uncommon with students long accustomed to bend over a table. His manner was very gentle and unassuming [Pellew 238, with credit for the quotation to Sullivan, *Letters on Public Characters*, 59].

John and Sarah Jay were truly devoted to one another. As Sarah's brother Brockholst wrote to their sister Kitty (3 September 1781): "Mr. & Mrs. Jay can be unhappy no where. They love each other too well." Their separations pressed hard upon them, especially upon Sarah. But both were willing to sacrifice their time together in order for John Jay to pursue his political career and serve his country.

The Mail

Since letters are the core of this book it is important for the reader to understand the conventions and peculiarities of keeping in touch by mail.

When John and Sarah Jay began corresponding in 1775, a colonial mail service set up by Americans in opposition to the Royal Post was just beginning to operate. This so-called "constitutional post" came into being after the Boston Tea Party when Committees of Correspondence were organized to keep people in the various colonies informed with regard to British actions and local sentiment. This alternative private service was created because Americans justifiably feared that mail sent by the

British Post Office would be opened. By the time the Second Continental Congress met in Philadelphia in 1775 the fledgling system was operating between Maine and Williamsburg, Virginia, mail being collected or left at designated post offices, taverns, or postriders' homes. It was short-lived, however. Recognizing the importance of communication among the colonies and the role the post office could play in uniting them, the Second Continental Congress established an official system in July of 1775 and extended service to Georgia.

Many people, including the Jays, preferred to entrust letters to family or friends who were traveling to or near intended recipients. John Jay wrote to Sarah (29 September 1775), " My last to you was by Mr. Graham which I hope you have recd." Whether sent by post or borne by acquaintances, mail almost always was slow. "But one Letter from you has for some long weeks arrived. I fear your Letters like mine make long Journies," John wrote to Sarah (12 December 1775). Needless to say, mail frequently miscarried. Sarah lamented in a letter to John (12 February 1779), "I am utterly at a loss to account for the miscarriages of my letters having frequently wrote & sent my letters by what I then thought safe conveyances." Copies were often posted in case the original was lost. To keep track of correspondence, letters usually began with a list of mail recently received and sent. "The last Evening I had the Pleasure of recieving your kind Letters of the 25 and 27 June last," wrote John to Sarah (3 July 1777).

The postal system was of crucial importance during the Revolution. Even though the Continental Congress and state governments employed special couriers for official business— the Jays sometimes used Samson Dyckman — the postal service, often at great risk to postriders, played an important role in maintaining lines of communication between a government, whose seat changed frequently, and its armies in the field. It also enabled soldiers to keep in touch with their families. Because letters by members of Congress, as well as of the armed forces, were carried free of charge, the post office ran up a huge debt. Sensible of its importance, Congress appropriated money to keep the system functioning.

Mail frequently fell into enemy hands. And letters were often published in Loyalist newspapers! John Jay was not being overly cautious when he recommended to Sarah that great care be taken not to include in letters information that would be damaging if revealed. "In your Letters be as particular on every interesting topic as may be consistent with Prudence, for in times like these we should be cautious what we commit to Paper" (20 May 1775). John Jay also recommended the use of ciphers, and not just for official letters. Kitty Livingston sometimes wrote to the Jays in Europe using a simple code, that of assigning numbers to the prominent people about whom she was writing.

In spite of the many problems that continued to plague the postal system under the government established by the Articles of Confederation, improvements were made and service extended. By the time the Constitution took effect in 1789, there were 75 post offices and more than 2,400 miles of post roads serving a population of three million (Fuller 40). The post office in New York City for the greater part of the year 1789 was at the home of the postmaster William Bedlow, Number 8 Wall Street, where mail from Philadelphia and points South arrived three days a week at 3 P.M.

and departed on three alternate days at 10 P.M. The mail from Boston arrived at 7 P.M. and left at 10 P.M. (Monaghan and Lowenthal 21). Stagecoaches came into use on certain routes. Writing to John from Rye (15 July 1799), Sarah thanks him for "three affectionate letters" she received from Mamaroneck where Peter Jay Munro had left them. "Had I known that he [Peter] was there I should have wrote by him, but since he is gone, Sylvia [a servant] has promised to watch the stage early in the morning."

In addition to surface mail, regular packet boats carrying mail sailed along the Atlantic coast between major ports. Which service was faster? The answer probably depended on the time of year. Roads were certainly bad, indeed sometimes impassable, but packets were at the mercy of wind and weather. In any case, the postal system continued to grow rapidly: by 1800 there were 903 post offices and 20,817 miles of post roads. Inland service had been extended to Pittsburgh and Albany, and "cross posts," or secondary routes, were being established.

Sending a Letter

Letters were commonly mailed without envelopes. They were merely folded and sealed with a wafer, a disk made of dried colored paste, or hot wax into which a stamp was pressed. A broken seal was clear evidence that tampering had occurred. Envelopes were not in general use because postage was based on the number of sheets in a letter and an envelope was counted as a sheet. Postage was also rated according to the mileage to a letter's destination. In 1792, for example, a single-page letter directed to a recipient 30 miles away was charged six cents; one being sent 450 miles cost 25 cents (Fuller 43). Letters were "rated up" by the office of origin. The charge was written by hand, and the date and the name of the town from which the letter was being sent were either written or indicated by a round hand stamp, making it possible to determine how long it had been in transit. A franking postmark identified mail sent free of charge. Postage stamps were not yet in use. Although postage could be prepaid by the sender, it was most often paid by the addressee upon delivery, a safer choice. Sometimes postmasters allowed patrons to run tabs and defer payment for months. Because letters were expensive to send, those who were frugal wrote in a fine small hand and sometimes turned the page 90 degrees and wrote over the text, making it difficult to make out the words.

John Jay kept careful records of the mail he received, both official and personal. On the back of each letter in the left corner at the top he noted when it had been received as well as the date on which he had answered it.

Letter Writing

In the latter part of the eighteenth century personal letter writing was considered a genteel pursuit, a presentation of self as revealing of status, education, and accomplishment as was speech, dress, or behavior. To write a good hand was an important goal, and to this end writing masters were employed. Models of good letter writing were studied with the intention of emulating them in content and style. There were more or less acknowledged conventions that applied to letter writing. The correspondence between Sarah and John Jay, as well as with friends and members of their families, illustrate many of these. Formal letters to men from men always closed with words like "I am your obliged and affect[iona]te friend & Servant" (John Jay to George Washington, 6 March 1795), or some variation thereof. Formality was the norm even when discussing the details of daily life. Sarah Jay always began a letter to her husband with "My dear Mr. Jay." And every letter to her from him, no matter how familiar in tone and content, was always signed "John Jay." (Lest she should have forgotten the name of the man to whom she was married!) There is a certain formulaic quality about letters of the period evident in expressions like "I did myself the pleasure of writing to you," and "I flatter myself that...." The Jay letters, like those of others of their class, are sprinkled with literary, historical and classical references, intermixed with lofty sentiments, Biblical allusions, Latin expressions, and French phrases. Good manners seemed to require the writer to adopt a deferential, often self-deprecatory tone; apologies for shortcomings, whether real or imagined, were profuse. References to Divine Providence occurred frequently, and calm resignation in the face of trials and tribulations was consistently recommended and aspired to.

Writing Implements

The writing instrument used by correspondents was of course the quill pen. Made from a primary feather taken from the wing of a bird, usually a domestic goose (because it was readily available and its feathers possessed the required flexibility), the quill had to be pared to a point. Enter the penknife or quill-cutter. This special knife was used both to cut and mend the quill and to correct mistakes by scraping the error off the paper. To achieve the flexibility needed to execute the thin upward strokes and thicker downward ones characteristic of the script of the day, as well as the flourishes affected by some, notably John Hancock, which served both to impress and to preclude forgery, the quill had to be slit. Finally, the actual writing edge of the pen had not only to be shaped so as to hold ink and dispense it smoothly but also angled to suit each individual's hand. The nib was in constant need of attention as it often broke or wore down. It had to be sharpened frequently — sufficiently to make possible small writing, yet not so sharp as to pierce the paper. Quills had to be cleaned after each use and kept in water to prevent them from drying out. The Jays could have purchased quills at several shops in New York City. Francis Turner, a quill-maker at 93 Queen (now Pearl) Street, sold various grades of quills: cheap ones went for four shillings a hundred while a hundred of the best sold for 15 shillings (Monaghan and Lowenthal 21). In addition to quill pen, penknife, paper and inkpot (the ink for which could be purchased but was sometimes handmade), a "pounce pot" was kept handy. This contained a powdered substance — pumice, or sanderach, a form of resin — which was sprinkled on writing paper prior to use to make it less porous, thus preventing the ink from being absorbed. Elaborate silver writing stands incorporating the necessary implements and accessories became fashionable, and the writing desk made its appearance in the library or front parlor of upper class homes.

Sarah Jay frequently complains in letters about her quill pen and penknife. She writes to her daughter Maria (1 April 1795), "My pen is intolerably bad & my knife not better." And to John (28 July 1800), "Our quills are cut up.... I am writing with the stump of a pen that is as stiff as my knife." Young Peter Jay Munro, writing from France to John Jay in London (20 November 1783), asks for a new penknife: "I have been so unfortunate as to break my penknife and I would be very much obliged to my uncle if he would bring me another." Not a bauble for an indulged adolescent but a necessity. In a letter to John from Persipiney (27 June 1777) Sarah bemoans the lack of suitable writing paper: "There is not any writing paper to be bought here. I think you had better get one or two Quires more of Gasharee." And again writing to John (8 May 1792), "I have no paper at hand—excuse therefore these scraps."

Although Sarah often apologized for the poor quality of her handwriting this could not always be blamed on the quill or her fatigue, for she was afflicted periodically, even at a young age, with rheumatism in her wrists and hands that made writing painful. The handwriting of both John and Sarah Jay is pleasing and remarkably legible; it does not seem to have changed very much over the course of their lives.

The Transatlantic Mail

For many years communication with Europe was more important than it was among the colonies. Settlers were naturally interested in maintaining contact with kin in their native lands and had little inclination—until commerce, political concerns and intermarriage made it desirable—to be in touch with their counterparts along the Atlantic seaboard. Because John Jay and members of his family lived abroad on two separate occasions in the latter part of the eighteenth century, the hows and wherefores of overseas mail are of interest.

Government correspondence was generally carried by warships or naval vessels. For regular mail there was a packet service. Specially designated mail boats or packets—small fast brigs, usually armed, carrying little or only light cargo so as to minimize turn-around time, and perhaps a few passengers—were commissioned to make regular round trips between certain American ports and Falmouth in Cornwall. Overseas mail service was, as might be expected, unreliable, what with the dangers from bad weather, privateers and enemy ships. Should a packet or naval vessel be in danger of capture, bags containing mail and documents were supposed to be weighted and thrown overboard. Packet charges were quite high: a single-page letter went for one shilling, a double for two, and one weighing an ounce for four shillings. For a letter that accompanied a parcel or box (on which freight had been paid), there was no charge. This loophole was often used to avoid paying postage. By 1783 regular packet service between the new nation and England had been restored: vessels left New York or London on the first Wednesday of every month. Not long afterwards packet service to France was also resumed.

Mail of a personal nature was often entrusted to friends crossing the ocean on merchant ships, who upon landing would find a way to forward the letters to addressees. Alternatively letters could be given to the captains of commercial ships who would deliver them at the port of arrival to designated coffee houses or taverns for pickup by recipients or to the post office if there was one. Lists of vessels and their sailing dates and destinations were posted in public houses, with mail pouches for each in which letters could be deposited. Transatlantic mail took from six to twelve weeks. Vessels in crossing often "spoke" to each other, that is, made contact with ships they met sailing in the opposite direction, to learn the latest news and to pick up letters which passengers had written on board and wished to send to those they had left behind.

When a vessel docked the mailbag had to be handed over to the post office before cargo could be unloaded or passengers allowed to disembark. According to William Strickland, a Yorkshireman on a visit to the United States in 1794, "The first that is required on a vessel landing at New York is for the Captain to deliver his letter bag at the Post-office; till that is done, and a receipt for it shewn at the Custom House, no permit can be obtained for clearing the ship or landing any part of the cargo, or property of the passengers, nor are the passengers themselves allowed to remain on shore."

References to mail sent by merchantmen — so-called "ship letters"— always included the name of the vessel and captain. "By the *Hope* Captn Haley I have written to you," notes John Jay to Sarah (16 August 1794). Ship captains usually received one penny per sheet above the packet rate for this service. Correspondents shopped around trying to find the most expeditious way of dispatching overseas mail, sometimes sending copies of the same letter by several means, hoping that at least one would get through, and in a timely fashion.

Transatlantic mail was slow and chancy, and continued so until steam ships replaced sailing vessels. Every school child knows (or should know) that the battle of New Orleans which took place on January 8, 1815, need not have been fought, for the treaty that ended the War of 1812 had been signed in Ghent on Christmas Eve. But neither the Americans nor the British in the field had received this news in time to prevent the battle.

Chronology

1745	Dec. 12	John Jay is born in New York City
1746		The Jay family moves to Rye, New York
1753		JJ attends the Latin School at New Rochelle
1756	Aug.	Sarah Van Brugh Livingston is born in New York City
		JJ is tutored at home in Rye
1760		JJ enters Kings College
1764	May 22	JJ is awarded the B.A. degree
		JJ studies law with Benjamin Kissam Esqr.
1767	May 19	JJ is awarded the M.A. degree by King's College
1768	Oct. 26	JJ is admitted to the bar
		JJ forms a law partnership with Robert R. Livingston, Jr., which is dissolved by 1772
1769		JJ is appointed secretary to the commission established to settle the boundary dispute between New York and New Jersey
1772		The Livingston family moves into Liberty Hall in Elizabeth Town, New Jersey
1774	April 28	Sarah Livingston and John Jay are married at Liberty Hall
		JJ is elected a member of the general committee of the City of New York
		JJ is sent to the First Continental Congress in Philadelphia
	Oct. 20	JJ's "Address to the People of Great Britain" is adopted by Congress
1775		JJ is elected a member of the New York Provincial Convention
		JJ is sent to the Second Continental Congress in Philadelphia
	Nov. 3	JJ is appointed colonel of 2nd Regiment of New York militia
1776	Jan. 24	SLJ gives birth to a son, Peter Augustus

	July 9	JJ drafts a resolution for New York State endorsing the Declaration of Independence
		JJ drafts substantial portions of the New York State Constitution
	July 16	JJ becomes a member of the secret committee to obstruct the Hudson River
1777	Oct. 17	JJ is appointed chief justice of the State of New York
1778	Nov. 4	JJ is sent to the Continental Congress by New York State
	Dec. 10	JJ is elected president of Congress
1779	Sept. 27	JJ is elected minister plenipotentiary to Spain; he resigns as president of Congress the next day
	Oct. 20	The Jays sail for Europe on the *Confederacy*
1780	July 9	SLJ gives birth to a daughter, Susan, in Madrid
	Aug. 1	Baby Susan dies
1781	June 15	JJ is named one of five American peace commissioners
1782	Feb. 20	SLJ gives birth to a daughter, Maria, in Madrid
	May/June	The Jays journey to Paris
	Nov. 30	Preliminary Articles of Peace to end the Revolutionary War are signed in Paris by Richard Oswald (for the British) and John Adams, Benjamin Franklin, JJ, and Henry Laurens (for the Americans)
1783	April 15	Congress ratifies the Preliminary Articles of Peace
	Aug. 13	SLJ gives birth to a daughter, Ann (Nancy), in Paris
	Sept. 3	The Definitive Treaty of Paris is signed in Paris
1784	June 1	The Jays sail for New York from Dover, England
		JJ is presented with the Freedom of the City in a gold box by the Corporation of the City of New York
		JJ is appointed by the New York State legislature to be a delegate to Congress
		JJ is appointed secretary for foreign affairs
1786		JJ is elected vice chancellor of the University of the State of New York
		JJ is a founder and is elected the first president of the New York Society for Promoting the Manumission of Slaves
		JJ is elected a member of the New York convention to consider the ratification of the Constitution of the United States
1789	June 16	SLJ gives birth to a son, William
	Sept. 26	JJ is appointed chief justice of the United States

1790		JJ is awarded the diploma of doctor of law by the University of Cambridge in Massachusetts (Harvard)
1790–1794		JJ rides circuit for the Supreme Court
1792	Feb. 20	SLJ gives birth to a daughter, Sarah Louisa (Sally)
1794		JJ is appointed envoy extraordinary to Great Britain and travels to London with son, Peter Augustus
	Nov. 19	JJ signs a treaty with Great Britain
		The Jays begin building a retirement home on their property in Bedford (now Katonah) in Westchester County, New York
1795		JJ is elected governor of New York for a three-year term
1798		JJ elected governor for a second three-year term
1801		JJ retires from public life and moves to the Bedford farm with his family
1802	May 28	Sarah Livingston Jay dies
		JJ remains in Bedford overseeing his farm
1829	May 17	John Jay dies

PART I

Ardor and Pain Amid the Anxieties of War

January 11, 1773–October 7, 1779

On May 5, 1774, *Rivingston's New York Gazeteer* carried the following newsworthy item:

> Jay, John, Esq, eminent barrister of New York City was married last week to Miss Sally Livingston (third daughter of William Livingston Esq) at her father's estate near Elizabeth Town, East Jersey.

A contemporary reader might have thought, "Interesting," or (more unkindly), "I thought he was courting a De Lancey girl." But for the modern reader, this spare announcement reveals nothing about the love story that was Sarah Livingston and John Jay.

At the time of his marriage on April 28, 1774, the 28-year-old John Jay had a thriving law practice, was a member of "the Moot" (the legal debating society founded by William Livingston), and was a manager of the Dancing Assembly, a regular gathering place for New York's fashionable society. Although it was rumored that he had wooed and been rejected by two daughters of Peter DeLancey, it seems that John, unlike his friend Robert R. Livingston, Jr., was not entirely at ease in the company of women. In fact, he described himself to Robert: "You understood Men and Women early, I knew them not."

How then did he come to woo the young Sarah Livingston? Though born in New York City, Sarah and her family in 1770 had moved to New Jersey while the family home, Liberty Hall, was being built. Governor Livingston sought the tranquil life of a farmer but his children continued to participate in the social whirl. Sarah was particularly close to her older sisters, Susan and Catharine, known as Kitty. They were intelligent, lively girls and politically astute. Kitty, a bit of a flirt, had many suitors, one of whom was Gouverneur Morris; and it is he who gives us our first glimpse of Sarah Livingston, the "non pareil that Opening Rose" as she enters into society at 16 years of age.

(Gouverneur Morris to Kitty Livingston at Elizabeth Town) New York 11th Janry 1773

What do you think Kitty. I have adopted Sally for my Daughter beleive me I will pay her the same Attention I would were I really a Father. To tell you a Secret I have a great many who pretend to the Honor of being my Son in Law. Never was a Little Creature so admired (I speak seriously) God send it don't turn her Head to prevent which no Endeavours shall be wanting on the Part of your Friend. As to her Heart when in the Midst of her Admirers it singeth with Joy. Never was any Creature happier. The rosy Fingures of Pleasure paint her Cheeks with double Crimson. Her Eyes sparkle with Delight. And so it will continue if the Whim does not take her to get in Love. And if it does some gentle Strephons must go hang.

Oh I go to Lynnes Coll in a Corner and see the most serious Scenes. Well bless us all but your tender Loviers are the most extraordinary Creatures that ever were invented! I would make you laugh Nay laughing would not serve the Turn you must do more. One bending forwards rolling up his Eyes and sighing most piteously. Another at a Distance sitting Side long upon his chair with melancholic & despondent Phiz

A plan of the harbour of New York. Engraved by John Carwitham (active 1723–1741). The Jays often sailed from Manhattan to Elizabeth Town, New Jersey, to visit the Livingston family. Reproduced by permission of Holkham Hall, Norfolk, England. From *Manhattan in Maps: 1527–1995,* by Paul E. Cohen and Robert T. Augustyn. Rizzoli International Publications, Inc., 1997.

prolongated unto the seventh buton Hole of his Waist Coast. A third his Shoulders drawn up to his Ears his Elbows fastened to his short Ribs his Brow wrinkled and the Corners of his Mouth making over his Chin a most rueful Arch.

In the Midst of all this sits Miss with seeming Unconsciousness of the whole one would be led to imagine she is unconcerned. On my Word this Picture is not beyond the Life. I shall dispose of her before the Winter is out I beleive provided Mamona has no Objections. I mean what I say....

I wish you the full Fruition of your own Wishes for as many years as your Life may consist of. Pray make the Compliments of the Season acceptable among all & beleive me

Dr Kate
very sincerely your Friend
Gouv. Morris

Morris was not quite accurate in his "before the Winter is out" time estimate, for it was a year later that Peter Jay picked up his pen to write to Sarah's father.

(Peter Jay to William Livingston at Elizabeth Town) Rye the 31st January 1774.

Sr.

My Son having informed me of his Inclination of being connected in your Family, and your favourable reception of his application, I take the earliest opportunity of acquainting you with our Concurrence.

Tho we have not the Pleasure of knowing the young Lady, yet the confidence we have in our Son's Prudence, satisfies us of the Propriety of his choice. Give me leave, Sr. to assure you, that I will always readily adopt every measure that may conduce to their happiness, and tend to render the connection between our Familyes agreeable to both.

Be pleased to present our Compliments to Mrs. Livingston and the young Lady. I am,

Sr. yr. very humble Servant
Peter Jay

Who was at the wedding? Surely members of the Livingston family, and perhaps John's younger brother Frederick. Who officiated? It may have been John's brother-in-law, the Reverend Harry Munro, but this is not certain. What is known is that the newlyweds began their life together with a trip to Rye, New York, so that Sarah could meet her husband's family. Subsequently, the two would endure many separations as the events of the conflict with Great Britain engulfed their lives.

(SLJ to her mother at Elizabeth Town) Poughkeepsie, May 6th, 1774

My dear Mamma,

This evening I had the pleasure of meeting Cousin Harry Livingston who informs that he is going to New York to morrow & will be so obliging as to forward a letter to you & as I know how generously you interest yourself in the Welfare of your children I shall take the liberty of troubling with an account of my little jaunt thus far.

On Monday we left New York & arrived at Rye in the afternoon where we were received with a hearty welcome. I was not by any means so much affected at seeing the blind children as I feared I should be. There was such an appearance of chearfulness & good humour in all they say that instead of depressing they rais'd my spirits which had been not a little damped at the sight of their afflicted Mother who we found extremely ill & who was amazingly affected at seeing me. But after a little Chat she appeared much better & the next morning she was in very good spirits & wanted Mr. Jay exceedingly to leave me with her. But since she could not obtain her request I am to spend a week with them on my return in which I have my Mamma's ease in view (tho' I am sorry to think how much trouble my dear Mamma will have at any rate). Mrs. F[rederick] Jay is to meet me there & stay with me while Mr. Jay's business calls him at West-Chester.

On Tuesday We left Rye & lodged about twelve miles from Peekskill. Wednesday we went from thence to Cousin Robinson's where we were very politely received & did not leave them till to-day. She beg'd to be remembred to you & to tell you she would be amazingly glad to see you & sister Catesy [Kitty] or any of the family. Today we met Judge Livingston at Poughkeepsie. He goes home very early to let his family know that we drink tea with them to-morrow & spend a week with them. I do not go to Sopus. Mr. Jay will be there very little while. The Land-Lady for this evening is waiting for this table to lay the cloth & I am obliged [to] conclude abruptly again but tell sisters I will write them from the Manor.

I beg my dear Mamma not to be offended at these scrawls. I assure you it is not [in] my power to write well in this room where there is such a collection of country-men talking politicks. Good night my dear Mamma, God bless you & all your dear family.

Believe me to be

your ever grateful & affectionate daughter
Sa. Jay

Mr. Jay joins with me in love to all. He begs Mamma will take care of her Cold.

Shortly after their marriage, the news arrived from England that the British Parliament had closed Boston harbor as punishment for the damage done during the Boston Tea Party five months earlier. New York merchants quickly proposed a committee to consider what to do and to determine "the most effectual Methods to advance the Interest of the common cause." John, a political novice, was named to this committee and assisted in drafting a letter to the Boston committee, suggesting "that a Congress of Deputies from the Colonies in general is of the utmost moment...." Though this was John's first dip into New York's political maelstrom, he did not neglect his law practice. John left his bride to travel to Albany, which he reached "after a Passage as agreeable as Absence from you and the Filth of twenty dirty lousy Scotch Passengers would admit. I am now surrounded at a Tavern with several Clients on Business...."

After his return to New York City, John was chosen as one of four delegates to represent New York at the first meeting of the colonies. Both John and his father-in-law were present in Philadelphia at the opening session of the First Continental Congress on September 5, 1774, and also at the Second Continental Congress on May 10, 1775.

Once again, John and Sarah were apart.

(JJ to SLJ at Elizabeth Town) Schoolkill, 23 May 1775

My Dear Sally

Your kind Letter of the 16th Instant was delivered to me last Evening; it relieved me from much Sollicitude, and I take the earliest opportunity of thanking you for it.

If I am not mistaken you promised to be chearful and in Spirits. How comes it then that pensive Contemplation has become a favourite Companion? Forbear my dear Sally to put yourself in the Power of Fortune. In the many Changes of this mortal Life occurrences unfriendly to our wishes must be expected, and that Philosophy is worth cultivating which teaches us to meet the Frowns of the fickle Goddess with Composure. The Sensibility however from whence these Anxieties result is amiable, and tho I can never discharge the obligations I am under to your Tenderness & Attention, I should be happy indeed were it in my Power to contribute as much to your Happiness as you do to mine. I am much obliged to you for being so mindful of my good Mother. It would give me pleasure to hear of the family. I have recd. one Letter from Fady. I am anxious about them, and most sincerely wish I could be more instrumental than I am to their Prosperity and Ease....

Sally! this State of Separation presses hard upon me. God grant it may be of short Duration. Remember me to all the family, & believe that I am and always will be

your affe.
John Jay

(JJ to SLJ at Elizabeth Town) Philadephia July 10th 1775

My dear Sally

It unfortunately has happened two or three Times that I have been told of opportunities of writing to you, the moment the Persons were about to set off. Yesterday Mr. Livingston for the first time informed me of his Intention to go to New York, and that so soon before he went that I was obliged to omit writing to you.

I am exceedingly happy to hear of your Health and am much obliged to you for your last Letter, which I have recd. I am a little surprized however that you have recd. only one from me, as I wrote you by a Person who went immediately to Elizabeth Town.

The weather here grows very warm, & I am heartily tired of it. I wish I could exchange our Situation for one more northerly, but it is very uncertain whether we shall adjourn to any other Place. It would give me Pleasure to inform you that I expect very soon to see you. I am not able to declare when, but this I can assure you that it will be as soon as I possibly can leave Congress with Propriety.

I have twenty little Things to say to you, but the Fate of Letters is so very precarious that I think it prudent to write with a Kind of Reserve, which however disagreable, I must be content to submit to.

Adieu my dear Sally
I am your affe.
John Jay

John visited Sarah when he could, but his frequent absences were not easy for her. Deeply in love with her husband, she missed him when they were apart and feared for his safety. She also was not of a robust constitution and seems to have suffered from several ailments, including arthritis. Though John's loving solicitude for her well being intensified after Sarah became pregnant in the spring of 1775, he felt it his duty to remain at Philadelphia. However, he was at her side when their son, Peter Augustus, was born on January 24, 1776.

(JJ to SLJ at Elizabeth Town) Phil. 18th Septr 1775

My dear Sally

Accept my Thanks for your kind Letter of the 13th Inst. It would have been cruel to have apologized for writing it: Excuses of this Kind you know pay ill Compliments.

Your Fathers absence gave me Reason to suspect your Mama was still much indisposed. I am sorry to find these Apprehensions confirmed, but still flatter myself you don't think her dangerous, or you would have mentioned it. I assure you her Illness gives me much Anxiety, & the more so as your Sensibility is as often awakened by the Apprehension as the Reality of Misfortunes. Resist this Tendency in your disposition, believe me it is unfriendly to human Happiness. I thank Heaven that you are well. May you never be otherwise. Again let me beg your never ceasing Attention to your Health. Reflect on its Importance!

This City is most intolerably wet and hot. We have not had a single fair or cool Day since my Arrival. It has however, thank God, had no influence on my Health of which I am extremely careful.

To your great Joy and my Satisfaction, the Horse I bought of Mr. Troup is sold & paid for. Claas has a Fever & sore Throat, but not very bad.

I hope your Sisters have regained their Spirits & Appetites. Remember me to them, & to your Mama. Your kind attention to my Father gives me Pleasure, forward the inclosed Letter to him. It might not be amiss to send it covered by one of your own. He will take it kind. But let me apprize of one Circumstance to be particularly attended to in writing to him, that should you be disposed to say civil things, do it very tenderly; rather let them be implied than expressed. I have often heard him censure the neglect of this Caution & inculcate this Rule to me when a Boy. Age indeed generally does away these Refinements. After a certain Period, People advance in Indelicacy as they advance in Years. This observation you know is not applicable to him, we both have Reason to think otherwise. Forgive my troubling you with Remarks so obvious to your Discernment. I always speak & write to you without that Circumspection which Prudence dictates in our common Converse with Mankind.

Adieu my dear Sally
I am your very affe.
John Jay

(JJ to SLJ at Elizabeth Town) Ph. 29 Septr. 1775

My dear Sally

My last to you was by Mr. Graham which I hope you have recd. It would give me Pleasure to have an opportunity of acknowledging the Receipt of one from you. I sometimes fear you are indisposed and that your silence proceeds from a Desire of concealing it.

Your Papa is hearty & well. The Congress spent yesterday in Festivity. The Com[mitte]e of Safety were so polite as to invite them to make a little Voyage in their Gondolas as far as the Fort which is about 12 miles from the City. Each galley had its Company & each Company entertained with Variety of Musick &c. &c. We proceeded six or Eight miles down the River when the Tide being spent & the wind unfavorable we tacked about & with a fine Breese returned, passed the City & landed six Miles above the town at a pretty little Place called Parr's Villa. It appears to have been the Property of a Gentleman of some Taste—a Garden, a close Walk, a Summer House &c. much out of order & partly in Ruins. I wished you & a few select Friends had been with me. This Idea tho amidst much Noise and Mirth made me much alone.

Adieu my beloved
I am most sincerely yours
John Jay

(JJ to SLJ at Elizabeth Town) Philadelphia 27 Nov 1775

My Dear Sally

Your Letter of the 23d. Inst. is come to Hand. I thank Heaven you were well, and am obliged to you for being mindful of telling me so.

We did not get further than Woodbridge the afternoon I left you. There Mr.

[Silas] Dean lost his Surtout*, and Claas his Shoes, Buckles and Brushes. It was dark when we arrived, and these things were taken out of our Carriage between the time of our leaving them and the Landlords coming to the door with a Candle, which was I believe less than two minutes. Our Search & Inquiries proved fruitless.

I have not heard from my Father or Brother since I left them. I have written, & hope my Letters have reached them. If you should have heard any thing of them pray let me know it. I am thank God well, and provided you continue in Health & Spirits, few occurrences can make me very unhappy.

I am my dear good wife
Your very affe.
John Jay

(JJ to SLJ at Elizabeth Town) Philadelphia 4 Decr. 1775

My dear Sally

When shall I have the Pleasure of acknowledging the Rect. of a Letter from you? I have been favoured only with one since I left you. Our Letters I fear often miscarry, and cant forbear suspecting that an idle and criminal Curiosity has proved fatal to several of them. It is really cruel thus to interrupt an Intercourse so innocent and interesting to us.

I begin to wish for the holy Days as much as a School Boy ever did. I flatter myself with being able then to pay you a visit as it is very probable the congress will then make a short adjournment. My dear Sally! be attentive to your Health, and be assured that the most acceptable office you can do me, is to neglect [no] means of rendering yourself chearful & happy. Adieu my beloved!

I am most sincerely yours
John Jay

(JJ to SLJ at Elizabeth Town) Philadelphia 23 Decr. 1775

My dear Wife

I have now the Pleasure of informing you that the New York Convention has at length made some Provision for their Delegates vizt. 4 dollars per day for their Attendance on the last, and this Congress, so that I shall not be so great a Sufferer as I once apprehended. The Allowance indeed does by no Means equal the Loss I have sustained by the Appointment, but the Convention I suppose consider the Honor as an Equivalent for the Residue.

The Congress this Day refused to give me Leave of absence for next Week. There are but five New York Delegates here, Coll. [Gouverneur] Morris and Mr. [Francis] Lewis being absent, so that should either of us leave the Town, the Province would be unrepresented. We expect however soon to adjourn, and your Papa has engaged Mr. Hooper to accompany him to Elizabeth Town, where I hope we shall soon be all

**A man's fitted coat or overcoat.*

very happy. My Horses were new shod, Wheels greased, Cloaths put up and every thing ready to set off early in the Morning, when on going to Congress this Morning all my pleasing Expectations of seeing you on Christmas Day were disappointed. Don't you pity me my Dear Sally? It is however some Consolation that should the Congress not adjourn in less than ten Days, I am determined to stay with you till ______. And depend upon it nothing but actual Imprisonment will be able to keep me from you.

At present I find the Objections of the Congress so reasonable that I am sure you would blame me, were I to attempt leaving them without Permission. I must endeavour to resign myself to my Fate, and I am sure you have too much good Sence and too much Regard for _____ to permit the Disappointment to occasion unavailing Anxiety. Tomorrow or on Tuesday next the Congress will I believe determine the Time of Adjournment so that it is probable I shall have the Happiness of wishing you a happy New Year. Adieu my beloved

I am most sincerely,
Your affe.
John Jay

P. S. I have received a Letter from Rye of an old Date. They were as well as usual. I dined with your Papa to Day. He was very well. Once more let me intreat you to be chearful and keep up your Spirits. I know by my own Feelings that these kind of Disappointments are disagreeable but when I reflect how much more happy [we] are than thousands of our Fellow Mortals my Uneasiness is lost in Gratitude.

(JJ to Robert R. Livingston at Clermont) Eliz. Town 26 Jany 1776

Dear Robert

The Concern occasioned by the many misfortunes lately attending your family, is greatly augmented by a Report which has for some Days prevailed of you being much indisposed. Did not Mrs. Jay's Illness forbid my leaving her I should most certainly pay you a Visit. She was the Day before Yesterday delivered of a Boy, and tho there is no Reason to apprehend Danger at present, yet the precarious Situation of Life in such Circumstances makes me the Subject of many fears & much anxiety....

God be with you my dear Robert
yr. F[rien]d.
John Jay

GLC 3107.04189. John Jay. Autograph letter signed: to Robert R. Livingston (1746–1813) re: advice for Robert's health, 26 January 1776 (the Gilder Lehrman Collection, courtesy of the Gilder Lehrman Institute of American History, New York).

(JJ to SLJ at Elizabeth Town) Philadelphia 3 March 1776

My dear Sally

Your Letter of the 17 Inst. made me very happy by informing me of your Health and our Son's Recovery, which I hope is by this time perfect. Tho your Tenderness in concealing his Indisposition merits my thanks, yet be assured that I shall never hesitate more in sharing your Anxieties, than in partaking of your Pleasures.

I am glad to hear Mrs. Lawrence was in such good spirits as to entertain you with the Story of the Conch shell Beauty, which together with its Embellishments, I dare say afforded much mirth & amusements to the Company. This little Incident happened in November last, and at the time was the subject of Wit and Raillery in the little circle of our acquaintances, but soon growing thread-bare it ceased, like other matters of the same kind, to be the object of attention, and I don't remember it once presented itself to my Recollection during the Time I spent at Elizabeth Town.

However as the story has excited your Curiosity, and may contribute to your entertainment, I will acquaint you with such of the Particulars of it as I can now recollect.

On a Saturday in November last, Coll. Morris and myself, invited by sunshine and good Road took a walk to Gray's Ferry with Intention [to] dine and spend the day there. On our arrival we ordered Fire to be made in a private room, and while it was preparing, sat down in the common Room with many travellers and country People who were returning from Market, with whom we entered into familiar conversation about Whigs and Tories and Beef and Butter and Congress too.

We had not been long engaged in this way, before a most beautiful country girl about seventeen, in a coarse but clean Dress, alighted from a waggon and came in to warm herself. She was tall, extremely well made, and of most delicate and well proportioned features; an uncommon sweetness was diffused thro' her countenance, and that kind of truely virgin modesty which Innocence and simplicity of manners inspire, marked her whole Deportment. Her Complection beggared all Description, nature had exerted her utmost skill in forming it. Her teeth were as good and her eyes of the same colour, and almost as fine, as those of my fair Correspondent. An object so charming immediately diverted our attention from the Herd around us.

The Coll. asked her very politely which way she was travelling; she blushed and answered, that she had been to town and was returning home. A conversation ensued. _____ _____ _____ _____ each Sentence borrowing Eloquence and Grace from Lips on which even a Right Reverend audience would readily consent to hang. Every Reply was accompanied by Blushes, which alternately rising and retiring, and each varying in Degree, formed a sweet Succession of such pleasing Shades, that one would be inclined to suspect that Beauty had shown the Countenance of this lovely girl, as a proper Field for showing the vast variety of modes, in which she could display her numerous Charms.

After a few compliments the Coll. told her he had a son a little older than herself whom he would be happy to marry to a pretty country girl that would not be above minding the Business of the farm, & would not (like some more fashionable Ladies) attend to nothing but dancing & Dress— that he was much pleased with her, and would, if she had no objections send him to pay her a Visit. She blushed, she smiled, her Eyes sparkled, and her whole countenance became agreably confused. She replied that she could not believe him to be in earnest. She was sure such a gentleman's son could not marry a poor country girl without a Fortune. I observed that Industry, Beauty, and Innocence composed a fortune more valuable than money, and that in these she was far from being poor. She was embarrassed, and Humanity forbid us to increase it.

The waiter soon after called us to Dinner, to which we retired after having in vain invited her to partake of it. We indeed inquired her name and Place of abode, of both which she informed us. We then parted after wishing her all the Happiness, which the Possession of so many Charms seemed justly to claim.

The pretty girl furnished Conversation for us the whole afternoon. Coll. Morris thought she bore a great resemblance to the Lady who will open this Letter, and I assure you his opinion was not ill founded, which probably was the Reason of my being the more pleased with her.

Before we left the Ferry, we considered of the Propriety of saying any thing about her, & finally agreed to do Justice to Merit, but to conceal her Name and Place of abode lest by being exposed to the Flattery and Snares of those who admire and caress one, destroy. Her Innocence beauty and Simplicity might be instrumental to her ruin.

But you may ask, how came she to be called the conch shell Beauty. It happened thus. In speaking of her complexion, which really exceeded any I had ever seen, I compared it to the inside of a Conch shell which is of the most exquisite Flesh color in the World.

You will readily imagine that on our Return to town we were not parsimonious of Praise. We were asked her name and where she lived, both of which Questions we declined answering. The curiosity of our friends was increased by this refusal, and they called us not a little on the motives they assigned for our Secrecy. All which we chearfully submitted to, rather than suffer her to be visited by a Swarm of Beaux who like so many Bees, often find a way to the Bosoms of the fairest new blown flowers, and after robbing them of their Sweets, ungratefully neglect and forsake them.

This is the History of the Conch shell Beauty, which I have endeavoured to render as minute as possible, and I am persuaded you will think it very particular, considering the little Time we were with her. A further acquaintance or even a second interview would probably have discovered to us many other graces which must then have escaped our Notice.

I have more to say, but it is so late and I am to sleep that I must bid you a good night.

Adieu my dearest Sally
John Jay

GLC 1220. John Jay. Autograph letter signed: to wife Sally Jay re: "Conch Shell Beauty," 4 March 1776 (the Gilder Lehrman Collection, courtesy of the Gilder Lehrman Institute of American History, New York).

(JJ to SLJ at Elizabeth Town) Philadelphia 12 March 1776

My dear Sally,

You will recieve this from the Hands of my good friends Mr. and Mrs. Lawrence.... Abrahams, the Jew of whom I bought the Mustard, could not give me

Change. Be so kind therefore as to pay him, or send the money to Grahams for him. The two shoemakers, Halsey and Carmichael are also unpaid. Settle with them. Tradesmen you know ought not to wait long for their money. I am sorry to give you this trouble. I intended to have done it myself, but intirely forgot it. I have written to Fady to send my Desk, Cloaths Press, & Bed to you.

Kiss the dear little boy for me, and believe that I am and always will be

your affe.
John Jay

(JJ to SLJ at Elizabeth Town) Philadelphia 31 March 1776

My dear Sally,

I have recd. your complimentary Letter of the 24th. March Inst. & should be happy to merit half the civil Things you say of your Husband.

How does our little Boy do? Have your apprehensions of his getting the Dow Worm proved groundless? By your Silence for these eight or ten Days I fear all is not well. It gives me Pleasure to hear of your being in perfect Health, tho' I confess your continuing so thin is an unpleasing circumstance. Perhaps being a Nurse disagrees with you. If so, I hope you will decline it. Let no consideration induce you to injure your Constitution.

I suspect your attention to your Son and too much Industry renders you negligent of Exercise. The Roads will now admit of riding. The Weather is often pleasant, and I am sure frequent Airings would do you more good than a Physician. Have you played Battledore & Shuttlecock* since I left you? God bless you, and give you Grace to take Care of the Health of your Body as well as your Soul. With my love to all the family

I am my dear Sally
your affece. Husband
John Jay

John Jay was an active member of several Congressional committees dealing with foreign affairs. Hoping for reconciliation with Great Britain, he slowly became convinced that a break was inevitable, that Americans were "impelled to independence by necessity, and not by choice."

In April 1776, after being elected to the New York Provincial Congress, he left Philadelphia for New York City to participate in the affairs of the state. Threatened by a British naval attack, the New York Provincial Congress was forced to move to White Plains. There the vote was taken to approve and, as John Jay wrote, "at the risk of our lives and fortunes" to support the Declaration of Independence.

**A game of ancient Oriental origin that evolved into badminton.*

(JJ to SLJ at Elizabeth Town) Philadelphia 5th April 1776

My dear Sally

Your Letter of the 2d. April Inst. relieved me from much Anxiety. Your not writing to me since the 24th of last month, and sending a Bundle without a Letter, led me to suspect that your Silence proceeded from a Fear of disclosing to me some disagreable Circumstance; which you know had been the Case once before. I am happy to hear the Boy is well. You don't tell me whether he has had the Sprue*, or whether the Symptoms of it mentioned in one of your former Letters, have disappeared.

The Intelligence you give me of my Father and the Family at Rye affords me great Satisfaction; and the more so, as I have not heard from them this Fortnight. His kind Attention to you and our son is perfectly consistant with that uniform attachment to his children, which has always distinguished and rendered him dear to them. I hope the next month will put it in our Power to pay him a Visit, and to increase his Happiness as well as that of my very good Mother, by a Sight of this grandson. Don't however depend too much upon it, for should the Commissioners arrive or be then expected, it is more than probable that I shall do Violence to my Inclinations, and deny myself the Pleasure of seeing you, till I shall be able to leave the Congress with Propriety.

Mrs. Gibbons has been so obliging as to give you a little Glass of the kind your Letter alludes to. It shall be sent by the first good opportunity that may offer. If any can be purchased here, you may expect to recieve two or three of them.

I hope your next Letter will inform me of your Mama's Recovery. Be so kind as to present my Respects to her, & Compliments to your Brothers & Sisters.

I am my dear Sally
your very affe. Husband
John Jay

(JJ to SLJ) White Plains 12 July 1776

My dear good Wife

You may easily concieve the Satisfaction I recd. from your Letter, when I inform you that it was currently reported here, that the enemy after landing on Staten Island had marched to Elizabeth Town and taken Possession of the Barracks there. This Report was so current & so confidently asserted to be true, that I confess I felt most sensibly for you, and immediately dispatched Dyckman Express to you, with orders in case he could be of any use to you to stay and afford you all the assistance in his Power.

I much commend the Coolness and Presence of Mind with which you recd. the alarm. My dear Sally continue to cultivate it. I am glad the Boy is weaned and does well. Kiss him for me. Are you still at Baskenridge? Above all things consult your Health. Let neither Expence or Complaisance induce you to omit any Thing conducive to it....

**Also known as thrush, a disease affecting the mouths of very young children.*

I am my dear Sally
your very affe. Husband
John Jay

(JJ to SLJ at Elizabeth Town) Poghkeepsy 21 July 1776

My dear Sally

In a hot little Room, in Spite of Importunities to hear the pompous Chauncey Graham preach, & in Defiance of the God of Sleep whom the Bugs & Fleas banished from my Pillow last night; am I set down to write a few Lines to my good little Wife.

On leaving Rye, I informed you of my intended Journey, which Letter you have doubtless ere this recd. We have paid a Visit to the Forts in the Highlands, and after a Jaunt of three Days which afforded us Pleasure as well as Exercise, I arrived here about an hour ago in perfect Health. Should I continue this kind of Life for three Weeks or a month my Cloaths would be too narrow for me.

I have recd. no Letter from you since the one by [Samson] Dyckman. Have you recd. mine from the White Plains? Direct for me at Rye. I am impatient to hear of your Health, my Sollicitude on that Head however was abated by Kitty's telling me at Morrissania that Doctr. Bard had seen & left you better. May God of his infinite mercy perfect your Recovery!

I am happy in a kind of Confidence or Pre-Sentiment that we shall yet enjoy many good Days together, & I indulge myself in imaginary Scenes of Happiness which I expect in a few Years to see realized. If it be a Delusion, it is a pleasing one, & therefore I embrace it; should it like a Bubble vanish into Air, Resignation will blunt the Edge of Disappointment, and a firm Persuasion of after Bliss give me Consolation. Then my dear Wife shall we fear no Tyrants Power, neither shall we know Anxiety any more, and, if   , I cant fill up the blank, we shall again join Hands & Hearts & continue our virtuous Connection forever.

My Return is uncertain. I hope our Boy is well. God bless & keep you both. My Compliments to all the Family.

I am my dear Sally
your very affectionate Husband
John Jay

As a member of the Provincial Congress, John served on a secret committee to protect the Hudson. He journeyed to Salisbury, Connecticut, to acquire cannon and shot for fortifications. He also was an active participant on the Committee for Detecting and Defeating Conspiracies, interrogating suspected loyalists, among whom were family members and friends.

The dangers were many; no one was safe. Fear of capture by opposing forces kept John on the move. Father Peter Jay had to abandon his farm in Rye, move inland and then to Fishkill for safety; even there, he was robbed. Sarah moved between her parents and her parents-in-law, often leaving her son with the Livingstons. Her health continued fragile. John was concerned for her: "My dear Sally! Are you yet provided with a secure Retreat in Case Elizabeth Town should cease to be a Place of Safety? I shall not be at Ease till this be done. You know my Happiness depends on your Welfare ...."

John Jay was right to be concerned about the Livingstons. On February 29, 1779, a British raiding party broke into Liberty Hall, where they found Susan and her mother. Not finding the Governor, the British demanded his papers; Susan cleverly was able to persuade them to take a box of unimportant documents instead of the official correspondence with George Washington and other leaders. Her brother Brockholst commended her: "They must be chagrined at the Trick played on them...."

(Peter Jay to SLJ at Elizabeth Town) Rye ye 6 augt 1776

Dear Sally

I have received yr letter your kind Sister miss Catharine has favour'd me with, and to wch. I would now write her an answer with great pleasure if my nervous complaint, (wch is much increased, did not prevent my puting pen to paper without ye greatest difficulty, and wch I beg may induce her to excuse my declining it. The long continuance of your indisposition gives us great pain, and it's our ardent prayer to God to bless you with a speedy recovery. It would give us inexpressible pleasure to see your kind Sister and our little dear Boy here, and still more so if you should be so happily recover'd as to admit of your accompanying them, a happiness that is I apprehend at too great a distance occasion'd by our unhappy Times, but should affairs take a favourable turn, so that yr. Journey can be preform'd with safety, Fady will wait upon miss Catharine agreeable to her proposal. In case some of ye Men of War should come in ye Sound, as it's expected they will, our Situation so near ye water will not be safe, and therefore I have hired some Rooms about 3 miles back in ye Country to move what is most valuable, & ourselves too in case it be necessary, so that at present we are in an unsettled Situation.

About ten days ago I heard Johnny was well and gone from Poughkeepsie to Connecticut but what place I could not learn, so that yr. Letter to him remains still here. We desire to assure Mr. & Mrs. Livingston & yr good Sister of our respects. Embrace our Little dear Boy for us & also little [Peter Jay] Munro if you should see him. Be assured of our greatest affection, I am my dear Sally

yr very affect Father
Peter Jay

(Susan Livingston to JJ at Fishkill) Eliz:Town 1:st Novr [1776]

Dr Sir

Mr. Fine returned last Evening, & delivered me your Letter, we were not without fear on his account, hearing such alarming reports of the rapid progress of the Enemy in your Province we feared he might be taken....

I am distressed for poor Mr & Mrs Jay to be obliged to abandon their House at their time of Life, & leave their Effects at the mercy of lawless Power must be very trying, the Havoc of War is dreadful.

Our little Boy grows finely, we have not seen Dr. [Samuel] Bard since you left us, & thank Heaven he has not needed his Assistance. Solomon tells us you intend sending for young Master. I hope it's only for a visit, we know not how to part with him even for a short time, if you will let him come back again Hannah Benjamin will go with him, she will not consent to stay the Winter at Fish kill as all her Relations are in the Jersies & the Child is so shy he will hardly suffer a Stranger to look at him. If it will not incommode you, or there is any Place near you where I could Lodge, I think to Escort our young Squire, I beg you will tell me plainly if it's inconvenient.

Mama begs an Affectionate Remembrance to your Fathers Family & we all unite in love to you & Sister

I am
Your affecte Sister
S.L

Sally must let us know what she wants that it may be sent when Peter goes. If he is to remain with you I shall return with Hannah Benjamin. Mama does not think it prudent to entrust him to Abbe's* care on such a Journey neither would he be contented with her.

(JJ to Kitty Livingston) Fish Kill, 8th November 1776

My much respected and very <u>respectful</u> Sister

Your Letter dated on some Wednesday in October last came to Hand when I was so engaged as to be deprived of the Pleasure of acknowledging the Reciept of it. My Fathers Family with such of their Effects as have escaped the Ruin to which the Property of the Whigs in that Part of the Country was exposed, are now here. Sally returned two Days ago from the Manor in much better Health than she went. Her appetite is as good as any Body's. The Rheumatism still <u>vexes her Bones</u>, tho less than formerly.

How shall we contrive to remove your little Friend to the Arms of his Mother? I am sure my Father and Mother are desirous of seeing him, tho they appear unwilling that he should be exposed to the Fatigue and Trouble of the Journey. If I could have three or four Leisure Day's I should certainly fetch him, and I am not certain that it will not be in my Power before the End of the Month. It will however not be without Reluctance, for I am so well convinced of the kind Attention paid him by his Grandmama and Aunts, that I am persuaded it is impossible to change his Situation for the better.

The Cravat you was so kind as to purchase (for which accept my Thanks) came safe. I wish Sally's Fur Gown may be as fortunate, but that continues uncertain, as the Movements of military People often depend as much on adventitious Circumstances as more uniform Principles.

The Enemy's Army is retreating to I know not where. Perhaps to a <u>less moun-</u>

**Abigail, known as Abbe, is a Livingston slave.*

tainous Country. Some suspect they are going into Winter Quarters which I think improbable.

Brockholst was at the Manor before Sally left it in exceeding good Health and much improved. He is a fine young Fellow, and will do Honor to the Family.

Sally took so little Thought for the Morrow as to bring only one pair of Shoes with her. They are almost worn out, and Shoemakers are as scarce here as Saints in Sodom. Be so obliging as to get a Copple of neat Pair, at any Price, made for her, and send them by the first good opportunity.

Thank Mama for the Rice &c she sent us.

Our Love to all the Family.

I am Dear Cate, or Catharine or Kitty your affectionate Brother
John Jay

P.S. Sally has read this Letter. She directs me to subjoin the following explanatory note vizt "The Rheumatism is now only in her Right Hand. Her Bone Waistcoat, and purple and white Calico Gown and the Cuffs thereunto belonging would be very acceptable to her."

(JJ & SLJ to Kitty Livingston at Baskenridge, N.J.) Fish Kills 20 Jany 1777

Dear Kitty

When I just now told Sally I was going to write you a Letter by General Morris she made a Point of it that I should tell you she was very well. So that notwithstanding my Scruples of Conscience I accordingly give you this Information. To tell you however the plain Truth, she is much better and has scarce any Remains of the Rheumatism, except now & then a few fly-about Pains of short Duration & no great Moment. She has learnt her spin on the great wheel, and from hence you may conclude not only that she pays proper Attention to Exercise but that She has regained the use of her Finger, of which she intends to give you further Proofs by writing you a long Letter one of these Days.

Doctr. Foster & his Lady arrived here two Days ago, & by them Sally recd. the Letter[,] Gloves &c mentioned in one of your former Letters.

The late Successes in Jersey have I hope raised your Spirits and diminished your Anxieties. We daily hear favourable accounts from that Quarter, and God grant that a deserved victory may soon reward our Exertions & Toil.

My Father is much indisposed, & I think wears away fast. Tho he does not express his Sollicitude in plain Forms, yet he frequently hints a Desire to see his Grandson. I wish he could be gratified in This, and if it could be conveniently done would give me great Satisfaction. The Business of Convention takes from me the least hope of soon paying you a Visit, and therefore must refer the Business of your nephews Journey to the Discretion of his Grandmother & Aunts. If Brockholst & you or Susan could come with him I should be easy. The River is very hard frozen at Staatsburgh & the Road from the opposite Shore to your House they say very good. If a covered Waggon could be procured, I should think it would [be] the most proper kind of Carriage & I would most chearfully pay the Expence of the whole. That is a Consideration of no weight with me in this Case, or indeed in any other whether the Happiness of my Parents is concerned. Mention the matter to Brockholst. I would write to him, but really have not Leisure. It is now near nine oClock at night & I have but just risen from Dinner.

Sally is much obliged to Mama for the Gloves &c &c and is uneasy lest she should want her Tippet*.

[In Sarah's hand] Do my dear Kitty be explicit, in the first Letter you or any of the family write me, about your health, if I should not be so happy as to see you here. I am afraid the Journey Mr. Jay has mark'd out for you will be attended with too much difficulty at this Season of the Year. The petticoat, Tippet, & some more things which I fear Mamma could but ill spare I wish I had it in my power to return as I am well provided. It is for want of opportunity alone that I do not Send my fur-gown to wrap the dear little rogue in but you may assure my dear Mamma if she will trust either of Sisters with hannah & the Child I will take care to wrap them very warm when they return. My Wrist which seldom pains me when I make any [use] of it, will not permit me to write another line, otherwise I am extremely well.

[In John Jay's hand] Tell Hannah we are much obliged to her for the Attention she pays to her little Charge. Adieu

I am your Friend & afft. Brother
J. Jay

In the face of escalating military activity, the members of the Provincial Congress, now called the Convention of the Representatives of the State of New York, retreated again, first to Fishkill, then to Kingston. A committee of which John Jay was a leading member was formed (August 1776) to draft a constitution for the state. During the debate on the draft in March 1777, John was summoned to Fishkill where his mother lay gravely ill. She died on April 17. Even as he comforted his bereaved family, members of the Convention conferred with John, seeking his opinions and approval of the new constitution.

(SLJ to JJ at Esopus) Fish Kill March 23, 1777

The happiness of my dear Mr. Jay is so nearly connected with my own that it is impossible for mine to be intire when I have reason to apprehend that yours is in any-wise diminished, which I fear has been the case when I wrote you that I was unwell with a cold. It is in order to remove any anxiety you may feel on that account that I again trouble you with another letter, as I am perfectly recovered.

Your father and mother still continue very much indisposed. They desire to be affectionately remember'd to you. Accept my thanks for your last letter. I assure you I felt a secret pleasure when I observed that in sending those letters to the Post-office (which I did the day after your departure) and in sometimes visiting & often inquiring about your horse I had been before-hand with your wishes. Thinking of your horse

A tippet is a long hanging end of cloth attached to a sleeve, cap, or hood.

reminds me of an odd accident that happened yesterday to Claas, who I had sent to your father's for grain in the morning. He return'd at noon without his bag, and in tears, inquiring for the docter [Theodorus Van Wyck], at which I was alarm'd, & asked him the cause of his uneasiness; After a few sobs he replied that in his way home being asleep, he was awaken'd by a couple of men who were holding his horse, & insisted upon having his whip to rouze him, which accordingly they wrested from him & after awaking him sufficiently, they took his bag of grain, & bid adieu. The Docter not being at home he return'd alone in pursuit of the men who had so unpolitely disturbed his rest, and overtook them at Mr. Wickoff's, to whom he related his story. But to the surprise of Claas they absolutely denied there having ever seen him before, & insisted upon it that if he had been asleep he had likewise dreamt; but the whipping was too recent in his memory to admit that thought, & he return'd without receiving any satisfaction, or obtaining any intelligence from them about his bag. But near the place that they had stop'd him he found it hanging on the fence. The impatience with which he had pursued the men had prevented his percieving it before.

Our dear little boy is well & in fine spirits. He has been setting on my lap playing with the pen, by which means he interupted me till Fady came in, & inform'd me that General Scott was going to Esopus to-morrow. I shall trouble [him] with this letter.

I have heard this afternoon that there are transports in the north river, about 4 miles below Croton ferry. It's thought forage is the object they have in view, in consequence of which I hear it's ordered to be removed. This very instant the Docter came into the room, his looks bespeaking the utmost discomposure. Bad news Mrs. Jay. Aye Dr. what now? The regulars madam are landed at Peekskill. My own & other Waggons are press'd to go instantly down to remove the Stores. Wherever I am, I think there are alarms. However I am determined to remember your maxim, prepare for the worst & hope the best. The Dr. is now going to Fish-kill. I leave my letter unseal'd till he returns.

Sister Caty gives her Compts. to you. She intends writing a letter to be inclosed in this for mamma & begs youll forward it as soon as possible. May the blessings of peace be soon restor'd to us!

And that health & safety may ever attend you is the sincere prayer of

your affectionate Wife
Sarah Jay

Monday Morning

The Dr. returned at midnight. He says that Mr. [William] Duer is come to Fish-Kill & that he says not less than twelve hundred of the Enemy landed at Peekskill, that General [Alexander] McDougal with the men under his command (a small number) were upon the high hill near the place where the regu[lars] landed & that they had been firing some time. I wish I knew what is to be done with your white chest. It is not perhaps safe [or at] least the stores being all ordered from Fish Kill make me think not. All the forrage & other Stores (except ammunition) are burnt at Peeks Kill. The melitia are all order[ed] down. This morng Frank* was here. He tells me

A family servant.

Peter [John Jay's brother] came home last night, & that Mamma [John Jay's mother] is very Ill. A line from you by the first opportunity to advise me in what manner to proceed will much oblige.

your Affe. Wife
Sarah Jay

On May 3, 1777, the Provincial Congress elected John Jay chief justice of the New York State Supreme Court of Judicature. He was thus, as he wrote Sarah on April 29, 1778, often

> engaged in the most disagreeable part of my Duty—trying criminals. They multiply exceedingly. Robberies become frequent. The Woods afford them Shelter & the Tories Food. Punishment must of course become certain & Mercy dormant—a harsh System repugnant to my Feelings, but nevertheless necessary. In such Circumstances Lenity would be Cruelty, & Severity is found on the Side of Humanity.

(SLJ to JJ at Fish Kill) Kingston, May 3, 1777

My dear Mr. Jay,

How shall I express my thanks to my dear friend for his tenderness, such extreme attention is too rare, as well too unmerited not to excite a gratitude & affection that is only excel'd by your generosity. The letters you mention have not been recd. either by the gentlemen or by myself & yr silence gave room to flatter myself that I should have had the pleasure of seeing you before now. Pray don't let that naughty irruption detain you at Fish Kill; indeed I would risque its being any thing. Besides, the Congress are impatient for yr return, & several of the Members say that they intend writing to you, as they are oblig'd to defer some important business 'till they can have your advice, so that you see the Public advantage requires your immediate presence.

Sister Caty is with Mrs. Jones at Herley, and Antie is at her mothers, so that I am sole Mistress, & as you may suppose have leisure to meditate from the rising to the setting of the Sun; now I think a word from you now & then would contribute vastly to enliven, direct, & improve my meditations. What is your opinion? I have just been interupted by the Miss Clemendorfs, who have paid me a social visit. After they had taken leave, and I had time to make enquiries of Frank about the family, I found that your company was so necessary to Papa, that I was displeased with myself for being so rapt in the idea of my own happiness, as not to perceive, that when I was requesting your return, I was likewise endeavoring to deprive him of a very considerable consolation. Be assured, my dear Mr. Jay, that from that consideration, instead of desiring to influence your conduct, you cannot determine any thing that will not be agreable to your

affectionate wife
Sa: Jay

(SLJ to JJ at Kingston) Troy, New Jersey, June 17th 1777

My dear Mr. Jay,

I have just heard that Mr. [Samuel] Ogden knows of an opportunity to send a letter to Esopus, I shall therefore embrace it with pleasure to assure my dear Mr. Jay of my confirmed health, & of the welfare of our family. Little Peter continues active & well, I dare not trust myself to say more of him lest I should say too much, suffice it therefore that I will tell you he speaks a few words, & that every acquisition in way of tricks &c. have from us the approbation that should be bestowed upon real merit.

Our situation here, altho' retired is by no means unpleasant, and if my friend who is now absent could make one of our party, I should even pronounce it happy. When Mr. [Gouverneur] Morris was here he desired Mrs. Ogden to supply us with any books from his library that were most agreable to us, which, together with those we had before, make quite a clever collection. Since I have been at Troy we have entertained ourselves with reading from breakfast time 'till noon, & when alone of an afternoon a play of Shakespears furnishes an elegant amusement. The history of Madame de Maintenon was my yesterday's study, & I intend to continue it 'till I have finished it: ....

After having given you an account of the manner in which we pass our time, you'll readily percieve (or if you would not any one else would) the great advantages that our little party might derive from the observations of my dear sage friend.

I believe I omitted telling you in my last that Grand Papa French had left this confused world of ours. I hope that the exchange which he has made is an happy one.

Papa return'd from Haddonfield a saturday and the Council of safety are to meet on tuesday at Morris Town. Pappa, mamma & sisters unite in desiring to be remembred to you and our other friends where you are.

I am my dear Mr. Jay, with unalterable affection,

Yours
Sarah Jay

(SLJ to JJ) Persipiney, June 25, 1777

My dear Mr. Jay,

Coll. [Matthias] Ogden has very politely sent me a billet this evening, to inform me that he is going to Esopus early in the morning & will take my commands with pleasure. I think myself extremely happy to have the power to thank my dear Mr. Jay for his kind letters. The last was left for me at Papa's when I was at Elizabeth Town upon a visit with Mamma, or I should have answered it by the Express. Our country seat appeared to me more delightful than ever, but I could not forbear lamenting the sad depravity of mankind, when I beheld the ravages committed by our neighbours upon the estate of a man in whose readiness to serve them they acknowledge the utmost confidence.

I congratulate you my dear, upon the safe arrival of your trunk with Cloaths, and to add to your satisfaction I can tell you that I found in your trunk a doz. & half of beautiful shirts, so that you need not be under any apprehension on that score. As you mention finding some summer necessaries at Fish Kill I shall defer sending more 'till you inform me particularly what will be most agreable. I fear the gloves I sent you are too small, the pair I now send I think are larger, but if they are not let me know & I'll knit another.

I have heard that Jewel wants to pay the sum for which he is bound to you & I think it will not be improper to send the bond & mortgage to me by Mr. Ogden in case it should be apply'd for.

How does this warm weather agree with you? This day especially, has been intensely warm.... In my haste I had almost forgot to tell you that your son is well. The eveng. is too far advanced to indulge myself with the pleasure of scribbling longer to my dear Mr. Jay.

I am, my dear,
Your affte. Wife
Sa. Jay

(JJ to SLJ) Kingston, 3rd July 1777

My dear Sally

The last Evening I had the Pleasure of recieving your kind Letters of the 25 and 27 June last. My anxiety occasioned by your Excursion to Eliz Town, has I assure You been amply compensated by the Benefit and Pleasure you received from it. One of the first Reports which reached us after the Evacuation of Brunswick, was that when the Enemy arrived at Bonum Town they separated, and that one division filing off towards Springfield marched to Staten Island through Elizabeth Town. This Manoeuvre it was said was occasioned by a strong Post taken by Gen. [William] Maxwell at bonum Town where we had before heard he was stationed. On comparing the time when you went to Eliz Town with the Time of this March, they corresponded so nearly that I was not a little uneasy at the Prospect of your being much terrified and perhaps made Captive by them.

I am much obliged to you for the gloves and druget*. The former fit me well. The Express delivered them to me....

I am your very affectionate Husband
John Jay

(JJ to SLJ) Kingston, Sunday, 6th July, 1777

My dear Sally,

Having a few leisure hours allotted me by this day of general rest, I shall divide them between Heaven and yourself; being persuaded that while I do my duty to both, my expectations of happiness will not be in vain.

When I consider that one of the reasons assigned for the creation of woman was, "that it is not good for man to be alone," I find my present situation condemned,

**Drugget: fabric made wholly or partly of wool used as a protective covering for a carpet.*

not only by my own feelings, but by divine authority. I assure you, I am tired of it; and, were there not many reasons to conjecture that the enemy will bend their course this way, we should not remain much longer separated; but, as it would be cruel to expose you to scenes of anxiety and distress, I must endeavour to bear your absence at least with patience, and to please myself with the expectation of shortly seeing the return of those happy days, when we shall again "sit under our own vine, and under our own fig-tree, and there be none to make us afraid."

As soon as the Council of Safety dissolves, which will be at the meeting of the Legislature, you may expect to see me for a few days; but when that event will take place is uncertain. Should this State become the seat of war, and be attacked on both sides, it will not be practicable to convene the Legislature, nor indeed would it be proper for me, in such a conjuncture, to be absent.

As the enemy are now expelled from Jersey, and Liberty Hall is again free, I fancy Susan has become as joyous as ever, and that the whole family are not a little anxious to put an end to their exile.

I returned last Wednesday from Fishkill. My father declines fast. His late loss affects him exceedingly; he gives way to silence and retirement, spending hours every day in that melancholy room; and though he appears calm and resigned, the effects of this inauspicious event are visible upon him. How few possess such sensibility, or are capable of affections so permanent and so delicate!

Whenever leisure and opportunity offer, remember, my dear Sally, how acceptable a line from you always is to

Your very affectionate husband,
John Jay

(SLJ to JJ at Kingston) Persipiney, Septbr. 3d, 1777

My dear Mr. Jay,

No less than three weeks have already elapsed, and not a single line from my beloved friend....

I long to know my destination next winter, and yet I could wish not to wait so long as winter neither before your abode is mine; I am the more earnest to be with you upon our son's account; the dear child has been very fractious these two or three weeks, & I know not whether to impute it to ill health or impatience of temper. If the latter be the only cause, I need not tell you how effectually you[r] presence would obviate any difficulty on that score since his implicit obedience to whatever appeared to be your pleasure is too recent not be recollected.

Mamma, Cousin Nancy, and Sisters present you with their esteem, and if you'll write me soon, you may assure yourself of the love of your

Ever affectionate
Wife
Sarah Jay

(Susan Livingston to SLJ;
Kitty Livingston to JJ at Kent, Ct.) Nov. 1st 1777 — Morris County

Dearly beloved Sarah

I am in expectation of the arrival of the Post every moment, he usually comes in on Fryday Evening, & returns next Morning as he goes no farther than Morris Town. Last Evening he did not come. Mama received a Letter, but the Post did not deliver it till his return from Morris Tn which deprived me of the pleasure of acknowledging it at that time; the things you mentioned were already taken care of. I hope to receive one when the Post arrives. He told us last Saturday, that he saw Mr. F. Jay, at Loudons who told him you were all moving at your Fathers; so that I do not know where to direct to you; we are afraid Mr. Jay has lost his Clothes that were at Kingston; Mama says if your warm Petticoat is lost, she can spare you one, rather than you should suffer for want of it.

Papa has been home since Sunday Evening, the accounts he brought are old now, & not worth writing. On the 23. Inst. 5 or 6 Men of War, warped thro' an opening they had made in the lower Chevaux de Frieze*, & came up to attack our Fort & Ships & Gallies but they found the Navigation so difficult, that they set Fire to the *Augusta* of 64, & the *Apollo* of 32 Guns, & the rest made the best of their way back again.

A few days before 2500 of the Enemy (most of them Hessians) under the command of Count Donolp, attacked Fort Mercer, or Red Bank, & were soon obliged to retreat in a most shameful & confused manner, leaving behind them killed & wounded 1500. The Count is a Prisoner; they also left 12 pieces of Artillery.

The 22d our Troops attempted a stroke upon a Detachment of six Regts. lying at Grays Ferry where they had thrown a Bridge over the River. They marched all night & reached the Ground about Sunrise, but the Birds were flown: they had suddenly the preceding night deserted the Post, left all their works unfinished & broke up the Bridge.

To day Se'nnight there was a very warm Engagement, but reports respecting it are so vague, & contradictory, I cannot pretend to give you any account of it.

The Articles of Capitulation that appeared in Loudon's last Paper are not relished this way, neither by Whigs, nor Tories, the latter say if Mr. Burgoyne was in a Situation to obtain such Terms he ought to have fought, the Former say if Burgoyne was obliged to surrender at all, Gates might have brought him to what Terms he pleased, so that it looks as if the two Generals wished to avoid fighting. The Troops will go home & Garrison the Forts abroad, & let those Garrisons come to America, so it will be only an exchange of Men.

The Dr. proposes to Inoculate our little Fellow next week; he is now a Fit subject for it, his blood is well purified, he has pretended to inoculate him often, so he will not be afraid of it. You know old Woodruff, that carts for us, his Son that lived next door to Dr. [John] Darby, died a few days ago of the Small pox the natural way & now his Widow & Child have it. The Old Man has never had it, he stayed in the same House with his Son till a Day before he expired; they are not entitled to much pity, for they say the Avarice of the old Man prevented their being inoculated. The Child will perish with it, it is thought.

**An obstacle of heavy timber and spikes which could rip the hull of a vessel.*

A few days after you left us Mama went down with Johnny to Eliz:T. to see about some Business, John was taken ill, & Mama was obliged to come back the very next Morning. Our House is a Barrack: there was a whole Artillery Company in it, so I expect every thing will be destroyed.

We have not heard from B[rockhol]st since the last Action to the Northward, (I have no doubt but his Letters have miscarried) but Mama has allmost persuaded herself he is among the Slain, & if there was any mourning to be purchased, I do not know but she would exhibit a dismal Spectacle of bombazeen* & crape.

Where can Gates stay with his Army? I wish he would quicken his Diligence to join Genl. Washington.

We have had the Taylor here (that you engaged) these 3 weeks, which has kept Kitty lightly employed; she is his Journey-woman. Mr. Jay's green suit is turned. Papa has brought home Cargo of broken things, so that we have not eat the bread of Idleness since you left us.

Mr. Jay's Letter is this instant brought in, it mentions a former that has never reached us. We want to know whether your Fathers Family is removed to Kent. Kitty desires me to leave a little blank Paper that she may reply to said Letter. I think this, scrawl as it is, with the first I wrote, entitles me to a few Lines from your fair hand. This I submit to you & whether you write or not, I am your most Affectionately

Dr Sir

Just now we were made happy by the receipt of yours of the 24 ult: your first not coming to hand we were extremely anxious to hear from Sister, you, & your good Family; of them we are yet ignorant; as indeed we are of the welfare of all our Friends, who have by our cruel & implacable Enemy been obliged to desert at an unfriendly Season, their once Comfortable & Peacefull abodes & be necessitated to implore shelter among entire Strangers. God only knows, how often we sha[ll suffer] the cruel effects of War, a Calamity indeed greatly to be de[plored]. Saturday Nov. 1st 1777 This morning your little Boy was inoculated. As the Dr. had for some time past practiced on his arm, he was quite reconciled to its being done in reality; he has not till now been a proper subject for the small pox, for after his illness, (of which Susan has informed you,) he had a cankered mouth, & the Dr. choosing he should be in perfect health we submitted to his Judgement. In Peters late indisposition he discovered great tenderness & attention to him, he is very anxious for the Child, would not have him die his patient he frequently says for fife hundred pound. Hannahs illness has hitherto I think proved fortunate as to that we owe the pleasure of having the sweet fellow with us; a pleasure greatly heighten'd by the reflection of its being an agreeable Circumstance to you in your flight, not to say any thing of the timely assistance he had in his dangerous distemper.

As I am arrived to the extent of my limits I can only assure you
I am your affectionate Sister

**Bombazeen or bombazine is a twilled or corded dress material of silk and worsted.*

(Kitty Livingston to JJ and SLJ at Fishkill) Persippiney, Novr. 21st 1777

My Dear Sister & Brother

It is with very great pleasure I announce to you, the recovery of your little Boy from the Small Pox; please to accept of the Congratulations of the Family on the happy event. No person ever was more favor'd in that disorder, he had only one pustule, & scarce a days illness. The Dr. bid me tell you that he had behaved manfully thro the whole. He intends sharing the Thousand pounds with Hannah*. If Sally you have at any time felt a regret at having left him least he should be spoil'd, be assured there never was a better Child. I have my doubts if ever any equaled him in goodness, I have but one Complaint to lodge against him, & that is, that we cannot make him talk; it is something extraordinary in our Family; but I flatter myself he will prattle every thing before he leaves us. I have more than one reason for wishing that to be the case....

Gen: Washington is reinforced with two Thousand Troops from the Southward, & Five from the Northward, & some hundreds from this State, of the Militia, of the Pennsylvania Militia only twelve hundred have lent him their assistance. The Philadelphians have lent Gen: Howe twenty thousand pound sterling & He has given the Old money of Pensylvania, New Jersey, & New York a Currency. The Quakers mount guard & do all Military duty that is required of them. Billy Allen is full Col: in the Enemys service, & is to raise his Regiment in his native State. Young Nat Philips died in Philadelphia of the wound received at Brandy-Wine. They write from our Camp that the Philadelphians come out in shoals, that some of them had not bread for several days before they left the City. Gen: [Sir Henry] Clinton did not Sail with the fleet, he has been seen very lately at New York, & on Staten Island. Lord Petershem is gone with Bur: [goyne] dispatches. He has said that if he should lose them he would not be beleived in England. He intends joining the minority as he is convinced of the impossibility of their conquering us. I hope our successes to the Southward will be more favorable than those to the northward, but I fear something serious will happen before the close of the Campaign tho it is late in the Season....

Yesterday I returned from Elizath. Gen.[Philemon] Dickenson is at that Post with between eight hundred & a Thousand Troops. My Fathers House for six weeks was made a Guard House, for a Bullock Guard the first instance I beleive of a Governors House being so degraded. I do not exaggerate In telling you the Guards have done ten times the mischief to the House that the Hessians did; they have left only two locks in the House taken off many pains of glass, left about a third of the paper hanging, burnt up some mahogany banisters, a Quantity of timber, strip'd the roof of all the lead, one of the men was heard to boast that he had at one heat taken 30 pd. of Lead off. The furniture that mamma left there when Sally & myself was last down is stolen except a few things of which there is only some fragments. It is as in the time of Pharoah what the Canker worm dont eat the Locusts destroy....

your truly Affectionate Sister

**Peter Augustus Jay was offered a bribe to behave when inoculated.*

(JJ to Kitty Livingston at Baskenridge, N.J.) Fish Kill 21 Decr. 1777

Dear Kitty

You cant concieve what Pleasure the Rect. of your last Letter afforded us. The Indisposition of our little only Boy, our Distance from him, and the long Time we were in Suspence about his Fate, had rendered us not a little anxious. We think it very fortunate that Hannah's Sickness prevented our bringing him with us, especially as the operations of the Enemy, would have rendered it necessary to remove him. He is now thank God! in a Place of Security, & with Relations from whom he will recieve all the Tenderness of Parents, & by whose attention I am greatly obliged.

That Tenderness however leads me to fear the Consequences of Indulgences. It is unhappy when Children have any Thing to unlearn, & when improper Habits instead of useful ones are permitted to direct their Conduct. Let him not be the Sport of Passions of any Kind, for, if he lives, the Time will come when they must be changed for other Principles of Action: and it frequently happens that sad & dear Experience only can work this Change. I wish to see him possess a sound Mind in a sound Body, and to grow up free from Those unreasonable Humors & Impertinencies by which favourite Children are too often distinguished. Nature will doubtless give him his Share of Fooleries; it would be a Pity that this natural Stock should be encreased by Education.

Sally is with me & well. Remember us to all the Family. I am Dear Kitty

your afft. Brother
John Jay

(JJ & SLJ to Susan Livingston at Persipiney) Fish Kill 16th March 1778

Dear Susan

Sally returned from Rhinebeck about ten Days ago in good health, & except now & then a short Visit from her old acquaintance, the Rheumatism, has continued so ever since. You cant concieve how easy she is about You all, and is quite content to live the ensuing Summer without her Son. Indeed there is no great Prospect of her committing her delicate Frame to the rough treatment which Travellers thro your Roads meet with. The nine Partners* will probably be our abiding Place this Summer, and it is not altogether certain that we shall not request the Favor of master Peter's Company. His mother expects that by the Time she sees him his Education will be considerably advanced, and that he will by that Time have been Taught to d—n the King & say the Westminster Confession of Faith. However the first may be the Case, I tell her she will be disappointed as to the latter, for you may remember you promised before Parson Charlton to make a Churchman of him.

Sally says if I write such Things she wishes I would conclude my Letter, so that as I always mean to be a very civil Husband I have concluded to write no more at present except to desire you to present my Compts. to all the Family & to assure you that I am your affte. Brother

John Jay

**The Nine Partners is an area near Poughkeepsie, New York.*

What a critical situation, my dr. Susan, is that of yr sister at present, to contradict the assertions of my Lord & Master may for aught I know be esteemed Petty treason in the eye of every man who has the honor of being a husband, & to let the above assertions pass in silence would by the ladies at Persepone be thought an indication of insensibility in a mother that is blest with so lovely a son I will only therefore ——— submit it to your own Judgment. I am my dear Susan

your's affectionately,
Sarah Jay

[In John Jay's hand] P.S. Mrs. [Janet] Montgomery offers to let you have a clever little Yellow Boy about seven Years old provided you will keep him till he is 18 or 21 years old. I think he would be a great relief to Belle, & a Convenience to the whole Family. What adds to his Value in Sally's Estimation is, his being the Son of a Wench brought up in your Family, as to the residue of his Parentage I know not.

On December 10, 1778, John was elected president of the Second Continental Congress and nine months later was appointed minister plenipotentiary to the Court of Spain. This time Sarah would not be left behind. John and Sarah Jay sailed for Europe on the *Confederacy* on October 20, 1779; their son, Peter Augustus, remained with his fond grandparents and aunts in Elizabeth Town.

(Samuel Adams to his wife Elizabeth Adams) Philadelphia Decr 13 1778

.... [P. S.] I forgot to tell you that last Friday Mr. President [Henry] Laurens discharged the Duties of his Station for more than one year with Fidelity & to the Acceptance of the Members, resigned the Chair, and John Jay Esqr a delegate from New York was chosen in his Room. To this Gentleman I chearfully gave my Vote.

(William Livingston to Nathaniel Scudder) Princeton 14 December 1778

.... P. S. Please to give my respects to your new President, & to tell him that his present office appears rather obstructive of the performance of the promise he has made me of using his best endeavours to get me another Grandson as soon as possible.

(SLJ to JJ at Philadelphia) Persipiney, Decbr 28th, 1778

My dear Mr. Jay,

I should have troubled you a second time, & have wrote you by the last Post had I not entertained the hope that it wou'd not be long before I should have the pleasure of acknowledging at least one favor from you. I have been disappointed, 'tis true, but still I will not relinquish the pleasing idea of being affectionately remembered by my beloved friend. To prevent future mortifications of the like tender to nature, permit me to remind you that there is a Post that takes letters from Morris-Town for Philadelphia & returns every week.

I had the pleasure of finding by the news-paper that you are honor'd with the first office on the Continent, and am still more pleased to hear this appointment affords general satisfaction. Will you be so kind as to inform me whether our State has prolonged your stay beyond the first of March or not? As by your present Appointment your personal attendance upon Congress I imagine can't be dispensed with, I am very solicitous to know how long I am still to remain in a state of widowhood; upon my word I sincerely wish these three months may conclude it; however, I mean not to influence your conduct, for I am convinced that had you consulted me as some men have their wives about public measures, I should not have been Roman Matron enough to have given you so intirely to the public, & of consequence your reputation & claim to the gratitude of your country would have been as much diminished as theirs who have acted so imprudent tho' tender a part.

It will give you pleasure to be informed that your son & myself are still favored with health, & if you can spare time to give me the same grateful tidings of yourself, you can hardly imagine what happiness you'll confer upon your

affecte. Wife
Sa. Jay

Wednesday Morng. Eliz. Town Decbr. 30th [1778]

I wrote this letter on monday, but as I knew of no opportunity of sending it, left it unsealed, & in the evening was agreeably surprised by Papa's arrival at Persipiney, but still more pleased when he handed me your letter of the 10th Inst. which I have the pleasure of acknowledging at present. Accept my dearest friend of my sincere thanks for your never-ceasing attention to my happiness. You tell me, my dear, that the greatest gratification you derive from the honor of your late appointment is it's being an additional recommendation to my esteem. And do you really imagine that my esteem for you can be heightned by any public testimony of your merit? No, no my dear, my sentiments of esteem have long since been confirmed, nor indeed has the public acknowledgment of your merit been wanting to convince me that the respect I felt for you was founded on your virtue.

Yesterday Papa prevailed upon me to return with Kitty & himself to Eliz. Town, and by way of inducement assured me there are more frequent opportunities of hearing from you here than if I staid at Persipiney. He tells me likewise to inform you that unless there is an order of Congress to the contrary he shall certainly fetch your little Boy very soon. Papa is just going to church, I'll seal my letter in hopes that in town he'll hear of some way of forwarding this to you. Please to remember us to Brockholst and be assur'd that I am unalterably

Yours

Kitty begs that Brockholst will remind Major Clarkson of a feather that he promised to send her.

(SLJ to JJ at Philadelphia) Eliz. Town, 3d. Jany. 1779

My dear Mr. Jay,

I was making inquiries just now for pen, ink &c. in order to write to my absent friend when papa return'd from town. What going to scribble again my dear? Were I in your place I would not give myself any concern about such a naughty husband who is too lazy to write to his little wife. So unusual an expression from papa commanded my attention & percieving a smile upon his countenance I demanded a letter from him, when after a few Presbiterian evasions he handed me yours of the 26th Decr....

Sister Kitty is much obliged to you for your polite invitation, & already anticipates the pleasure of being with us. Papa too has made her happy by his acquiescence with your request, tho' it's my opinion you could not make a request with which he would not chearfully comply. As to me, you know, that the pleasure of your company is my prime enjoyment & therefore your proposal to send for me is very agreeable. If you think it probable that accomodations will be provided by the 1st Feby. let that be the time for the Col: [Henry Brockholst Livingston] to attend us: I think it will not be amiss if Jacob should come with the waggon for our baggage, unless Brockst. can procure a continental one; but be that as it will, order your Secy. to inform us of yr. determination previous to his leaving Philadelphia.

The company of your dear little boy proved a great consolation to me since you've been absent, & I should not have forsaken him for Eliz. Town had I not found my spirits a key too low, which I thought a ride would contribute to enliven. As soon as a convenient opportunity offers Kitty & I shall return to Persipiney & wait there the Colonels arrival. Adieu, my dr. Mr. Jay. I dare not ask you to write frequently, if the time to be so employed, must be deducted from sleep; for certain I am, that if a sufficient portion of time is not alotted for repose, your too intense application to business will inevitably impair your health.

Accept the Compts: of the season from our little circle & may we repeat the same to each other fifty years hence. Once more my beloved Adieu.

Yours affectionately
Sa. Jay

(JJ to SLJ) Philadelphia, 18 January 1779

My dear Sally

Yesterday I had the Pleasure to hear of you tho not <u>from</u> you. Your Brother recieved a Letter from Caty, who was then at Elizabeth town. I imagine from her Letter that you must have returned to Persipiney. This Letter will nevertheless go to Elizabeth Town. I suppose there is constant communication between the two Families.

No Home yet, about the Middle of February we shall have one. But that will be so near the 1st of March, when my Delegation will expire, that unless it should be prolonged I doubt whether I ought to put you to so much Trouble, for the Sake of spending only a Week in Philadelphia. But more of this hereafter. Whether our Legislature will think proper to leave me here longer, is uncertain. I expect soon to be informed, and shall give you the earliest intelligence of their determination whatever that may [be]. At any Rate I hope they will not keep me here in the summer Months; until May or the first of June I should be content, but no longer.

God bless you my dear Sally.

I am your affectionate Husband
John Jay

(SLJ to JJ at Philadelphia) Persipiney, Feby. 12th, 1779

My dear Mr. Jay,

I am utterly at a loss to account for the miscarriages of my letters, having frequently wrote & sent my letters by what I then thought safe conveyances, & I am more surprised still that neither you nor your brother have received those which Susan & I wrote by Mrs. Ferguson who promised Susan to send them as soon as she arrived at Philadelphia. I will not trouble you with a repetition of my anxiety to see you. Permit me however to transcribe a couple of lines that [William] Mason gives us from the lips of his amiable Elfrida as very expressive of my own impatience.

With what a tedious and retarding weight
Does Expectation load the wing of Time.

Left: **John Jay, 1779. Engraving after a drawing by Pièrre E. Du Simitière (c. 1736–1784). The now-lost drawing was done in Philadelphia when Jay was President of Congress. John Jay Homestead State Historic Site. New York State Office of Parks, Recreation and Historic Preservation (JJ.1958.563.1).** ***Right:*** **Sarah Livingston Jay, 1779. Miniature, watercolor on ivory by Pièrre E. Du Simitière (c. 1736–1784). The artist wrote in his notebook in May 1779: "miniature of Mrs. Jay, the Lady of the president of Congress, larger than usual." Owned by Arthur W. Schwartz.**

Poor Kit is very anxious to know her fate as she calls it whether she shall spend the months of march & april agreably at Philadelphia or waste them in obscurity & dullness. We last evening received invitations from General [Henry] Knox to celebrate the Alliance with France at his Quarters the 18th inst:. As Brockholst dropt a hint in his letter to the girls of being at Camp at that time if business would admit, I am very solicitous that Kitty should be there, especially as there has been several dances at which she has been invited but been present at none.

I wrote to sister [Mrs. Frederick] Jay some time ago desiring she wou'd send me the gloves she had of mine & in an answer to my letter she informs me that she has sent them to you. Pray, my dear, have you recd them?

Our dear little boy has had two severe fits of illness occasioned by worms; during his indisposition my suffering I think was little inferior to his as he was only affected by immediate pain & not by any apprehension of future consequences. Happy negligence of disposition that attends the state of child-hood!

I have been bless'd with a great share of health the whole winter. The weather is very dull at present, perhaps the transition from such lovely weather as we have been accustomed to lately may effect my spirits, whatever it is, they are not as I would wish when writing you.

I will therefore bid you adieu. Perhaps when Montanie returns he will bring me a letter from you which (should the depression of my spirits continue till then) will effectually chear the gloom & for the time banish every disagreeable sensation. Once more my Love, adieu.

Believe me to be most affectionately yrs.
Sa. Jay

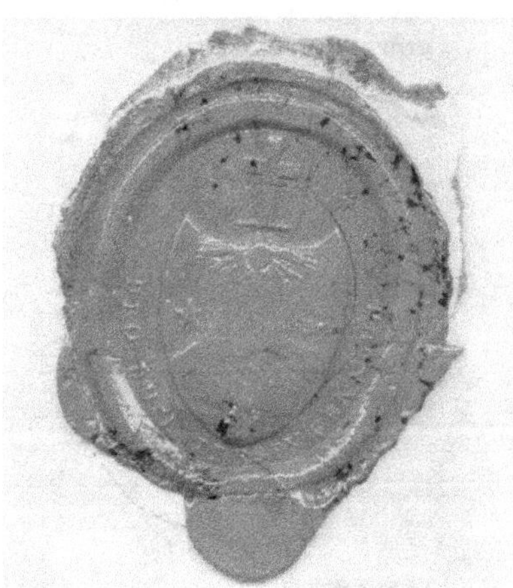

Top: **This seal with the Jay motto, _Deo Duce Perseverandum_ ("God leading we must persevere"), is on a letter from John Jay to Peter A. Jay of 10 February 1799, and is a rare example of a complete wax seal. Most seals would be broken upon opening a letter. John Jay Homestead State Historic Site. New York State Office of Parks, Recreation and Historic Preservation (JJ.1980.568). _Bottom left:_ Facsimile of John Jay's signature. From letter to Sarah Jay, 12 October 1783. John Jay Homestead State Historic Site. New York State Office of Parks, Recreation and Historic Preservation (JJ.1986.23). _Right:_ Facsimile of Sarah L. Jay's signature. This signature comes from a letter to her son, Peter A. Jay, of 17 June 1800. John Jay Homestead State Historic Site. New York Office of Parks, Recreation and Historic Preservation (JJ.1980.275).**

(SLJ to JJ at Philadelphia) Persipiney, February 18th, 1779

I thank you my dear Mr. Jay, for your kind letters of the 31st. of Jany. & 5th of Feby. Be assur'd the advice contain'd in them was as welcome as indeed it was requisite....

Sister Kitty & brother Jack are at Pluckemin. They dine to-day at General Knox's quarters where he has prepared splendid entertainments of Fire-works, Balls, &c. We had an invitation from the ladies at Baskenridge to take their house in our way. Several reasons induced me to decline making one of the party. I hope Kitty will not be disappointed in her expectation of meeting Brockholst at Pluckemin.

Why enjoin me my dear so frequently to be particular about my health. I remember Papa once told William when at school that he would always take that for granted that he was well, provided William mentioned nothing to the contrary. Will not that be a sufficient assurance likewise for you if I promise to inform you when I am indisposed.

You can't imagine what satisfaction I receive from the increasing fondness of my little boy who frequently inquires where his papa stays so long & if you never intend to return. In telling him stories & teaching him to spell I deceive many hours that would otherwise linger on unamused & sometimes unemployed.

Mamma & William desire to be remembered to you & yr. Secy. Susan & Judy are at Eliz. Town with papa. Mr. [John] W[atkins] urges his suit with great ardour; I fancy I will be prevailed upon to resign her hand & liberty to his guardianship next autumn; he pleads for happiness in the spring but prudential reasons incline her to wait 'till fall.... I have examined the trunks, but found no moth in them.

Adieu my dear. May providence smile upon your endeavors for the public weal & reward your constancy. I am

most affectionately yours
Sa. Jay

(JJ to SLJ at Persipiney) Philadelphia March 5, 1779

... It is now nine o'clock, my fellow lodgers out, and, what seldom happens, I am perfectly alone, and pleasing myself with the prospect of spending the remainder of the evening in writing a letter to you. As it rains and snows there is less probability of my being interrupted, and for that reason I prefer it to moonshine or starlight....

(SLJ to JJ at Philadelphia) Persipiney, March 11th, 1779

I thank you my dearest love for your favor of the 1st instant, tho' I regret exceedingly the interuption that prevented you from indulging me with a larger share of your attention, than which there are few things could give me greater pleasure. I imagine the british officers have deprived me of no small consolation when they pocketed your letters at Elizabeth-town. But that is only one of a thousand they are in my debt.

What will you think of me, my love, when I tell you that for some time past I have relapsed into the opinion I formerly entertained that in order to avoid misery we ought to endeavor to attain an indifferance of disposition that can view, unmoved every occurrence that we are liable to meet with however unpleasing. And yet, pardon me my dear, your scheme of resignation is certainly a more rational as well as more christian scheme for happiness; that indifferance I have in vain been sighing for could only be dictated by despondency that bane to comfort. I wish your example may have due influence on my conduct & that I may not fail to imitate what I so greatly admire....

Abigail begs I will ask permission for her attendance if I go to Philadelphia, but as I am ignorant how long you are to stay, & absolutely dispair of seeing you there I give her but little encouragement....

Mamma desires to be remembred to you & Brockholst. Peter sends you many kisses; the little urchin pretends frequently to have just come from Philadelphia & delivers me letters that you would be diverted to hear him read.

I have knit a couple of pair of under-stockings for you this winter that I think would be acceptable if I knew how to send them. I am my dear Mr. Jay,

Yours affectionately
Sa. Jay

(JJ to SLJ at Persipiney) [Philadelphia] March 17, 1779

... I esteem it a blessing that (when absent from you) solitude is so far from being irksome, that I often court and enjoy it. Hence it is that, altho' few are more fond of society, I oftener walk and ride without than with company. There is a kind of satisfaction in being able, without any breach of politeness, to pursue one's own inclination, to ride as fast or as slow, to stop as short or as long, to take this or that road, as may be most agreeable.... In this unfriendly month, Nature, you know, appears in a rude and dirty garb; so that as yet I must be silent about 'lonely devious walks' thro' 'verdant fields' or 'shady groves;' nor would it be in season to say a word of 'gentle breezes,' 'melodious birds,' or 'the hum of bees inviting sleep sincere.'....

(JJ to SLJ at Persipiney) Philadelphia 21 march 1779

My dear Sally

It gives me Pleasure to inform you that Mrs. Gurney appears now to be moving in earnest. I have got Possession of the Cellar and Stables, and unless some cross Accident should again happen, the House will be ready for me by Thursday next. In this Case your Brother will set out the Day after. Do not however be too sanguine in your Expectations—another Disappointment, tho not very probable, may take Place. It is with great Reluctance that Mrs. Gurney can prevail on herself to go to the Country, & perhaps this Disinclination may occasion further Delay. Believe me my Love, my Sollicitude for the Pleasure of seeing you is such that not a Moment shall be lost;

& it is not without Difficulty I can persuade myself not to let your Brother go for you, till I see the House free from its present Inhabitants.

My Love to all the family.

I am my dear Sally
very affectionately Yours!
John Jay

(William Livingston to SLJ at Philadelphia) Trenton 7 October 1779

Dear Sally,

It is with great pain that I am obliged to part with you across a wide Ocean, & to a foreign Land. Considering the Mortality of Man, and my time of life, it is probable I may never see you again. O may God Almighty keep you in his holy Protection, & if it should please him to take you out of this World, receive you into a better! And pray my dear Child, suffer not the Gaities and Amusements of the World, and the particular Avocations of what is call'd high Life, to banish from your mind an habitual sense of an all-present Deity, or to interrupt you in paying him the homage you owe Him. With my most ardent Wishes for your good Voyage & safe Return I am

your affectionate Father
Wil: Livingston

(George Washington to SLJ at Philadelphia) West-point Octobr 7th 1779

General Washington presents his most respectful compliments to Mrs. Jay. Honoured in her request by General St. Clair, he takes pleasure in presenting the inclosed*, with thanks for so polite a testimony of her approbation & esteem. He wishes most fervently, that prosperous gales an unruffled Sea & every Thing pleasing & desirable, may smooth the path she is about to walk in.

(William Livingston Jr. to SLJ at Philadelphia) Persippany 16th Oct. 1779

Permit me my dear Sister to mingle my Joy with yours on the honorable Distinction which Congress have been pleased to confer on Mr. Jay.

It is not the Dignity of Embassadorship, nor the Lustre of high Office, considered in themselves, that did create, or that can authorize the uncommon Satisfaction, with which your Friends felt themselves impressed on that Occasion. But it is the Benefit & Advantage your Country is likely to derive from the Appointment of one, who, having manifested every Testimony of his Zeal & Abilities in her Services here, is destined to carry abroad & raise her reputation in foreign Countries. The

**A lock of the General's hair [in Sarah's hand]. John Jay had the lock of hair incorporated into a pin while in London in 1784.*

Regret we feel in the temporary Loss of a firm & unshaken Patriot from a Community in which his Assistance is so necessary and useful, is Silenced, when the nature of his Mission is called in question — every Desire of his remaining among us must be laid asleep when we consider the grand Object of his Embassy.

But since you are no Partner in the Commission, can you Madam plead the same Apology with your Friends, for the Loss they are to sustain from your Absence? However sensibly they may feel themselves affected by this Seperation, they must all allow the Wisdom of your choice. To gratify a laudable Curiosity & to travel in the Pursuit of Knowledge under the Advantages that will attend you, thro' the Progress of your Journey are motives that appeal to your Friends & yourself with equal force. With a Gentleman capable of directing your Enquiries, & a Judgment & Disposition to make the best Use of his Directions, you can not fail attaining the greatest Improvement to yourself, & reflecting the brightest Honor on your Family & Country.

And so Madam, you are in good Earnest to become the Castilian. We have already been tracing your Rout on the maps. What think you of the Pyrenean Mountains? But your Fortitude I suppose, has e'er this, levelled them with the Plains. But what think you of your inveterate Foe the Flea? France abounds with them. Spain too, is infested with the hostile Animal. But this say you shall not terrify the mind of an American: very Right. And if neither mountains nor Fleas can cool your Intrepidity nothing more formidable will I hope obtrude themselves. You are to travel we find thro' the most Southern & consequently the most fertile Provinces of France. But even there, one Object will present itself, that will at once call upon your Humanity & remind you of your native Country. The Poverty I mean of the Husbandman & his half-cultivated Fields. O happy America, will you say, thy Farms are better tilled, because thy Citizens are more free. But I find I am attempting the History of the Country, which you'll soon be perfectly acquainted with from your own Observation.

When you get to the Land of the renowned DonQuixot you will not fail to select & give us an Account of every Piece of Knight Errantry that falls within your Notice — that is the fairy Land of Fancy — there Immagination frolicks in all her Wattonness. Many are the Romances she has given birth to. You will let us know whether the ravishing Wit & Beauty of the Ladies & the valorous Gallantry of the Men riegn in them only. And if the Coll [Brockholst] turns Cavilier, enters the List & carries off some celebrated fair-one you will give us the earliest Intelligence.

And now my dear Sister I shall bid you Adieu. May the great Ruler of the Universe make you his peculiar Case, shield you from every impending Danger & restore you in due Season to your Friends Family & Country, enriched with every valuable Acquirement you wish to possess. These my dear Sister & many more are the most fervent Hope & Desire of

Your Affectionate Brother
William Livingston jun

PART II

Together in Europe

December 12–26, 1779–
December 30, 1783

The Jays set off on their four-year voyage to Europe from Philadelphia on October 20th, 1779. On board the 185-foot frigate *Confederacy* with the Jay party were Sarah's brother Brockholst Livingston; her personal maid Abbe, a Livingston slave; John Jay's 12-year-old nephew Peter Jay Munro; and his private secretary William Carmichael.

It took the *Confederacy* six days to sail down the Delaware River and out into the Atlantic. Once at sea, disaster struck in the form of a severe winter storm. Here is Sarah Jay's account of what happened.

(SLJ to her mother)

On board the *Confederacy*
12th to 26th Decbr. 1779

My Dear Mamma,

When at Philadelphia I was favor'd with your affectionate Letter. I dared not trust myself to acknowledge it: The Voyage I was then so soon to take, and which was to seperate me so long a time from my indulgent parents and other partial friends, was a circumstance that engross'd my thoughts more than I chose to confess, and I was aware that to write either to Papa or you would be the ready way to reveal a Secret I wish'd to conceal even from myself.

How wise and tender in my dr. Papa & Mama to recommend their Children to the care of that being whose power is unlimited, and whose goodness & mercy are equal to His power? Nor have the prayers of my kind parents been disregarded: that providence which they implor'd has kindly preserv'd us through uncommon dangers. May we never by our ingratitude forfeit its further protection!

We embark'd at Chester on the 20th of Octbr., but did not lose Sight of land 'till the 26th:, when we launch'd out to Sea with a brisk gale. The very first evening we were all Seized with the most disagreeable Sickness peculiar to our Situation. My Brother, Peter, & myself soon recovered, but my Dear Mr. Jay suffered exceedingly at least five weeks & was surprisingly reduced. I imagine his health would have been much sooner restored, had not our passage been so very unpleasant.

About 4 o'clock in the morning of the 7th of November, we were alarmed by an unusual noise upon deck, & what particularly surpris'd me, was the lamentations of persons in distress. I call'd upon the Captn. to inform me of the cause of the confusion that I imagined to prevail, but my Brother desir'd me to remain perfectly composed, for that he had been upon deck but an half an hour before & left every thing in perfect security.

Perfect security! Vain words! Don't you think so Mamma? And so indeed they prov'd. For in that small space of time we had been depriv'd of nothing less than our bow sprit, fore mast, main mast, & missen mast; so that we were in an awkward situation rendered still more so by a pretty high South-East wind & a very rough sea that prevail'd then: however our misfortunes were only began, the injury receiv'd by our rudder, the next morning, served to compleat them as we were ready to conclude. The groans that distress'd me were uttered by two men who had suffered from the fall of the masts; one of them was much bruised, the other had his arm and hand broke: The former recovered, but the latter, poor fellow! surviv'd not many days the amputation of his arm.

Will it not be painful to my dear Mamma to image to herself the situation of her children at that time? Her children did I say? Rather let my benevolent Mamma imagine the dangerous situation of more than 300 souls toss'd about in the midst of the Ocean, in a Vessel dismasted & under no Command, at a season too that threatened approaching inclemency of weather. And would you for a moment suppose me capable of regretting that I had for a time bid adieu to my native land in order to accompany my beloved friend? Would you have dispaired of ever again embracing yr. affectionate children? Or would you have again recommended them to Him who appointed to the waters their bounds, Who saith unto the waves, thus far shalt thou go, And to the winds, Peace be still? Mama's known piety & fortitude sufficiently suggest the answer to the two latter queries: and to the former it becomes me to reply. I do, and assure you that in no period of our distress though ever so alarming did I once repine, but incited by his amiable Example, I gave fear to the winds & chearfully resign'd myself to the dispensations of the Almighty.

Your whole family love Mr. Jay, but you are not acquainted with half his worth, nor indeed are any of his friends, for his modesty is equal to his merit. It is the property of a Diamond (I've been told) to appear most brilliant in the dark; and surely a good man never shines to greater advantage than [in] the gloomy hour of adversity: in scenes of that kind I have lately beheld with pleasure, & even admiration, the firmness & serenity of mind that evidently shone out in the countenance of our invaluable friend. May he long, very long, be preserved a blessing to his connections & a useful as well as disinterested friend to his Country. Pardon me Mamma, if I appear to prolix in the praises of the person we so highly love & esteem. Am I not writing to a partial mother? And is it not a consolation to her, that the guardian of her children is worthy of her confidence? Besides, I have the pleasure to hope that none but friendly eyes will peruse this scrawl, & I therefore indulge myself as though I were actually conversing with my dear family friends: I hope every letter I receive from them will be equally free from restraint.

After our misfortunes on the 7th & 8th of November (the memorable aera from which we now date all events relative to ourselves) a Council of the Officers was held to consider where it was most expedient to bend our course & it was unanimously concluded by them that it wou'd be impossible to reach Europe at this season, with a ship in the condition that ours was. They were likewise united in opinion that the southern direction was the only one that offered a prospect of safety, & of the Islands, Martinico was the most eligible, for its commodious harbour & the probability of being supplied with Materials to refit. Accordingly the first fair wind that offered (which was not 'till near three weeks from the above mentioned aera) was embraced in pursuance of the advice given by the Officers: & after having passed thro' very blustering, squally latitudes, we are now in smooth seas, having the advantage of trade-winds, which blow directly for the Island; nor are we, if the calculations made are just, more than 220 miles distant from the destin'd port. Thus while our american friends are amusing themselves by a chearful fire-side, are we sitting under an awning, comforting ourselves with the expectation of being refreshed by some fine southern fruits. I expect in a few days to write to papa & the girls from Martinico, &, if what I hear of crabs, fresh fish, & Oysters be true, I'll make papa's mouth water, & make him wish to forego the pleasure of pruning trees, speechifying Assemblies, & what not for the greater pleasure of messing with us.

And now let me recollect. Is there nothing that has occurred in the space of seven weeks worth Mamma's attention? Why let me see. There is the celebration of Mrs. Gerard's birth-day. When we first came on board, Monsieur Gerard among other subjects mentioned that he hop'd for the pleasure of our company at his house the 7th of Decbr., as it was customary for his Lady to entertain her friends upon the aniversary of her birth day. The accidents I have already related account for our not arriving in France. Mr. Jay therefore surprised our friend by inviting all the Officers of the ship & Gentlemen that were passengers to breakfast & spend the day with us, mentioning in the cards the occasion. Early in the morning we were amused by a small band of musick, & the discharge of a number of cannon, which led Mr. Gerard to enquire the reason that gave rise to the apparent Joy; & when the gentleman waited upon him to congratulate him upon the occasion, he received them very politely, & waited upon them into the dining-room (alias Cabbin) where a very genteel breakfast was prepared.

The vessel rolls so intollerably, & Mr. C[armichae]l & the Coll. who are playing at drafts at the same table leave me no chance of writing legibly, so that I must lay aside my pen 'till some quieter opportunity offers. Thank fortune the gentlemen have thought fit to walk out & leave me at leisure to proceed with my narrative, and as to waiting for an easy motion of the ship, I believe it will be needless, for I begin to be of the Carpinter's opinion, that she would hardly lay still again were she put upon the stocks.

So much by way of digression and now I think we'll return to the gentlemen in the Cabbin, & as they have had quite time enough to finish their breakfast, I'll conduct them up stairs, where the whole deck is covered with an awning for their reception. There they continued to amuse themselves with Chess, cards, & Drafts; musick still heightening their pleasure, 'till 4 o'clock, when they where invited to (what in our situation might be call'd) an elegant dinner: after which a number of pertinent toasts were drank, to each of which was a discharge of cannon. I then withdrew, & the gentlemen had coffee, tea & cakes sent them, & then concluded the evening with dancing.

That day happened to be a merry one to the sailors likewise, for crossing the Tropick they insisted upon an ancient custom of shaving & ducking every person that had not cross'd it before, excepting only those who paid their fine. I could not for-bear smiling at Peter's fate, who had been diverting himself with observing the operation perform'd on many of them, 'till they exclaim'd at the injustice of exempting him, & insisted upon his being tar'd at least, which by the by was their method of shaving. Peter, sobbing, declared that had not his new coat been spoilt, he would not have regretted so much the difficulty of getting rid of the tar. Apropos of peter, his behaviour throughout this Voyage has charm'd me. I thought I could trace his grand-father's firmness in the equanimity of the child. May the resemblance be increas'd & perpetuated in every disposition & action of his life.

Writing of one child but reminds me of the other. How I long to see the dear little varlet! I could ask a thousand questions about him, but to what purpose? When should I be answer'd? There was a diffidence in the dear child's disposition when I left him that I hope does not continue to distress him; do, my dear Mamma, guard well his tender mind against such impressions, you know that honour & firmness are the parents of many virtues. How many inconveniencies, & even Vices are young people frequently led into thro' a false shame? Teach him therefore betimes to say no as well as yes. But to whom am I dictating? Pardon me Mama, I forbear. And may God Almighty bless you & your instructions. God bless my child!

Decbr 14th

....A land bird! A land bird! Oh! the pleasure of being near land! A pleasure I more than once since I left Chester had reason to fear never being sensible of.

Wednesday, 15th Decbr.

Early this morning we were awaked by a report that light was discerned a head of the ship, & the master of the vessel, concluding it to be from and as his reckoning was out the preceeding eveng., hove the ship too, fearing to run aground; but the Captn. arose to make preperations for an action, thinking it equally probable that the light proceeded from a sail. However, when day appeared, no sign of sail or any thing else was visible, nor any further indication of land save only a small flock of birds that are known to deposit their eggs on shore....

Martinico, Decbr. 26th '79

Join with me, my dear Mamma & sisters in grateful acknowledgements to that supreme Being whose indulgent care has preserved your friends thro' every danger, & permitted them to arrive in health in a most delightful Island, furnished with every thing necessary for health & almost every thing that can contribute to pleasure. On the 18th inst. early in the morning I was most agreeably surprised to find, that we were sailing close along the [shore of the] most verdant, romantic country I ever beheld. In that instant, every disagreeable sensation rising from unpleasing circumstances during our voyage, gave place to the more mild & delightful emotions of gratitude.

At breakfast we were visited by some of the planters who live near the shore, & from them we learnt that Mr. Bingham was still at St. Pierre; when we arrived opposite to that City Mr. Jay wrote him a letter, & my Brother waited upon him, upon which Mr. Bingham very politely return'd with the Coll., & insisted upon our residing with him during our stay at Martinique; & never was I more charm'd with any thing of the kind than with the polite friendly reception we met with from that gentleman.

The two families most dear to me would be delighted with this Island. The neatness that prevails here cannot be exceeded & I frankly confess I never saw it equal'd. How mistaken was I as to the character of our allies! The Admiral Le Motte Piquet has granted to Mr. Gerard's request a Frigate to convey us to France, & we shall sail from this place the 28th inst. I regret exceedingly the perpetual hurry I have been involved in by the shortness of our stay in this place, but for nothing more than its preventing me from having the pleasure of writing to more of my friends, & to you, Mama, more explicitly about this Country.

It's with pleasure I can inform you that Mr. Jay, Brockst., & Peter never enjoy'd better health than at present. As Peter was suppos'd to be my son upon my first arrival, I had the pleasure of being complimented as the mother of a very lovely Boy; & indeed his engaging behaviour added to other circumstances attach me to him, that it would be difficult to convince me that he really was not my own child.

The prices of every thing are so immensely high, that I think you will not be displeased if I defer sending to you at present those articles that I know would add to your convenience. Mr. Bingham expects to return to America 5 or 6 weeks hence & has promised to take charge of a few Boxes of sweet meats to be divided between the two families. If you knew how many hundred times I've been interupted since I began the two last pages you would indeed make many allowances for me.

As I find it is impossible for me to write Mr. Jay, will you be so kind as to send this letter to him after your family have perused it. From his former indulgence, I have reason to expect his future partiality & tho' I should dread the eye of an impartial person I fear nothing from that amiable family. When on board the Frigate I hope to pursue the subject, & flatter myself that the variety which has presented itself in the course of 10 days will furnish my friends with more entertainment.

And must I now bid adieu to my best beloved [friends]. Think not any one that I have forgotten you. Mamma's miniature profile, & Kitty's picture with which she favor'd me partake almost every day my most affectionate embraces. And tho' I've not the same memento to the rest of my friends in both families, yet are their memories impressed on my heart in indelible characters.

May! the Almighty guard, protect & bless, my ever dear! my ever valued friends. Embrace my little blessing. My heart is too sensibly affected to proceed, & to discontinue is like parting a new. Adieu!

Sa. Jay

The *Confederacy* suffered too much damage to continue on its voyage. It put into Martinique in the Caribbean where the Jays enjoyed the hospitality of William Bingham, the American agent there.

The French admiral at Fort Royal arranged for the Jay party to take passage on a smaller frigate, the 66-foot *Aurora*, so that they could continue their voyage to Europe almost immediately. They departed from Martinique on December 28th for Toulon, France. Chased by a British frigate off the coast of Spain, they put in instead at Cadiz on January 22, 1780.

(SLJ to her father at Elizabeth Town) On board the *Aurora* frigate
December 30th 1779

It was my determined resolution to write to my dear papa from Martinico, but to my great regret was prevented by the shortness of our stay there. A few days after

The frigate *Confederacy* passing Cape May. Painting by Nowland Van Powell, 1974. This American frigate was built as a 36-gun ship by Jedidiah Willets of Norwich, Connecticut, in 1778. The vessel, carrying the Jays to Europe, was severely disabled during a gale in the northern Atlantic Ocean but, with jury-rigged sails, made it to Martinique. From *American Navies of the Revolutionary War* by Nowland Van Powell, © 1974 by Nowland Van Powell. Used by permission of G.P. Putnam's Sons, a division of Penguin Group (USA) Inc.

our arrival at St. Pierres, Mr. Bingham accompanied Mr. Gerard and Mr. Jay to Fort Royal to wait upon the Admiral & General who were there, from whom they had a very polite reception; and the Admiral was so obliging as to consent to part with the *Aurora* frigate for the purpose of conveying the gentlemen immediately to Europe, and also assured Mr. Bingham of his readiness to afford the Capt. of the *Confederacy* every assistance in his power.

The two days those gentlemen were absent I intended to devote to my american friends & for that purpose declined accepting any of the invitations I receiv'd, but the weather being very warm, & having indiscreetly indulged my taste for fruit (which was increased by the want of it during a long voyage) I was too much indisposed to pursue the bent of my inclination.

The first approach to Martinico is extremely beautiful: tho' the grounds are vastly uneven they do not appear like the unfinish'd work of nature, but rather as if in a sportive humour she had display'd a whimsical fancy. It is not more than sixty miles in length & therefore the inhabitants have found their advantage in cultivating every part of it: you can hardly imagine how romantic an appearance the whole

Island offers. I wish'd exceedingly for papa's pencil at the time I view'd it, and not less now for his pen to describe it. The heights and plains (or rather the intervals between the hills) are equally verdant, and it is really surprising to trace the effects of industry on the very summits of the hills which are all covered with coffee, coconuts and cane: every here and there the eye is surpris'd [by] settlements aside & amid the hills belonging to the negros who are employed upon the plantations. Then again a plain of small extent with genteel houses diversify the prospect: but nothing in my opinion has a more pleasing effect upon the sight than the falls of water that come tumbling down, murmuring as they roll over projecting rocks & broken grounds.

St. Pierres is the capital of the Island and a very pretty city it is: directly behind the town a fine river descends from the mountains [which] waters the city in a most delightful manner, through each street there runs a small stream that cools & cleanses them at the same time, and every inhabitant that chooses may have a sufficiency of water admitted into their dairies and rooms for bathing. The bathing rooms of the gentlemen are really very elegant as well as convenient: they have by a very simple contrivance the advantage of warm as well as cold baths, both of which are very useful as well as agreeable in that warm country, and I'm told that one or the other serve as a remedy for almost every Disorder incident to the climate: so that you may suppose phisicians there are rare.

The gentlemen live in a very genteel stile; & their hospitality is really captivating, nor is it possible to be less pleas'd with the perfect cleanliness that is universal in the city. The easy manners of the gentlemen & ladies freed from any embarrasment that I might have been sensible of among strangers had they been less polite. I was very sorry that the shortness of my stay & the many engagements I had, prevented me from making as many observations as we were invited by our situation, every thing almost having an air of novelty to me; and if the observation so often made by gentlemen upon our sex, that novelty has peculiar charms for them be just, it is not surprising that I was so much pleased. A Gentleman was so obliging as to have some cane gathered tho' out of season on purpose to gratify our curiosity by shewing us the process of making sugar.

It was some satisfaction to me to distinguish for myself in what manner the Coffee grows as I received very different accounts from different persons: the grain is inclosed in red berries that grow upon trees resembling our cherry trees the leaves of which are not unlike those of our peach and the trees would be equally tall were they not trimmed but those who cultivate them find that by keeping them low they spread and produce more. As cotton is rais'd in America it's needless to say any thing of that tho' the manner in which it's produc'd was new to me.

The cabbage peculiar to the West Indies, in my opinion is vastly inferior to those in your kitchen-garden; nor can I imagine why it takes it's name from a plant that it bears not the least resemblance to either in taste or appearance: it is the pulp that grows in the midst of the trunk of the tree, of a whitish colour which they cut in small strips & boil; but there is another way of dressing it which I think preferable, that of mincing and frying it in oyl like fritters. Altho' it was not the fruit season, we were agreeable surpris'd with a great variety of it.

You would be pleased with the variety of fish they have at Martinico, which they dress extremely well as indeed they do every thing that appears upon table. Crabs I did not see: their lobster tho' different in shape from those in our part of America, are nevertheless excellent. I can't say much for the oysters, they grow upon trees in the water, and are when taken out of the shell about the size of the small crabs we sometimes find in our oysters: suppose I had sent you some to plant in your pond, wou'd it have been much more difficult to supply it with salt than at present with fish? They have a small shell fish call'd crevisse that are very sweet and exactly resembles in shape our lobsters; they are larger than shrimps, and tho' seldom served upon table when they exceed three or four inches in length, I am told they would, if left to mature attain the size of lobsters.

Mr. Petault, a gentleman at St. Pierres inform'd me that until he sent for a swarm of bees (which was not longer than 18 months ago) there was not one in the Island, and that single swarm has in that short space of time increased to the number of 46 swarms & produc'd as much wax as is necessary to supply four families with all the candles they use. The honey is very beautiful and fine tasted, and as the bees work the whole year they never destroy them: but does not this, sir, derogate a little from the sagacity usually attributed to those industrious little insects, since we now find that laying up stores is rather to indulge a natural propensity, than a wise provision for an inclement season?

If I have too long detain'd your attention from subjects more interesting than those of my letter, I'm sure you'll pardon me for the intention sake which you will readily believe was to amuse you and entertain myself for while writing to you I'm flatter[ed] with an idea of being in your company and so pleasing to me is that illusion that it's with reluctance I quit it even to assure you that I am my dear papa,

Your very affectionate and dutiful daughter
Sa. Jay

(SLJ to Peter Jay)

Aurora frigate,
sailing sweetly before the wind
Jany. the 9th, 1780

Little did I think when last I parted from my dear papa, that so many months, nay perhaps years would have elapsed before we shou'd again have the pleasure of an interview: but the ways of Providence are mysterious! And tho' beyond our ken, we know it to be an act of Wisdom to submit with chearfulness to its dispensations. May you, sir, still possess that amiable resignation which has heretofore sustained you under many severe tryals, & I hope we shall again rejoice together.

Our Voyage from America to Martinico was rather an unpleasant one, rendered so by several accidents & the degree of uncertainty naturally attending them; but the pleasure we received there wou'd have amply compensated for the inconveniencies we suffered on our passage, had our own gratification been the sole motive that induced us to leave America. The variety, verdure, & fertility of the Island, afforded me not less pleasure than the hospitality, good breeding and cleanliness of the Inhabitants.

The climate was not disagreeable at the time we were there, tho' we could have dispensed with a few rays of the Sun, had they been disposed to visit you in your retirement. I could not but reflect Sometimes upon the different manner in which my Fish kill friends were solacing themselves from that in which we found relief. On Christmas day I imagined that Peter [John Jay's brother] was calling for still more Wood, adding that the influence of a cheerful fire enliven'd the Company: and indeed, Brother, I am of your opinion, for never at that season did I feel so languid as on the last, tho' in the midst of an agreeable circle of friends, not that I by any means suppose that more warmth had been requisite to animate my spirits but rather that they languish'd for want of that charming North West wind that renders a good fire so necessary in our Country.

Mr. Bingham, a young Gentleman from Philadelphia, and Agent for Congress at St. Pierre's, favored us with every mark of politeness, & introduced us to many genteel families at there who likewise were very civil. The Viscount Damas was so polite as to review his regiment in compliment to us, for which he chose a lovely piece of ground, situated in a level Spot, (one of the rarest things to be met with in the Island, or at least near the Town) between two rows of trees that are tall & very handsome, and on either side fields, tho' somewhat hilly, covered with cane. The regiment made a very good appearance, to which their neat uniforms, their fine musick, and even the beauty of the adjacent country contributed. It was a satisfaction to me that in viewing such fine troops, I recognized the friends of American Liberty, nor was it without emotion I heard that eight hundred men of that same division had already, since this contest, yielded to the too frequent fate of War. Justly may it be said that "The paths of glory lead but to the grave."

Having mentioned the cane, perhaps Peter may be curious to know the construction of the mills for making sugar. Had Mr. Jay been sufficiently disengaged from writing to have seen one, he could have given a better description to his Brother. I think it very like those we have for cyder, only that the rollers are of iron & the reservoirs for the Juice directly under the rollers. The wheel is turned by another wheel, which receives its motion from a stream of water; the juice is conducted from the reservoir, that immediately receives it to a large bason by a gutter, and from thence by the same kind of conveyance into a large boiler.

When it has considerably boiled away, it is then put into the next of a smaller size, & again when diminished to a certain quantity put into the third & last, to which they then pay a great attention, throwing it up continually with a large flat shovel to prevent it from burning, & when it attains a consistency the syrup is poured into large earthen pans in the form of sugar loaves with holes in the bottom which they stop till the sugar begins to chrystallize, then unstopping them, they are set in jars & the syrup that contains no grain drains off, & is what we call molasses.

There is a convent at St. Pierre's, but I had not an opportunity of visiting it as our stay was short. I should regret it but that I expect to have the pleasure of seeing several before I return. There are very few carriages at that place, nor are they requisite for the town & country are so very hilly that it would be impossible to use them. It was at the risque of my neck that I ventured in one to visit a sugar plantation.

We left Martinico on the 28th of December, in the *Aurora* frigate, commanded by the Marquis de la Flotte, & have been favored with fair winds ever since, so that there is a great probability that we shall reach Toulon sometime next week. The hurry we were in while at Martinico has cautioned me not to defer writing untill we make land again! As Toulon is pretty distant from Paris, I flatter myself with the expectation of a very agreeable ride, & when arrived at our Journey's end, hope for the pleasure of reassuring you of my constant regard. Will you be so obliging as to remember me affectionately to sister Jay, Nancy, Mrs. Munro, and Brother Peter and Sir James. Mrs. Munro may be perfectly satisfied about her son, he is in good health and fine spirits, & is quite the favorite among the Officers of the Frigate, some of whom he instructs in the English language, and receives lessons in French in return.

I have never known Mr. Jay [to] enjoy his health more perfectly than at present: The rest of our family are likewise very well. Adieu, my dear sir, may tranquil days and peaceful slumbers soon succeed to those stormy & restless ones that unfortunately have disturbed your repose, & may no anxious cares invade your bosom for the safety of your children, in the number of whom its my pleasure & pride that you acknowledge

your truly affecte. daughter
Sa. Jay

(SLJ to her sisters Kitty and Susan at Persipenny) Cadiz 4th March 1780

But one Vessel has left this port for America since our arrival, & the Captain of that has letters from me for my father, Mr. Jay & Hannah Benjamin, & should like wise have written to my dear Sisters had not extreme indisposition prevented me.

Two or three days before we made the Bay of Cadiz, we were chased by an English frigate & while a number of sailors were preparing the cabbin, for the expected engagement, I went upon deck & staid there till the chase was over, when it was already ten o'clock, & I had caught a severe cold, the effects of which did not leave me untill five weeks after: I am now, thank God! perfectly recovered but have by my confinement been prevented from Seeing any thing that can be entertaining to you.

We are now very agreeably accommodated, & I do assure you the view from my window reminds me of that dear spot that gave me birth.

There is an Irish brigade stationed in this City, officered by gentlemen who do honor to humanity, from whom we have received every mark of attention. Think how pleasing to me are the praises bestowed upon my worthy Countrymen by those as well as other gentlemen. Do you think, girls, that distance diminishes my affection for Americans, or my concern for their interest? Oh! no; it encreases my attachment even to enthusiasm. Where is the country (Switzerland excepted) where Justice is so impartially administered, industry encouraged, health and Smiling plenty so bounteous to all as in our much favored Country? And are not those blessings each of them resulting from, or matured by freedom, worth contending for?

But whither, my pen, are you hurrying me? What have I to do with politicks? Am I not myself a woman, & writing to Ladies? Come then, ye fashions to my assistance! Alas! Sisters, it mortifies me exceedingly that the vessel which Sails to morrow is bound for Boston, & will therefore prevent me from sending you a specimen of them. The prevailing mode, however, is here the Same as it was in America last winter, with only a trifling variation. Every thing bears a most extravagant price here; only think of my being asked 60 Dollars for a table cloth only large enough to cover one table, & a dozen napkins, & every thing in proportion.

If, my dear sisters, you have any compassion for me, do let me hear from you soon & direct to me at Madrid, for next week we begin our Journey thither. This week I shall pay visits, & shall see all the rarer shows that this City affords, & then girls, prepare yourselves for a folio. Give my love to Mamma, & tell her that I often wish for her own Satisfaction She could now & then by looking into her mirrour behold our little circle, innocently happy, & most frequently conversing of our friends on the other Side [of] the Atlantic. Mama must write me, indeed she must, & tell me that she confides in that Providence who has never ceased to bless me. My little lovely Son must not believe those insinuations which his uncle has interspersed in his letter to his Mama. Kiss the dear little fellow for me, I know he deserves it, for I am Sure he is a good boy.

....Give my love to Papa, & request the favor of a letter for me from him. Tell William he has described the hosts of fleas in such terrific colours, that he has awakened my apprehensions at the thought of encountering them, more than when in hourly expectation of a naval engagement.

Mr. Jay joins with me in love & best wishes to Papa, Mama, & the rest of the family. Adieu. God bless you all. When you write, be very particular, for you know how dear your welfare is to

Your affectionate Sister
Sa. Jay

The Jays had a difficult and disappointing two years in Madrid. As minister plenipotentiary for the United States, John Jay found that he was neither welcome nor accepted. Spain was not ready to recognize America as a new nation nor was it willing to lend it money. Despite following the Spanish king from palace to palace, John Jay was never invited to present his credentials at Court.

(Brockholst Livingston to his mother at Elizabeth Town) Madrid 30th April 1780

My dear mother,

...Mrs. Jay ... is determined to keep Mr. Jay to his promise of returning in two years. She counts Six months of these past and at the End of Eighteen more expects to bid adieu to Madrid.... She was indisposed almost the whole of her time at Cadiz. But you may take my word for it when I assure you that She never looked better nor never enjoyed better health since she was married than she does in this City. Could she forget America, You and her little Boy she might enjoy as much happiness as she does health. However we have all lived long enough to know that this is not the Planet of Happiness. When Mrs. Jay has made some acquaintances here, & understands the language, I am persuaded She will spend her time tolerably agreeable. There are no amusements here at present but Comedies & Bullfights.... And as for the Bull-fights, I don't believe Mrs. Jay will ever go to one of them, they being the most Inhuman diversion I believe ever practised by a christian nation. The Spanish Ladies are very fond of them and rarely omit going....

[On the journey from Cadiz] The coachman either drunk or asleep left the mules to their own discretion in choosing the Road. This like to have cost us dear, for the mules on going down a hill took it in their heads, contrary to their usual custom, to trot, and carted us of the side of it. Altho the overset was very violent & we were four in the coach Sally had the good fortune not to receive the least hurt. She was hardly frightened. Mr. Jay received a slight bruise in the forehead and as for myself, except a black eye, a bruised side & a squeezed foot I came off very well. The hurt in my side was the worst.... Had not the mules luckily disengaged themselves from the carriage, as it overset, we should have been in a much worse situation then in the dismasted frigate....

Mrs. Jay is very busy in furnishing her house. This she finds difficult & very expensive.... When the house is furnished we shall be comfortably situated. Being near one of the Gates of the city we shall have some of the Country air which is of some consequence in a town where the heat is so intense in Summer that Scarcely any one appears in the Streets till the Evening....

Harry B. Livingston

(Brockholst Livingston to his father) Madrid May 5 1780

Dear Sir,

....Mrs. Jay is well. She has taken a Master for the Spanish. Indeed we all find so many difficulties for want of this tongue that we find it our Interest to apply closely to it. From the little I know of it I will venture to pronounce it much easier for an Englishman than the french. The construction comes much nearer ours than that of the French. Altho' I did not apply to it till our arrival at Cadiz, & the two months we were there, I studied without a Master, I can now write it with much greater facility than I do the french of which I have had some smattering these several years. Not to forget the french, certainly the most useful language of the two, I have taken a Master here who speaks only spanish & french, by which means I shall learn something of the two tongues at the same time, by translating alternately from Spanish into french & from French into Spanish & having a person perfect in both to correct my errors.

We wish much to hear from You & the family. We doubt not there are letters on the way tho' they have not yet reached us. You will find some herewith enclosed for our Family, of which I beg your care & am with much Esteem

Your affectionate & dutiful Son
Henry B. Livingston

(JJ to Margaret C. Meredith at Philadelphia) Aranjues 12 May 1780

Dear Madame,

It is a delightful evening, and I am just returned from a long solitary walk to pay my Respects to you. While the Court were enjoying a Bull Feast, I amused myself in the Gardens and ornamented Grounds which surround me, some of which are beautiful; but I forbear describing them or the Reveries they suggested. Mrs. Jay is at Madrid, and her absence makes me feel the force of the Reflection which concludes Milton's description of the charms of Paradize.

You will naturally suppose that the delicious Retreats to be found here, would give a romantic Complection to an Imagination less inclined to it than mine. Nor will it be difficult for you to believe, that the fairy scenes which present themselves in the Reveries I often indulge in these Retreats, are peopled from America, when I assure you, that the ocean has not been able to wash from my Remembrance, any of the many agreable Ideas impressed upon it in that country.

Could you perceive the direction of my thoughts, you would see them daily bending their course to the Hudson and the Delaware, sometimes sporting at the Hills, that seat of Hospitality, and at other Times admiring the Delicacy of sentiment and manners which created the esteem and friendship that prompt this letter. There are Recesses about this place that would please you, and to those who wish sometimes to enjoy Solitude, they afford it in Perfection. They are frequented by few except the Gardners who keep them in order.

The beau monde preferring a grand public walk, planted by Charles the fifth, where they see and are seen, where every evening they pass and repass each other, where the Courtier bows to his Patron, the Belle displays her charms, the pettit maitre his pretty person, the Grandee his Equipage, and all have the Happiness of Seeing the Princess of Asturies* take her evening Ride in a splendid carriage, drawn by six fine Horses, richly caparisoned, and surrounded by Guards well dressed and well mounted, and holding naked sabres in their Hands.

This Pageantry may be proper in Monarchies, and may entertain those who seldom entertain themselves. For my own Part I readily exchange it for the lonely devious walk, the water falls, the fountains, the Birds, and above all the ancient Elms bound to each other by innumerable vines of Ivy, and whose tops intermixing exclude the sun. But as much as I am in love with these, I would gladly leave them for less decorated scenes on your side of the water, and for the pleasure of spending the Remainder of my Days in that Peace Tranquility and Retirement, in which alone virtue and Liberty reward their Votaries for all their sacrifices— neither the whistling of a name, or the Fascination of ambition will be able to detain me from your shores, when the duties of a Citizen will permit me to return from this honorable Exile, for as such only can I consider it. Then Madam! I shall again have the Pleasure of seeing you shine in the Dance, at the Tea Tables, and in those polite and proportioned attentions which bespeak Discernment as well as Grace.

But you may ask me how it happens that in thinking of Balls and Tea Tables I

**The Princess of Asturies was Louise Marie of Parma, daughter-in-law of Charles III.*

should forget the silks etc. we were to send you? If you understood Latin, or if I had an English Translation of Virgil I should exclaim in the words of Aeneas, when the Queen desired him to relate his adventures. The winds and waves madam, have been cruel to us, and your Disappointment was involved in ours. Had we gone to France your orders should most punctually have been obeyed, or had we possessed more humble Ideas of your Taste, I should have employed some Person there to execute them. Unfortunately for these orders we were brought here, where fashionable People import handsome Things at a great expence and charged with very heavy Duties from abroad; unfortunately too, I knew no Person in France to whom I could trust the Task of choosing for you. If my Fellow Traveller's Taste in Dress had been like yours, I should have requested the favor of him. Thus circumstanced, I was obliged to acquiesce in the mortification arising from your Disappointment, and I assure you nothing but the Reflection that to some Persons artificial ornaments are of little importance, can diminish it. As to this Country, believe me, it would be as difficult to find very elegant things manufactured in it, as Mrs. Merediths, and I have no reason to believe they are very often met with any where....

I imagine you have had a very gay winter, and that the French minister has given you some little specimen of Paris. What has Hymen been doing? if he has been half as busy the last winter in making matches, as Mercury was the one before in making Lies and mischief, you have had fine times. Tell us something about these matters. You cant conceive how interesting every thing from America is, especially such as relate to our friends. I know I can give you in Return nothing equally so; but as I am sure you are disinterested I wont dwell on that circumstance. Adieu. Assure Mr. Meredith of my Regards and esteem and believe me to be very sincerely

your Friend & Servant
John Jay

P.S. Mrs. Jay wrote to you from Cadiz.

(SLJ to her mother) Madrid, 13th May 1780

Here my dear Mama are we at last arrived after an absence of six months from our native Country. The goodness of Providence has been exemplified to us in so many instances, that I can neither recount them, nor without ingratitude pass it over in silence.

I think I promised William an account of our journey hither & therefore will not demand your attention to any circumstances that occured in our route, but rather proceed to tell you that I am pleased with Madrid, & expect that my satisfaction will be increased when I have acquired the language of the Country. As yet I've made but few acquaintances among the ladies & the chief amusement I have hitherto taken has been in the riding way.

Mr. Jay is at present at Aranjuez, where His Majesty has a very beautiful seat & which is at present the residence of the Court. It is seven leagues from the City & the road that Leads to it is the finest I have ever seen, adorned on either side by handsome trees, that owe their flourishing state to the unremitted attention of persons appointed to water them, which they effect by means of canalls that conveys the water from one tree to another. What a defect in this climate is the long droughts that prevail thro' the country & renders the produce of the finest soil extremely precarious. What do you think Mamma of being nine months successively without any rain? We are not yet in the middle of may, & the fields already begin to fade & change their verdant appearance for one of an yellower hue.

The King is much fonder of his Country palaces than being in Madrid, and therefore spends so little time here, that in the whole year it does not amount to more than 30 or 40 days. This may be very agreeable to his majesty, but it is both inconvenient & expensive to the foreign Ambassadors & Ministers who are obliged to follow the Court; & I confess mortifying to me to part with Mr. Jay, whom Congress has scarcely ennabled to maintain a family in one place, much less to remove with him to half a dozen different ones in this expensive Country.

We have been so fortunate as to hire a very convenient house; which has the advantage of a fountain in the yard, a circumstance that but few of the inhabitants can boast as they are supplied with all the water they use from publick fountains.

It has given me great concern that it has not been in my power to send you those articles that I know would be useful to yourself & family. My sisters have been disappointed & I fear have blamed me, but indeed they would not if they knew how we have been circumstanced.

Mr. Jay intends upon his return from Aranjuez to write to a Gentleman in Holland (from whom he has received offers of service) requesting him to send some things for both families to St. Eustatia with orders to be re-ship'd on board an American vessel for Philadelphia, with proper directions.

I find by an American paper that the last Winter has been extremely severe there. How I pity our soldiers for the sufferings they must have sustain'd, & yet that pity is mingled with Admiration of the magnanimity with which they supported every difficulty. The Americans are highly esteem'd by the Europeans, & in my opinion they greatly merit it. May Peace and tranquility soon succeed those scenes of war & toil that at present occupy my Country-men & may they long enjoy the liberty for which they have so nobly struggled....

Pray Mamma have you had any more appearance of the scurvy? If you have, let me intreat you to try the following prescription, which I recd. from a very skilful Physician of this City.

To a pint of old Madeira wine, add 9 spoonsful of Lemon juice & 5 spoonsful of loaf sugar, mixing them together in a bottle; provided you drink that quantity every day it is immaterial whether it is at mealtimes or any other part of the day. The Doctor tells me, he never knew the most inveterate scurvy [to] resist this remedy 8 days.

It is more than a year since I left Mamma & my little son. When shall I have the pleasure to re-embrace them? Tell me my dear Mamma will my beloved Child answer the fond expectations of his partial mother? Is he amiable? Is he healthy? Does he still cultivate the acquaintance that had commenced between his little Neighbours & himself while I had the pleasure of residing among you. There is no Reflection from which I derive more satisfaction than the certainty I have of his imbibing with his earliest acquirements that probity & generosity that reigns throughout the family that has kindly taken charge of him. In short, if in his mind & actions he as much resembles his father as he did in his Countenance when last I saw him I ask no more for him of Heaven.

Please remember me affectionately to Papa. I have ventured on a subject that unfits me for writing more at present; but to-morrow I'll resume my pen & devote an hour or two to my Sisters and William....

Adieu my dear Mamma. May the great Protector of Virtue be ever near you. And may he inspire with goodness like your own

Your ever Affectionate
Daughter
Sarah Jay

John Jay was constantly in need of money. While his main diplomatic mission was to seek funds for America, in fact he had difficulty supporting his own household. The high cost of living forced him to travel about Spain without his wife. Under these circumstances it is no surprise that Sarah was often lonely. On June 4th, Brockholst wrote from Madrid to his sisters Kitty and Susan:

> You will hardly beleive me when I tell you that although Mrs. Jay has been in Madrid near two months She has not Seen a Spanish Lady of this place in her house, & you may Swear her American blood will not let her visit them first. A Bilboa Lady, whose husband has large connections with America, is the only female acquaintance ... [she] has in this City.... Mrs. Jay, very fortunately for herself, is always happy at home, (& there happiness is only to be had) or She would be badly off here. However I have hopes that when the Court comes here, which will be this month, ... [she] will not be So lonesome.... Mrs. Jay is as well as She can be. We are fortunate in having an acquaintance with an high Physician of Skill & experience, in case of Mrs. Jay's being otherwise....

Sarah was not only lonely, she was pregnant.

(JJ to Robert R. Livingston at Philadelphia) Madrid 23 May 1780

Dear Robt.

Accept my Thanks, and cordial ones they are, for your friendly Letter of the 22d Decr. last, which I had the Pleasure of recieving a few Days ago.... You have the same Place in my Esteem and Affection which you have filled for near Twenty Years, and neither has or will be diminished by Absence. In one Sense I percieve we are coming nearer to each other.

I am approaching the Age of Ambition without being influenced by its Allurements. Public Considerations induced me to leave the private Walk of Life. When they cease, I shall return to it. Believe me I shall not remain here a moment longer than the Duties of a Citizen may detain me; and that I look forward with Pleasure to the Day when I shall again follow peaceably the Business of my Profession, and make some little Provision for my Family, whose Interests I have so long neglected for public Concerns. My Conduct moves on fixed Principles, from which I shall never deviate; and they will not permit me to leave the unfortunate part of my Family destitute of my Care and attention longer than higher Duties call me from them....

I am here in a disagreable Situation. Congress have made me no Remittances. The small Credit I had on Doctr. Franklin is expended. The Idea of being maintained by the Court of Spain is humiliating, and therefore not for the public Good. The Salary allowed me is greatly inadequate. No part of Europe is so expensive, nor did I ever live so Economically. The Court is never stationary, moving from Madrid to the Pardo, then to Aranjues, thence to St. Il Defonso, thence to the Escurial, in perpetual Rotation. To keep a House at each place is not within the Limits of my Finances. To take ready furnished Lodgings and keep my own Table at each, is beyond Belief expensive. I live at Aranjues, in a Posada, in one single Room, with but one Servant, and without a Carriage. When I left Philadelphia, every Thing was cheaper There than here.

Spain does not cloath its Inhabitants. Their Butter Cheese fine Linnen, fine Silks, and fine Cloths, come from France, Holland &c. They have imposed an exorbitant Duty on all foreign Commodities, and a heavy Tax is laid on Eatables sold in the market. The Sum allowed me will let me live, but not as I ought to do. A paltry post Chaise drawn by three Mules costs me every Time I go to or from here to Aranjues (7 Leagues) ten Dollars, all Things in that Proportion. To Day I am to try a pair of Mules for which I am asked 480 Dollars. They tell me they are very cheap. Yesterday I refused a pair, the Price of which was 640 Dollars. I cannot get a plain decent Carriage and Harness under 870 Dollars. Judge of my Situation. So circumstanced I cannot employ Couriers to carry my Dispatches to the Sea Side or to France. My Letters by the Post are all opened.

Fortunately on this occasion Mr. Harrison now going to Cadiz will take my Letters. With whatever allowance Congress may make, I shall be content. I know how and am determined to live agreable to my Circumstances. If Inconveniences result from them being too narrow, they will be public ones. They therefore merit the Consideration of Congress....

Inform me of the Health of Mrs. Livingston your Mother & Family, to whom Mrs. Jay joins with me in desiring you to present our Compliments and best Wishes. Adieu my Dear Robert

I am your Friend
John Jay

(JJ to his father) Madrid, 23 May 1780

Dear Sir

Various have been the scenes thro which I have passed since last we bid each other Farewel. Some of them have been dangerous, and many of them disagreeable. Providence has however been pleased to bring me safe thro them all to the Place of my Destination, and I hope will restore me to my Country & friends as soon as the Business committed to me shall be compleated. Then I shall have the Pleasure of entertain[ing] you with the Recital of many interesting matters which the Risque to which all my Letters exposed forbids me to commit to Paper. I will nevertheless give you some little account of our Journey from Cadiz to Madrid, because the manner of travelling here differs entirely from that of our Country it may afford you some Amusement.

The Distance is between three and four hundred English Miles. We were told at Cadiz that it would be necessary to take with us Beds, Hams, Tea, Sugar, Chocolate and other Articles of Provision as well as Kitchen utensils for dressing them, for that we should seldom find either on the Road. We were further informed that these Journeys were usually performed in Carriages resembling a Coach and drawn by six mules the pre[sen]t hire of which was from a hundred and thirty to a hundred and fifty Dollars and that they would carry near a thousand weight of Baggage.

We accordingly made the necessary Provision for eating and sleeping comfortably by the Way & set out the Marys day of March last. We crossed the Bay to Port St. Mary's in very pleasant Weather, and a handsome Boat which the Brother of the Minister of Indes was so kind as to lend us. We staid a night at that place waiting for our Carriage, and were very hospitably entertained by Count Oreilly—the same who established the Spanish Government at New Orleans at the Conclusion of the last War. He is a Man of excellent abilities and great knowledge of men as well as things. He has risen to be Inspector and Lt. General of the armies of Spain, into which he has introduced a Degree of Discipline to which they had long been Strangers, and Captain Gen. of the Province of Andalusia &c. &c.

The next Day we set out for Madrid. There are some peculiarities in these Carriages. The hind wheels are very high and heavy. The fore wheels are low and are made to play under the Carriage so that they turn very short. The Nails that fix the Tire have Heads as large as half a middle sized apple. They are driven thro the Fellow & Clinch. Over each axle Tree is Room for two large Trunks or Chests and Beds upon them. Under the Frame which supports the Trunks behind, there is a Netting of Rope capable of containing a large Hamper and under the Floor of the Carriage there is a Place of about seven or Eight Inches Deep the whole Length and Width of the Floor in which many things may be stowed as well as under the Seats & some other lesser nettings about the Coach.

The hindermost mules were harnessed to a Bar run across by the foot of the Pole & secured by Irons from each End to the fore axeltree, but the Traces of each of the other four were all laid in a Notch made in the hinder Part of the Pole & had no sort of Connection with each other. Instead of Collars they had Haims constructed with a Groove that admitted a Piece of Wood exactly like our Hog Yokes strongly fastened in the Crotch by an Iron spike or Rivot that passed thro it. The Ends of the Trace were tied near the Points of this Yoke, which was run into the groove whenever the Mules were put to the Carriage & taken out again as often as they were turned into the Stable.

As to the Harness they never were taken from the mules during the whole Journey. Each of their Necks was ornamented with six or Eight little Bells & made no little noise. A Driver setting over the fore axle tree guided the two hindermost Mules with a pair of leading Lines. The other four went as they pleased in fair Roads, but in common a Man walked or ran by their Sides to take the foremost by the Head and guide them in Places where they could not safely be left to their own Discretion.

These Animals are fed entirely on cut Straw and Barley, & I am told are constantly going. We traveled at a Rate of between twenty and thirty Miles a Day and the same mules brought us to Madrid that we set out with from Cadiz, at which they had arrived from Madrid only a Day before we left it. We stopped but once in the Course of the Day. At the End of the Journey they appeared in as much flesh and Spirits as when we set out. The manner of driving them is in my opinion greatly to their Disadvantage, very fast up and down Hill, & slow on plain Ground.

I had no Idea of there being animals of this Kind in the World so fine. I have seen some near sixteen Hands high. In common they are from 14 to 15, a great many 14½, very active and well limbed. I am convinced that they are stronger as well as more durable than Horses tho not so handsome.

One Reason perhaps why the Mules of this Country exceed those of others is that the Generalty of their Horses are better. The Andalusian Horses of which you have often heard are noble animals, handsome, sprightly, and well tempered. Many of them are rather too small and delicate, but it is not uncommon to meet with them strong & full sized. They are formed much like English Horses, and tho I have scarce ever seen any of the latter with so fine an air as many of the former, yet I have met with none of the Spanish so perfectly well made as some of those from England I have seen. They cannot be exported without special Licence from the King.

The asses are of two kinds very large and very small, they being of distinct Breeds, as much so as our common Horses & Poneys. The little asses are by far the more common, because they live with less than the others, and are the chief Porters of the Country, Carts and wagons being very little used. The large ass is very ugly—they call them fine, I suppose when compared with those of other Countries. I have seen none yet that exceeded fourteen Hands and I think them rather heavy limbed. It is more than probable that when I return I shall bring a couple of them with me. I am satisfied that for Labor two very good mules are at the least worth three very good Horses.

The Po[s]adas or Inns were more tolerable than they had been represented to us. Many of them had very good Rooms, but swarming with Fleas and Buggs. The Mules were generally lodged under the same Roof and my Bed Room has frequently been divided from them by only a common Partition. The Innkeepers give themselves little Trouble about their Guests further than to exact as much from them as possible. I found no Reason or Justice among them. They furnish scarce anything except Food for the Mules & House Room for the Passengers, I may indeed add such Beds as nothing but necessity wd. induce one to use. Thoroughly Dirty. For all these they charge extravagently, and what you will hardly belief they have the Impudence to charge for what they call the noise of the House, and this seldom costs us less at each Po[s]ada than from three to four Dollars.

At one Tavern, which it seems keeps something to eat, we arrived and dined late, & excepting the Coll. went to Bed without supper. We took Breakfast in the

Morning. Our Servants, 4 in number, except a little Bread and Milk, eat of the Provisions they brought. We all slept in our own Beds. When the Reckoning was called it amounted to 477 Reals— that is £ 9-10-9 York Money. They charged us for 14 Beds tho our Number, including Servants, amounted only to 8 (for as to the muleteers, we had nothing to do with them or their Mules). On observing this to them we were told that there were many Beds in the Rooms in which we had slept and in others communicating with them, and that we might have used them all if we pleased. We remarked that it was impossible for Eight persons to use Fourteen Beds; they replied that was not their Fault. There was no Remedy and I paid it after taking an acct. of the particulars with a Rect. at the Foot of it which I Keep as a Curiosity.

I am told that these Impositions arise from this Circumstance. The Houses in which these Po[s]adas are kept generally belong to Great Men, who from Rent & License to keep Tavern demand from the poor wretches much more than they can honestly get by that Business and thence they are driven to make up the Deficiency by these iniquitous Practices. The Landlords know this and so enjoy these high Rents support their Tenants against Travellers, and take Care that the latters be the Losers by all Disputes with Innkeepers. Besides as Travellers cannot remain long enough at one Place to prosecute and abide the Event of such Litigations they generally put up with the first Loss.

My next will probably contain a continuation of this Acct. which I hope will be confined to the Family.

On the Subject of politics I make it a Rule to write to none but Congress. We have no News except that the Dutch are grumbling and have half a mind to make War with England. I would send you News Papers if I had any besides Spanish, but as you don't understand that Language they wd. be useless.

My Brothers must consider this Letter as an apology for none to them. I have not at present Time to write to each of them separately. We are well. Peter had had the Fever and Ague but is recovered. He behaves well, but I find it difficult to make him apply.

I have ordered several little Articles for Family use. They will I hope arrive before cold weather. Don't however depend on them, for they may be taken.

Our Comps. To Doctr. & Mrs. W. Vwyck. Our Love to all the family.

I am Dr Sir Your Dutiful and Affe. Son

P.S.

I bought a very fine negroe Boy [Benoit] of 15 years old at Martinico, from whence as well as from Cadiz, I wrote you several Letters. No Lettr. from the Family since I left Pha.

(Benjamin Franklin to JJ at Madrid) Passy, June 13. 1780

Dear Sir,

....Yesterday, and not before, is come to hand your favours of April 14 with the Pacquets and Dispatches from Congress, &c. which you sent me by a french Gentleman to Nantes. Several of them appear to have been opened, the Paper round the

Seals being smok'd and burnt as with the flame of a Candle us'd to soften the Wax; and the Impression defac'd. The Curiosity of People in this Time of War is unbounded; some of them only want to see News, but others want to find (thro' interested Views) what Chance there is of a speedy Peace....

Mrs. Jay does me much Honour in desiring to have one of the Prints that have been made here of her Countryman. I send what is said to be the best of 5 or 6 engrav'd by different hands, from different Paintings. The Verses at the Bottom are truly extravagant. But you must know that the Desire of pleasing by a perpetual use of Compliments in this polite Nation, has so us'd up all the common Expressions of Approbation, that they are become flat and insipid, and to use them almost implies Censure. Hence Musick, that formerly might be sufficiently prais'd when it was call'd bonne, to go a little farther they call'd it excellente, then Superbe, magnifique, exquise, celeste, all which being in their turns worn out, there remains only divine; and when that is grown as insignificant as its Predecessors, I think they must return to common Speech, and Common Sense: As from vying with one another in fine and costly Paintings on their Coaches, since I first knew the Country, not being able to go farther in that Way, they have return'd lately to plain Carriages, painted without Arms or figures, in one uniform Colour. With great and Sincere Esteem, I am

Dear Sir
your most obedient
& most humble servant
B. Franklin

(Brockholst Livingston to his father) Madrid 12 July 1780

My dear Sir,

I know not what has been the fate of the Letters I have already had the Pleasure of writing to you, not having had a line from America since our departure.... This however shall not deter me from sending you congratulations on the birth of your Spanish Grandchild. I fear your Persippeney Grandson has so monopolized the Affections of his Grandpapa that his sister at more than three thousand miles off will stand but little chance for her share. Mrs. Jay is well & bids fair to continue so.

I dare say that you are all pleasing yourselves with the hopes of very soon hearing good news from Spain. I wish it was in my power to encourage these hopes. This court seems disposed to give us nothing but professions. They have suffered Mr. Jay to accept Bills drawn on him by Congress for about 12,000 dollars & that with Reluctance. They insist, if they enter into treaty with us, on the Navigation of the Mississippi. You may be sure our misfortune to the southward will not make them abate in their demands. Mr. Jay is not yet acknowledged. They do not seem to wish to entangle themselves with us. The Nation is sick of the war. Their resources are already nearly exhausted. They are obliged to borrow money, altho' they have plenty of [it] in the Indies but dare not draw it home at present. Their commerce is almost ruined by British Cruisers....

Indeed from what I have seen & heard since our arrival in Europe I am more than ever persuaded that America must trust to her own Exertions more than to the Professions or alliance of any Power on this side of the water. Tho' to do the French Justice they have really behaved cleverly. There are now in the Bay of Cadiz 39 Ships of the Line, Spanish & French. They are on the Point of sailing. If they & Geary meet there will be warm work.

Mr. Jay & myself went yesterday to a Bull-fight which is almost the only diversion this town affords—& a cruel one it is. I will not shock you with a description of it. Except the Gladiators I never heard of any thing more inhuman. In the morning one of the knights who fought on horse-back was killed & two wounded—this was something very uncommon, as the men very seldom get much hurt. But the horses which are torn to pieces by the Bull, & the tedious tormenting death of the Bulls themselves is a most shocking part of the Entertainment. What surprized me most was the pleasure the Spanish Ladies received from the death of the poor Animals. Indeed unless a great many horses are killed they call it a very poor feast. The Activity & Strenght shewn by the fighters is really surprising. The danger they put themselves into is still more so. I have seen a Man hoped over a fence 5 or 6 feet in height on the Bulls horns, return to the fight again in an Instant as if nothing had happened to him.

Besides these Bull-fights, they have a Comedy every evening. But as I do not know enough of the Language to understand the Actors I have not derived much pleasure from any I have yet seen. The Devil has a great Part in their Comedies. I have been in one shop where there were more than 3,000 comedies of different kinds to be sold, & I have been told by an Abby here that above 500 of these are now actually in vogue & represented on the two theatres in the City. I am dear Sir Yours &c.

HBL

(JJ to William Livingston at Trenton) [Draft]

Madrid 14 July 1780

Dr Sr

I give you Joy. There is a little Stranger here, who I hope will one Day have the Pleasure of calling you Grandfather. On the 9th Inst. Sally was deliverd. of a Daughter as like her Brother as two Children can be. The Mother is in a fair Way & the Child thrives finely. It has as yet no Name nor am I certain what it will be. The old goody has a great Mind to save it from Limbo (a spanish name for a dark Receptacle for the souls of Infants who die unbaptized). About Eight Days ago she presented Mrs. Jay with the Pictures of [______] who I presume have succeeded the ancient Goddesses in presiding over Births. If these Saints had any thing to do with it we are much obliged to them, for she had a fine time of it.

When the Child was born she proposed (as being customary here) to give it the Name of the Saint of that Day, for they are so happy as to have at least one Saint for every Day in the Year. But as the Saints are at War with us Heritics we shall name it after some Sinner that will probably have more Affection for it. Besides on looking over the Almanack I found that the 9th July was the Day of St. Cirilo who was a pope, and as neither that Name or Office except in the Case of pope Joan ever appertaind. to a Female I did not see how the old Ladys Advice cd be followd. in this Instance. I was nevertheless mistaken in supposing this Difficulty insuperable for in similar Cases it seems the Name of Papa wh. is spanish for pope is taken, as being Sufficiently feminine for the most delicate Virgins. However as the popes are as clever as the old Norman Lawyers were in drawing extensive Conclusions from weak premisses, and might possibly from such a Circumstance claim some Right to my little Girl, whom I wish not to embarrass with any Disputes with the See of Rome, I think it will be most prudent to let her take her Chance under the Name of Susanna who was a good Sort of a Woman & nobly resisted the lascivious Attacks of two Inquisitor Generals, whom the Latin Bible have in Complim[en]t I suppose to the Presbyterians stiled Presbyters.

I am Dr. Sr. with sincere Regard
Your most obt. Servt.

(SLJ to her sister Susan) Madrid, August 28th 1780

Your letter of the 29th March I recd. this morning.... I feel more for what my friends have suffered for me than ever I did for myself. It's true we have been in imminent dangers & to be candid I did once think I never should have seen relations, friends, or Country more; but to confess the whole truth (as if inspired by our example the preceding winter) I determin'd with Cornelia to fall with decency, or rather with submission to acquiesce in the dispensations of Providence; our Resignation was accepted & Providence was pleased kindly to deliver us from every real & apprehended danger & conducted us in safety to Martinique; where we were much refresh'd & hospitably entertain'd. Mr. Bingham's politeness deserves the warmest acknowledgment. Susan, how agreeable, nay absolutely delightful to meet in a foreign Climate a person whose native soil is that of one's own Country!

The generous wishes of our friends for a safe passage from Martinique were not without effect. It was more than safe it was pleasant.... We had very brisk gales all the way, as you may imagine by our performing a voyage of 4000 miles (encreas'd to that length by the circuitous course we were oblidged to take to avoid encounters with our british friends) in 24 days.

In one of my Letters to papa I have assigned the reasons that induced us to make the port of Cadiz: while we continued there, I was constantly confined by indisposition, arising from two circumstances, one of them was the length of time we had been at sea & the other I leave you to conjecture.

Immediately after our arrival, Mr. Carmichael set out for Madrid with dispatches from Mr. Jay for that Court, & we remained at Cadiz until Mr. Jay recd. permission to proceed on his Journey. How to give you a just idea of the inconveniences that occur in travelling thro' this Country is somewhat puzzling, as our Country is exempt from the like circumstances.

From Cadiz we went to Port St. Mary by water in a very handsome Barge, belonging to Mr. Galvez Commandant of the Bay & brother to the Minister for Indian affairs: it was ornamented by a crimson damask canopy handsomly fringed & the benches covered with cushions of the same, the Rowers were 16 or 20 in number, in a uniform that was after a fanciful taste, & not unpleasing: the day was perfectly serene, & vastly different was the appearance of the sea from what I had lately beheld it! The regularity of the Oars, the musick, the serenity of the weather, the mildness of the sea, and the beautiful prospect presented from the bay conspired to render our passage extremely agreeable. Upon our arrival at the Port we found General Oreilys coach had been some time in readiness for us, & we were immediately conducted to his house, where we were recd. with great politeness by the Count & Countess, & were introduced to a large circle of their acquaintances who had been invited in compliment to us. Port St. Mary is a pretty town, greatly improved & much ornamented since Count O'Reily has made his residence there: & it was not without regret that we left it the next day to pursue our journey.

Altho we had been apprised of many inconveniences to be expected in our route, my surprize was not less than if silence had been observed upon that subject, so greatly did the awkwardness & filth of every thing exceed description: the two carriages in which we were to travel were the first outre figures that caught my attention; they've the impudence to call them Coaches, it's true they are made of wood & have four wheels, but there the resemblance ceases; & for a passage for ourselves and servants in two of these pretty vehicles we were obliged to pay seventy six doubloons, tho the distance is short of three hundred miles; the coachmen do not differ less from the human species in looks, dress and manner than the Carriages they drive differ from those of other countries; in short drivers, mules, & Carriages are admirably suited to each other, & not to be equal'd elsewhere.

We had in consequence of the advice of some Gentlemen provided every thing we thought would be necessary upon the road; but the very first evening we found that a broom was absolutely essential; was ever a broom deem'd part of travelling equipage before! With some little difficulty the servants purchased one in the village, & while we waited in the Court-yard, Abbe and an Irish woman I brought [with me] from Cadiz clear'd the Room of some half dozen filthy beds & several loads of dirt in which were contain'd not [less] than two or 3000 fleas, lice, buggs, &c. if we may form any Judgment by what still remained.

We then had our Catalonian bed open'd which is the most compleat of the kind I've seen: having in one trunk, bed, bedstead, Musketto net &c. and indeed I would advise all persons who travel thro this Country by all means to provide something of this kind, for by that we were enabled to get some sound repose in spite of the many preventives that every where surrounded us, for the want of every thing convenient in our lodging place and the super-abundance of every thing we did not want was far from being the whole amount of the inconveniences that fell to our share. The adjoining apartment to ours was allotted to our Mules, & indeed they would have disturbed us less than any of the guests, had they been freed from the bells that the vanity of their drivers had encumber'd them with, but unluckily for us they slept not much & we had the mortification of being serenaded with the tinkling.

After leaving Jeres we travell'd on in the Jog-trot way till we arrived at Cordova an ancient City, of which we had a most beautiful view from a height about [a] league this side of it: indeed we never saw any thing more enchanting than that prospect; its true it had an advantage from the very time that we gain'd the ascent, it being just before sunset, & then you know the shades by being lengthened vary the scene prettily; nothing can be imagined more luxuriant than the meadows which we beheld below us, upon which were a great number of Cattle grazing & enjoying a respite from the toils & fatigues impos'd upon them by restless and insatiate man: indeed I believe I recd. the greatest pleasure I felt upon that occasion from the appearance of innocence & ease that was visible in the whole scene, the flocks & herds peacefully contenting themselves with the provisions supply'd for them by bounteous nature, while the goats wantoning & frisking along the edge of the surrounding mountain seem'd delighted with their elevation. The vineyards & groves of olive trees (oh! how I wish I could send you a branch from one of them) are here and there interspersed as if with matchless art, & appear as if intended to form a rural garden for the inhabitants of those piles of buildings that the City presents to view.

We all by mutual consent requested the coachman to wait 'till we indulged ourselves with this attracting landscape; for now the Sun was retiring behind a dark & heavy cloud that was hanging over Cordova & now and then shot forth lightning like a trail of fire & the thunder was re-echoed from the mountains that terminated the view; but tho' the prospect was greatly improv'd by the alteration in the atmosphere we could no longer enjoy it, our driver being absolutely averse to a wet skin.

Excuse me my dear Sister for staying so long near Cordova, the Coachman was perfectly right to be peremptory & we arriv'd at that City an hour after dark. The next day we continued there and recd. much civility from a number of Irish gentlemen who had arrived from the Sea-ports & made that their residence: Mr. Moyland ... waited upon us when we visited the Bishop's palace gardens &c. and was one of the Gentlemen that went with us to see the Cathedral, I doubt whether it is exceeded by anything in Spain, it was formerly a Moorish mosque & certainly gives us an high idea of their proficiency in Architecture, but I am quite incapable of giving you an adequate idea of it; leaving that for the Coll: I'll only mention one circumstance that will convince you that it is a vast & splendid Edifice, since it contains not less than 999 pillars of polished marble, elegantly wrought and of every kind that has been discover'd. The Spaniards have made great additions to it equally magnificent & curious.

There are many things in Cordova worth seeing but as Mr. Jay's maxim is to prefer business to pleasure, we the next day proceeded on our Journey & I don't recollect any agreeable circumstances that occur'd after quitting the province of Andalusia. We very frequently pass'd little wooden crosses on the highway which had been plac'd there to denote the burying places of those who had been found murder'd there, it being the custom to inter them in the same places they were found. When we came to La Mancha we naturally recollected the exploits that had been there atchieved by the renowned knight of the rueful countenance & looked but in vain, for those large trees that sometimes afforded a safe retreat for the affrighted squire.

Few marks of cultivation after quitted Andalusia; there are to be sure some Vineyards and Olives groves but the greatest Industry is visible in the Siera Morena which is chiefly inhabited by Germans that have been invited there by his present

Majesty & who by his encouragement have made the barren wilderness to smile: for until his reign that large tract of Country was perpetually infested by Robbers & Murderers. But to what a length am I proceeding, surely your Patience is almost exhausted & as there is not the same necessity for you to travel through a country so barren of entertainment as there was for me to undergo that toil that I think I'll ev'n land you at Madrid without further ceremony or even refreshing ourselves at Aranjuez.

I am frightened to see how much Paper I've blotted and dare not begin to review it: if you find many words misplac'd or mis-spelt & a whole train of blunders instead of criticizing, consider if such a journey is not sufficient to fatigue and distract such a feeble mortal as myself and don't conclude from your own perfect and beautiful manner of writing at all times and upon all occasions that there should be no allowance made for others who have not arrived to such Improvements.

You tell me that our Army still improve & mention an instance of generosity in some of the troops that charms me. Nothing delights me more than the praises of my Countrymen. Tell me therefore in every letter some of their Actions, for but to mention them is a sufficient panageric. May an Auspicious Heaven! smile upon their noble efforts for liberty & crown their Council & their Arms with success.

Altho' I have already encroached upon your time, indulge me while I request you to embrace my dearest Son, thank him for those whishes he has express'd for our return, I do indeed most ardently long to see him: but he is ignorant of the excess of my love for him & grief for the loss of his lovely Sister. Indeed my Susan, she was a lovely babe.

Tell Hannah I've not forgot her but will write some time this week, tho' I shall divide the Chances by sending some of my letters to bilboa and others to Cadiz. Brockholst and myself are surprized that William has not favor'd us with some of those lively sallies of wit which was so agreeable to us when in his company and so entertaining in his absence. If he has not recd. my letters, let him tell me so and I'll write another.

Give my affectionate love to Kitty, as soon as my fingers are a little supled I shall devote a large share of my Time to her. If it is convenient, you'll oblidge me by letting our friends at Fish Kill know that we are all well.

Adieu my ever dear Sister.

(SLJ to her mother) Madrid August 28, 1780

Had I wrote to my dear Mamma a fortnight ago, while my whole heart overflowed with Joy & gratitude for the birth of a lovely daughter I am sure every line must have conveyed pleasure to the best of Parents, who well knows the affection of a mother. Every circumstance united in rendering that event delightful to us. Excluded the Society of our most intimate friends behold us in a Country whose customs, language & religion are the very reverse of our own, without connections, without friends, judge then if heaven could have bestowed a more acceptable present. Nor was the present deficient in any thing that was necessary to endear it to us: rather let me say that every wish of my heart was amply answered in the precious gift, in her charming countenance I beheld at once the soften'd Resemblance of her father & absent brother, her little form was perfect symmetry and Nature, by warding off those disorders that generally attack Infants, seem'd to promise a healthy constitution added to those circumstances; her very name increas'd my pleasure & I even flatter'd myself with a hope that Kitty & Nancy would be charm'd with their little God-child. When I used to look at her every idea less pleasant vanish'd in a moment. Scenes of continued & future bliss still rose to view, and while I clasp'd her to my bosom my happiness appear'd compleat &c. Alas! Mamma, how frail are all sublunary enjoyments! But I must endeavor to recollect myself.

On Monday the 22d day after the birth of my little Innocent, we perceived that she had a fever, but were not apprehensive of danger until the next day when it was attended with a fit. On Wednesday the Convulsions increas'd, and on thursday she was the whole day in one continued fit; nor could she close her little Eye-lids till friday morng the 4th of Augst. at 4 Clock when wearied with pain the little sufferer found rest in _____. Excuse my tears—you too mamma have wept on similar occasions, maternal tenderness causes them to flow & reason, tho' it moderates distress, cannot intirely restrain our grief, nor do I think it should be wish'd. For why should Heaven (<u>in every purpose wise</u>) have endowed its lovely Messenger with so many Graces but to captivate our hearts & excite them by a contemplation on the beloved object of our affection, to rise above those expectations that rather amuse than improve & extend our views even to those regions of bliss where she has arrived before us. While my mind continues in its present frame I look upon the tribute my child has paid to nature as the commencement of her immortality, & endeavour to acquiesce in the dispensations of the all-wise disposer of events; & if my heart continues in proper subjection to the divine will, then will she not have sicken'd, not have dy'd in vain.

But let me not be so wrapt in my own feelings as to forget that you, Mamma are not without yours: doubtless you are solicitous to know the state of my own health; & I am happy that I can gratify your generous curiosity, & at the same time give you the pleasure which I know you'll receive from my assurances of my entire recovery. Never was any person more favor'd by Providence than myself during my late confinement for I not only escaped many disorders incidental to women in child bed but was even free from the lightest fever, & indeed from all kind of pain: this climate is peculiarly favorable to women in that situation, of which I could tell you instances that are really surprising; but letters are no longer the free medium by which distant friends un-bosom themselves to each other; every thing therefore that prudence bids us suppress at present, we'll entertain ourselves with when sitting together by an american fire-side. You see, Mamma, I don't despair of the happiness of seeing you again.

The attention and proofs of fidelity which we have receiv'd from Abbe, demand, & ever shall have my acknowledgements, you can hardly imagine how useful she is to us, for indeed her place cou'd not be supplied, at least not here.

I am so strangely bewilder'd when I attempt to write to any of my American friends that its not to be wonder'd at if my letters are unconnected. Would you believe that this is the third time I have attempted to finish this? Usually my thoughts make such rapid excursions toward my native Country that it's with difficulty that I can confine them within due limits but at present I can scarcely detain them a single moment from the subject of the first part of this letter, perhaps it engages my attention the more as Mr. Jay is at present absent the Court being at St. Ildefonso between thirteen & fourteen leagues from hence and I own I never feel so entirely myself as when in his company, for tis then that the silent encouragement I receive from his steady modest virtue, operates most powerfully upon my mind, & I may add upon my conduct; for what can I fear or how can I repine when I behold him who is equally interested, composed in danger, resigned in affliction, & even possessing a chearful disposition in every circumstance. Excuse me, my dr. Mamma, excuse my officious pen perhaps too ready to obey the dictates of my heart but he really is virtues own self. I am interrupted. A Servant is arrived from Mr. Jay who has rode all night to bring me a paquet of letters from America that were delivered to his Master at St. Ildefonso. My emotions are so great that was not the Coll: to open the seals, I should certainly tear them in my haste.

I thank God! my dear & ever worthy friends are well my Child too is in perfect health! tho' I have been deprived of one, the other is still preserved. Oh Mamma I never fully comprehended the affection of Parents for their children till I became a Mother, & never even then was convinced how closely they were twisted with the fibres of the heart until a late painful seperation....

My love to Papa & the rest of the family, numberless embraces to my dear boy & affectionate remembrance to Hannah.

I am with the sincerest affection

ever yours
Sarah Jay

(JJ to SLJ in Madrid) St. Ildefonso 21 Sept 1780

My dear Sally

I begin to flatter myself with the Pleasure of seeing you soon, but as it will depend in some measure on the will of others, I am afraid to say how soon. The Manner in which you keep up your Spirits consoles me, and as the next week will certainly put an end to my Absence, probably for five or six Months, I shall endeavour to bear it with Patience. You know my being here is not of choice, but rendered necessary by objects which I am sure you wd. not have me neglect. Remember therefore that you are an American, & persevere in that command of yourself, from which you have already derived so much Reputation.

Your Letter of the 17th gave me much Satisfaction. It was cheerful, and it assured me of your Health. Don't suffer either to be impaired. Be yourself, and

Believe me to be
Your very affte. Husband
John Jay

(SLJ to JJ) Madrid, 22d Septbr 1780

Ah my dear! how obliging is your letter of the 21st inst; even yr flattery is inhanced by the graceful manner in which you convey it; & I confess without hesitation that you have charm'd me by your praises, and encourag'd me to hope that I may one day merit them. True, I am an American, & it is from that consideration that I relinquish the pleasure of your company, when your attention to business which may prove of utility to the public weal renders a seperation necessary.

I am very well indeed & in good spirits; and am rejoyc'd that you still enjoy your health. May heaven continue to bless & prosper whatever you design or wish shou'd succeed.

Adieu my dear

yours affectionately
Sa. Jay.

Just as I was dating this letter, a packet was handed me from America, containing a letter from Mr. Bingham & 3 from Kitty; unless the Coll: when he comes home advises to the contrary I shall send them to you. No news. All friends well. The printed paper inclos'd in one of Kitty's letter, be sure take great care of. I am prouder than ever of my charming country-women. Excellent Women!

(Benjamin Franklin to JJ at Madrid) Passy Oct. 2 1780

Dear Sir

I received duly and in good Order the several Letters you have written to me of Augt 16. 19. Sept. 8 & 22. The Papers that accompanied them of your writing, gave me the Pleasure of seeing the Affairs of our Country in such good Hands, and the Prospect from your Youth of its having the Service of so able a Minister for a great Number of Years: But the little Success that has attended your late Applications for money mortified me exceedingly; and the Storm of Bills which I found coming upon us both, has terrified and vexed me to such a Degree that I have been deprived of Sleep, and so much indisposed by continual Anxiety as to be render'd almost incapable of Writing.

At length I got over a Reluctance that was almost invincible. And made another Application to the Government here for more Money. I drew up and presented a State of Debts and newly expected Demands, and requested its Aid to extricate me. Judging from your Letters that you were not likely to obtain anything considerable from your Court, I put down in my Estimate the 25,000 Dollars drawn upon you with the same Sum drawn upon me, as what would probably come to me for Payment. I have now the Pleasure to acquaint you that my Memorial was received in the kindest & most friendly Manner; and tho' Court here is not without its Embarrassments, on Account of Money, I was told to make myself easy, for that I should be assisted with what was necessary....

You will not wonder at my loving this good Prince: He will not ruin the Hearts of all America.

If you are not so fortunate in Spain, continue however the even good Temper you have hitherto manifested. Spain owes us nothing, therefore whatever Friend ship she shows us in lending Money or furnishing Cloathing, &a. tho' not equal to our Wants and Wishes, is however tant de gagne; those who have begun to assist us are more like to continue than to decline, and we are still so much oblig'd as their Aids amount to. But I hope and am confident that Court will be wiser than to take Advantage of our Distress and insist on our making Sacrifices by an Agreement, which the Circumstances of such Distress would hereafter weaken, and the very Proposition can only give Disquiet at present. Poor as we are, yet as I know we shall be rich, I would neither agree with them to buy at a great Price the whole of their Right on the Mississippi than sell a Drop of its Water. A Neighbour might as well ask me to sell my Street Door....

If you find any Inclination to hug me for the good News of this Letter, I constitute and appoint Mrs. Jay my attorney to receive in my Behalf your Embraces.

With great and sincere Esteem I have the honour to be,

Dear Sir,
Your most obedient
and most humble Servant
B. Franklin

(JJ to William Livingston) Madrid 22 Novr. 1780

Dear Sir

Your favor of the 17 March last did not reach me till September. My Letters to you in August mentioned the Situation of our Family, which tho then encreased has since been reduced to its former number. Mrs. Jay has more than usual Health, and her Spirits continue to produce that easy Chearfulness which constitutes so important an Ingredient in human Happiness....

When Peace shall again afford you Leizure & opportunity to cultivate your Garden at Liberty Hall, Seeds of the best Fruits in this Country shall not be wanting to enrich it. The Melons & Grapes are very good, but I have met with no other Fruits superiour, if equal, to those you already have—among them melons (I mean muskmelons). There is a species which keep thro' the winter till late in the Spring. I eat of them in April last. Tho not equal to the others, they are far from bad. Some of yours at Eliz. Town were as good as the best I have seen here. The Herbs & Roots to be found in Spanish Kitchen Gardens are very good particularly Sallads, Cabbage, Colliflowers & onions. The latter far exceed ours in Size and are generally white. You shall in due Time have Samples of them all and also some Slips of a species of Grape whose Clusters are in general so large as that many are often found which weigh ten, fifteen, & twenty pounds. The present king, I am told, speakes of one that had been presented to him which weighd above five & forty. Perhaps that kind of grape was cultivated by the Canaanites. For my own part, I have as yet seen none of these Clusters, which I thought exceeded seven or Eight pounds....

Be pleased to remember me affectionately to Mrs. Livingston and all the Family. I am Dear Sir your obedient Servant

J. J.

You will be pleased to hear that Brockholst speakes Spanish & French fluently, and that his application in acquiring useful knowledge promises much.

(JJ to Kitty Livingston) Madrid 23d Novr. 1780

Dear Kitty

You are without Exception the best Correspondent I have in America, and for that & twenty other good reasons, every Letter I write to Congress shall enclose one for You. Sally has recd. & answered your last, it was dated in July.

You will be a little surprized when I tell you that we have not as yet been favored with a single Line either from XXIII—II—III—or XXII. The first I can excuse, but not the others. This omission is very unpleasant, and if you know any Thing of them, I wish you would be particular in your next. I hear that II has spent sometime this Summer in Philadelphia, do you know for, or to, what Purpose? We wonder at your Silence respecting X especially considering what passed before we left you. Where are V & VIII and what are they doing.*

In a Letter which I write to Mr. Robt. Morris by This opportunity, I have requested him to pay you Twenty pounds Sterling, and to draw upon me for the amount. Give a half Johans† to Hannah Benjamin, and do us the Favor of considering the residue as designed for some of those little Artickles, which we should have sent to mama, Susan, yourself and Peter, had we been nearer the Sea, and the Risque of Transportation less. In the Spring this Credit shall be repeated.

You have probably had some interesting Tete a tetes with the Lilly of the Valley—if so, how comes it that none of your Letters mention any Thing of it?....

Dont forget to be particular about our little Boy—take Care of him dont let him be spoiled; remember that he is not a Girl, and that an untanned Face is one of the last Things which will recommend him to me or to others. I think it is Time for him to begin to learn to read—close Attention or long Confinement I by no means approve, but two Hours in the four & twenty divided by proper Intervals would not be too much. Idleness is too agreeable to human nature to be indulged without Risque, and Habits of application are best acquired in Youth. Let him at least rise with the Sun.

About three or four weeks ago a young virginia gentleman near Eighteen years old, joined us. He is in the Family, and is sensible & well tempered: his name is Lewis Littlepage.

Remember me affectionately to all the Family, and believe me to be very sincerely

Your Friend & Brother
John Jay

**Although the code has not been deciphered, the numbers probably refer to family members, friends, and acquaintances.*
†A johans is a Portuguese gold coin called a half joe in America.

Kitty Livingston had made a bet with the Chevalier de La Luzerne: did Sarah observe the Sabbath by not wearing make-up and by not going to plays. In her letter of July 10, 1780, she wrote Sarah:

> Do you know that I am trading on your stock of firmness; and if you are not possessed of as much as I suppose you to be I shall become bankrupt, having several wagers depending that you will not paint nor go to plays on Sundays. The Chevalier is not to be convinced that he has lost his bet to me, till Mr. Carmichael informs him you do not paint. Mr. Witherspoon informed me that he was questioned by many at Martinique if you did not.

(SLJ to her sister Kitty) Madrid, 1 December 1780

How invaluable my dear Kitty! is a real friend; had I been ignorant of its worth till now, the pleasure I've deriv'd from your affectionate attention to our happiness would have taught me to estimate the blessing in a proper manner. I am at this instant overjoy'd with the rect. of three charming long letters from you just handed to me, which added to those I had recd. before makes eleven that I return you my sincere thanks for: sister susan has wrote me one letter, & one I've been favor'd with from Mrs. Meredith, not a single line has reach'd us from any of the family at Fishkill. Thus you see how extravagantly kind you have been, & how highly we must value your correspondance.

I willingly flatter myself that even those of my friends who have not time to throw away in writing to me, may yet have no objection to hear that I'm still in the land of the living, & therefore have taken the liberty of introducing myself to their recollection by scribbling to them. Whether or not my letters have been lost I can't tell, tho' I almost believe they have since they have not provok'd an answer. You alone seem sensible of the interest I take in the concerns of my friends, since but for your letters I should remain in ignorance of any alteration that takes place in my absence. Some of my friends indeed have experienced changes that I much lament; but others again have received an increase of happiness. Among the latter it's my joy to find the Chancellor and Mrs. Livingston. The pleasure I felt upon hearing of the birth of their little daughter induced me to trouble Polly with a letter to tell her that I shared her felicity. Notwithstanding Peter's caveat I had hopes to engage his affection for a lovely little sister, and yours for a sweet god-child, but alas! my dear Kitty, she is now beyond the regards of either.

When I first took up my pen, I thought I should be unable to quit it, but really so many things crowded upon my mind that one displaces the other. Let me see, I'll begin with a reference to your last letters, & pray my Lady, why was the place you was at omitted in the date? And why did not you inform me of your retrogade manoeuvre from Eliz. town? Whether the family still reserve the house at Persipiney or not? And whether my little heroe shar'd in the glory of the retreat? Was you not asham'd to abandon a post that susan alone had once maintain'd with so much good conduct? But jesting apart, I assure you I suffer'd exceedingly on your account ....

I wish our dr. susan wou'd visit our friends on the banks of the Hudson, their society & the change of air wou'd be agreeable & useful to her. I long to receive a letter from Mamma were it to contain but three lines; methinks I could kiss the name written with her own hand. Pray give my love to Papa. I fear he is less fond of his pen than gratitude to that little instrument of his fame will justify. I repent my not bringing with me some of his compositions....

The betts depending between you & the Chevalier I hope are considerable since you are certainly intitled to the stake (I don't mean a wooden one, but such as I suppose a Lady like yourself wou'd naturally lay as a Cap, Fan, &c) for I have not us'd any false colouring nor have I amused myself with plays or any other diversions on sundays....

I thank you my dear, for the plan inclosed in yr. Letter which the ladies have adopted for the relief of our worthy soldiers. You must know that I perceiv'd the folded paper I immediately fancy'd it contain'd your picture, & should have been much disappointed if it had not been so agreeable & honorable a representation of my lovely Country women. I am quite charm'd with them and indeed with every thing truly american. One piece of advice I'll whisper in your ear; whatever false notions travellers may endeavor to palm upon you: don't you ever say that such a lady is handsome enough to please even at Court; believe me it requires a greater degree of beauty to be only passable in America, than to out-shine all the Grandees of ——— I won't say where.

I wou'd not wish to damp the ardor of a youth who has enter'd the service of his country but I must confess I don't think Jack will be pleas'd with the Region of Neptune: however, he has my best wishes. My fingers are tir'd of holding the pen. If I recollect any thing more before an opportunity offers I'll resume my pen & begin another sheet.

In the mean time believe me

most affectionately yours,
Sa. Jay

Please to present my most respectful Compts. to General & Mrs. Washington.

(JJ to Kitty Livingston at Elizabeth Town) Madrid 17 decr. 1780

Dear Kitty

It is uncertain whether this Letter will ever come to your Hands. Two or three others are now on the Way to you. I fear your late Letters have been unfortunate. The last that reached us was dated in July, since which we have not heard any Thing of the Family. We suspect that several Letters from our Friends were committed to Mr. [Henry] Laurens Care. If so, they may one of these Days have the Pleasure of seeing themselves in Print. It is said all his Papers fell into the Enemy's Hands. He poor Man is still in the Tower, where his Reputation as well as Person lies at the Mercy of the Ministry. They have insinuated that he has said many Things, which without better Evidence than their words, I cannot believe he ever said.

All the World here are cursing Arnold & pitying his Wife. <u>Arnold's Plot</u> is the Subject of every Conversation. Do you know at what Price he sold his Conscience &

Reputation? A Report prevails here that Gen. Clinton agreed to give him 80,000 Sterl. & a Majr. General's Commission, & Majr. Andrews [Andre's] Life in the Bargain....

Your Brother is gone to Bilboa, from whence you will probably hear from him. How long he may stay is uncertain. Some say it has more Charms than any other part of Spain. If he should be of that opinion, I shall not expect to see him again very soon.

We are daily promising ourselves the pleasure of recieving some very long Letters from you. You have hitherto been very attentive — dont fall off. Your Letters are always doubly welcome. The Hand that writes them has few equals, and they contain more interesting Information than most others we recieve.

Kiss our little Boy for us. I will repay you when we meet; in the mean Time accept my best Wishes. I assure you they extend to every Thing that can make you happy here & hereafter. Our Love to all the Family

I am Dr. Kitty
your afft. Brothr.
John Jay

(William Livingston to SLJ at Madrid) Trenton 14 January 1781

My dear Child

I cannot express the pleasure I felt on the News of the birth of your Daughter in a foreign Country, where, having so few connections, it must have given you still more joy, than mothers generally receive from so joyful an occurrence. I was proportionably afflicted by the account of her death, tho' I cannot pretend to form an adequate Idea of the distress into which you must have been thrown by so unfortunate an event. But the magnanimity & resignation with which you have borne that, as well as the other disasters with which it has pleased Providence to try your Patience & submission, do you great honour, & give me not a little comfort. I hope my dear Child that you will be restored to my arms as soon as circumstances will admit, & that the same kind Providence that protected you in your voyage to Spain will grant you a safe return to your native shore. I ardently long for the happy day.

Peter is a very fine boy, & I have within these few days received a Letter from him written with his own dear little fingers, tho' guided by his Aunt Suky's hand. The writing was his own, & he tells me that if I will buy for him a continental Primmer, he will mind his book. I immediately procured & sent him one with the picture of his favourite, General Washington in the frontispiece, & a Letter which I wrote in Characters in imitation of Printers types, which he was able to read & understand.

In your correspondence with the rest of the family, I am sorry that you have hitherto not included

your affectionate Father
Wil. Livingston

(JJ to his father at Fishkill) Madrid 29 Jany 1781

Dr Sir

As yet we have not recd. a single Line from any of your family. Several Letters from me to you are on the way to America, and I hope many others have arrived. Allowances however in these times must be made for Captures, and other miscarriages. I have lately sent you another little parcel of Salt (I think twelve or fifteen bushels) from Cadiz to Philadelphia. If they should come safe Mr. Morris to whom they are consigned will inform you of them. If you should hear nothing from him on the Subject you may depend on their being lost. Don't however rely on these uncertain Supplies.

In the course of these Troubles you have suffered much by the Enemy, and may suffer more. Should you be pressed by the Difficulties Remember that you have a Right to all I can do, and to a Share of all that I have. I hope the Trunk I sent you last Summer from Bordeaux arrived safe. It would give me Pleasure to hear of the welfare of my Brothers & Sisters. As Peter and Nancy did not enjoy very good Health when we left them, we are particularly anxious about them. I need not add how sollicitous we are to hear of You. We are all, thank God, well.

Our love to all the family & Compts. to the Doctor & your Neighbour

I am Dr. Sir
Your very affte Son
John Jay

John and Sarah Jay's son, Peter Augustus, had been left with his grandparents in New Jersey. Sarah's sister Susan, in charge of his education, guided 5-year-old Peter's hand across the page so that he could write to his grandfather.

(PAJ to William Livingston) Tuesday night 30th January 1781

My dear Grandpapa

I give you a thousand thanks for your letter which I this day received. I was very sorry the messenger was in such haste that Aunt Susan could not make time to guide my hand — but I write as soon as possible in hopes of sending it by the Stage. I thank my Dear Grand Papa for the money, & intend to pay the Taylor with it, as far as it will go towards it, for making my waistcoat & overalls, but he has spoilt your little P. clothes so, that he deserves nothing but his labour for pay.

You must not have so bad an opinion of little P. as to think he loves money better than his book, no, no, Grandpapa, I have learnt three or four lessons in my primmer that you sent & I know a great deal of my catechism already.

This morning when it began to Snow, grandmamma said if it came good sleighing she woud take me in a sley & go to see Grandpapa, at Raritan or wherever he could be found but the snow turned to Rain & so disappointed us.

Peter wants to see his Papa & Mama very much, tho his grandpapa & grandmama are so good to him, that their absence is not so great a loss as it would be if he had not such good friends.

Grand-papa has forgot my face I believe, he has made it very queer indeed in the letter with such curled hair; but P. has not forgot Grand Papa's face—and he can't think of any more to write—& so he remains your very dutiful Grandson

Peter Augustus Jay

(Brockholst Livingston to SLJ at Madrid) Nantes 1st march 1781

My dear Sister,

Your favor of the 4th Ult. was delivered me Yesterday.... Mrs. Johnson has been too unwell to execute your Commissions yet. In a few days she will venture out. She has shewn me a riding suit for Mrs. Bingham. It is very rich & elegant. The feathers alone in the hat cost several Guineas. Our Affairs must be in a promising train while the Ladies can afford such Extravagance. Several gentlemen lately from America assure me, the female Headdresses in Philadelphia exceed by some feet those of their fair Allies on this side of the water.

I went last night to a masquerade. It was the last of the Season, & the first I had ever seen. It was too crowded to be agreeable. There were not far short of fifteen hundred men & women the greater part of whom resembled Demons more than human beings. I wonder any Lady who has the least Pretensions to Modesty will be seen at a place where disorder, double-Entendres, and Indecency are so prevalent. Perhaps none there laboured under this Embarrassment. It was certainly fortunate for me not to be sufficiently acquainted with the language to understand the half of what was said. By this Ignorance the delicate organs of my hearing escaped, and spared me the Imputation of Modesty, which must often, in spite of every effort, have discovered itself by the blushes which would have overspread the cheeks of a much less bashful fellow than myself. It was not till sometime after Sun-rise the Company broke up.

These diversions only prevail during Carnival which ended Yesterday. Lent of course commenced to day, tho' from what I have seen the People of this Country are not quite so Scrupulous in the observance of it, as their neighbours of Spain. At the Hotel where I dined to day there was scarcely a dish of fish to be seen, unless they had assumed a masque which a great many dishes here wear even after Carnival, & often puzzle a Stranger to know what he has before him; nor is his taste always Sufficient to determine the doubts of his Eyes.

I will not forget the Umbrella. Don't neglect to increase your commissions thro' fear of giving me trouble. You will find by a former Letter of mine that I had advised you to do it. I wrote to Mr. Jay yesterday. With my best wishes for you both I am Dear Sister

Your very Affectionate Brother,
Henry Br: Livingston

(SLJ to her father) Madrid 14 March 1781

My dear Papa,

The receipt of your letter last evening gave me inexpressible satisfaction but it was rendered less compleat than it otherwise would have been by a hint that you entertained some doubts of my remembrance of you. As I always preferred the virtues that flow from the heart before any accidental acquirements in any one, I cannot feel satisfied till every doubt of that nature is banished from your mind. I must therefore inform you that while on board the Confederacy I wrote to nobody but Mamma unless that letter was written jointly to you and her, the weather being too tempestuous to admit of handling the pen with convenience....

You were too well acquainted with my Sensibility to be mistaken when you thought it had been greatly wounded by the death of my lovely babe, nor was my dear Sir mistaken when he concluded I had obtained resignation on the occasion, that gently soothed my grief and made me view the providence as if some guardian angel had offered to conduct her home without encountering the dangers of the sea when we were about returning to our native Country. And is she not gone home before me escaped from a more perilous ocean than that which parts me from my Country? Yes she is safe, but what trials may await her surviving friends is concealed in the bosom of futurity...

Some gay ladies there are who if they perused this letter would conclude it was written during the influence of spleen and vapours but they would be greatly mistaken. I am unacquainted with those disorders which I believe seldom visit any bosoms but those which are destitute of Thought. My situation is as agreeable as absence from my very dear friends will permit. I'm neither so hurried with company and trifling amusements as to exclude more rational entertainments, nor so much alone as to be tired of myself. My health is perfectly restored and I feel as happy and as chearful as if inspired by the season which is really enchanting. You would be pleased with this climate in the winter; already the leaves are opening and the trees blooming as with you in May.

The present King of Spain has greatly improved this City and the adjacent Country by beautiful walks, handsome fountains and excellent roads; the trees alone with which he has adorned the roads and walks would be to you sufficient proof of his taste. He has four sitios or Country seats with palaces which he alternately visits and as he takes great delight in the Chase he prefers them to Madrid. Aranjuez is generally thought to be the most beautiful but as I only saw it en passant in my way here I cannot form any opinion of it, but intend in the month of May to make a short visit there, our finances not permitting me to spend all the time with Mr. Jay that he will necessarily be there. In the king's Armoury is some very curious and very compleat armour. I had no idea that the ancients were so well guarded from spears. As they are preserved with great care they really make a pretty appearance. There are three equestrian statues in it of the Emperor Charles the 5th one of which represents him with the very clothes he wore and the saddle he rode on that occasion as Conquerer of Tunis. The other when crowned king of the Romans and a third as King of Spain. The horses are likewise in armour and upon their sides is a kind of styrup to support one end of an immense spear. Poor Montezuma's wooden spear and painted Armor make but an humble appearance among those of the Europeans. The large Mourning coach in which the foolish queen (for that is the epithet given her) used to ride and always carry with her the corpse of her dead husband the Arc-duke father of Charles is likewise preserved in that place.

There are a great many things here very worthy of notice. The Palace is magnificent, and the Cabinet of natural curiosities well supplied, but of those things I suppose Brockholst has given you discriptions as his pen can do them more justice. Don't you already think me unconsci[on]able to engross so much of your attention when so small a portion of your time is your own.

Heaven grant success to your unremitted attention to the benefit of our country. May peace and tranquility soon succeed to the toil and dangers of my Countrymen: the sun shines not on a more worthy people, even in their errors virtue is conspicuous, for does not the generosity that governed the actions of those soldiers who were lately discontented cast a veil over their precipitation. As the season advances that must open the Campaign my solicitude increases though but certain I am that victory will one day give to the Americans that liberty they have had the virtue to defend. Adieu my dear Papa. Never again admit one idea to the disadvantage of the affection with which I am

your very dutiful daughter,
S. J.

As you are often absent from the family I shall likewise write to Mamma but as we often divide the pacquets perhaps both letters may not arrive at the same time and if that should be the case please to remember me affectionately to her.

I felt the tenderness you express for my little boy with a great deal of gratitude and am very thankful for the continuance of his health. You have encouraged me to write to him by telling me that he begins to read. If we are absent more than a twelvemonth I hope his Aunt Susan will teach him to write.

John Jay had been the person on whom his father, and the family in general, relied. In his absence and due to their father's illness, his younger brother, Frederick (Fady), assumed John's responsibilities. The family was beset by troubles during these years, including the forced relocation of the household from Rye to Fishkill and eventually to Poughkeepsie; robbery by marauding bands of soldiers and others; and the difficulty of producing enough food because of the shortage of labor.

(JJ to his brother Frederick at Fish Kill) [Draft]
Madrid 15 March 1781

My dear Brother

I was just dispatching the enclosed Letter to you when yours of the 28 Decr. last was delivered to me....

The short Stay you purposed to make at Philadelphia pleases me; it evinces your Attention to our good old Father & his Family. The Proofs you have given of filial Affection make me love and esteem you more than ever I did, & be assured I shall never neglect a single opportunity of giving you higher Evidence of it than words.

I am exceedingly happy to hear you left the Family well. God grant that they may long continue so and that every obstacle to my seeing them & contributing to their Welfare may soon cease. The account you give me of my dear little Boy is flattering. I fear he will soon begin to lose by my Absence, it is hard (tho proper) to make such tender Sacrifices to public Good. I neither do or shall much regret his not going to Fish Kill. I have doubts on that Subject. I have recd a ridiculous Letter from Mrs. M[unro] but neither have or shall answer it. I wish to be excused from that correspondence at present. Have no Hand therefore in conveying any of her Letters to me. As to our Knight of the Order of Sisiphus [brother James Jay], I am not much surprized to hear of his being still at Philadelphia, where I suppose he is labouring hard to roll some new Stone up Hill. I wish he may succeed for once. Had I flattered his foibles & been less sincere I should have been more agreable.

Tell Peggy I charge her to keep up her Spirits, give the same Injunctions to Peter & Nancy. We shall all yet be happy together, and I shall be much mistaken if the Time does not come even in this world when we shall rejoice for the Days wherein we have seen adversity. In the next we certainly shall. Comfort each other, & be assured that I shall not delay joining you a moment longer than Duty to our Country may detain me from you.

You may remember that I left a Chest of Law Books at Poughkeepsie. Take a Catalogue of them and let Mr. Hobart have them on his signing a Rect at the foot of it. Present my Complts to him. I Esteem him much.

Dont neglect drawing upon me for the 50£ Ster. mentioned in the enclosed Letter, & in three months after draw agn. upon me for the like Sum out of which pay twenty pounds (that is fifty hard Dollars) to Polly Bancker, twenty to Peter, twenty to Nancy, and you will be pleased to lay out twenty more in something clever & present to Peggy. Sally & Peter are well and desire to be affectionately remembered to you all.

Write often to our Elizabeth Town Friends. We have frequent Letters from them. As to Letters for me, send them often by the Way of Boston. You have several acquaintances there who wd. readily enclose them in some of their Correspondents in this Kingdom and many more Vessels come to Spain from New England than from all the Rest of the Continent. Remember that you have a Cypher, and that you will greatly oblige me by frequent, long, & particular Letters.

Remember me to my old Friends.... Tell all the Servants that I remember them, the Trunk I sent from Bordeaux containd something for each of them; it is lost & I am sorry for it.

Adieu my Dr Friend, continue to comfort and aid our good old Father & the Family & rely on the Gratitude and Sincere attachmt. of

Your afft. Brother
J.J.

P.S. Don't let Mrs. M. want but be guided by her real not ostensible necessities. I am sure you wont forget poor Guss [brother Augustus Jay].

(JJ to his father at Fishkill) [Draft]

Madrid 24 ap 1781

Dr Sir

The number of Letters I have lately written to you & Fady leaves me very little to say in this. I have as yet recd no other Letter from him than the one he wrote at Philadelphia.

I send you enclosed a Print* of one of your Family, and flatter myself that the Time allotted for the absence of the original is already more than half spent. You will recieve by this Opportunity a long Letter from Sally which I hope will compensate a little for the Brevity of this. Indeed as the Gentleman who carries this to America is waiting for my Dispatches, I cannot indulge myself in writing such long ones as I should otherwise do.

It seems one little parcel of Salt I sent you from Cadiz has arrived safe at Philadelphia so that you will not be greatly distressed for Want of that necessary article. I wish the Trunk from Bordeaux had been equally fortunate. You wd have found in it a little of almost every Thing for Family Use.

Peter is busy in writing you a french Letter, which I shall send in Statu quo that you may the better Judge of his progress. He never looked better in his Life. He has Masters both for Head & Heels.

We have had a charming winter, clear mild Sunshine almost every Day. The Spring is very favourable & there is a better prospect of a plentiful Crop than has been known here since the Year 1756. It has already lowered the price of Grain & Barley wh. is the common Food of Horses & mules & which was at the long price of fourteen Shillings for a measure a little larger than a Bushell is now sold for Eight Shillings (your money). The most disagreable Season here is Summer, the Heats of which exceed any thing you experience in America. The Droughts are also excessive so much so that the Face of the whole Country looks as if Fire had passed over it, no verdure to be seen except a pale sickly green in the withering Leaves of the Trees of which there are very few. Wood for Fuel is sold here by Weight. Chimnies are not common, a pot of live Coals being a cheaper tho less pleasant Substitute.

Be pleased to make my Compliments to the Doctr & your Neighbours.

My Love to all the Family

I am Dear Sir
your very dutiful & afft. Son,
J.J.

(Susan Livingston to SLJ at Madrid) Elizth. Town May 10th 1781

My ever dear Sister

...My little god-son is very well, & there is no danger of his forgetting his Papa & Mama for he talks of them every day; & used to challenge the red gown I wore of

Jay sent an engraving of himself, done by Benoît Louis Prévost after Pierre E. Du Simitière.

yours last winter very often. He is at play out of doors every day when the weather permits, & begrudges time for his book & meals.

William is now answering Henry's letters dated from France, & will give him an account of the recent misfortune of your Father at Fish Kills which I have already done in a letter to him about a fortnight ago: & least that should miscarry, & as Billy & I purpose sending our letters different ways, I shall mention again that mr. Jay was plundered on the 8th of April of every thing useful & valuable by a party of robbers; to the amount of near 3000 pounds; mr. Jays Age & infirmities render such a disaster peculiarly distressing; if aught could have inspired the cruel perpetrators with an human sentiment, one would have thought that this reflection would have stayed their hands; but they are above discrimination, so that even virtue herself affords but little safety to her Votaries. They had so much generosity as to spare mr. Peter Jay his Clothes.

This unfortunate circumstance puts it out of Fady's power to fetch his little nephew; which is a great disappointment to him, his intended visit to his Grand-Papa Jay, has been the topic of his harangues these many months; he very often upbraids me for not taking him down to Phila to see his Pa, & Ma, before they went to Spain, I could if I had pleased he says.

Mr. John Reade, & mr. Comfort Sands have likewise been robbed: what corner of our Land has escaped these villains! It appears as dangerous to retire back into the Country as to live on the Frontiers....[Incomplete letter]

(SLJ to her sister Kitty at Philadelphia) Aranjuez, May 18th 1781

Thanks to heaven my dear Kitty's 17th letter, dated the 4th of April has arriv'd safe, & thanks to my lovely sister for so frequently favoring us with intelligence, 'tis almost from you alone that we have any tidings of our friends, Mr. Jay seldom receiving any letters.

You have surpris'd me by that little anecdote respecting the conduct ascrib'd to us at Cadiz. The usual tenor of our letters will convince you that circumspection has not been wanting on our part: Mr. Jay not only return'd every visit he receiv'd, but paid the first compts. to those whose rank intitled them to that attention. As for myself, tho' it was with difficulty I bore the fatigue of dressing, I return'd those visits I received, & when the Governor's lady waited upon me accompanyed by a Coll: of the Hybernian regt. who officiated as interpreter they were introduced into my chamber where I was confin'd by my indisposition, having been inform'd that a denial would be taken ill. Her Ladyship was very polite, & requesting me to name a day when it would be agreeable to me to dine with her, I did, tho' I much fear'd my inability to perform my engagement; however I went & we were politely presented to a very large circle of genteel company among whom were several foreigners of distinction that spoke english very well; but my apprehension of my weakness was but too well founded as I was obliged to retire from table & was with difficulty prevented from fainting, remaining however too ill to wait the arrival of our carriage the Governor's was ordered & I returned to my lodgings where for some time I was again confin'd. As to the Hybernian Officers Count Oreilly the Commander in Chief of the whole province & others of distinction were of the number we found there, they were very polite & very useful to us; their first Physician attended me with the most friendly assiduity & from his skill I deriv'd much benefit.

As to Mr. Carmichael's not being included among those accused of disrespect to the inhabitants is perfectly intelligible to me & the author of the letter might have known that his stay there did not exceed a week & in that time was kept too constantly employed in copying papers &c: to be much abroad ~~& were you acquainted with all the events of our two voyages you wou'd not be surpris'd that a french letter should commend him & deny us.~~ Thus you see my dr. kitty, that we almost daily experience that the utmost integrity, attention, & circumspection are not sufficient barriers against designing calumny, which not only surprises the careless but even attacks prudence by sly indirect insinuations. I flatter'd myself & even am still persuaded that we made many friends at Cadiz having recd. various polite instances of attention there & since our arrival here. You have done wisely in mentioning the contents of that letter, it was intended no doubt to injure us & I wish you would continue to let me know every thing you may hear to our disadvantage that I may immediately remove misapprehensions.

It is a great consolation to me that you are with my dear Mrs. Morris, embrace her for me & tell her I often anticipate the joy I shall feel when I may tell her in person how much I love her & how sensible I am of her attention to you.

Mrs. Lawrance's affection for me gives me the sincerest pleasure; if a grateful attachment can merit that honor I hope I never shall lose it. Do not suffer any of my friends to forget me, if any thing in my conduct towards them appears inattentive let them consider the disadvantage I'm under: I've wrote to many of my friends & recd. very few answers, but still make the necessary excuses for them: the loss of the esteem of one friend would impair the pleasure I propose to my self upon re-visiting America, & yet I should not be surpris'd if the sly & mean artifices with which we are persecuted should affect it. The distress introduc'd by our enemies into the southern provinces have made my tears flow very plentifuly I assure you & lessen'd the pleasure I should otherwise enjoy in this enchantg. place....

I am just now engaged to walk with Madame Gautier (the Lady of a Brigadier General) in the street of the queen as it is call'd where her Royal highness the Princess of Asturias rides & walks every afternoon & all the Court & other persons of distinction meet to pay their respects to her.... [I] assure you of the uninterrupted affection which you & the whole family possess in the heart of dr. Kitty

your very sincere friend & sister
S. Jay

~~Is Hannah Benjamin with you still? If she is do remember me to her~~. Abbe is well & would be glad to know if she is mistress of a husband still.

In Spain, the Jays became caught up in a swirl of innuendo and rumor related to purported disrespect to their hosts.

There were problems within their household as well. Sarah's brother Brockholst was proving to be especially difficult, publicly airing impolitic views. Neither Sarah nor John Jay was able to reason with him. In desperation, Sarah wrote a letter to her father about him in June. The letter was sent to sister Kitty to be delivered should Brockholst misrepresent his behavior. The letter was never forwarded.

(SLJ to her father) Madrid, 24 June 1781

My dear Papa,

I had the pleasure of writing you a long letter by Mr. Toscan & likewise sending a duplicate of one which had been written a long while ago. I hope you will soon receive them as they may serve to show you that those sentiments of gratitude & esteem to which you are intitled from me have not been obliterated by absence. The reluctance I feel to lessen the satisfaction of my dear Papa, already sufficiently involved in cares, has prevented me from disclosing a circumstance from which we have receiv'd not a little distress. I scarcely know where or in what manner to introduce a subject which I could wish buried in eternal silence. But since justice to ourselves as well as duty to you require it, I will undertake the painful task.

You know my dear sir in what manner the prospects both of your family & Mr. Jay's in respect of wealth have been destroyed by this war; that both you & Mr. Jay had disregarded all private considerations & intirely devoted yourselves to the service of the public. In the midst of the career you was elected Governor, Mr. Jay was appointed Minister; neither of those offices impeded your public services but rather prepar'd a prospect of more extensive usefulness: they were accordingly accepted. You resign'd the repose which you had long ardently wish'd; Mr. Jay consider'd in what manner he might render his appointment beneficial to his friends as well as serviceable to his Country: education so necessary to render men useful to Society being interrupted, he concluded to take his Nephew with him, that he might at the same time that he inspir'd him with patriotic sentiments ennable him to render future services to his Country.

My brother has rec'd his education it's true, but Mr. Jay still thought Brockholst might derive advantages from making the voyage with us, for which purpose the consent of Congress & yourself was obtained, & Mr. Jay hop'd that the pleasure you relinquish'd, by giving us his company would be compensated for by the advantages Brockholst would receive by residing some time in Europe; as I've often heard Mr. Jay say that here he might perfect himself in two useful languages, gain a knowledge of mankind, form useful connections, & at the same time make such a proficiency in the study of the Law as might ennable him with a little practice on our return to make himself master of it if Congress should not choose to place him in a political line.

But alas! instead of an affectionate & chearful Brother we too soon discover'd a discontent & disgust which astonish'd us. My brother's temper I always knew to be irritable to an unhappy excess; but I flatter'd myself that that generosity of disposition which I had remark'd with pleasure in our family, would secure us from impoliteness except at times when his passions were not under the influence of his reason

& which I would readily have pardon'd. But I was mistaken. A constant captiousness & sulkiness has without ceasing mark'd his conduct, & I'm sure that if you had been a witness of the forbearance that Mr. Jay has impos'd upon himself, even when most insolently treated by him, you would not have been less surpris'd at his moderation or less wounded by the want of delicacy in B––t than myself.

To confess the truth, my feelings have been too much hurt always to admit concealment which has induced me two or three times to bring on an explanation, hoping that when he perceiv'd how much I was pain'd, he would endeavor to cultivate a more happy disposition. But Mr. Jay always disapprov'd those éclaircissements in the presence of B––t as well as when we were in private, telling me that his situation with respect to Brockholst was too delicate to admit of those remonstrances which friendship would justify, & that he hop'd to conquer his disgusts by a repetition of good offices; but Mr. Jay was mistaken in his opinion of Brockholst; instead of being gain'd by gentleness the idea of his own importance rose with our condescension & he has twice or thrice threatned to return to America which Mr. Jay with uncommon meekness as often disuaded him from.

When he return'd from France we resolv'd to continue the utmost caution, & even to avoid such subjects of conversation if possible as might excite his captiousness not omitting our endeavors to please him. Unfortunately the other day ye Coll: & a young gentleman from France who had din'd with us, conversing on the manners of different Countries, the Coll: took occasion to be very severe on the Americans on the score of sobriety, adding that it was more rational to drink wine like the French with their dinner than to oblige their Guests to get drunk after, as was the custom in England and America. The gentleman who had been educated in England ask'd permission to assure him that that barbarous custom was at present abolish'd there, & I took the liberty of rescuing my country-men from the same disgrace. However, the Coll: did not relinquish his assertion but was polite enough to believe that I thought as I spoke, since the ladies were excus'd from that ceremony. The gentleman smiled & inquired if Congress gave into that fashion. Congress, reply'd the Coll: I have seen them all drunk at a time. Coll: said I, it may have happen'd that upon the celebration of our Independance or some other public festival those gentlemen have drank more freely than usual, but surely you would not infer from that, that it was a practice they were often guilty of. Oh Congress are like other men & the custom of getting drunk after dinner is general.

Soon after the two young gentlemen retir'd; and I observ'd to Mr. Jay that my brother's remarks upon Congress appear'd to me imprudent considering the Country we were in, & that he himself was a servant of that Assembly, since such reflections might make deeper impressions than if dropt under other circumstances. He told me that his sentiments corresponded with mine upon that subject but that he fear'd to mention them lest he might provoke him, & that there was a probability the like conversation might not soon happen again.

The next day I was amusing myself with drawing when the same gentleman came in to thank Mr. Jay for the permission he had obtain'd through him to reside at Toledo some time, adding that he should have fear'd to trouble him had he thought so much time & difficulty would have been necessary to acquire a permission that might be granted in a few hours, but these monarchical governments, continued the gentleman, choose sometimes to shew their power. Mr. Jay made the usual reply to the gentleman's Compts., but the Coll: took up the reflection upon these kind of Governments & said that Congress exceeded them far, for that to his knowledge a person had been detain'd at Philadelphia three months to receive a pass-port from that Assembly after they had resolv'd to grant him one. Ay but, says that gentleman, they ought to be excus'd from the consideration of the multiplicity of business that demands their attention. Mr. Jay with his ordinary good humor said they should at least be spar'd the censure of Americans, & then as he had his hat in his hand when the gentleman came in, he recommended him to my attention & bid us good-morng.

The Coll: was displeas'd with that observation, & after Mr. Jay withdrew said that for his part he thought the Americans ought to speak their sentiments of Congress with the utmost freedom; that they were like other men, & he doubted not but that there were among them as great rascals as in other assemblies, & that indeed he knew some. I said that in America no ill could arise from scrutinizing their conduct, but that here, as the independance of America had not been publicly acknowledged, we should be careful not to lessen the respectability of the representatives of our Country.

Some conversation pass'd on that subject in the course of which I could not forbear requesting that even if he differ'd from me in opinion on that matter he would spare my feelings in future whether they arose from prejudice or esteem, promising likewise that I would observe silence on any one topic that would be disagreeable to him, upon wh. his warmth increas'd & he declar'd he was sorry to find me so deficient in good sense, then turning to the stranger, ask'd him to go with him to Mr. Carmichael's. He, says the Coll: can abuse Congress, tho' formerly a member of it, & thank God! there we can say what we please.

When Mr. Jay return'd I mentioned to him what had pass'd. He told me he fear'd I had been angry, since he had sometimes observ'd that when my brother was unpolite I appear'd too sensible of it. In the evening, B. return'd from Mr. Carmichael's, & after supper he told Mr. Jay that he had reflected on the conversation that had pass'd between Mrs. Jay & him & that he prefer'd going to America to remaining like a slave here. Mr. Jay endeavor'd to reason with him but that was in vain, & indeed some indecencies in B––'s conversation made me quite as angry as himself, which Mr. Jay perceiving, told us we were both too warm to be reasonable & advised the Col: to go to bed and me to compose myself.

I slept but little that night; the insinuation of slavery which the Coll: had dropt was an idea I could not account for as it was impossible to act with greater delicacy than Mr. Jay had observ'd towards him. From the time that Mr. Jay's sallery commenced he allow'd the Coll: two hundred and fifty spanish dollars a year to furnish him with Clothes & pocket-money; his washing and mending being done in the family & even chose that the money should pass thro' my hands to him to avoid giving rise to any disagreeable feelings that B–– might be sensible of upon those occasions. As to any restrictions upon his pleasures, there have been none. Few persons in Madrid are less acquainted with the manner in which he spends his time than we are; he is studious, I believe, but we are both unacquainted with his studies. Mr. Jay's advice was never kindly taken by him. On the contrary, Brockholst has not been sparing of his sarcasms on his brother for advising him to pay considerable attention to some particular books as preludes to the study of the Law: offering at the same time to send by the way of Holland for such Law-books as would have been necessary. But as B––t treated almost every thing recommended by Mr. Jay as unessential & frequently as ridiculous, that plan was not executed. Thus my dr. Papa have I day after day experienc'd mortifications that can only be imagin'd by those who have the welfare of a brother as much at heart as myself, who, like me, admire the tenderness & delicacy of a husband, &, like me, lament his endeavours for a brother's happiness repaid with hatred.

But, think not, sir, I ascribe the whole of my brother's conduct solely to the dictates of his own head or heart. No, there is another cause & one that has not given us less pain. Good God! papa, so dearly as we love America! that all our unquiet should proceed from those who rec'd their birth in that favor'd Country. My emotions are very great when I reflect upon the insidious and cruel manner in which Mr. Carmichael has treated Mr. Jay: the friendly part he had assum'd while we were at Philadelphia was thrown aside soon after the *Confederacy* was dismasted, & tho' the masque has at times been re-assum'd, the cloven foot was not conceal'd as formerly. With this gentleman the Coll: has form'd the strictest intimacy, swallowing unwarily his artful baits: I soon perciev'd the seeds of jealousy grow in the breast of Mr. Carmichael. He knew the reputation which you sustain'd in America & fear'd a rival in your son; he saw the strong attachment of Mr. Jay to the Coll: & likewise was sensible of his application & speedy attainment of the spanish language. He observ'd with pain that Mr. Jay was anxious for the advancement of my brother and employ'd him in copying for Congress, which increased his jealousy so much lest Congress by that sh. be reminded of him, that he could not conceal it, but told Mr. Jay in my presence, that it had so odd an appearance that a Member of Congress had inquir'd of him in a letter the reason why the papers were not in his hand-writing? But for his part he said he suppos'd it arose from Mr. Jay's desire of making the Coll: acquainted with business & of promoting him.

A variety of circumstances too tedious to enumerate in a letter leave me not the smallest doubt that he has made B––t act a part so foreign to the welfare of himself & the interest of the family: I'll only mention one instance by which you may judge of B––t's devotion to him. Last summer Mr. Jay gave B––t a paper to copy, which not choosing Mr. C––l should be acquainted with, desired my brother, who had acted always as his private secry not to mention it to him. Yet in a few days after he did, & Mr. C––l spoke to Mr. Jay about it & said he had it from the Coll: shortly after I myself heard Mr. Carmichael apologizing to the Colonel for mentioning it, upon which the Colonel reply'd Oh, it's no matter, I'm glad of it, such caution is all d––n nonsense. In short, I'm well persuaded he has in the most artful manner endeavor'd all along to make Mr. Jay and the Coll: disatisfyed with each other, which tho' Mr. Jay saw thro' I'm sure the Coll: did not.

I remember last fall Mr. C––l happen'd to be present when the Coll: in one of his ill-humours threatned to return to America. After B––t had withdrawn Mr. C––l said he was very sorry for what had pass'd. Mr. Jay said he was the more hurt by such conduct as he had a great affection for B--t. Upon which Mr. C--l replyed that young folks would often abuse the affection their friends had for them, that he himself had done so when in Scotland with the Uncle that brought him up but that when the Coll: grew older he would know better. Mr. Jay thought that an extraordinary manner of apologizing for the Coll: who, you know sir is no child, but seeing that those observations were rather calculated to irritate than reconcile matters, determin'd to frustrate his unfriendly designs by behaving to B--t as if nothing had happen'd.

Though I'm well convinc'd that Mr. C--l for a long time fear'd a future rival in Brockholst & took immense pains to infuse into his mind discontents against Mr. Jay in order to make the stay of both of them in this Country disagreeable to themselves, yet I begin to suspect that having accomplished his aim on the part of B--t & not only made him an enemy to his brother, but also persuaded Brockholst to think that his own interest & his were united, he would rather the Coll: should stay here not only to trumpet him, as is the present system, but also to lessen & behave rudely to Mr. Jay which B--t very frequently does, even at our own table before company, & that in the most indecent & unprovoked manner, which Mr. C--l is not ignorant of, having been present more than once upon those occasions. Had I been in Mr. Jay's place I never could have observ'd such moderation & civility to that gentleman after being acquainted with his baseness as he has done, but if moderation & prudence are virtues, I'm sure [he] has enough of them.

The subjects I've been obliged to dwell so long upon are so interesting that I know not where to stop; I would avoid a single hard reflection on B--t that was not necessarily occasioned by the justice due to ourselves; but I value your good opinion too much to be willing to forfeit it when I know that I have not ceas'd to deserve it. If the Almighty answers our wishes for the safe arrival of B--t in America, my breast will be compos'd, & I will continue to trust in his providence to be one day delivered from the snares with which we are beset by a designing man. Indeed, were I not bless'd with confidence in Heaven I never could have supported a chearful disposition at such a distance from friends whose value is enhanc'd by the dangers that surround them, separated from my son, depriv'd of a lovely daughter, distress'd by a mistaken brother, and convinc'd too late of the insincerity of a person I believ'd our friend, when already in a foreign Country. Yet there is sweet consolation in innocence which soothes the mind under every perplexity & prevents the most disagreeable circumstances from destroying our peace. Should my brother attempt to excuse his return with plausible reasons, I wish they may be accepted. You cannot but see the disadvantage it would be to him should his conduct be scrutinized or exposed.

I wish that when I write again to my dear papa a more agreeable subject may employ my pen. At present I'm sure we are both too much fatigued for you to read or me to write more than that I am, with the greatest sincerity,

Your affectionate daughter
Sa. Jay

(PAJ to SLJ) Elizabeth Town, 18th July 1781

I thank my Dear Mama for her kind letter, & good advice; & my dear Papa for his remembrance.

I hope when you return to our Country you will find your little son as you expect, & not be disappointed.

Aunt Susan teaches me to read; every hour the bell rings, & then I go in the office to say my lesson. Aunt Caty sends me books from Phila:. I learn in a very pretty book of Tales, one page has a picture & the opposite one a tale to explain it, all the book thro'. I have finished with the Continental Primmer & given that & the dull Ass to cousin Betsey.

As soon as I read well Aunt Susan will teach me to write, & then I can have the pleasure of writing to my absent friends. I have a pocket-book full of letters that Grand-Papa printed for me last winter. Every fortnight allmost I received a letter from him, & last month Grand-Mama & I went to meet Grand-Papa & spend a few days with him at Cousin D[avi]d Clarksons, who lives three miles this side of Princeton. It was a long ride for such a little fellow as me.

Aunt Caty sent me a top, & Uncle Watkins made me a Kite for pastime. I am quite a country boy clad in a striped linen waistcoat & trowsers, and sometimes I hoe in the garden & gather the gooseberries & currants, & I helped to rake hay on the Lawn in the hay harvest.

We have plenty of fine fruit this summer, while we had cherries, the boys collected from all parts of the Country here, not less than fifty in a day, & soon stripped our trees.

Mama says I must write her what I wish her to bring me. I should like a hat, a pr. of shoe & knee buckles, & a pr. of sleeve buttons—if she pleases.

Hannah says I must not forget to mention her, but she won't tell me what to say about her. She has not left me, & is very good to me; & gives her love to Mama. She has received the fine handkerchief & is much obliged to Papa for it.

Wealthy has been to see her mother 3 or 4 weeks, & is not the better for her visit. She does not learn her book as well as I do.

Please give my love & duty to Papa & my love to Uncle Henry & Cousin Peter. I am dr. Mama,

Your very Affecte. Son,
Peter Augustus Jay

(SLJ to her sister Kitty) Madrid July 22d 1781

I have my dr. Kitty recd. with infinite pleasure yr letter of the 6th of June, & susan's of the 27th of May, for which you have both my sincere thanks. Susan's fears may be dissipated, as those letters she thinks had miscarried have all arrived safe & been punctually answered. Of yrs. twenty have arriv'd safe, but not one unperus'd, however, since your correspondance is not treasonable continue the same familiar style....

This Court parted from Madrid the 18th inst. for St. Ildephonso, & we shall set out for that place with all the family next week. I cannot promise you a description of it, for I'm told that the royal gardens there surpass in magnificence those at Aranjuez, & you know I told you that they surpass'd my capacity for description: form to yourself an idea of a terrestial paradise & [perchance] ... it will resemble the enchanting Sitio of Aranjuez. The frequent changes of the court are very agreeable to his Majesty & I doubt not contribute to the health of the good old King, but really all the attendants of the Court had need be kings also to support the expence. I often think papa would be fond of amusing himself in the manner that the king does, that is hunting, fowling, & fishing, for which purpose he rises very early, dines at twelve o'clock, & betakes himself soon to rest. Every thing in & about Madrid bespeak the attention he has discover'd to render Madrid healthy & beautiful; indeed the character he sustains for honesty & virtue renders him a great favorite of mine, & I sincerely wish him to triumph over his haughty enemies of Briton; don't you believe I do?

This country has been favor'd with a very plentiful season, which was the more happy as the want of it wd. have reduc'd the people to great distress, not having had for several years before even a tolerable harvest.

I'm sorry the tea, gauze, ribbons, silk shoes &c. &c. that were sent from France did not arrive safe, but we wont despair, but only send a few articles now & then & some of them will reach you; at present I'll beg you'll accept (if you can get it) of twenty yards of straw-colour'd lutestring for a polinese or negligee* & with my love give mama the little paper enclos'd for her. I will by this conveyance send sister Jay the same quantity of the same silk & by a gentleman who will likewise go to America very soon & will deliver a bundle to you at Philadelphia. I intend to send Mama, susan & sister Nancy purple lutestring & trimmings.

I recd. my sweet little fellow's letter & was so pleas'd with his attention, & the accounts that I receive of his good disposition & application to his books that I desire you will make him a present in my name of any thing most agreeable to him. I order'd one of the servants to buy him a pr. of handsome shoe & knee-buckles, but I saw none worth sending to him. With your parcel I shall put a piece of linnen for his use, & shall likewise send him a suit of Clothes for next winter of the same cloth that his Majesty & the Princes wear every day while they amuse themselves wh. the Chace. It is a proper color & kind for a little republican to play about in & pursue those exercises which strengthen the Constitution & thereby enable him one day to serve his Country in those employments which require vigour of body as well as strength of mind.

I would wish you to keep in his view two great objects for his pursuit, that of endeavoring to please his maker by an humble imitation of the example he has given us, & that of rendering himself useful to his fellow creatures, especially to his own Country, which after the Deity has the first right to his services, not excepting his life itself. Perhaps you'll think me premature in my advice, but really I'm of a different opinion, & think the human mind susceptible of great & good impressions at a very tender age, & I'm sure, that yourself, Mama & susan, can recollect a number of examples that will create in him an admiration for virtue & a detestation of the reverse.

**An easy robe or dressing gown.*

Excuse me my dr. Kitty for presuming to dictate to you in an affair which I ought rather to take your advice upon. But the deprivation of the most delightful task in the world does not prevent my ideas sometimes following those in it who are more happily thus engaged.

Remember me affectionately to Papa & Mama, Susan & my little Peter; & kiss his Cousin betsy for me. [no closing or signature]

(SLJ to her sister Kitty) Madrid, 25 July 1781

The happiness I rec. from my dr. Kitty's affectionate attention wd. be compleat did I not regret that by the miscarriage of a number of my letters she herself loses the satisfaction of knowing that hers are recd. with the sensibility they deserve. Your disappointment upon the arrival of vessels from Cadiz have as often arisen from our ignorance of their sailing as from the miscarriage of our letters for I doubt not but that Mr. [Carmichael] has frequently recd. intelligence of vessels from Mr. Harrison who has naturally concluded that it wd. be mention'd to us; but he was less acquainted with [Carmichael] than unfortunately for us we are, for permit me to assure you my dr. sister that in whatever style policy may induce him to mention me to those whom he thinks already my friends in america, neither Mr. Jay nor myself are in the least indebted to him for acts of friendship or even justice in this country: but in a letter from Aranjuez I've already explain'd to you my ideas of that gentleman, & as his conduct towards Us has not ceas'd to give us more pain than pleasure we'll quit the subject....

My heart is quite dilated wh. the information of the amiable disposition of my dr. little son & I'm confident that mamma & susan will omit no opportunity to cultivate it: I shall desire Major Franks to purchase if possible a set of maps in France like those which Miss Louden Robinson once had, for Peter, that he may learn geography while he only thinks of amusement.

I confess that I regret with you the step that my father-in-law's family have taken in quitting Fish Kill, but really they have been so persecuted by misfortunes that I'm not surpris'd they shd. be embares'd in their measures. Poor Mr. Jay's feelings are so affected by their difficulties that he can't mention them to me w[ithou]t emotion.

In the 2 years that we have been absent from America Mr. Jay has recd. but two letters from Fady, & not one from Sr. James, tho' he has written to both, to Fady frequently. You may imagine our anxiety is not a little increas'd by their silence, but patience is a virtue, ... & I think we are in a way of acquiring it. Three weeks ago I was distress'd by my dr. Mr. Jay's illness, but my fears have given place to the more delightful sensation of gratitude for his recovery. His situation is not in general the most desirable, for besides the perplexity often times of his business, he receives little pleasure or satisfaction from some near him who ought to behave differently from what they do: one of them is the most insidious & deceitful man I have ever known & is unfortunately too much the others tutor. Indeed I never shall in future expect any virtue to spring from a soil that has not been soften'd & enrich'd with filial & fraternal affection. I acknowledge that the delicacy & forbearance that Mr. Jay has observ'd towards him, have heighten'd if it was possible my esteem & affection for him, while the unfeeling, sulky rudeness of the others conduct daily wears away my attachment, & sometimes puts me out of all patience.

As I'm not sure but what I shall commit this letter to the flames as I've done several before now in which I had mention'd this unfortunate circumstance I shall bid you adieu at present & resume my pen after dinner. Let me charge you however not to mention a syllable of this in or out of the family. Indeed I shd. not have ventur'd to say what I have at present, but as this letter will be carry'd by Majr. Franks I've not reason to be afraid that it will be open'd by any body but yourself. Be cautious therefore of this secret, shd. it be expos'd it might do harm & can do no good.

May you my dr. Kitty never lament the insensibility of those you love, but may all who are favor'd with your friendship feel for you an affection not less ardent than

Your ever affectionate sister
S. J.

(SLJ to Mary White Morris) San Ildefonso Sept. 1781

As we are at St. Ildefonso it would be inexcusable to be intirely silent about the Royal Gardens here, which its said are unequaled in Europe but still in mentioning them I can only say that they surpass description. I had often heard of them as being very magnificent, but still the Idea I had formed of them was inadequate as would be that of a person who should take his Idea of a first-rate ship of war from the view of a ferry-boat. Here you have ye whole heathen mytholigy & the metamorphoses of Ovid represented in an admirable manner by figures vastly larger than the life: the fountains, Statues & marble urns are almost innumerable, & the water which forms the cascades, & that which is thrown up by the fountains (by some of them upwards of a hundred feet) is perfectly transparent; in short the whole discovers a royal master. Nor is the Palace less worthy of observation since it is stored with an immense number of very valuable antiquities: in the lower apartments I think I shd. have remained immovable had not our conductor too frequently interrupted my attention by informing us there yet remained a vast deal to be seen. No imitation of nature can be more successful than that which is displayed in the admirable statues of Castor & Pollux; the case which is thrown into their attitudes, tho' it proves a masterly hand, yet for a time it banishes the Idea of art [incomplete letter]

(JJ to Kitty Livingston) Madrid 21 January 1782

Dear Kitty,

Sally will mention the Date of the last Letter we had the Pleasure of receiving from you. Mr. Ridley was the Bearer of it, as well as of a Picture for which I esteem myself greatly indebted to our good friend Mr. Morris. I think it greatly resembles you, and that Circumstance gives it a value with us, which it is neither necessary nor easy to express. I have seen & admired many ancient Paintings of celebrated masters, but their Effect on ones Feelings is cold & momentary, compared with the Impression made by a less finished portrait of a favorite absent Friend.

Simitiere really appears to have done his best, and I confess has somewhat softened by his Pencil, the Resentment excited by the Impropriety of his Conduct. I think he has given you a few Years too many, and if there be any other material Fault, it is in not having transfused in to the Eyes, the exact and full Expression of the originals, but this I believe can seldom be accomplish'd, except in Cases where nature has not been very liberal. I like the neat Simplicity of the Head Dress, but the Ringlet on the Shoulder might have flowed in Lines more easy. The air and mien of the whole Picture is graceful, the Dress well fancied, and tho the Countenance is rather sedate, it is nevertheless free from Severity, serene, and pleasing.

.... A Letter dated the 27 Augt. last from my old friend & Companion Mr. Benson arrived here ten Days ago. He gives me the most particular & satisfactory acct. of my Fathers Family wh. I have as yet recd. I have not had a Line from Fady of later Date than April, and I have been too plain & sincere with no. II [brother James Jay] to be admitted into the Number of his Correspondents. What is he doing?

In one of my former Letters I mentioned to you that my Family would probably be increased this Spring. We expect this Event will take place in march. Sally's Health is in some Respects better than usual, tho still delicate. The Rheumatism has left her, but her Strength is not in proportion to her Spirits.

I much fear that your apprehensions about the Saratoga are too well founded. We can hear no Tidings of her. It is possible nevertheless that she may have been captured, but the Probability of it decreases daily. A Regard for your Feelings as well as my own, prevents my enlarging on this Subject. Our Inquiries shall be continued and you shall be informed of the Result of them.

Mr. Morris it seems has sent his two eldest Sons to Europe. They have had a fine Passage, and I rejoice at it. I have desired Mr. Ridley to send me their Address, when settled at Geneva. I have always found myself strongly attached even to the Children of my Father's Friends, and unless my Heart decieves me, the children of my own Friends will always find a Place in it. My Ideas of an European Education were never very exalted, and I confess they are less so now than ever.

.... Sally has sent Mr. Johnson at Nantz an order, of which the following is a Copy vizt.

No. 1 to contain
2 white embroidered Patterns for shoes,
4 pr Silk Stockings,
a Pattern for a negligee of light pink colored Silk, with a Set of Ribbands suitable to it,
6 pair of Kid Gloves,
6 Yards of Cat gut, and Cap wire in proportion,
6 Yards of white silk Gauze.

No. 2 to contain
The same as above, except that the Silk for the Negligee must not be *pink* colored, but of any other Color or Colors that Mrs. Johnson

may think fashionable and pretty. The shoes and ribbands to be adapted to it.

No. 3 to contain
The Same as above, except that the Silk for the Negligee must be of a different Color from the other two, and the Shoes and Ribbands of a proper color to be worn with it.

We hope that one at least of these parcels will reach you, and be agreeable to your Taste. You will be pleased to observe that they are not merely sent to your Care but for *your* wear....

Adieu. I am sincerely Dear Kitty, your affectionate Friend and Brother,

John Jay

(SLJ to her father) Madrid, Jany 31, 1782

The great distance that seperates me from my dr. Papa makes me solicitous to inform him of such things as would amuse him, or at least give him an account of this part of his family; & with those intentions have frequently taken up my pen; ....

The many distressing incidents that have arisen in our part of the world in consequence of the cruel war that has been prosecuted against us are sufficient to contrast the former bounties of Providence to our Country & to raise our gratitude for the prospect which the happy conclusion of this Campaign has open'd to Peace & Independence. Our once haughty foe now finds himself depriv'd of [a] great part of his Empire, Dignity & the confidence of many of his subjects....

The 6th of Febry. Count De Montmorin the French Embassador will give a very splendid entertainment at his house in celebration of the birth of the Dauphin, & you may judge whether or not it is likely to be elegant when I tell you that it is said that the ten thousand dollars allowed by his Court for the occasion will be insufficient to defray the expence that will be incur'd; your daughter tho' invited, I fancy will hardly partake of the ball tho' it wd. be perfectly agreeable to her inclination, since its probable that about that time or very near it, she will have the pleasure of giving you a little name-sake. Your attention to my dr. little boy encreases my gratitude, & makes me wish you may one day be repaid by his own amiable conduct, being sensible that a generous mind is most agreeably rewarded when it percieves that it's benefits have been useful.

Please to remember me to my dr. Mama & brother Wm. & believe me to be, my dr. Papa with great sincerity

your very dutiful daughter
Sarah Jay

Sarah Jay was delighted to announce the birth of another daughter in Madrid. Maria was born on February 20th. Although Peter Jay, John's father, died on April 17, 1782, the Jays did not hear of his death for many months.

(SLJ to Peter Jay) Madrid April 29, 1782

My dear Papa

If a longer time than usual has elapsed since you have heard from me, I hope that you have not imputed the silence to omission in me, but rather to accidental miscarriages, some of which I have been inform'd of. By a letter from Mr. Harrison Mr. Jay has just recd. intelligence of the Capture of a Brigg from Cadiz bound to Philadelphia on board of which was a box for your family containing 15½ yds of silk for sister Nancy, black & red silk handkerchiefs for you, Peter, Fady & Nancy & likewise for the servants; besides stockings, tape &c. I was so indiscreet as to put the letters I had written to you & sister Jay in the box which I regret extremely.

Mr. [Egbert] Benson & sister Kitty have in some measure lessened the anxiety we felt about your family by informing us of your situation. Mr. Jay has recd. but two or three letters from his brother during his absence, which is two years & an half. I am very happy that my son is with you & wish as much that you may find amusement in his artless prattle as that he was of an age to receive instruction from your example & advice. May the pleasure he affords you now be a happy presage of the satisfactory manner in which he will perpetuate the memory of his ancestors. How much we wish to be of your family party, your own affection for us will suggest; for I'm sure the affection we have for each other is mutual. I flatter myself that by this time you have recd. Mr. Jay's letter informing you of the birth of your grand-daughter. She still continues very healthy, but what will surprise you a little is, that she was born with her tongue ty'd, which they say girls seldom are, nor can I account for it other wise than by imputing it to the taciturnity of her mother. Nursing does not yet disagree with me, & I shall omit no caution necessary to continue to me that pleasure, especially as it will prevent embarresments on that score when the signal for our return shall be given.

Though the tranquility which at your age is so desirable, & which indeed from your circumstances you was intitled to expect, has been unhappily interrupted by the clashing of arms, yet I rejoice with you my dr. sir that the clouds which obscured American freedom are breaking away, & that you will have the satisfaction of seeing the exertions of our Country crowned with success.

Papa writes me that little Peter had lamented to him in a letter, his want of powder to make squibbs to join in the public rejoicings for the capture of Lord Cornwallis. Tho' he is yet too young to be entrusted with powder, I am glad to find that my little spark had kindled upon that occasion, & am pleas'd when I reflect that where he is, the sentiments of Liberty will be cherish'd in him by education, & not suffer'd to expire like his own little squibbs in the first effort.... I am glad that brother Peter has so agreeable a neighbour in Mr. Benson, & I hope that sister Jay & Nancy find their situation at Poughkeepsie at least as eligible as it was at Fish kill, & as to you my dear sir who have so long practic'd resignation, I am convinc'd that no local circumstances will disturb your peace while you have your little family around you.

Please to remember me to my brother & sisters & believe [me] to be with the greatest sincerity

Your affectionate daughter
Sa: Jay

Mr. Jay will have the pleasure of writing to you & sending you the portrait of Peter Munro.

In the spring, John Jay was called to Paris by Benjamin Franklin to participate in the peace negotiations that would lead to the Treaty of Paris of 1783, the formal end of America's war with Great Britain. The Jays left Madrid on May 21st. Mr. Jay wrote to his friend, Robert R. Livingston:

> Our Journey thus far afforded much Variety, & excepting some bad Roads, Fleas, & Bugs, was not unpleasant. Both Spanish & French Biscay contain a number of romantic pretty Scenes, & I assure you we found ourselves perfectly disposed to enjoy the Beauties of this charming Season.

On June 23rd the Jays arrived in Paris, where they were welcomed by American as well as French friends.

(Adrienne de Noailles, Marquise de Lafayette, to SLJ at Paris)

Paris tuesday 25 June 1782

Madame de Lafayette has just learned that madame Jay has arrived in Paris. She is very eager to have the honor of meeting her, and would have liked very much to do so as early as this evening, to personally hear of her trip but she is not able to go out today due to her health. She begs Madame Jay to find a way so she can make amends tomorrow and to tell her at what hour it might be convenient to visit her.

Madame de Lafayette dares to hope that the kindness and friendship which M. Jay has for M. de Lafayette, of whom he has so often spoken, will allow Madame Jay to comply with an eagerness, perhaps a little tactless, and will with forbearance accept her initial respects. M.de Lafayette is at Versailles from whence he will return tomorrow, to have the honor of seeing Monsieur and Madame Jay.

(SLJ to her sister Kitty)

[Draft]
Paris, 14th Augst 1782

My dr. sister,

I have regretted extremely the miscarriage of 8 of your letters which occasion'd a space in the intelligence I had Recd of my friends of 5 months which solicitude magnifyed into an age. The Capture of the *Jay* and *Lady Jay* must have prevented you likewise from hearing from us a very long time, especially as I've not written to any of the family since I left Madrid which was on the 21st of May.

We did not arrive at Paris till the 23d of June and was then so ill with the intermitting which I catch'd at Bordeaux that I could scarcely quit my bed. No sooner had the bark succeeded in breaking it, than I was severely attacked by a disorder which from its very general influence was call'd the <u>influenza</u>. The Physician told me that he had not seen any persons so severely attack'd as Mr. Jay & myself. When that disorder abated my fever return'd & its but 2 days since I've again left my bed. To compleat my distress my dr. little babe as well as her Cousin took the Hooping-Cough in our Journey & the difficulty of struggling with that was increas'd by a fever which she caught from me & frequent fasting when I was too ill to suckle her. Since my arrival here I've met with a Clever Nurse for her but she is still ill tho' I hope now out of danger.

The uncommon Coolness & frequent rains that has prevail'd here this season has render'd it very sickly. I was inform'd 3 Weeks ago that the Lieutenant de Police had a return of 100 thousand sick persons in this City so that you see our whole family (for a fortnight ago we had not one person well in it) are very fashionably dispos'd....

The Marchioness de la Fayette is a most amiable woman; she is confin'd to her house by indisposition, the consequence of an expected addition to her family.

In the packet Mr. Vaughan had from me were letters from every one of the family not excepting master Peter. If Mr. V. could only reserve the Band-Box Master Peter has lost his Clothes which Mr. V. took in his Chest. I'm very anxious about that Child I must own to you for time slips away unperceiv'd at his age & if unimprov'd I think the detriment cannot be name'd. Do my dr.Kitty let me know exactly whether [he] reads well & even condescend to let me know what he reads. I think some short agreeable History might be put in his hand & I could [teach] him to learn to spell very well that his Opportunities for learning may increase [&] he may not be retarded in his progress.

(Frederick Jay to JJ at Paris) Poughkeepsie 15th Augt. 1782

Dear Sir

The preceeding is a fourth Copy of my last to you, since which I have been favour'd with yours of the 29th April by Major Franks, who on his way to Philada. was kind enough to call upon me. The Acct. he gave me of your health and that of your Family were very pleasing to us all; may you and they long experience that great Blessing.

I was in great expectation to have had it in my power to have given you a full and Satisfactory acct. of our Fathers Estate, but from the present Situation of the times it is impossible. Mr. Benson and myself have taken an Acct. of the Bonds and find them fall very short of what I expected, being not more (exclusive of Interest & Loan office Certificates) than one half as much as was received from Mrs. Chambers.

We have not as yet been able to collect in any monies due to the Estate, and it is very uncertain when we shall, as the greater part of the bonds are due from People in the power of the Enemy & very little dependence is to be made from the rents. However we shall do the best we can and endeavour to support the Family in as easy and comfortable a manner as circumstances will admit, hoping the time is near at hand when we shall again enjoy our former happy state.

Your son is still at Eliz: Town. I would have fetch'd him some months ago, but the weather has been so exceedingly warm that we did not think it prudent. Next month I shall go for him and you may be assured that he shall want for nothing. None of the Articles you have sent us ever came to hand except those mentioned in mine of the 20th April last. The silk you sent Peggy still remains at Eliz Town. She is much obliged to you for it.

Peters picture* came Safe to hand, and if the Original mind contains as much beauty (and I make no doubt it does) he must be handsome indeed. I've shewn it to several young Ladies, who all declare that they would rather die old maids than not have a chance of getting this Young Beauty.

Peter enjoys good health, Nancy very indifferent, Mrs. Jay better than when we were at Fish Kill. Gussy continues to behave well and remains at Kingston. Mrs. M. lives in her own house in Albany. Her going there was contrary to my advice and that of her Friends. Indeed it was a most imprudent Step at this time.

Whether I shall remain here longer than the Fall will depend upon Circumstances. Was it not for Peter & Nancy I would move out of the State, as it is impossible for me to do any business here, especially as I have such a charge upon me. Whether I stay or not be easy about your son, I shall take care of him. Plato stays with me and behaves well, your man Lewis is Peters A.D.C.[aide-de-camp] and is a pretty good Boy. Clarinda is sold and her sister Mary is for Sale, the other Mary boards with Zilpha at Fish Kill. Moll is with me & Susan† at Mr. William Van Wycks. I am &c

Fred. Jay

(SLJ to her mother) Paris, 28 August 1782

My dear Mamma,

I had the pleasure of writing several letters to you & the rest of the family just before I left Madrid, but since my arrival here the indisposition of my family has prevented me from writing, ...

I'm much pleased with France. It seems to be one of the favorite spots of Nature if we may judge of her disposition towards it by the enchanting prospects & fertile fields that perpetually engage the attention of a Traveller; but nothing pleased me more than the gaiety & industry of the inhabitants. I could not but remark their natural inclination for chearful objects displayed in their little flower gardens, for there is scarce a peasant's cottage without the appurtenance of a garden & many of them have little bowers that discovers a very pretty taste; in short such was the impression which their apparent content & good Humour made upon me that I became again reconcil'd to the lot of humanity, tho' some scenes in the preceding part of my Journey had almost disgusted me.

Today I had the pleasure of the Company of Mr. Morris's two sons, Mrs. Montgomery's son & one of Mrs. Izard's sons, & you can't imagine how happy I feel in seeing them. It's true there could be an addition to the little society that would increase the pleasure I have in my little company of Americans & I sincerely wish my dear

**Peter Jay Munro sat for a miniature portrait while in Madrid.*

†*All were Jay family slaves except Zilpha and Old Plato, who had been given their freedom when Peter Jay died.*

boy was with me, but have not resolution to send for him. I wish mamma you would be so good as to inquire what is the state of Jersey College at present and at what age the youngest that can be admitted at the Grammar school there must be. Should any thing retard our return for any length of time it would be proper to consider in what manner the dear little fellow might profit most.

Will you be so good as to give my love to him & tell him that I expect to be informed from his own pen how he liked the stuff I sent him by Mr. Vaughn for Spring clothes, & the buckles & buttons I ordered out for him from France before I left Spain.

Sister Susan is many letters in debt to me for I've not received one from her of a later date than October, so that I quite long to hear from her, and shall thank her if she will when she writes to me enclose a lock of Peter's hair. I regret exceedingly the loss of a box sent out last fall for the two families, for had it arrived safe the contents of it would have contributed to their convenience. We have just heard that a Vessel has arrived safe for the south-ward in which was a box for Kitty with a pink lutestring negligee, 6 Eels* of Gauze and as much Catgut, 4 pair of embroidered silk shoes, 4 pair of silk stockings, 6 pair of white kid gloves and a suit of broad and narrow ribbon; but we have likewise had the mortification to hear of the capture of another vessel which contained a like parcel only differing in the Colour of the silk and ribbons. There has been still a third parcel shipped which we have not heard of since, but our frequent disappointments have discouraged us from risqueing any thing further until there is a peace concluded. When that will be God only knows....

I am my dear mamma

Your very affectionate daughter,
Sarah Jay

(SLJ to her father at Trenton) Paris 14th Oct. 1782

My dr. Papa,

General du Portail's departure from Paris for America furnishes me with an excellent opportunity to write to my friends ....

After two or three months indisposition I again begin to respire & my friends flatter me that my countenance begins to near the appearance of health. God grant that the appearances may not be fallacious. My dr. Mr. Jay is still very much troubled with a pain in his breast; if he does not soon obtain relief I shall be apprehensive for the consequences. We are at present infinitely more agreeably situated than we have been since our arrival in Europe.

Maria grows charmingly & amuses us exceedingly. If we do not return to America next Spring the first language she speaks will be the french, but to that I've no objection since she'll soon acquire the english in our own Country. I long beyond expression to see my son, & I owe you a thousand thanks my dr. sir for the attention you have been so kind as to show him: will you add to the obligations you have

**Sarah writes "eels" but means ells. An ell is 45 inches.*

already confer'd, by devoting a leisure hour to telling me exactly what you think of him? Favors do not sour me, for I can receive & confer them with equal pleasure....

The time allowed me for writing is almost expired & I will therefore take leave of you, my dr. sir, in the words of Isaac Anis to his friend Aaron Moneca: "Porte toi bien: vis content et heureux; et que le Ciel te comble de prospérités, te donne une santé parfaite, et te rend Vainqueur de tes ennemis."*

Your affte. daughter
Sa: Jay

(SLJ to Mary White Morris) [Draft]
Paris, 14th Novbr. 1782

With what pleasure my dear madam do I take up my pen as a medium of or substitute for a conversation with you; by admitting no other idea to rob me of your image, I enjoy, at least for the moment the most pleasing delusion....

If during my stay in Paris it is in my power to serve you, nothing my dr. Mrs. Morris can give me greater pleasure than receiving yr. commands. At present the prevailing fashions are very decent & very plain. The gowns most worn are the robes à l'angloise which are exactly like ye italian habits that were in fashion in America at the time I left it. The sultana, resembling the long polinese is also à la mode, but as it is not expected that it will long remain so, every body makes them of slight silk. There is so great a variety of hats, caps, cuffs, &c. that it's impossible to describe them. I forgot that the robe à l'angloise if trimm'd either with the same or gauze is dress, but if intirely untrimm'd must be worn with an apron and is undress: negligees are very little in vogue: fans of 8 or 10 sous are almost the only ones in use.

At the Marquis de la Fayette's table I had the pleasure of hearing you my dear Mrs. Morris mentioned the other day as well as Mr. Morris in terms to me the most grateful imaginable. The Marchioness is a most amiable woman; she expressed her inclination to see America in very flattering terms, and I could not forbear assuring her that if she ever honored us by a visit, she would find that her Character there had already prepared the Americans to receive her in a manner, that would convince her that the Marquis, though much esteemed, was not the only one of his Family that they respected.

The Queen has lately returned to Versailles after a residence of 8 or 10 weeks at Passey. While there, I us'd sometimes to have the pleasure of seeing her at the Plays. She is so handsome & her manners are so engaging, that almost forgetful of republican principles, I was ever ready while in her presence to declare her born to be a queen. There are however many traits in her character worthy of imitation even by republicans, & I cannot but admire her resolution to superintend the education of Madame Royale her daughter, to whom she has alotted chambers adjoining her own, & persists in refusing to name a governante for her. The Duchess of Polniac is nam'd for that office to the Dauphin.

*"*Stay well, be content and happy; and may Heaven fill you with prosperity, give you perfect health, and allow you to be victorious over your enemies.*"

I have just been interrupted by a visit from the Princess Mazarin, who inform'd me that the Count d'Artois would be here in 8 or 10 days hence & the Prince her husband soon after, so that I conjecture the seige of Gibralter is to be abandoned.

I have had so many interruptions since I've been writing this short letter that I must entreat you will impute some of the blunders with which it is filled to that cause....

I have the honor to be, my dr. madam,

Yours sincerely,
Sa. Jay

(SLJ to her sister Kitty) Paris, Nov 16, 1782

My dearest Kitty,

I have this inst. recd. a letter from Major Franks but as he informs me of yr. indisposition I have little satisfaction in reading it; & my thoughts are so much occupied by my concern for it, that I have as yet scarcely bestow'd a thought upon his peculiar misfortune.* If your indisposition has been only a fever & ague I flatter myself you are by this time perfectly recovered, & even much heartier than before: the reason that I thus flatter myself is its having had that effect upon me, for I enjoy much better health than I've known since my arrival in Europe.

Mr. Jay has but tolerable health, a continual pain in his breast, the consequence of the influenza & too much application, still continues to alarm me: our little girl grows charmingly; I long to hear her lispe your name. Peter was well when I heard from him last & I hope is still: does he yet begin to write? I had the pleasure of receiving a letter from mama the other day that was dated in April. I've often experienced the truth of an observation I've heard from her that Children rarely know the extent of their obligations to their parents until they become parents themselves; & I'm sure I am more sensible than ever of what I owe to mine, since by being by my distance from them depriv'd of their advice, & sometimes when most necessary, of their consolation; I have learnt the real value of those blessings: Mr. Jay's extreme tenderness for me could alone have reconcil'd me to so long an absence from them.

I sympathize with sister Watkins on the loss of her child; but should not, if untaught by an event that will be ever recent in my memory, have thought the task so difficult, to be reconcil'd to the death of an infant. I hope to have the leisure to write to Judy as well as Mamma before the Captn. sails, but if disappointed, you'll be so good as to remember me to her & Mr. Watkins. If my friends hear from me less frequently than they wish, I hope they have the justice to conclude that my letters miscarry, which must be the case since numbers remain unanswered & unacknowledged: should they impute my silence to the love of dissipation which reigns here, they would do me injustice, for tho' dissipation has too great a share of my time, it finds no place in my heart. I long, & even sigh for rural retirement & friendly society; in fashionable life, politeness supplies the place of friendship, but my heart as

**In a letter to John Jay, David S. Franks mentions having been jilted by a Philadelphia lady, who got married on the very day he returned, and also having "been left out of the Army," i.e., discharged (28 September 1782).*

well as judgement convinces me that the substitute is inadequate; and that conviction endears to me my former friends....

I've heard that there is not a perfect cordiallity between the Ladies of Carolina & those of Philadelphia, but I hope that I've been misinform'd, & indeed upon reflection I'm sure of it, for such a coolness does not at all accord with the character of the American Ladies....

Take good care my lovely sister of yr. health.... [incomplete letter]

(SLJ to Mary White Morris at Philadelphia) Paris 25th Novbr 1782

My Dear Madam,

It was not without regret that I heard of Captn. Barney's leaving Paris without having those things in charge which you had requested might be sent by him....

The measure for yr. gown, cannot it seems be found: but it is of less consequence as Mr. Ridley has sent out for Mrs. Powel two habits; a sul[t]ana & an English habit, which you can see before you have yours made. The Pistache & rose colour were most fashionable last Autumn, but what will succeed them in the spring is difficult yet to divine: the trimming is made by the first miliner & will either suit a sultana or habit, with both of which dresses they wear the petticoat of a different colour. You'll pardon the liberty I've taken in adding an handkerchief; for as it was new, & consequently admir'd, I could not resist the inclination: it's to be ly'd on before the gown, & then pinned down to the stays & when the gown is on to be put under the shoulder straps & then the tippet* is put around the edge of it & renders a tucker† unnecessary. I can't imagine why it's call'd a Chemise,§ for I cannot discover any resemblance that it bears to that part of dress. The hat & Cloak are fashionable at all seasons of the year, tho' in the Winter the Cloak is only worn in dress. Your Stays tho' made according to yr. direction is perfectly the mode, stiff ones having long since been laid aside, but you forgot that your waist has length as well as breadth, & therefore you'll be so obliging as to pardon yr. Taylor if he has not guess'd right. Am I at liberty to draw any inference from yr. partiallity?

As black & white riding hats are equally worn, I've sent both, the one trimm'd in the present taste, the other without ribbon that your own may be consulted. They are likewise very much worn of a morning with the hair dress'd without a cushion as for riding. Should I have been so fortunate as to give satisfaction in the choice of things, I shall think myself vastly happy, & always proud in being honor'd with your commands.

May I flatter myself, that this scarce legible scrawl, will as well as some former ones, meet with your indulgence. With my best wishes for Mr. Morris & my dr. Kitty, I remain my dr. Madam

your very sincere & affecte friend
S. Jay

**Tippet: a long hanging end of cloth attached to a sleeve, cap, or hood.*
†Tucker: a piece of lace or cloth in the neckline of a dress.
§Chemise: a woman's one-piece undergarment or a loose straight-hanging dress.

On November 30th, the Preliminary Articles of Peace were signed in Paris by Richard Oswald for Great Britain and by John Adams, Benjamin Franklin, John Jay, and Henry Laurens for the Americans. John Jay had taken it upon himself to negotiate independently with the British, thereby disregarding instructions from Congress to involve the French. He was subsequently criticized for doing this, in spite of the fact that the terms of the Preliminary Articles were extremely favorable to the new nation.

While in Paris, the Jays had a large circle of friends. Among them were Matthew Ridley and his English wife, Anne Richardson Ridley, Alice DeLancey Izard of New York, Benjamin Franklin and his grandson, William Temple Franklin, Lady Juliana Penn, John Adams and his sons John Quincy and Charles, and of course, the Marquis and Marquise de la Fayette.

(SLJ to her father) [Draft]

Paris Decbr 14th 1782

Fourteen months have elapsed since the date of the last letter I've recd. from you my dr. sir & I leave you to judge of the effect which so long a silence must have had on my sensibility....

At present my dr. sir those Clouds which have long obscur'd the serenety of our distress'd Country begin to disperse & give rise to the pleasing expectation of brighter days. The dawn of peace seems to approach, for the Court of Great Britain has accorded to the American Commissioners the most honorable terms to take effect when the terms for Peace are agreed to by France & England. Permit me to congratulate you on this happy event.

Mr. Jay begs to be remembred to you in the most friendly manner. He has not either been favor'd with a line from you I believe this year. I think his health is a little improv'd since this attainment of that great object I've just mention'd, & I hope that if it sh'd. be succeeded by a little suspension from business, it will continue to amend for there is still great room for it. A cruel pain in his breast has render'd writing tho' absolutely necessary very irksome to him.

Myself & my little girl thrive tolerable well at present. Please to remember me affectionately to my dr. mama & condescend my dr. sir to convince me by a few lines that you still remember

your affectionate & dutiful daughter
Sa. Jay

(SLJ to her sister Kitty at Philadelphia) Paris, 14th Decbr. 1782

....Let us my dr. Kitty rejoice together & bless God! for the prospect of approaching Peace. I already begin to enjoy in imagination some delightful scenes. Oh! Kitty perhaps the time draws near when we shall fold each other to our bosoms, and when our Domestic felicity shall again be compleat.

....Among all the pleasures which Paris affords (& they are not few) none of them gratify me like the frequent opportunity of seeing my Country-men. At present you would be surpris'd to see what a Circle we form when collected. We have recd. an agreeable addition to our society by the arrival of Mrs. Ridley the day before yesterday. Mrs. Price & Mrs. Montgomery have the suit of rooms over my head in this same Hotel & Mrs. Izard lives directly opposite & has two daughters that are grown up. There are three days in the week that we take tea & play Cards at each others houses, besides meeting upon other occasions. I was telling young Franklin the other day that he must aid me in contriving a Ball when Peace is concluded.

I fear my dr. you begin to think that the idea of amusements is the only one that I attend to, & to convince you that that would be a mistake, I assure you I regret nothing more than the omission of a Chaplain to the Doctrs. appointments. All the foreign ministers have one & I think it would be particularly useful here as there are always a great number of Americans at Paris & having no public worship, they seek amusements, but you know how much easier it is to contract bad habits than to quit them. Besides there are likewise some young Americans here for their Education & it really distresses me that they shd. be brought up without any idea of religion. Being unprejudiced they see the absurdity of many things taught in their school but they have none to direct them aright.

Remember me my dear sister to mama, susan, sister Linn, sister Watkins, William & Peter. When you write again let me hear from Hannah & tell me whether Mama remains at Eliz. Town & whether Papa has been re-elected. Peter writes me no more letters. Adieu my lovely sister spare no attention to your health, remember it is absolutely necessary to the happiness of

your affectionate
Sa. Jay

In the spring of 1782, Brockholst Livingston decided to return to America. His ship was captured and he was taken prisoner by the British who locked him up for several weeks in the Provost Gaol in New York City.

(William Livingston to JJ at Paris) Elizabeth Town 8th Janry.1783

Sir

I have just now received your Letter of the 14th October. Next to your being here, I rejoice at your being in France, as I presume that if Madrid can please a Spaniard it is as much as can be expected.

I hope that my little grand daughter is by this time recruited from her tedious Journey; & thrives on the salubrious milk generated by lawful matrimony. As to Master Peter, all the pains the family takes with him, carry with them their own reward: <u>labor ipso voluptas</u> [work itself is a pleasure]. He is one of the most sagacious boys of his age that ever I met with; & has almost every fable of Aesop & Gay at his fingers end....

As poor Brockholst lost his whole collection of garden Seeds by his capture, I shall be much obliged to you for the Seeds of any such horticulary vegetables in which the french gardens excell ours, as well as for those of any pretty flowering shrubs that are not to be found amongst us. This, you will Say, is an odd commission for an Ambassador, but as Mr. Oswald will probably lead you thro' many thorny paths, it may be well enough to amuse yourself sometimes with collecting a few flowers that you may accidentally meet with during the Journey. I am Dr. Sir

your most humble Serv.
Wil. Livingston

(William Livingston to SLJ at Paris) Eliz. Town 8th Jany 1783

My dear Mrs. Jay

I received your Letter of the 15th Octr. on my way to this place where I had not been since the beginning of October last. It is the first letter I have had from you since your arrival in France. I am glad to hear you was recovered from your indisposition; & wish I could felicitate Mr. Jay on the like fortunate event respecting himself.

I long to see you both, & my dear little french grand-daughter Maria: My sweet little Peter is now standing at my elbow; & as you desire me to tell you what I think of him, I will give you my Opinion with the greatest impartiality. He is really and without flattery one of the handsomest boys in the whole country & exceedingly sprightly and active; of a very quick apprehension and an exceedingly good memory. Of late he is as fond of his book as can be wished, & he reads well for a boy of his age.

I think that he has lost but very little by his not having been at school since he left Poughkeepsie. However we were determined to comply with his father's request as to sending him thither again; & should have resigned him into the hands of his Uncle Fady whenever he had called for him for that purpose whatever mortification our parting with him might have cost us. But Mr. Benson's Sentiments upon that subject (which I am told have been transmitted to Mr. Jay) will I hope reconcile you to his being still with his grand mama Livingston, who notwithstanding her great fondness for him, is far from spoiling him, as there is really not a boy in the Country more orderly or under better command than Master Peter.

We had some thoughts last Fall of putting him to school in this Town; but considering the expence of boarding and how little more he would learn by that means than at Home, we concluded to defer it till Spring, when he can foot it from Home with his Basket containing his dinner, & need not return till after the Second school, which I think will greatly contribute to his health & strength by the due quantity of excersise it will afford him. Mr. Jay's directions in the interim shall however be the rule of our conduct respecting him. He has lost much of his bashfulness; & begins to go to & converse with strangers with considerable freedom. I am sorry that he still retains his bad pronunciation of some words occasioned by his not being able to pronounce the G & C, substituting the D for the former & the T for the latter. Gold for instance he calls Doold & Come tome. But I hope this will soon wear off, as most of my children were long puzzled with the pronunciation of certain letters of the Alphabet which they afterwards articulated as well as others.

A few days ago a number of transports arrived at New York from Charles Town in consequence of the evacuation of that Garrison. I long earnestly for their leaving New York that I may again be able to live with my family which labours under many inconveniencies on account of my absence from it, as I do in my turn in being obliged to live at a distance from them.

I long exceedingly to see you & Mr. Jay in safety over that Element which has been so fatal to mine. I am,

your affectionate Father,
Wil: Livingston

P.S. Peter does not yet learn to write, but I enclose you a specimen of his Genius for imitation in that way. [We have n]ot received your Letter with [your acco]unt of the Pyrenees.

(SLJ to JJ at Rouen) Paris 17 Janry. 1783

My dr. Mr. Jay,

I had just sent for paper &c. to write to you when your letter of the 13th Janry. was handed me. I hope before this you have recd. mine by Mr. Johnston, who persisted in his resolution of following you, tho' I told him that you would probably have left Rouen before he would arrive there. You have my thanks my dr. for both your kind letters. I am sorry that your health has receiv'd so little benefit as yet from your journey; my hopes of service were so very sanguine that that consideration almost banish'd the dread of a seperation. My disappointment will even exceed my former hopes if our absence is not compensated for by additional health. I believe your sleep & mine have fled together, perhaps to drown the cares of some less happy persons, for my waking hours are not painful ones.

Mrs. Ridley, her Cousin, & son drank tea with me last Eveng. She is not well, but as the cause of her illness is a natural one, there is less reason to regret it.

Yesterday at 3 o'Clock Mr. [Caleb] Whitford waited upon me to desire me to inform you that a fine bay horse of Lord Mount Stuart's which you have seen (but not the unsound one) is to be dispos'd of at present for 40 Guineas with saddle & bridle, & for 36 guineas without. Mr. Whitford wishes to know as soon as possible whether you would choose to make the purchase. Did I tell you Mr. [Richard] Oswald was going to England? He went last wednesday afternoon after calling upon me for my commands & requesting to be remembred to you.

I've recd. a letter for you from the Marquis de la Fayette who is at Cadiz but am ignorant whether you would wish to have it forwarded: the expectations of a Peace seem to be again revived but on what foundation I can't tell. I suppose you have heard that Captn. Hill has brought some Prizes to the L'Orient & left a few American Privateers amidst a fleet of Merchantmen consisting of twenty sail & without a convoy so that it is supposed they will have their choice. The family are all very well

& the servants conduct themselves to a charm. Our Neighbours are very friendly & we pass our time very sociably ensemble.

Maria runs about in a kind of Go-cart & continues as fond of me as ever. Adieu my dr. Mr. Jay, believe me to be most

Affectionately yours
Sa. Jay

(JJ to SLJ at Paris) Rouen 18 Jany 1783

My dear Sally

A little Letter I wrote you this morning, contained a promise of another by Tomorrows Post, and to perform it I am now retired to my Room.

I fear your Expectations respecting the speedy Recovery of my Health are too sanguine. As I lost it by almost imperceptible Degrees, the Restoration of it will doubtless be gradual, and I shall think myself happy if I regain it on those Terms. If my Endeavours succeed, I shall be grateful; if not, I shall be resigned. I hope you will always consider these matters in their true Points of View, and not permit vain Hopes or causeless Fears to distress either you or me. The more easy & happy you are, the more I shall be so also, and consequently the better prospects we shall both have of future Health. I am better than when I left you, tho' not much. The weather has been and still is very unfavorable, but it must change soon, & thank God it cannot change for the worse.

...This Town is daily amused with contradictory Reports respecting Peace. They are anxious about it, and with Reason, for the uncertainty of its taking Place, holds Commerce suspended, and injures the mercantile Interest greatly. I am pleased with this City and the people of it. They are industrious and hospitable. Their manufactures are very considerable & very proper for our Country, with whom they will certainly have a great Trade unless it be fettered & embarrassed with superfluous Regulations and ill-judged Restrictions. I suspect the Trade of this Country stands in need of Revision very generally.

Present my Compts. and best wishes to Mrs. Ridley & your neighbors. I am glad the Servants behave well, they shall be rewarded for it. Kiss our little Girl for me, and believe me to be,

my dear Sally,
your very afft. Husband,
John Jay

(SLJ to JJ at Rouen) Paris 21st Janry. 1783

My dr. Mr. Jay,

Immediately upon the rect. of your letter of the 18th, I sent to request the favor of Mr. Whitford's company a few minutes & communicated to him yr. sentiments of the horse. He promised to mount him & give me his opinion after the tryal, but as the signing the preliminary articles yesterday was an interesting event, he seem'd himself too much agitated to execute his intention. This instant Mr. Whitford has left me, he call'd upon me booted & spurr'd for the experiment, but as it is already past twelve I fear I shall not have an answer for you before the post leaves Paris. My spirits are quite exhausted, for tho' I have in some Measure been prepared to expect the welcome tidings, I never was so overcome with joy. At first my spirits were only elevated as upon ordinary pleasing occasions but that was succeeded by such lively emotions of gratitude & wonder that my sensations would have been too painful to support had I not been reliev'd by a very plentiful effusion of tears. I long my dear to embrace you now as well as a deliverer of our Country as an affectionate & tender husband.

Mrs. Ridley has been so good as to send me word that she will spend the day with me, & as I expect her every minute I hope you will excuse this scrawl. My Compts. to Mr. Ridley & congratulations to you both.

I am my dr.
yours affectly.
Sa. Jay

(William Livingston to PAJ at Poughkeepsie) Trenton 13th February 1783

My dear Peter Jay

Don't you remember that you promised to send me a Letter as soon as you got to Poghkeepsie? But I fear that you have forgot it: But you see that Grand Papa has not forgot you. Since you have been taken away from Elizabeth Town to be put to School at Poghkeepsie, I hope you will mind your book, and try to be the best Scholar in the whole School. I know that you can learn very fast if you please, and you must tell me in your Letter what book you are in. Uncle Fady will write a Letter for you, but then you must tell him what to write.

We have good news about a peace, and that king George is forced to lett us alone, and how foolish will the Tory-boys look then, Master Peter? And then I hope we shall soon have Papa and Mamma Jay back again to this Country, and that will make Grand Papa very glad indeed, and my little Peter too. I am

My dear little P.
Your affectionate Gr.Father
Wil: Livingston

As Matthew Ridley wrote from Paris to Kitty Livingston on March 26th:

Mr. & Mrs. Jay & the little Spaniard are bravely. Whether the next [child] is to be a Spaniard, French, or English will depend on Master Congress. I think if they do not decide soon it may probably be French.... This Night we are going altogether say the old Folks, to the Opera of Theseus & tomorrow go to St. Cloud to eat mattelottes. You must enquire [of] your French

> Friends what they are...." [Matelotes are fish cooked in wine, onions, herbs, etc.]

Although pregnant and devoted to her little Maria, Sarah Jay nevertheless had an active social life.

(SLJ to her mother) Paris, 15th April 1783

My dear Mamma,

I flatter'd myself that among the numerous blessings restored to us by the Peace, that of a free communication between absent friends would not have been the last; but to my great regret I've not recd. a line from any body on your side of the Globe since the 3d of Janry. Indeed my Correspondents are contracted to a very small number, scarce any body but my dr. Susan & Kitty condescending to write to me. I can account for & excuse the silence of many who at first favor'd me wh. their correspondance, & lament the necessity which impell'd my silence in the letters to my friends on subjects which from their novelty would certainly have been interesting; but if they'll have the goodness to suspend their curiosity 'till my return among them, they shall command all the little store of events that my Journey has furnished me with.

How sincerely my dear Mamma do I rejoice in the restoration of tranquility to our friends & country. Now that the weather begins to be pleasant, I fancy I see you at Eliz. T., walking & conversing with Papa on the subject of reducing the Farm to its former order whilst he, with his pruning-knife in his hand is almost at a loss where to begin his operations. Doubtless my dr. Papa was surprised to behold all the effects of his former care effaced by the wilderness that had sprung up in his absence; & yet the astonishing changes that have taken place in the fortunes of our friends, & the politicks of our Country in the short interval of those rural amusements so far exceeds all ordinary subjects of admiration that they vanish upon the recollection. Oh when! my dr. mamma will it be our happy lot to be restored to our friends & our country. Sometimes my imagination amuses itself with a recollection of former scenes, & former prospects, & for a moment regrets the loss of them, but then is again chear'd by hopes of the future enjoyment of my friends & of retirement. Such ideas however must not be too frequently indulged at present while our mode of life is still likely to remain so opposite; least I sow seeds of disgust that may produce thorns & briers where already the path is not too smooth: I mean shd. we return to Spain, which in all probability will soon be the case.

You will not pardon me if I don't say something of Maria, nor indeed would my own partiality permit me to be silent. Tho' some fashionable ladies would be surprised to hear that even in Paris she makes one of my chief amusements, you my dear Mamma I'm sure will not: she resembles her sweet little brother exceedingly, but is much smaller than he was at her age; nor does she yet walk without the aid of a finger from her nurse or myself, yet it is only owing to her timidity for with that slender assistance she runs about continually. Since we have been here, the weather 'till within a fortnight has been very unpleasant, but now it is quite delightful, & I therefore suffer no engagements either of business or pleasure to prevent my riding out with her & walking every day, for she has not yet recovered the shock her tender constitution receiv'd in her journey from Madrid. The extreme delicacy of her frame has prevented me hither to from weaning her but some of my friends think she will thrive more on more substantial food, & therefore I intend to let Abbe wean her next week.

How does my dr. little boy do? I long beyond discription to see him, & find it difficult to reconcile myself to a longer absence. Will you be so good as to give him ye little tooth-pick case inclos'd? I forbear sending him other things because I'm convinc'd every thing is now to be had in America, & it's asking too great a favor of a traveller to burden himself with bundles, as Paris is so distant from the Ports. I wish my dr. Susan would give me a circumstantial account of the family, where they are & how employ'd; & if she hears any thing of Mr. Jay's family pray let her communicate it....

Give my love to Papa, & tell him that if I dar'd I would continue to scribble to him now & then, but 6 or 8 letters which I have written to him remaining unanswered, discourage me from addressing him again. Adieu my dr. Mamma. Happy in the return of Peace! happy in the hopes of being again re-united to each other, let our confidence in Providence prevent all anxious cares, and rest assured that whether accidents intervene to prevent my letters from reaching you, or whether you punctually receive mementos of my gratitude & affection I shall never cease to be

your dutiful & affectionate daughter
S. Jay

(SLJ to her sister Susan at Elizabeth Town) Paris 16th April 1783

My dr. Susan,

I've been pelting you wh. letters ever since a Peace has encreas'd the probability of yr. receiving them, but as yet have had no returns from America. Are you all napping or are the merchants attending the certainty of a treaty of Peace? Whichever be the case I long for a change, & wish you would speedily tell me of all the new arrangements that are likely to take place on the alteration of our affairs. I do not mean political changes. Thank heaven! I've no interest in them, at least no personal ones; for nothing could add more to my happiness than being mistress of a plentiful dairy & comfortable farm house; & nothing be more distant from the mark than a return to Spain, yet the latter is likely to be my fate, so that you see the worst that can happen to me, if it be but a change, must be to my advantage. But the alterations I allude to are the domestic ones of my friends. As soon as N. York is evacuated let me know it, & who of our friends return there....

Do you remember that you was so good as to lend me a fan when I went to Philadelphia & that it was never return'd to you? Pray favor me wh. the acceptance of the one Mr. Mason will charge himself with in it's place. I shall order a little box of common fans for mamma, as summer is approaching they will be useful; indeed there are hardly any others used here even by persons of the first quality; but the whole dress of the Ladies as well as gentlemen is remarkably simple & pleases me wonderfully.

Adieu my dr. Susan. I fear'd I should not be able to write to you by this opportunity, but if a few lines will convince you of my attachment I'm glad that Mr. Mason deferr'd his departure 'till this morng., & that I rose early enough to scribble them.

Remember me to all the family & embrace my little boy; suppose my dr. that with a little of yr. assistance he should resume his Correspondance....

Believe me to be my dear Susan

yours affectionately
S. Jay

(SLJ to her sister Kitty at Philadelphia) Paris 24th April 1783

My dr. Kitty,

This morng. Mrs. Izard sets out for Bourdeaux from whence she expects to sail for America. I intended to have troubled her with a large packet for you & the family, but a severe pain in my face these two or three days past have prevented me from having that pleasure. The reason for my delaying to write so long was that I might give you the latest intelligence of the health & intentions of our little family. As to the latter, they are yet almost unform'd since Mr. Hartly, the Gentleman appointed to sign the difinitive treaty with the Americans is not yet arrived, & our return to Spain or not this summer must depend upon the time of the Completion of that business; for shd. it be protracted 'till June, in my situation a Journey at that season would be very dangerous. Mr. Jay's health I think is rather better within this week, & the little girl bears her weaning better than I expected....

Present my Compts. to Mrs. Morris. Tho' she won't write me I'm sure she'll envy me the pleasure I'm to have this afternoon, when I tell you that her little sons are to drink tea & eat whiggs* with me. Mr. Jay joins with me in love to our little boy & our friends.

Adieu my dearest sister. Believe me to be

most affectionately yours
Sa. Jay

Direct your letters to the Care of Doctr. Franklin, for I would not choose that any letters intended for us shd. arrive in Spain before we do.

(SLJ to her sister Kitty) [Draft]
Passy 11th June 1783

How shall I make you sensible my lovely sister of the inexpressible pleasure I recd. from yr. letter of the 23d Janry? The happy tidings it contained of yr health dissipated my fears, gratifyed my wishes, & I am certain had a beneficial influence on my own health which had languish'd for some time.

**Whiggs or whigs: small, wedge-shaped cakes.*

You'll be surpris'd to rec[eiv]e. so short a letter from me by Mrs. Izard, but I really intended to have forwarded others to her care before her embarkation & nothing but ill health shd. have prevented me; for my cough which before her departure had made but little progress gain'd strength very rapidly, & soon became the most violent one I have ever experienced; and as it prevented me from rest at night I found my whole frame very much rack'd by it, nor did I find the relief I expected from being bled as it continued very obstinate until I came here, when the change of air affected the cure of it. I hope we have done well in embracing Dr. Franklin's advice & joining families for the summer; for Air & Exercise we all wanted & Mr. Jay thinks he already finds a change for the better in his appetite, digestion & sleep. Maria likewise thrives, altho' she suffers from teething, & her Cousin grows as fast as ever. Poor Abbe is one third of her time confin'd with tooth-ach & another third wh the Rheumatism.

....I shd. write you still more frequently were I not so often troubled with indisposition: at present I'm troubled with a dizziness in my head which I don't expect to be free from until I lye-in, since it has attended me in similar situations every time since I've been in Europe, but I hope that in the month of Augst the cause wh[ich] occasions it will cease....

Pray tell my dear Papa how infinitely I'm obliged to him for his kind letter of Janry last; as it is the only one I've recd from him since the capture of Lord Cornwallis, you may judge if it was not welcome. I am much obliged to him for the pleasing portrait he gives me of my little boy; I could not forbear examining & re-examining the charming description, at once thanking Providence for its bounty to my child & asking blessings for those friends who have so kindly watch'd over him since his birth. I was sorry to see by my dr. Susan's letter to you that he has been again taken from Mamma: how could any one imagine that we shd. wish the child shd. be deprived of the benefit of mamma's care, or her of the amusement she took in rearing her little grand-son? It's true, while yet there was a prospect of aleviating the cares of Mr. Jay's father by the child's prattle we wish'd the project to be try'd, not doubting but Mamma's good constitution & prospect of many future years, wd. afford her opportunity for much of that kind of pleasure when the dr. old gentleman would be insensible to it, & time has justifyed our conjectures. I expect Maria will know you at the first interview if you retain yr. resemblance to the portrait I have of you for she embraces it often enough to remember it nor will she be content unless I imitate her, tho' the little puss is not aware that I rec[eiv]e. as much pleasure from it as herself....

Please to remember me affectely. to Papa, Mamma, Susan & the rest of the family & believe me to be my dear sister

yours sincerely,
Sa. Jay

On the 4th of July, the Jays celebrated the Anniversary of the Independence of the United States at Passy. Sarah Jay enclosed a copy of "the toasts Mr. Jay prepar'd for the occasion" in a letter, dated July 16th, to her sister Kitty. Since the toasts are in Sarah's hand, it has long been thought that they were given by her on the occasion of the signing of the Treaty of Paris. However, upon close reading, it is clear that they are more appropriate for an Independence Day celebration and were most likely given by John Jay on July 4, 1783.

(SLJ to her sister Kitty) Passy l6th July 1783

My dr. sister,

Captn. Barney's arrival here has made me much happier than before I recd. your last letters as I began to be discouraged by the silence of those I lov'd & flatter'd myself were my friends; the only diminution to my pleasure proceeded from an appearance of dejection of spirits in your otherwise charming letter. Should that dejection proceed from a relapse into your former indisposition, & that be occasion'd by our absence I shd. indeed be unhappy, but I hope that my dr. sister is too sensible of the intimate connection between her health & my happiness to neglect any means for the preservation of it. Will you permit me to recommend to you, what I have found vastly beneficial to me, I mean frequent anticipation of our mutual happiness at meeting: since Mr. Jay has declar'd his wish & intention to return to America next spring I seem animated by another spirit, & my health has certainly been much improved by it. How much our view of things depend upon circumstances! A year's absence from my friends would once have appear'd insupportable to me, & now, even the prolongation of absence for another year appears but like to-morrow, so much has the certainty of returning seem'd to shorten the distance between us. In like manner, I remember that while incapable of steering we were toss'd for 3 weeks on the banks of New-found-land, it was impossible to feel interested about the winds whether they came from the North or from the south; but no sooner was a port determined upon, & means invented to guide the Ship, but every breeze that fill'd our sails gave me new pleasure & I continually counted the time past as so much deducted from what we were destin'd at first to pass at sea.

On the 4th of July we celebrated the Anniversary of our Independance here at Passey, but the next I hope to celebrate in yr. company, & I'm sure that our pleasure will not be less animated even tho' we shou'd substitute butter-milk in lieu of champagne to commemorate the illustrious event. I'll inclose you a copy of the toasts Mr. Jay prepar'd for the occasion & of a song composed and sung by a french gentleman who was of our Party. How nearly my dear Kitty! does extreme felicity approach a painful sensation. I've more than once experienc'd it; nor were my feelings divested of that kind of sensibility on the 4th of July, for I found it difficult to suppress the tears that where ready to flow to ye memory of those who in struggling to procure that happiness for their country which we were then celebrating had fallen in the glorious attempt....

The idea of a return to spain was as disagreeable to me as it could have been to you, but heaven be prais'd! my apprehensions on that score are at present dispel'd. Indeed I think Mr. Carmichael who is already there the only <u>American</u> who is capable of enjoying himself there; for of all my country-men I know not his equal for duplicity of soul, or one who can so readily smile upon & court the man he hates or despises, or fawn upon the man who treats him with contempt. The pleasure he rec.

from making himself the subject of conversation has sometimes led him to relations of actions & sentiments below the dignity of a man, & much more so below the more elevated sentiments of an American. However I'm rejoiced at the prospect of his continuance in Europe as I've not the least desire of ever meeting him again in America. I think it fortunate for the tranquility of America that the artful & interested will now aim at appointments in Europe as they can here indulge any of their propensities unobserv'd by their more virtuous country-men; for shd. they remain at home their restless ambition would only lead them to excite factions & defame true patriots. But I've trangress'd the line that I propos'd to observe in my Correspondance by dipping into politicks, but my Country & my friends possess so entirely my thoughts that you must not wonder if my pen runs beyond the dictates of prudence when engaged by those subjects.

You should not my dr. sister have heard of the prospect of my increasing family lst from a stranger, had not my fears of alarming yr. apprehensions induc'd me to be silent about it. However as Captn. Barney does not sail 'till the 25th perhaps the little stranger may arrive before his departure, tho' I'm more inclin'd to think it's appearance will not be 'till Augst. Apropos of Barney, he tells me that he has a Ship very convenient for passengers; I wish most heartily that he might come to Havre next Spring that our family might sail with him; can't you propose it to Mr. Morris? Perhaps public business might be advanced by it at the same time that our convenience was promoted.

I shall be very happy to see Mr. & Mrs. Bingham at Paris; shd. the business of the American Commissioners be compleated in the course of the summer, probably Mr. Jay will have the pleasure of seeing them in England as he has some family business to transact there relative to the Legacies of Mrs. Peloquin. I wish much that he may have leisure as I think the journey wou'd be useful to him, but I've no thoughts of accompanying him, as my love of ease begins to be more predominant than my curiosity & ones ease cannot be much indulg'd when travelling with infants, nor one's mind very tranquil in leaving them wh. strangers, & you know my dr. I've no tender mother here or indulgent sisters to protect them. Maria begins to run about cleverly & grows every day more amusing; tho' she can't speak, she understands everything we say to her either in french or english. I've scarce wrote half a dozen lines without interruption either from her caresses or importunities. She has been very liberal in the kisses she has given me for her Grand-Papa, Grand-mamma, Aunts, brother, &c. at my request, but her Papa is the greatest favorite she has.

....Lady Juliane Penn & Miss Penn are vastly amiable, & as they pass the summer at Serenne, which is but a few miles from Passy, we have often the pleasure of seeing each other; except my charming friend Mrs. Lawrance, this Lady is the only one that I feel dispos'd to call Mamma. She did intend to leave France the lst of Augst. but has promis'd to postpone her departure if my family is not increas'd before that time. Her Ladyship had the goodness to send to England for a few books for Maria, & among them I think there is one that may be useful to my dr. little boy, the rest are only proper for younger children. I am sorry as far as concerns me that you've left Philadelphia, but still I'm not so selfish as not to enjoy the satisfaction wh. your return diffuses thro' the little circle at Liberty Hall. With what pleasure do I contemplate the present tranquility & security which the family enjoy. May the happiness of the family & America in general be as permanent as their endeavors to obtain it has been glorious....

I am my dr. sister

yours affectly.
Sa. Jay

Enclosure

Toasts by John Jay, July 4, 1783

1. The United States of America, may they be perpetual.
2. The Congress.
3. The King & Nation of France.
4. General Washington & the American Army.
5. The United Netherlands & all other free States in the world.
6. His Catholic Majesty & all other Princes & Powers who have manifested Friendship to America.
7. The Memory of the Patriots who have fallen for their Country. May kindness be shown to their widows & children.
8. The French Officers & Army who served in America.
9. Gratitude to our Friends & Moderation to our Enemies.
10. May all our Citizens be soldiers, & all our soldiers Citizens.
11. Concord, Wisdom & Firmness to all American Councils.
12. May our Country be always prepared for War, but disposed to Peace.
13. Liberty & Happiness to all Mankind.

(SLJ to her father) Passy 18th July 1783

My dr. Papa,

I had the pleasure of recg. your favor of the 8th Janry. some time in May, & that of the 21st of may, the 2d. of July; and sincerely thank you for those instances of your remembrance. You was very obliging my dear sir to be so minute in your account of my son, & I have reason to hope from the examples as well as precepts of those who have been so kind as to watch his education that you have not flatter'd me; tho' really but for that circumstance I should have been a little apprehensive that the pleasing description flow'd rather from the partiallity than the Judgement of his indulgent Grandfather. If any thing could have encreas'd my desire to return to America, my wish to see the dear little fellow & to evince my gratitude to his friends wou'd have been the motives. If you should think of any thing not to be easily procured in America, that would facilitate the prosecution of his studies, & will be so good as to acquaint me what it is, I'll endeavor to procure it here & bring it with me; or if there is any thing besides the garden-seeds, which you, my dear sir, are desirous of having from Europe you cannot flatter me more than by letting me know what it is, that I may have the pleasure of being the bearer of it.

Mr. [Ferdinand] Grand, who has a well chosen collection of fruits, flowers &

shrubs in his garden has promised Mr. Jay that he will order his gardener to preserve seeds of the choicest fruits &c. which he has, & we will not fail sending them out in time to be sown next spring: but don't promise yourself much from them, for really the fruits I have tasted in Europe bear no comparison to those with wh. I've been so often regal'd from your garden, excepting only the melons & grapes in Spain. The last year it's true the season was unfavorable to the fruits in France, & I have not yet this year had an opportunity of judging of the peaches & pears, which ought to be fine if ever they are for the summer is confessedly a fine one, but the earlier fruits have still maintain'd their inferiority to ours.

Can you, my dr. sir, account for the backwardness of speech in my children? Peter indeed may alledge the want of his mother's example, but what excuse can be found out for Maria who is a great deal with me, & is very active expect [sic] with her tongue? Mr. Jay imputes her not yet talking to the confusion of tongues she has heard since her birth, since she must learn two or three words to express each individual thing she would speak of; & candor obliges me to confess that I'm of that opinion, for to do her justice she does not seem to want inclination.

I am a subscriber for a little work intitled L'Ami des Enfants par M. Berquin, of wh. we receive a volume the 1st of every month; & could Peter read French I would send them to him as they were publish'd, for I really think they merit the title the Author has chosen for them, as in those little volumes the excellence of virtue & the depravity of vice is contrasted by the example of Children of amiable & unamiable characters in so natural & easy a manner as cannot fail to impress the tender & uncorrupted minds of children with proper dispositions; perhaps when I return if you have leisure, & think any of the tales may be useful to my children, you will be so obliging as to assist me in translating some of them into english for their use.

Adieu my dr. Papa! may you long enjoy health & independance the well earn'd reward of your truly patriotic conduct, & live to see your children's children following your example.

As the packets from France & England will begin to Sail in Septr. for New York, I hope the intelligence between friends will be more frequent then formerly, & if indisposition does not prevent me from writing, you shall not Papa have reason to complain of the silence of

your dutiful & affectionate daughter
Sa. Jay

(JJ to Kitty Livingston at Elizabeth Town) Passy 26 Augt. 1783

Dear Kitty

You will recieve Letters from us by Capt. Barney, who is now on the Way to Philadelphia. On the 14 Inst. I wrote to your papa that Sally had the Day before been delivered of a Daughter. The Pleasure which that Letter occasioned in the Family must have been affected by the Suspence it unavoidably left you in respecting the Progress of her Recovery. I will not therefore omit any Opportunity of giving you Information on that interesting Subject.

I thank God that she continues to gain Strength, and that the Child is well. It was baptized this morning by the name of Anne, after her excellent aunt. I pray God that both of them may live to embrace each other next Summer. Miss Sophia Penn, the Daughter of Lady Juliana Penn, is one of the Sponsors, and Mrs. F. Jay & my good Friend Egbert Benson are the others.

Your little Maria thrives charmingly, and often kisses your Picture. Happy shall we be to see her in your arms.

I am less indisposed [than I] have been, tho' not perfectly well. Assure the Family at Liberty Hall of our warm and constant regard, and believe me to be Dear Kitty

your afft. Friend & Brother
John Jay

P.S. be pleased to convey the enclosed to my Brother & write me what you may hear of my Family. Kiss my dear Boy for us.

In Paris on September 3rd, the Definitive Treaty of Peace of 1783 was signed by David Hartley for Great Britain and by John Adams, Benjamin Franklin, and John Jay for the United States. Not only did Britain formally acknowledge American independence but it also agreed to terms extremely favorable to the new nation. Perhaps most important among these was recognition of the Mississippi River as its western boundary.

Although John Jay has been criticized for negotiating separately with the British, he considered his actions to be in the best interests of the United States. The Treaty stands as testimony to his efforts.

(Marie Joseph Paul du Motier,
Marquis de Lafayette to SLJ at Paris) Wensday Morning [Sept. 3, 1783]

Marq. de Lafayette Most Respectfull Compliments Wait Upon Mrs. Jay, and Will Have the Honor to Wait Upon Her to the French Play House, But is Sorry to find the play to Be Acted is a New and a Very Indifferent One, Which, What is the Worse, Has not yet been Printed. On Saturday We Have Phaedre, a Celebrated Piece of Racine, and if that is More Convenient the Same Arrangement that Was to take Place to day, will Subsist for Saturday on Every Point. And in the Mean While, the Ms de Lafayette Would propose Mr. and Mrs. Jay's Going on Friday Next to the Opera House, Where a Celebrated piece Castor et pollux* is to be Acted, and Where He Has got a Box.

He begs Mr. and Mrs. Jay Will please to Honor Him with their Orders, and will Be Happy to Hear they Both and the little Child are in Good Health.

**A lyric tragedy by Pierre Joseph Bernard, with music by Rameau.*

(SLJ to her mother at Elizabeth Town) Passy, Sepbr 12th 1783

My dr. Mamma,

When Coll. Ogden took leave of us the day before yesterday & told me that he was going early the next morning to England, from whence he would soon embark for America, I regretted that I had not been earlier apprised of it that I might have written to you & the rest of the family, as I fear'd I shd. be prevented that evening from writing, having in the morning recd. a note from the Dutchess of Manchester, informing me of her intention of visiting me in the evening; I therefore took Coll. Ogden & Mr. Thaxter (the young gentleman who is to be the bearer of the Official accounts of the conclusion of the definitive treaty) into my room to see my little girl, not daring on account of her cold to venture her out of the room. Coll. Ogden promises me that he will not be 24 hours in Eliz. Town before he waits upon you to inform you of our health & wishes for your & our happiness in a mutual interview, which I've charg'd him to tell you we flatter ourselves will not be retarded beyond the commencement of next summer.

I long to present my little girls to you & their brother whom I long to see beyond expression. I am sorry Maria is so backward in her speech for I wish to hear her prattle. She is an affectionate little puss & is already become so necessary to my amusement that I feel uneasy when she is absent. My little Nursling was as lovely a babe as ever you saw from its birth 'till 3 weeks after but I think her already changed with her Cold which has been attended with a fever & the most severe cough I ever saw so young an infant afflicted with. To confess the truth I am not without apprehensions for her still, tho' her fever is abated. I have myself been vastly favor'd in my Lying-in, & had I been so happy as to have had my dr. mamma or sisters with me, I do believe that 4 days would have re-established my health: but the custom which prevails with you of having a careful woman used to attend ladies in that situation does not extend here, so that one is often liable to colds & other inconveniences from the inattention or ignorance of ones own attendants.

Mr. Jay has written to Papa & Kitty since the birth of my little one, & Lady Julianna Penn was so obliging as to mention that circumstance in a letter to her son, desiring him to inform Kitty of it if she was still at Philadelphia. I regret the departure of that Lady for England as she was a very attentive & very valuable acquaintance. Mr. Jay I think mention'd in his letters, that Miss Penn was sponsor to the little française & that Lady Julianna & Mr. Granville Penn were Proxeys for Mrs. Fr. Jay & Mr. Benson.

I flatter'd myself that I should have oftener had the pleasure of writing to you & the rest of the family this summer, but really I've been so tormented by tooth-ach & ear-ach that I have scarcely enjoy'd myself & have regretted that I did not, tho' contrary to the advice of my acquaintances have my teeth that were affected drawn before I lay-in, for I suffer'd so much from them that 8 days after I was obliged to send for the Dentist who happen'd to be clumsy enough to leave two prongs in the gum & then told me that I was too weak to have them extracted at that time so that with the addition of a fever I was obliged again to have recourse to patience, which tho not always a Physician, is at least a friend. I hope my dr. susan will believe that nothing but indisposition could have made me so long defer answering her kind letters....

Please to remember me to all our friends, & believe me my dr. Mamma, that I shall ever esteem that situation most eligible that places me nearest you & admits most frequently of my assuring you of the affection with which I am

your dutiful daughter
S. J.

In the fall of 1783, John Jay went to England for his health and to finish some family business in Bristol. Having had a constant pain in his chest for many months, as well as a sore throat, he decided to take the waters at Bath. While he was away, Sarah moved the family from Passy to a house at Chaillot.

(SLJ to Lady Juliana Penn) Passy Octbr 8th 1783

My dear Lady

Next to the pleasure of seeing and conversing with our friends is that of hearing from them, & I therefore owe you many thanks for conferring upon me that satisfaction by your friendly letter of sepbr: it revived in my mind the pleasure I lately enjoy'd in the society of your charming family, & flatter'd my wishes that the friendship commenced between us here might be continued & cemented by mutual recollection....

I shd. write to you my dr. Lady with twice the pleasure did not the mortifying idea perpetually occur that I am not to see you again this winter. We have just hired the new house near the iron gate between Passy & Paris: perhaps you may recollect it. It has a terrace & portico. There I might have enjoy'd your instructive society in as much tranquility as at Serenne had not your Ladyship been so cruel as to quit us. But while I regret your absence I endeavor to derive consolation from the pleasure you most certainly receive from the company of your friends & relations. My little girls whom you are so obliging as to enquire about are well. Miss Penn's little godchild is a lovely babe & nursing her agrees with me perfectly. She is at this inst. in my arms & while I am gratifying my friendship by writing I am at the same time performing the tender office of a nurse to her. Tell Miss Penn that I look upon this little poppet as one of the Cords of friendship that I hope will long unite us....

Mrs. Ridley added another son to her family the 24th of sepbr. after a moderate illness of an hour & twenty minutes & has been much heartier since her lying-in than before tho' I'm sorry her cough still continues. She thanks you for the mention you made of her in your letter to me & desires me to present her Compts. to you as well as the other Ladies you nam'd. I shall say nothing of Mr. Jay who will probably soon have the pleasure of seeing you himself as he proposes setting out for England to-morrow....

Believe me my dear Lady to be

your faithful & affecte. friend
S. Jay

(JJ to SLJ at Passy) London 15 october 1783

My dear Sally

My Letters from Calais and Dover have I hope reached you. I arrived here last night, and find myself the better for the Journey. After a week or ten Days, I shall go to Bristol, & from thence to Bath. As yet I have seen nobody except mr. v. Schaack who breakfasted with me. He is in better Health than I have seen him these fifteen Years.

I shall pass this morning in paying the visits of Ceremony due from me, and among others, to the Embassador of France. Our Friend Vaughan I hear lives three miles off, so that I shall not see him until Tomorrow. An american Paper mentions the arrival of his Family at Philadelphia. By late advices from thence, it also appears that Sr. Guy Carlton has recd. Instructions to evacuate New York. A Letter from him to Congress on the Subject, is published.

You forgot to give me the Hair you wished to have worked. It can be done here exceedingly well, and I advise You to enclose it to me.

When you see miss Walpole, let her know that the Letters & Packets she committed to my Care, were safely delivered this morning. Lady Juliana is out of Town. God bless you my dear wife.

I am affy yours
John Jay

(SLJ to JJ at London) Passey Wednesday Eveng. 15th Octbr. 1783

My dear Mr. Jay,

Mr. Ridley tells me that a gentleman who is going to England on fryday, will call at Auteuil to-morrow to take his Commands; I've therefore advis'd Peter to write this evening, & am myself too happy in hearing of the opportunity, to defer 'till to-morrow the pleasure of telling you that myself & little family are perfectly well. The day after you left us, having occasion to go into your room, Maria saw the door open, & with her usual glee when going to see you, she came running into the room, when all on a sudden disappointment succeeded expectation & her little head droop'd. I catch'd her in my arms & while embracing her, thought her still dearer to me for the sympathy I found between her feelings & my own. My little Ann still continues to thrive. Ben[oit] has been quite recovered ever since sunday; & you may banish all apprehension of Maria's having catched the disorder since there is no appearance of it.

Mr. Adams call'd upon me to day to let me know that he shall set out for England next monday, & you may rely upon my profiting of that opportunity as well as every other that offers of telling you how we all do, & if we continue as well as we are at present, I am happy to think the satisfaction you'll derive from that circumstance, will more than compensate for the time you bestow in reading my letters.

I hope by this time you have arriv'd in London without meeting with any material interruption; & that your health will be so much benefited by the journey, that you will not be obliged to prolong your stay beyond what you propos'd: for I can assure you upon my word, that I find a deficiency, a vacancy, a something wanting since your absence that even surpasses what I expected. Do not however fear that I encourage unpleasant ideas, the reverse being the case, for I flatter myself that this little excursion will re-establish your health, & in that expectation have really enjoyed the fine weather we have lately been favor'd with.

Present my Compts. to any of our friends that you may see, & believe me to be, my dearest, best of friends

most sincerely & affectly yours
Sa. Jay

(JJ to SLJ at Passy) London, Harley Street no. 30
26 Octob 1783

My dear Sally

I have had the Pleasure of recieving your Letters of the 15 & 17th Instant, & thank You for them. Since my Arrival here I have written twice to You. One of those Letters informed You of my having been taken ill of a Dysentery, & of my being then far recovered. All Remains of that Disorder are now removed; and I find myself as well as when I left You.

I have consulted Doctr. [Richard] Warren (the Physician who atended me during my late Sickness, & who is at the Head of his Profession here) about the Pain in my Breast, and the Propriety of taking the Bath waters for it. He tells me that Pain does not arise from the Lungs, that the waters of Bath may be safely used, but that altho I may expect some Good from them, yet that Exercise & Relaxation from all Business which requires much Thought and application, can alone compleat the Cure.

The Duration of my absence will be entirely regulated by the object which occasioned it, vizt. the Recovery of my Health. If that was out of the Question, I should immediately return; for I assure you the Charms neither of this Country, nor indeed of any other, are sufficiently powerful to detain me from You.

On my arrival here I took private Lodgings. Mr. Bingham & Mr. Vaughan insisted on my going with them. The former reminded me of his Invitation when at Paris, and of my not having refused to accept it. The latter pressed me in the most friendly Manner to take a Room with him. Mr. Bingham's Invitation being prior and Mrs. Vaughan being ready to lay in, I removed to Mr. Bingham's. I fear our friend Vaughan is not quite pleased.

Lord Shelbourne has sent me an Invitation to pass some Days with him at his Country House. I think it is situated between this and Bath; so that the acceptance of this Invitation will be convenient as well as agreable....

Don't be in too great a Hurry to remove to your House. Unless it should be in order to recieve You, your Residence in it will not be comfortable, at least for some Time. The first or Second Week in novr. would be early enough.

Does Maria begin to talk yet? Mrs. Bingham has a little Girl of twenty months that prattles cleverly. I hope Nancy is not too much for You. Unless your appetite continues you should cease to nurse her.

My Complts. to our Friends. I am my dear Sally,

Your very afft. Husband,
John Jay

(JJ to SLJ at Passy) London 28 October 1783
Harley Street no. 30

My dear Sally

My last to you was dated the 26 Inst and committed to the Care of Col. Wadsworth who set out for Paris this Morning. As it enclosed one for Peter I omit writing to him at present.

Yesterday Mr. Adams delivered to me your Favor of the 19 Inst. enclosing Locks of your own and our Children's Hair, which I shall endeavour to have wrought in the best manner. As yet I have seen so little of London that I can form but a very imperfect Judgmt. of it.

I was last Evening at the Drury Lane Theatre, where the celebrated Mrs. Siddons* displayed her Talents in the Character of Belvidera, to which she did ample Justice. The House is neat and well lighted, but not so magnificent as those at Paris....

A Visitor has just come in, I must therefore postpone adding any thing except that I am,

my Dear Sally,
Your very afft. Husband,
John Jay

P.S. Mr. Van Schaack who is just entered desires me to present his best Compts. to you.

John Quincy Adams and his younger brother Charles accompanied their father to the Netherlands where Mr. Adams sought to secure a loan and negotiate a treaty of commerce with the Dutch. They then traveled with their father to Paris where he joined Jay and Franklin as a peace commissioner. In 1783, John Quincy and Peter Jay Munro, both 16 years old and at school together, became good friends.

(John Quincy Adams to Peter Jay Munro at Chaillot) London Novr. 4th 1783 Tuesday

Dear Moron

On Friday evening, I went in Company with your uncle, Mr. & Mrs. Bingham and some other gentlemen to see that wonderful, wonderful, wonder of wonders Mrs. Siddons The most capital performer upon the Stage; not only of Europe, at present,

**Thomas Otway's tragedy* Venice Preserved, *with Sarah Kemble Siddons (1755–1831), was presented at the Drury Lane Theatre on October 27, 1783.*

but that ever was seen. (N.B. While I am in England, I must talk like an Englishman.) She out Garrick's Garrick, Sir, cent per cent she play'd that evening Isabella in the Fatal marriage [by Thomas Southern]: you probably know nothing of this piece: it is the deepest Tragedy I ever saw or read: and I must confess I never saw any player, so possessed of the pathetic, as this said Mrs. Siddons. All the audience were in Tears and there was a young lady in the next box to us, who was so near falling into fits that she was obliged to be taken away. I am told it is not uncommon here it happens very rarely in France now what does that argue? that there is more Sensibility in this Country? that the Tragedies are deeper? or that they are better performed? I believe there is more Sensibility here: the Tragedies are beyond doubt deeper, but if we except Mrs. Siddons I do not think, they perform a bit better here than in France....

Adieu, my dear fellow
porte toi bien
O

(SLJ to JJ at London) Chaillot, 4th Novbr 1783

My dr. Mr. Jay,

I have this day recd your letter of the 26th Ult. by Coll: Wadsworth & on Sunday Evening I was so happy as to receive that of the 28th. Accept my dr. a thousand thanks for yr. very kind attention. I am rejoic'd to hear that you have recovered from the dissentery & hope you will be equally fortunate wh. respect to the pain in yr. breast if you follow Dr. Warren's advice: and tho' I long to see you exceedingly yet I assure you, that shd. you return without the consent of yr. Phisician it wd. give me pain as well as pleasure to see you, so that I would rather deprive myself of the pleasure of seeing [you] a little longer that when we meet our satisfaction may be compleat.

Please to present my Compts. to our friends Bingham & Vaughan. I am very sensible of their hospitality. Sunday Eveng. we lodged here for the first, & I hope that in two or three days time our affairs will be quite arranged; had I waited at Passy 'till the house was quite ready for me I fancy you would have found me still there at your return, but by coming here, Mr. Poussin finds himself obliged to exert himself, & I hope that to-morrow we shall receive the rest of our furniture. I am not less pleased with our situation than I expected to be & I think you'll be equally content. I shall be very happy to see any of your friends that come here & I think we can accomodate the young gentleman you mention tolerably well.

This morng. I went to Paris to speak to Poussin & to make some purchases, & while I was gone Mr. [Thomas] Walpole call'd at the house & left me an invitation to dine with his sister & daughters & to go wh. them to the Opera; but as I return'd late I could not avail myself of his politeness.

Our friend Mrs. Ridley still continues very low, & Mr. Ridley is very uneasy, tho' he seem'd a little consoled by the opinion of Dr. Gams the English Phisician that you've seen at Passey.

I could wh. pleasure spend half the night in writing to you, were it not necessary that my letters shd. be early in the morng. in the post office at Paris. The children are very well & so is Peter who has been very useful & obliging to me since you've been gone.

My health thank God! is extremely good, & my little one thrives accordingly. Adieu my dearest

Yours sincerely,

In Paris, the Jay household was beset by domestic problems when Abbe, Sarah's personal maid, ran away. Abbe seems to have been offended by the Jay children's nurse, Louisson, and when she was offered work for pay by an English washer-woman, she seized the opportunity. Sarah's reaction to this affront was to contact the police, who took Abbe into custody and put her in "a house of confinement," where she might come to her senses. On the suggestion of Benjamin Franklin, Sarah Jay sent William Temple Franklin and her nephew Peter Jay Munro to persuade Abbe to reconsider her actions.

(SLJ to JJ at London) Chaillot, Novbr 6th 1783

My dr. Mr. Jay

This Eveng. Mr. [Henry] & Miss [Martha] Laurens favor'd me wh. their Company, & as they set out to-morrow for England I could not suffer them to go without a little token of my remembrance, & that they might be ennabled to give you an account of yr. little girls I sent for them down, & was not a little flatter'd by Miss Maria's behaviour. She does not yet speak, but she improves in her health & looks. Louisson still continues to take great care of the Children & is quite delighted wh. her new situation. As the weather is very fine she walks wh. them on the terrace & I rarely omit giving them a ride.

Every body that sees the house now is surpris'd it has so long remain'd unoccupied; it is so gay, so lively, that I am sure you'll be pleased with it. Yesterday the windows were open in my Cabinet while I was dressing & it was even then too warm. Dr. Franklin & his Grandsons & Mr. & Mrs. Cays & the Miss Walpoles drank tea wh. me likewise this Evening & they all approve yr. Choice. As the sky is very clear & the moon shines very bright we were tempted to walk from the salloon upon ye terrace & while the Company were admiring my situation, my imagination was retracing the pleasing Evenings that you & I have passed together in contemplating the mild & gentle rays of the moon. Shd. the weather be less pleasant when you return I shall be mortifyed.

It is wh. regret that I'm obliged to quit subjects that afford pleasing ideas, for one that I fear has already given you pain; but as Mr. [William Temple] Franklin tells me that he has inform'd you of Abbe's leaving Passy, my further silence about it instead of preventg. anxiety would only appear misterious. I fancy her extreme jealousy of Louisson added to the inticements of an English washer-woman who promised to pay her if she would assist her in washing, as the cause of that mis-step. She had for some time treated Louisson so uncivilly that she had told me that were it in my power to dismiss Abbe, & I still chose to keep her, she should be obliged to leave me, but that as she found that Abbe was impertinent to me, she must bear it likewise. Immediately upon finding that Abbe was gone with her Cloaths Mr. Franklin wrote to the Lieutenant of the Police who had her taken up (at that washer woman's) & put in a house of confinement. Four days after Peter went to see her as if without my knowledge, & advis'd her to let him solicit my permission for her return, but she reply'd that instead of desiring that, she would run-a-way again were I to send for her, & that she wd. remain where she was 'till yr. return, or 'till she might be sent to America instead of returning home to be laughed at & work too. As she inquir'd about the family, Peter told her that the Children were well & that my Cook seem'd a Clever woman. She said she hop'd I was then Content since she was gone for that I was intirely govern'd by Louisson.

Today Peter call'd again, telling her that as he had come to Paris to pay some visits he could not forbear calling to see if she was more reasonable, but she remain'd still obstinate. Dr. Franklin thinks I ought not to take notice of her for 15 or 20 days; but I'm so afraid of her suffering from the Cold that I think it better that Peter shd. call now & then as if by accident that she may not suffer after her repentance. Pray don't let this affair make you uneasy. The irregularity of her Conduct for some time past has made me expect the step she has taken.

When you return bring me if you please 2 Doz. Knives & a silver tea-pot & tea-bowl.

Mr. Poussin has been very dilatory indeed; we have not yet half the Kitchin furniture but I hope after a few more messages he'll think fit to comply wh. his engagement.

I believe I did not tell you that 2 or 3 weeks ago I din'd with Mr. [William] Pitt at the Marquis de la Fayette's. You can't imagine how much I'm obliged to you for your frequent letters; I wish it was in my power to make you as agreeable returns, but you are so good that you'll take the will for the deed & be content with the assurance of the sincere regard of

yr. affecte Wife
Sarah Jay

(Peter Jay Munro to JJ at London) [Draft]
Chaillot Novr. 12th 1783

Dr. Uncle

My aunt recd. your favor of 7th inst. this very evening. We were drinking tea in her toilet alone and talking when your letter and one from young Adams to me were brought in. Since tea she has been continuing a Letter she begun this afternoon to you and tho' tis but half pass 8 she has retired to take a nap, declaring to be so sleepy as not to be able to write any longer but at the same time charging me to wake her at 10. I am now setting in her place and writing with her pen.

The reason why we did not mention abby's elopement at the time arose from a desire we had of keeping you ignorant of an event the knowledge of which would make you uneasy, when it was out of your power to afford my aunt any assistance in that Case. Tho' we knew mr. Franklin had mentioned it in a Letter to you, we thought best not to say any thing about her till we were sure you had recd. his Letter. She was taken up at the request of Dr. Franklin who at the desire of my aunt wrote to Lieutenant of the Police. She is confin'd in the hotel de la force. I have payed her three visits. This increased her Ideas of her own importance and the last time I saw her she was more sullen than at either of the former …

I am Dr. uncle
your Dutiful nephew
P. J. M.

(SLJ toJJ) Chaillot, 12 November 1783

My Dear Mr. Jay,

Last sunday evening your letter of the 4th inst. enclosing one from susan was handed me at Dr. Franklin's, and the same evening I recd. another from Susan dated the 19th of July, in which she mentions Peter's having recovered from the measles. You are perfectly right in disapproving Peter's leaving Mama for frivolous visits, & I am much obliged to her for withholding her consent.

I regret exceedingly those succeeding attacks which have prevented yr. journey to Bath, but hope before this that the inflamation of yr. throat has ceeded to prudent measures, but do not suppose that you will leave London 'till after you have seen the Ceremony that will attend the Prince of Wales's first taking his Seat in the house of Lords.

I hope the weather is fine in England for we have had a most enchanting Autumn here. You'll be pleas'd wh. our situation when you return, for which I most ardently long, tho' I would not have you leave England until you have given it a fair tryal.

From one of susan's letters it appears that brother Peter was already at Rye in July, and I can easily figure to myself the zeal with which he is endeavoring to restore order to the house and farm with the double expectation of immediate convenience & the hopes of procuring an agreeable surprise for you. This instant Ben has brought in a letter from Mr. Adams for Peter and one from you dated the 7th for me. I thank you my dr. for the repeated marks of your attention, & assure you, that if you do not hear as frequently from me it must be owing to the miscarriage of my letters, not to negligence since I have written 6 or 7 times at least.

Peter and the Children are very well, as well as myself. Maria's constitution seems to have regain'd its' former strength & my little Nancy is a perfect Cherub, without making the least allowance for the partiallity of a mother. Apropos, I am very much pleas'd with the plan you have design'd for my bracelet & sh'd it be well executed wd. entirely ans'r my wishes.

Yesterday morning Madame Cays & myself accompanied by Mr. F[ranklin], Peter and Ben, breakfasted with Major Monchfort at the Invalides & he was so polite as to attend us thro' the different appartments & explained to us the various designs in the Dome, which is really a most magnificent piece of architecture. The major told me that when the Emperor [Joseph II of Austria] visited it, he inquired of his Guide (who was ignorant of his Rank) whether the Door in the Dome might not be open'd, but was answered that it was only opened when the fête Dieu was celebrated, upon which the Emperor demanded if it was not open'd when the King came there? You may judge of the Emperor's surprise upon being told that the King had never been, for he immediately declared that he would desire him to come, & by the expression discovered his real rank upon which the man offer'd to open the Door but the Emperor would not permit him....

Adieu my dr. Mr. Jay. May Heaven soon restore you to Health and Me.

Yours affectionately,
Sa. Jay

Have I reminded you that when you return we shall have occasion for some plain English Knives. This Evening Count Montmorin call'd upon me, & desir'd his Compts. to you.

(JJ to SLJ at Chaillot) London, 14 Novr 1783

My dear Sally

However my Letters may be short and unentertaining, you will I am sure give me Credit for Punctuality, especially if you recieve as many from the Post Office as I send to it....

I have Invitations to pass some time in the Country with Mr. [William] Baker and Mr. [Richard] Penn, but am too anxious to be with you again, to avail myself of the Civilities of those and many other Gentlemen of this Country. I was yesterday at the Royal Society and afterwards spent the Evening with the Club of honest Whigs,* at the Head of which is the celebrated Doctr. [Richard] Price. Their first Toast was their absent Member Dr. Franklin of whom they spoke with Great Respect and affection.

America has many excellent Friends in England, and I may also say, many implacable Enemies. This People is immersed in Pleasure, and yet very far from being happy. A Stranger finds among them much to commend and much to blame. Nothing has as yet exceeded my Expectations, and I shall probably return to America fully persuaded that Europe collectively considered is far less estimable than America.

My Throat continues exactly the same. I shall probably set out for Bath on Wednesday next. Remember me to all our Friends. I long to be with You. God bless you my Dear Wife. I am

your very affte. Husband,
John Jay

P.S. Littlepage is here, for what purpose I know not.

**An informal London supper club known for its liberal politics.*

(SLJ to JJ) Chaillot, 18 November 1783

My dear Mr. Jay,

Last Saturday I was so happy as to receive yr. kind letter of the 10th & 11th instant. From the number, I perceive that not one has miscarried. I hope before this you've receiv'd a letter from me that was intended for the post, tho' by mistake detain'd too long, which Dr. De Butte has promised Peter to take charge of. In my letter, favor'd by Mr. Laurens, you have Abbe's history. She still remains where she then was. Peter offered her permission to return if she would behave well, but she refused to accept it, saying that she was very happy where she was for that she had nothing to do. Her being at Passy where she had so little occupation has been of great dis-service to her....

Today, & two or three days past, we have had windy, rainy weather & the Chimneys have smoked very much. Would you believe that I receive as much pleasure from the stormy weather as I did from the fine? It proceeds from the regret I had during the fine weather that you did not participate [in] it, & the hope I now have that the sun will again re-visit our mansion at yr. return....

Dr. Franklin charges me to present you his Compts. whenever I write you, but forbids my telling you how much pains he takes to excite my jealousy at your stay. The other evening at Passy he produced several pieces of steel, the one he suppos'd you at Chaillot, which being plac'd near another piece which was to represent me, it was attracted by that & presently united; but when drawn of[f] from me & nearer another piece which the Dr. called an english Lady, behold! the same effect. The Company enjoy'd it much & urged me to revenge, but all could not shake my confidence in my beloved friend. The Doctor has just sent me word that he will drink tea with me this Evening notwithstanding the storm....

The Children & myself enjoy perfect health, & I h[ope] [it] will not be long before my dear Mr. Jay will be able in person to make the same declaration of himself to his

ever affectionate Wife,
Sa. Jay

(Peter Jay Munro to JJ at London) Chaillot the 20th Novr. 1783

Dr. Uncle,

Young Mr. [John Quincy] Adams has Informed me that he never saw you look so well as you do at present: I am glad to hear it. Tho I long for your arrival, I hope you will not return before you are quite rid of all your complaints: my aunt says the same. Is the inflamation in your throat of the same kind as that which gave you so much pain & trouble some years ago?

As you say nothing of England in any of your letters, we expect you will tell us a great deal at your return.

Aunt Jay and the Children are well. Nancy is but little trouble to her mamma. Before I conclude I must tell you a Punn made up on you and Mr. Fox. I saw it in the Courier de l'Europe. Perhaps you have heard of it. A London wit hearing that you and Mr. Fox had had a conference, "Bon, dit il, nous y voila donc revenus au tem[p]s d'Esope, ou les Quadrupedes et les Oiseaux avoient le don de la Parole." ["Well, he said, we are once more in the time of Aesop, when four-legged creatures and birds had the gift of gab."]*

When you see my Father remember me to him, and believe me to be

Dr. Uncle
Your Dutiful Nephew
P. J. Munro

P.S. I have been so unfortunate as to break my penknife and I would be very much obliged to my uncle if he would bring me another.

In England, Dr. Robert Sutton and his sons worked to modify the technique for smallpox inoculation. Their method involved a shallow incision, rather than a deep one, and the use of infectious matter from another inoculee, rather than from a victim of the natural smallpox. The Suttons required that their inoculees be quarantined from the general public. This technique produced good results and fewer complications than previous methods.

(SLJ to her sister Kitty) Chaillot 22d Novbr. 1783

Its paying you but an ill compliment my dear sister to tell you that my intention is to scold you heartily for forgetting me, or at least for being too indolent to tell me that you do not....

My little Maria is as busy as a bee next to me & nothing less than pen & paper will satisfy the little mimick. As to little Ann, she is one of the loveliest children I've ever seen, always dispos'd to laugh & rarely cries. Yesterday I sent for a Physician to consult about the propriety of innoculating the children, but he appeard unwilling & told me he would ask mr. Sutton, an english innoculator to wait upon me. I confess the hesitation of Dr. James has a little stagger'd my resolution; but if Sutton thinks it safe, I wd. fain surprise Mr. Jay, as it will spare his feelings, tho' I know my own anxiety will be increas'd. How often! my dr. Kitty do I reflect upon the anxious moments that Mamma has pass'd for us— nothing surely can equal the Cares or transports of a Parent.

I hope that by the time we arrive in America some of our friends will be already re-established at New York. Have you been there yet? Susan gives a distressing picture of it.

The servant has just announced Dr. Sutton. My heart palpitates with doubt whether or not to put my intention in execution. Kiss my sweet little boy & believe me my dr. Kitty to be yours

affectionately
Sa. Jay

The pun refers to Charles James Fox (1749–1806), British foreign secretary at the time.

(JJ to SLJ at Chaillot)

London, 23 Novr 1783
Harley Street No. 30

My dear Sally,

....It gives me great satisfaction to hear that you are so well pleased with your House &c. I am anxious to participate with you in ye Comforts you mention. Sun Shine is a Rarity here, and "the Light of wax Candles" is a poor substitute for it. Is it not strange that Maria should not speake yet. Mrs. Bingham's Little girl of the same age prattles not a little.

I am much displeased with Abbys conduct. I think with the Doctr. that it would be best to suspend all attention to her for some Time. I hope she is separated from Wine and improper Company, and that, without being indulged in the Conveniencies, she has all the Necessaries of Life. If so, Sobriety Solitude and want of Employment will render her Temper more obedient to Reason. I am glad the other Servants behave well. I shall not forget your orders, and will readily execute any others you may favor me with.

My Throat continues a little inflamed. The next Letter you will recieve from me, will be dated at Bath, where my Stay shall not be a moment longer than the object of my going there may require. I am really home Sick, & find few Things more unpleasant than absence from my Family, A Smile from you and the Caresses of our little ones are worth more to me Than all the Pleasures of this Town.

Mr. & Mrs. Bingham, to whose very friendly attention I am much indebted, present their Comps to You. Remember me to Peter, and our Friends at Passy and Auteuil.

I am my dear Sally,
Your very affe.
John Jay

In June 1783, the first practical balloon, a large linen bag filled with hot air, rose over the town of Annonay, south of Lyon. The Montgolfier brothers, Joseph and Etienne, were responsible for its conception and construction. On September 19 a Montgolfier balloon was launched from Versailles, and on the 21st a manned flight rose from the château de la Muette in Paris. The latter flight is considered to be the first time human beings flew. A competitor, Jacques Charles, also sent balloons aloft over Paris, but these were filled with inflammable hydrogen. The public was enthalled, as was Sarah Jay, who witnessed at least two of these flights.

(SLJ to JJ)

Chaillot, 27 November 1783

My Dear Mr. Jay,

I had not received a letter from you of a later date than the 14th inst. until last evening, when your two letters of the 18th and 21st were handed me.... I am delighted to find you begin to wish yr. return & can answer that a sister-sentiment has long since found a place in my own breast: but since you are absent, rather prolong yr.

stay as long as may be necessary for yr. health than by returning too soon leave occasion to regret not having given the waters of Bath a sufficient tryal.

You'll find by my other letters that my little family was perfectly well when I wrote, & heaven be praised! we still continue so. The weather here is really delightful, & now that we are a little settled I shd. like to inoculate the Children, if you approve of it. The famous Inoculator, Dr. Sutton is here; so that if upon reflection you think it wd. be proper let me know.

The Coachman's wife was brought abed of twins the day before yesterday, & as he is anxious to see her, I can't detain him, but will write you a longer letter to-morrow.

Good night my Love,
Sa. Jay

Peter's letter is not yet ready, so that I've time to tell you that a Globe of Montgolfiers went up the other day from the Muette with two persons in a gallery that was fix'd to it: after the cord that detain'd it was cut, it asscended three thousand feet high, & the gentlemen that were attach'd to it, observing at one time that it descended rather to rapidly, threw into it a little more straw, & then it again mounted, by which means they remained in the air 'till they had gone from the place from whence they set out to Paris, pass'd over the whole City, 'till at length concluding they had stay'd as long as the experiment required, suffered themselves to descend gradually near the Boulevards, without having expended more than a third part of the straw they had provided. Next Saturday Monsr. Charles will entertain the public wh. a like experiment of a Globe fill'd wh. inflammable Air.

Don't you begin to think of taking yr. passage next Spring in a Ballon?

God bless you.

(JJ to SLJ at Chaillot) Bath 29th Novr 1783

My Dear Sally

Your kind Letters of the 12 and 18 Novr. which are the last I have recd. gave me great Pleasure. The apprehensions excited by the Lapse of three long weeks without a Line from You, were painful, & formd. a strong Contrast to the agreable Emotions occasioned by these chearful and affectionate Letters....

The English call this an uncommon fine autumn. It would not be commended in America.

... My sore Throat has abated a little, tho but very little. I impute it to the Climate, & I hope soon to quit the former with the latter. Lady Juliana told me it first appeared here about twenty years ago.

It gives me Pleasure to hear our Friend the Doctr. is in such good Spirits. Tho

Opposite: **Hot air balloon ascent with two men, October 19, 1783, from Paris. The ornate balloon, with Pilâtre de Rozier and Girond de Villete on board, reached an altitude of 330 feet. Library of Congress, Prints & Photographs Division, LC-DIG-ppmsca-02445.**

his magnets love Society, they are nevertheless true to the Pole, and in that I hope to resemble them. Make my Comps. to him and the young Doctr. Believe me I am as anxious to return, as you can be to see me. This has been a long Separation. May it soon & happily terminate. God bless and preserve you my Dear Wife.

I am yours affectionately
John Jay

Kiss our dear little Girls for me. Notwithstanding my being here, direct your Letters for me to the care of Wm. Bingham Esqr. Harley No. 30 London.

(SLJ to JJ) Chaillot, 30 November 1783

My Dr. Mr. Jay,

Your two letters of the 21st & one of the 23rd inst. have given me a degree of mortification that wd. be difficult for any one unacquainted with strong attachments to conceive. I flatter'd myself that not only Mr. Laurens had long since arrived in London, but also that you had receiv'd my letters of the 12th & 18th, & that those of the 20th & 27th would not have left a sufficient interval in your intelligence to have occasioned uneasiness. Did I not still hope that some of those little messengers of tenderness were from time to time arriving w[it]h evidence of my attention, I should be inconsolable, for really I wd. rather you should think me dying than suppose me indifferent where your pleasure is concern'd. If the Post did not go early tomorrow I shd. defer writing 'till the morning, for what with the too apparent, tho' half conceal'd doubts of my attention which your letters betray, & Dr. Franklin's telling me that you write him that you have not enjoy'd one day's health since you left France, I am so dejected that I can scarcely know what I say. Pardon me, my Love. I fear you are not candid & that while you amuse me with accounts of a sore throat you are more seriously indispos'd. Kind heaven! Avert my fears.

I'll endeavor to divert my uneasiness by re-perusing the latter part of your last letter.

You ask me if it is not strange that Maria does not yet begin to speak? I think it is & regret it, for there is something vastly amusing in observing the young ideas as they begin to shoot. The Children are both perfectly well at present, & if they continue so 'till yr. return, I'll answer for their recompensing you for any pleasures you'll leave behind. I don't know whether it's good policy to tell you so often what a sweet little babe my Nancy is, but really I love to anticipate your pleasure. You never saw a little creature more fond than Maria is of her sister, & I often find a trickling tear stealing down my face while regarding her caresses. Whether from a regret that you do not participate [in] that pleasure or from what other cause I leave you to decide, but certain I am there is a luxury in the sensation that I wd. not exchange for any other but the pleasure of seeing you.

Tomorrow Monr. Charles will entertain the public with the sight of a very large Globe which is to ascend from the Tuilleries, w[it]h a kind of Carr attach'd to it in which two persons will sit. As I can see it as well from the terrace as the Garden I'll inclose my ticket which may serve to give you an idea of it. Peter is writing to you & will, I suppose, give you further accounts of it as well as of the Procession at Paris when the Declaration of Peace was proclaim'd there.

For my own part I shd. be delighted to contribute to your amusement, but to tell the truth my uneasiness has made me more stupid than ever. Take care of yr. health, banish anxiety & believe me to be my dearest Life,

Yr. very affectionate
Sa. Jay.

(SLJ to JJ) Chaillot, 2d Decbr 1783

I wrote you my dr. Mr. Jay the night before last & as the post goes to-morrow, tho' no change has happened in the family, I will not omit writing, least you shd. fear there had. I was very much dejected that evening, but feel better now because I hope yr. anxiety has ceas'd with the arrival of the mail, which I hear had been detained.

You may recollect I then told you, that the next day Messrs. Charles & Robert were to make experiments with a very large Balloon fill'd with inflammable air; which they according did, asscending in a Carr exactly represented in the ticket I then sent you; which was supported by Cords that fastened it to a net that was thrown over the upper part of the Globe. Thro' the Globe pass'd a tube that descended into the Carr, which by means of a string serv'd to let out the air from the top at the discretion of the gentleman. The Balloon as before was made of taffeta & covered with elastic-gum. Nothing could have better answer'd their expectations, for they found themselves sufficiently masters of it, to make it rise or descend at pleasure, by means of the ballast they provided, for they took up as many sacks of sand as the Globe could raise, which made their Asscent very gradual, & when they chose to mount still higher they threw out some of the sand. It was 40 min. before two when they left the Garden, & as the wind was very gentle it remain'd a long time in sight.

The Dukes of Cha[r]tres & Fitz-James I am told, by taking relays follow'd it's Course, & arriv'd ¼ before 4 at a Village 9 leagues from Paris at the inst. the Balloon descended. There Mr. Robert alighted, & Mr. Charles remaining in the Carr, took the Certificates of those gentlemen & of the Curates of that & the neighboring villages; after which taking in some earth to replace the weight it had left by the descent of Mr. Robert, tho' not an equal proportion, Mr. Charles remounted to make some observations with the instruments he had provided for that purpose & went a league & an half further, but with much greater rapidity.

There is I am told an account of those transactions in the Journal de Paris of to-day, & I therefore sent to Doctr. Franklin for his, but while Lewis was gone, young Mr. F. call'd in to see me, & I told him I had sent for the paper to send to you. After he was gone Lewis stay'd a considerable time, & then return'd with it, but with a request that I would send it back to-night or early in the morn'g, as it was to be sent to England: so I order'd Lewis to return with it immediately with my thanks to the Doctr. & then to go to Auteuil & beg Mr. Ridley's.

I forgot to mention that a short time before the Cords that detain'd the great Balloon were cut, a little Globe of 4 feet diameter was sent up to amuse the people; & what appears extraordinary, was it's taking a direct contrary course from that which the other immediately after went & seems to prove that the wind differs at the same inst. at different heights, so that if the Balloon cannot lay too, it may at least avoid the effects of an opposite wind by diving or soaring. I am inform'd that the Gentlemen made some curious experiments while detach'd from earth & that they will be related in the Journal to-morrow. If they are I'll send it to you.

Lewis has just return'd with the paper & Mr. Ridley's Compts. to you. It's late, for I defer'd writing till I could have some tidings of a subject that I knew would before long become an important topic at your tea tables as well as of all ranks of people here. We are all very well & if I had 4 balloons to make a mercury of a common messenger you shd. not be 24 hours without hearing of us. Tell me in yr. next exactly how you do, how you rest, & how your appetite is. God bless you.

Your affecte. Wife

(SLJ to JJ) Chaillot, 4th Decbr. 1783

My dear Mr. Jay,

I long for a letter from you that will inform me of the rect. of some of those little fugitives, whose delay had occasioned you so much anxiety. I believe that none of your letters have miscarried, at least before the 23rd. Ult.; since which I've not heard from you, & therefore conclude you are gone to Bath, & that I shall receive a few lines on sunday. Peter recd. a letter last Eveng. from Mr. Adams in which he tells him that you was to leave London the 26th. Myself & family still continue well, & I shd. be happy could I flatter myself that you are so likewise, but what you wrote Mr. Franklin still dwells upon my mind & damps my hopes: I will not however regard only the mauvaise jamb, but continue to indulge the expectation of agreeable tidings from Bath. If I was not a nurse as well as Wife, I don't think I could command myself as well as I do, but the welfare of my child renders every effort for tranquility necessary.

Tuesday Evening I told you that Messrs. Charles & Robert had the day before made a tryal of their new-invented Machine. The next day they returned to Paris & recd. the Compts. of persons of the first distinction, and in the evening sup'd with the Duke de Chartres at the Palais-Royal, whither they were followed with the acclamations of a Crowd of People. This last essay has made more noise than any of the proceeding ones, & seems to have confirm'd the general idea of great utility resulting from the discovery. According to the calculation of Monsr. Charles wh. was made by means of the instruments he had with him, our adventurers were 1500 toises above the earth, which you know is equal to nine thousand feet. I hear he intends publishing an account of his observations, but 'till I can get them, I must content myself with sending you a print of the Globe....

Shan't I have the pleasure of your company at Christmas? Let me know what letters you've recd. from me since the 6th of Novbr.

I am my dr. Mr. Jay
Your affte. wife
S. Jay

(SLJ to JJ) [Draft]
Chaillot 7th Decbr 1783

My dear Mr. Jay,

As I have wrote you three letters last week, & having nothing new to tell you, I might say with the school-boys, that this is to let you know that I am well, hoping you are so likewise....

On Fryday, Peter call'd to see Abbe; she beg'd he would solicit leave for her return. As I fear'd she would not receive benefit from the society she had, I granted her request; & am glad to find her penitent & desirous to efface by her future Conduct the reproach her late mis-step has merited.

The Children are well & Peter I suppose will tell you that he is for he is now writing to you.

The Countess d'Artois has lost her only daughter & I really feel for her, for she is a princess of an amiable character & vastly fond of her children. Let me hear from you soon, for suspense is painful to

Your affecte. wife
Sa Jay

(JJ to SLJ at Chaillot) Bath 8 December 1783

My dear Sally

I have this moment received your agreable and affecte. Letters.... It gives me very sincere Pleasure to hear that you and the Children are well. God grant you and they may continue so. The civil Things (if I may use that Expression) which you say of Nancy raises my Curiosity as well as affords me Pleasure. It is a pleasing Subject.

I entirely approve of you having them both inoculated by Dr. Sutton. We may not have such another opportunity, and I think it ought not to be neglected. I fear the Coachman thinks his Wife too bountiful. How hard it is that such interesting Blessings should be marred by straightened Circumstances! Make him some Present on the occasion. He is a good Fellow & will thank you for it.

...I thank you for the Print* you enclosed, and the account you give me of Montgolfier's Experiment. I wrote to you and to Peter last post. Remember me to him and to our Friends at Passy and Auteuil.

Adieu my Dear Wife
Yours affecy.
John Jay

**An engraving by Charles de Lorimier of Montgolfier's balloon ascent; Jay later sent it on to Congress.*

(JJ to SLJ at Chaillot) Bath 10 Decr. 1783

My dear Sally

The number of this Letter will shew how frequently I write to you. I am persuaded you derive pleasure from it, and I assure You the moments I devote to that Employment are among the most agreable I pass. The 30 of Novr. is the Date of the last Letter I have recd. from you. Mine to you of the 8th Inst. mentions its having come to Hand. Lest that Letter should miscarry I again inform you that your Proposal to have the Children inoculated meets with my perfect approbation, and I wish you would without Loss of Time consult with Doctor Sutton about it; & if he thinks it adviseable, to let him do it. The season of Year appears to me to be favorable, and I presume from the accounts you have given of their Health, that they are in a proper State for the Purpose but of this you who are with them, & the Doctor who is on the Spot, can best determine. I know of no objection & therefore am clearly of opinion that so good an opportunity of having them inoculated should not be omitted, provided Circumstances, of which I am ignorant, do not forbid it.

There is a Report here that Doctr. Franklin is very much indisposed. I hope it is not true, and I doubt it the more as your Letter makes no mention of it....

I am very desirous to hear of our dear little Boy, and of our friends of Poughkeepsie and Eliz. Town. It is long since Caty has written to either of us, which is the more singular as she lives so near to new York, from whence several vessels have arrived in England since I left you.

I shall go in the Course of three or four Days to Bristol to compleat the settlemt. of certain affairs there after which I think my stay here will not be long. I am impatient to be with you, & to take our little ones in my arms. God bless you my dear wife. I am sincerely & affecty

Yours
John Jay

Remember me to Peter, & all our Friends at
Passy & Auteuil

(SLJ to JJ) Chaillot, 11 December 1783

My dr. Mr. Jay,

The arrival of several posts without any letters from you, as seventeen days had elapsed since the date of your last, had in spite of my endeavors to the contrary dejected my spirits; not that I thought you negligent, but because I feared some accident had prevent'd your writing. But last evening your letter of the 29th Ult. restored the tranquility of my mind, which had indeed been likewise interrupted by another cause. Will it be necessary before I relate the other reason for my anxiety to ask your forgiveness for the measure I adopted without attending your approbation. The tenderness of your friendship for me, will I know make you jealous of my having any cause for anxiety conceal'd from your knowledge & participation & it is on that score alone I fear your displeasure.

You may recollect my dear, that in one of my letters I requested yr. opinion about the inoculation of our Children. After I had written, upon more mature reflection, I concluded I already knew your sentiments sufficiently to Authorise my having the operation perform'd if Mr. Sutton should think it advisable, & that by attending the event without letting you know it, I should spare you a degree of solicitude that wd. be unavoidable & perhaps retard the recovery of your health. I therefore the next day sent for the Doctor, & finding him very sanguin about the success of it, I immediately prepared myself and children according to his directions, & a day or two after he inoculated them.

For 8 days after, they were both so well that I could with great sincerity assure you of their health every time I wrote, & last Sunday evening after I had finished my letter Louisa came into the parlour to let me know that she fear'd my little one was going into convulsions. She looked so terrify'd that Peter catch'd the alarm & you may suppose I did not remain insensible, but recollecting your fortitude upon a former distressing occasion I endeavored to imitate it, & desiring them to be calm, I took the babe in my lap & made Louisa hold a bason of luke warm water in which we bathed her feet about a quarter of an hour, sitting in a current of air, after which I walk'd with her in the dining room, the windows & doors being open, but the Child well cover'd except her head, 'till midnight when her fever was exceedingly abated and she fell into a sweet sleep that continued 'till morning, when we observed that several pustules had made their appearance.

In the morning when the Doctr. visited me he assured me that all danger was then over, & that the measures I had taken prevented her from having convulsions. Fortunately Maria's simptoms did not appear 'till the next evening, and then after a very smart fever the small pox discover'd itself; since which they have been bravely, & to-day quite gay & well. Sunday or Monday the Doctr. will give them medicine to carry off the humors & he begs me to assure you that they are quite recovered.

When shall I receive such charming tidings from you as that you likewise are perfectly recovered? You have stated your return upon such a footing, that much as I long to see you, I dare not yet wish it. Doctr. Franklin tells me that while he was in England he rarely saw an American there but what was troubled with a sore throat sometime after his arrival, & therefore shd. you not receive that benefit from Bath which we hop'd, I think with you that you'll get rid of the sore throat by leaving England....

I told you, I think that Abbe had returned: she has a violent Cold. As I've prevail'd upon her to remain in bed, I hope she'll recover in a week or two. As I have not slept for several nights on account of the Children I hope I shall to night rest well, for they are both in a sweet sleep.

Be assured my dear Mr. Jay that I enjoy my health perfectly and that I am most sincerely and affectionately

yours,
Sa. Jay

(JJ to SLJ at Chaillot) Bath 26 Decr. 1783

My dear Sally

...My approbation of your Proposal to inoculate the Children, was conveyed in three different Letters. I commend your Fortitude and rejoice with you in the Success of it. I am indeed happy & thankful that they are both recovered. I lament Abbys Death. It would have given me great Pleasure to have restored her in Health to our own Country. I am persuaded of your attention to her, and think with you, that her being at Home, and well taken Care of, are Circumstances of Consolation. The Situation of the Family during their Illness must have pressed hard upon you, & tho' the Recovery of our dear little Girls doubtless gave new Vigour to your Spirits, yet I fear they have been too much agitated by the variety as well as Degree of Emotions which you have lately experienced. That Consideration makes me extremely anxious to be with you, & were it not for the Bristol Business (to finish which I wait for Papers to be sent me from London by Mr. V. Schaack) I would set out for France Tomorrow morning. Let me entreat you my dear Sally to continue tranquil and composed. Amuse yourself a little by seeing your Friends at their Houses and at yours. I need not remind you that People passing thro' this World are not to expect to have all the way strewed with Roses. Let us be grateful for Blessings, & resigned to adverse Incidents.

I shall write to Mr. Johnson on the Subject of a Maid such as you mentioned. My Absence shall not be a Moment longer than may be unavoidable. My Health mends, and if with you would mend faster.

God bless and preserve you & our little ones. My Love to Peter, & Compts. of the Season to the Doctr. & our other Friends.

I am my Dear Sally,

Your affft. Husband
John Jay

(Kitty Livingston to JJ at Paris) Elizabeth Town Decr. 30. 83

Permit me my dear Sir to wish you and Sister, the Compliments of the season, and to assure you that no one more sincerely wishes the ensueing year may be propitious to your every wish than your friend who has now the pleasure of writing to you....

The Legislature of this State having risen we are hourly expecting my Father home. By the enclosed letter you will see its determined that Master Peter stays with us this Winter. He is very ambitious to write equal to his Aunt Susan his instructer. This morning as I was looking over him I read his copy for the day—Commend virtuous deeds. I must do more than that says he I must imitate them. He has read Robinson Crusoe & Don Quixote; he is now reading Nature Delineated [by Noel Antoine Pluche] and is exceedingly pleased with the natural History they contain. He begins the exercise of the day and closes the same with reading a few Chapters in the Bible. He has learnt many of the hymns in the book you sent him & frequently expresses a great desire to see you and his Mamma. He enjoys good health and is often complimented with having his Mamma's complextion. It is indeed sun and frost proof. His under teeth are like Sally's, the upper ones that have made their appearance are rather larger, they are perfectly white, but foul the soonest of any I ever saw. As we have paid attention to drawing the decayed & those that were in the way, they have every chance of being sound and well cut....

Kiss Sally and your sweet babes for me, and I'll pay you with interest when we have the pleasure of meeting....

Yr. Affecte F[riend] & S[ister], CWL

After an absence of several months, John Jay returned to Paris from London on January 22nd, 1784. While anxious to depart for New York, he wished first to settle the unfinished business of his accounts in Madrid. On leaving that city, the Jays had not given up the lease on their house or settled other financial business, diplomatic as well as personal. William Carmichael, who was in charge of tidying their affairs, had been extraordinarily slow in doing so; he finally arrived in March. The accounts were so complicated that it took until May 12th to settle them (Carmichael to John Jay, 12 May 1784).

The Jays left Paris on May 16th for England and sailed from Dover for New York on June 1st. Before their departure, Sarah Jay received the following note from the Marquise de la Fayette:

> The moment of departure which I have dreaded for some time is here.... Accept my wishes for a happy voyage, for the better health of M. Jay, & I beseech you to remember me sometimes, and then I hope that you will send me your news.... embrace your sweet little girls several times for me....

PART III

The Demands of Public Service and Family

November 28, 1784–July 13, 1793

The Jays arrived in New York City on July 24, 1784, after four and a half years abroad. Now that America was independent, John felt that he had done his duty in serving his country; he intended to return to private life and to his legal practice. No sooner had the family landed than John received the news that Congress had elected him to fill the vacant post of secretary for foreign affairs. His experience in dealing with the governments of France, Great Britain, and Spain made him an excellent choice.

Yet John did not immediately accept the appointment. In the next months he negotiated with Congress for an operating budget, more autonomy in choosing his clerks, and the promise that Congress would meet in New York. Before he was sworn in on Dec. 21, 1784, he was also elected a New York delegate to Congress.

As chief diplomatic officer, John Jay's wish was "to see the United States assume and merit the character of ONE GREAT NATION" (10 May 1785). In the next five years, he attempted to make his department more efficient, promoted the welfare of the United States as a whole and negotiated with other nations. All reports from abroad were funneled through the secretary to Congress, which would then frequently endorse his recommendations. However, sectional partiality as well as the poverty of the United States government, and his perceived defects of the Articles of Confederation often prevented Jay from reaching satisfactory conclusions in his dealings. Violations by both Great Britain and America of the terms of the peace treaty were serious problems. Discussions with Spain on the right to navigate the Mississippi River dragged on. Being secretary was a frustrating job, yet Jay's political influence increased daily. The French Consul General wrote home, "Congress appears to govern itself only by [Jay's] impulses" (10 January 1786). Of course, his power also aroused the enmity and jealousy of some members of Congress, but most continued to view him as honest, prudent, and patriotic.

John Jay's greatest asset was his wife Sarah. Happy to be home and reunited with her son and parents, she gracefully took on the role of hostess and aided John in his diplomatic duties by entertaining many important political figures. Her dinners were renowned and must have been delightful occasions. Abigail Adams Smith wrote to her mother on May 20, 1788:

> Yesterday we dined at Mrs. Jay's, in company with the whole *corps diplomatique*. Mr. Jay is a most pleasing man, plain in his manners, but kind, affectionate, and attentive; benevolence is stamped in every feature. Mrs. Jay dresses showily, but is very pleasing on a first acquaintance. The dinner was *à la Française*, and exhibited more of European taste than I expected to find.

(SLJ to JJ) Elizabeth Town 28 Nov 1784

Accept my dr. Mr. Jay a thousand thanks for yr. two charming letters. Were you not so tenderly attentive how much less happy shd. I be! I am glad, since Congress have not yet made a House, that you proceeded on to Philadelphia, & likewise that you've had some very fine weather to facilitate seeing yr. friends. I think that place must seem nearly as naturel to you as N. York, since it is from society that most places receive their stamp, & there we had a very agreeable circle of acquaintances....

The inst. I told Peter that you wd. be happy to receive a line from him, he ran for his pens & without hesitation began his letter; & I was very much pleased to observe that he wrote without study or difficulty as if happy in an opportunity to evince his obedience.

This evening the post will arrive, & I flatter myself that in the mail there is a little messenger of Love to gladden my heart & keep alive that softener of absence, all-chearing hope. Have you recd. my letter of the 21st. inst.? If you have, I suppose in yr. next I shall be favor'd with directions about Peter's schooling. Don't you think it wd. be well to write to Mr. Barclay to inquire whether he ever heard of the safe arrival of our China at Havre de Grace & if he has, to whom it was consigned. Perhaps if we know in whose care it was, Mr. Swanick might put you in a way to get it to Philadelphia....

Our little ones grow charmingly & are daily more interesting. The more I observe Peter, the more striking I find the resemblance he bears to his Grand-father. Mamma & family desire to be affectionately remembred to you: please to present my Compts. where you know my esteem is already placed. My Love is all your own.

Farewell & happiness attend you.
Sa. Jay

Only think of the naughty Post! Not a line: the next will be more favorable.

(SLJ to JJ at Trenton) Elizabeth Town, 5 Dec 1784

My dr. Mr. Jay,

Your letter of the 28th reached me last fryday; & from the date of that & yr. former letter I find that both were written at the same times, perhaps the same inst. that mine to you were wrote, & I enjoy'd the idea that we had been mutually employed in marking our attention to each other at the same inst. of time. How happy for us my Love! that space seperates not the minds as well as persons, for otherwise absence would be deplorable indeed. Mr. Renden informs me that Congress are at length assembled & I'm glad of it, for I now hope that by Christmas you'll be at liberty to pay me the promised visit.

As I suppose you are now at Trenton I conclude my letters have reached you. Since they were wrote the School master has left Eliz. Town, & it is now no longer in our option to place Peter wh. him. What therefore must be done? His Grand-father expects to return in a fortnight or three weeks, & then hopes to have the sole care of him. I confess I shd. regret the loss of his writing, which is yet by no means established tho' in a very fair way; & Mr. McWorther thinks that writing his lessons will entirely spoil it; nor will his cyphering, reading & spelling be more advanced at New-Ark. I own I wish him to be proficient in these first & not least necessary branches of Education before he leaves home & loses the parental care. Had the school-master stay'd at Eliz. Town all those advantages might have been united: at present I've been obliged to relinquish his grammer for I found that the time allotted for it was really lost since he did not learn that & neglected other things. I will however take care that he preserves what he has already learnt & be happy to receive your directions about him. He is a good boy & his backwardness to the grammer proceeds from a taste for what is more amusing & more apparently instructive not from obstinacy.

It is with difficulty I write & I believe it will be as difficult for you to read this scrawl, but Maria will not quit me & I've but one hand at liberty & more that but by spells. How imperfect my dr.! is human penetration. While the delicacy of little Nancy's appearance awakened our fears, & the florid complection of Maria assured us on her part, Nancy recovers health & strength & poor little Maria is attack'd wh. a fever. This is the first in 8 days that she has eat a mouthful. Last Sunday she was taken very ill, monday her fever still continued & her tongue & mouth appeared very sore. That alarmed me, for I apprehended she had the malignant sore throat, but the next day her fever abated, tho' her mouth continued & still does very sore, & her breath very offensive. The fever has intirely left her & it is wh. pleasure I've observ'd ever since I first apprehended the sore throat, that when she drinks she swallows without difficulty, & I now conclude she has the sprue, or as the English call it the thrush: if it is that it will be some time yet before she'll be quite well. To day she told me in the bed that Pappa Jay wd. come home bye & bye to see Maria....

Mr. Renden waited upon us this afternoon & has promised to call himself or send his servant in the morng. for this letter: Scrawl I might rather call it, & indeed I am quite ashamed of it, but if you knew under what disagreeable circumstances I've written, you wd. rather pity than blame me. I've just daub'd all my paper wh. syrrup that I had to mix magnesia for Maria. I'll endeavor to let you know from time to time how she does. Don't be uneasy, for if I think her dangerous I'll send an Express to you.

I've sent to the post-office but without success. Adieu my dr. Mr. Jay & believe me to be most affectionately

Yours
SA JAY

Tuesday — Reasons which you shall be acquainted wh. when I see you prevented my letter from being sent yesterday, but I'm not sorry, since it gives me an opportunity of telling you that our sweet little girl is vastly better, & I now think quite out of danger. I'm ashamed to add anything to this scrawl, but to-morrow I'll begin anew.

The delicate balance of amiable relations that John and Sarah tried to keep with all the members of their families was sometimes difficult to maintain. John, now that he was home again, resumed the role of primary caregiver to his extended family. His relationships with his siblings ranged from warm friendship to exasperation to aloofness. John and Sarah often had to tread a fine line between what proper etiquette on the one hand and their emotions on the other required of them.

(JJ to William Livingston at Elizabethtown) NYork 19 Feb. 1785

Dr. Sr.

It was not untill Eveng. that Brockholst delivd. to me yr. obliging Letter of ye

13 Instant. He supposing that he had given it to Mrs Jay, when he brought yr. public Letter, had left it in his great Coat Pocket, till this Morng when Mrs. Livingston accidentally found it.

I regret this Delay, both because it deprivd. me of ye Pleasure of sooner making my acknowledgmts. to you for yr. kind attention, & because it postponed my resuming that Line of Conduct towards him wh. our Relation to each other now renders requisite.

I have not been a little anxious I assure you, to slip away from Business, & unbend my mind in ye safe and agreable Society of my affecte. Friends at Liberty Hall, & in the innocent Prattle & Caresses of the Children. These are Pleasures which gladden ye Heart, & in some Measure gild this iron cage with Streakes of Gold.

It was my Intention to have crossed ye Bay last Saturday, & I had arranged my affairs accordingly, but thro' out that whole Day not a single Boat from Elizh. Town was to be found. An obstacle of another kind detain'd me here to Day, vizt. the sailing of a Packet for France, by wh. I was to send Dispatches respecting Circumstances too recent to admit of my preparing Letters in Time to leave Town. I hope the third attempt (wh. I expect to make next Saturday) will be more Successful; & that when ye Roads & ferries become more open & practicable, ye Frequency of my Visits will be more equal to my wishes.

With my love to all the family, I am
Dr. Sir &c.

P. S. Be so good as to cut and bury some Slips for me from your Vines.

Two subjects close to John Jay's heart were education and the abolition of slavery. He believed that education should be available to all, since a knowledgeable people would govern the country more capably. Jay acted on this belief by helping to found the African Free School in 1787 for the purpose of educating slaves, female as well as male; later he also supported the schooling of six needy boys in Rye, New York.

(JJ to Dr. Benjamin Rush) [Draft]
New York 24 March 1785

Sir

I have been obliged to trespass on my usual punctuality in private correspondences....

I consider knowledge to be the Soul of a Republic, and as the weake & the wicked are generally in Alliance, as much Care should be taken to diminish the number of the former as of the latter. Education is the way to do this, and nothing shd be left undone to afford all Ranks of People the means of obtaining a proper Degree of it at a cheap and easy Rate.

I thank you for the pamphlet you sent me. There is good Sense and just reasoning in it. I wish to see all unjust & unnecessary Discriminations everywhere abolished, and that the Time may soon come when all our Inhabitants of every Colour & Denomination shall be free and equal Partakers of our political Liberty.

I am Sir

With great Respect & Esteem
Yr most obt Servt

(JJ to Adrienne de Noailles, Marquise de Lafayette) 13 August 1785

Madam

I have recd, ye Letter, w[hic]h. you did me ye honor to write on the 15 Ap. last. Few Circumstances have given me more Pleasure than such Evidence of my having a place in the Remembrance & good Opinion of a Lady whose Esteem derives no less Value from her Discernment than from the Delicacy of her Sentiments.

Accept therefore Madam of my sincere & cordial acknowledgemts. for honoring me with a place among yr. Correspondents, w[hic]h. was the more obliging, as you was to afford more Pleasure by, than you would expect to receive from it. You know it is an old observation that Ladies write better Letters than Gentlemen, and therefore independent of other Considerations, a Correspondence between them is always so far on unequal Terms.

I can easily concieve that you whose Predilection for your Husband was always conspicuous, shd. experience so much Satisfaction on seeing him return from his Field of Glory with additional Honors; and I can with equal Ease form an Idea of his Emotions when on that, as on former Occasions, those Honors promoted him to higher Rank in your Estimation.

Even Remarks on the Marquis' Affection for his Children and the Value you set on domestic Enjoymts. must be pleasing to those who are capable of feeling their Force....

If you was not what you are, I would not encourage the Desire you express of accompanying the Marq' on his next visit to this Country, for I am sure you would be disappointed.

We have few Amusements to relieve Travellers of that Weight of Time & Liesure wh. oppresses many of them. Our men for the most part mind their Business, and our women their Families, and if our wives succeed (as most of them do) "in making Home man's best Delight" Gallantry seldom draws their Husbands from them.

Our Customs in many Respects differ from yours and you know that whether with or without Reason we usually prefer those wh. Education & Habit recommend. The pleasures of Paris & the pomp of Versailles are unknown in this Country; and their votaries must unavoidably experience a certain Vacuity or Blankness, wh. nothing but good Sense, moderate Desires and a Relish for less splendid, less various but not less innocent or satisfactory Enjoymts. can supply. Tho not a Frenchman, I shd. nevertheless be too polite to tell these things to those whom they might restrain from visiting us. On you they will have a contrary Effect. It wd. gratify the Friends of the Marqs. vizt. the Citizens of the United States to have the Honor of a visit from you. I flatter myself that consideration will afford a strong and additional Inducement.

My little Family is well. Mrs. Jay desires me to assure you of her Remembrance & Regard and permit me to add that I am with sincere Esteem and respectful attachment.

Madam
your most obt. & very h'ble servt.
John Jay

The Jays were careful not only in their conduct toward members of their families but also toward the government officials they entertained. John and Sarah were proud to be Americans, and polite attention from diplomats was appreciated but only as a mark of esteem for the United States. They were both too prudent to accept gifts of a personal nature without the prior approval of Congress.

(JJ to Don Diego Gardoqui at New York) [Draft]
NYork 4 Octr 1785

Dr Sr.

Mrs. Jay is greatly obliged by ye pleasing & polite attention wh. dictated yr card of Saturday last, & the valuable Present which accompanied it. She wd have replied to it immediately, but as I was then out of town, she wished to consult me on so delicate an occasion, especially as several considerations have weight with public characters, that do not apply to private individuals. These Considerations, wh I will take an opportunity of explaining to You, induce me to think it adviseable for her to return the Boxes. Be assured however that this mark of attention and the Friendship & Regard it manifests, will never cease to make the most agreable Impressions, and that we shall be happy in every opportunity of testifying the Sentiments of Esteem & Attachment which we entertain for you.

With the best wishes for your Health and Happiness I am Dr Sr

your most obt & very hble Servt

(Don Diego De Gardoqui to JJ at New York) New York 28th Feby. 1786

Dear Sir

You may remember that in one of the conversations which we had soon after I arrived here, you said that if you had returned directly from Spain to America you would have asked for a Permit to export a Spanish Horse for Breed, and that I offered to write and request such a Permit. I accordingly did write in June last to his Excellency Count de Florida Blanca who was pleased to mention it to the King; but his Majesty instead of Granting the Permit ordered a Horse to be sent to me for you, one was chosen afterwards and sent to Cadiz where he has been many months expecting a Vessel that might carry him to this Place. He has arrived at last after a voyage of 75 Days, and will be disembarked as soon as part of the Cargo is taken out—all which I communicate to you for your Information, repeating that I have the Honour to subscribe myself &ca

Diego de Gardoqui

(JJ to Don Diego Gardoqui at New York) [Draft]

NYork 1 March 1786

Dr Sr.

I have recd. the Letter which You did me the Honor to write Yesterday, informing me that instead of granting a Permit as you requested for me to purchase and export a Horse, his Majesty has been pleased to order one to be sent to You for me. This is indeed doing a Favor in a royal Manner. It demands my sincere and respectful acknowledgement, and I shall take the Liberty of requesting the Consul de Florida Blanca to express to the King the Sense I entertain of it.

I ought however to apprize you that I do not consider myself at Liberty to accept the horse without the previous Permission of Congress. I shall immediately lay your Letter before them, and acquaint you without Delay of the answer they may be pleased to give.*

Your application for the Permit was friendly & obliging. Accept my Thanks for it and be assured of the Esteem & Regard with which I have the Honor to be

Dr Sr

your most obt & very hble Servt

(PAJ to his Grandfather at Elizabeth Town) [New York] April 7, 1786

Dr Grandpapa

I would have wrote to you before now, but papa expected to go to Elizabeth Town & take me with him last Saturday, the weather proving bad were prevented: papa still intends going tomorrow, but if it blows so hard as it does this morning, I am afraid we shall be disappointed again. Mama also intends paying Grandmama a visit as soon as the weather is settled.

We have this day begun our house again. Our Stable is quite finished, but the other night two of the Tiles were blown off the roof. Two or three nights ago one of the willows which papa has lately procured was stolen out of the Garden, & the Cow has eat off the tops of those which he had before; but he says that next spring you may take your choice either to have the old one which will sprout again from the roots, or some which he had lately set out.

Please to give my love to Grandmama & thank her kindly for the Letter she was so obliging as to send me. The same reasons that has prevented my writing to you has prevented my acknoleging her favor.

I am your most

Dutiful & affectionate Grandson

Peter Augustus Jay

(SLJ to JJ at New York) Eliz. Town 5th May 1786

My dr. Mr. Jay,

**Congress, on March 3, granted Jay permission to accept the horse.*

Yesterday evening I recd, yr. letter of the 3d inst., & with pleasure acknowledge yr. friendly attention: I am happy to find that our dr. little boy is better, & hope his indisposition will continue to decrease. Your tender & affectionate care of him my dear Mr. Jay! is so very amiable, that I could not read in Susans letter of your having exchanged beds with Mr. Watkins for the purpose of attending the Child, without a pleasing & grateful emotion. Papa & Mama still flatter themselves that they shall see you to-day or to-morrow, & I cannot tell them of my doubts without informing them that Peter is unwell, which might retard the progress mama is making in the recovery of her health & spirits by creating anxiety which tho' natural would still be fruitless.

The two little girls enjoy a full tide of health. You would be delighted to see their transports; little Nan particularly seems to have given herself up to joy, all around calls forth her wonder & exstasy. Oh Mama! Mama! she every instant exclaims, now bringing me flowers, then asparagus &c. which with her Grand-papa she has been collecting and every now & then Papa strikes at the windows to call us to observe the little ones rolling on the Lawn & skipping & playing as gayly & not less innocently than the little Lambs they admire. When Maria rides with us, the whole time passes in answering her innocent & often-times sensible questions. The Country was really enchanting a few days ago & indeed is so still, tho' the fall of the blossoms have diminished a little the gaiety of the scenery.

The first evening of my arrival here, my mind was so much affected by the visible beauty & bounty of nature, that in my sleep I fancyed myself engaged in describing to you every thing that pleased me, in poetic numbers, & imagined that my verse flowed as natural as my desire of pleasing you, so that I was highly satisfyed with my dream. But the satisfaction arising from the dream was as transient as the slumber that gave it birth, for tho' return of light which had dispel'd the dusky reign of fancy, presented to my view scenes not less capable of exciting admiration & delight, than those which imagination had enjoyed during my slumbers. Yet with the powers of recollection, the reflection also return'd of my incapacity to impart to you any part of that pleasure which the charming views around inspire, & I felt, & I still feel the probability of the solitary state in which poor Adam found himself even in Paradise when destitute of a beloved Companion.

Remember me to Peter, tell him I am rejoiced to hear that he bears his indisposition with so good a grace, & I am sure the Chearfulness which his Aunt tells me he possesses will contribute to his more speedy recovery. Papa has written to you since I've been here. If Peter is better may we not hope to see you both? If not, tell me when you expect my return.

Adieu! my Love to Susan, & believe me to be unalterably

yours
S. Jay

Papa & Mama desire to be remd. to you. When you come pray bring with you fish & lobsters.

During the years of the Confederation (1784–1789), John Jay, concerned that the new nation would splinter into regional factions, focused his efforts on empowering Congress. On May 31, 1785, he wrote, "Our affairs are settling by degrees in order. If power be given to Congress to regulate trade and provide for the payment of their debts, all will be well." Of great interest were the new trade relations between New England and China. Jay asked Samuel Shaw, the U.S. Consul at Canton, to

> transmit to me by proper conveyances, whatever Intelligence and observations you may think conducive to the public Good. The mercantile and other Regulations at Canton, respecting Foreigners; the number and size of foreign Vessels, and of what nations, which annually enter there — their Cargoes and what articles of Merchandize answer best, are matters which merit attention. It might also be useful to know whether foreigners do or can carry on a circuitous Trade in that part of the World, either on their own account or by being Carriers for others, whether asiatic or European (30 January 1786).

Jay wished "to see the people of America become one nation in every respect" (4 May 1787). But this optimism would not last. The rise of political groups, an economic recession, and the lack of power that Congress had over the individual states colluded to increase fears that the new republic would soon fail. John Jay corresponded with Thomas Jefferson, George Washington, and other leaders on what changes might be desirable.

(JJ to George Washington) NYork 7 Jan 1787

Dr. Sir

They who regard the public good with more attention & attachment than they do mere personal concerns must feel and confess the force of such Sentiments as are expressed in your Letter to me by Col. Humphreys last Fall. The situation of our affairs calls not only for Reflection & Prudence but for Exertion. What is to be done? is a common Question, but it is a Question not easy to answer.

Would the giving any further Degree of power to Congress, do the Business? I am much inclined to think it would not for among other Reasons it is natural to suppose there will always be members who will find it convenient to make their Seats subservient to partial & personal purposes. And they who may be able and willing to concert and promote useful and national measures, will seldom be unembarrassed by the Ignorance, Prejudices, Fears or interested views of others.

In so large a Body secrecy and Dispatch will be too uncommon and foreign as well as local Influence will frequently oppose & sometimes frustrate the wisest measures. Large assemblies often misunderstand or neglect the obligations of Character, Honor and Dignity, and will collectively do or omit things which individual Gentlemen in private Capacities wd. not approve. As the many divide blame and also divide credit, too little a portion of either falls to each mans share to affect him strongly, even in cases where the whole blame or the whole credit must be national.

It is not easy for those to think and feel as Sovereign who have been always accustomed to think & feel as Subjects.

The executive Business of Sovereignty depending on so many wills, and those wills moved by such a variety of contradictory motives & inducements, will in general be but feebly done.

Such a sovereign however theoretically responsible, cannot be effectually so in its Departments and officers, without adequate Indicatories.

I therefore promise myself nothing very desireable from any change which does not divide the Sovereignty into its proper Departments. Let Congress legislate. Let others execute. Let others judge.

Shall we have a King? Not in my opinion while other Expedients remain untried. Might we not have a Governor General limited in his Perogatives and Duration? Might not Congress be divided into an upper and lower House, the former appointed for Life, the latter annually, and let the Governor general to preserve the Ballance with the advice of a council formed for that only purpose of the great judicial officers, have a negative on their acts? Our govt. shd. in some Degree be suited to our Manners & Circumstances and they you know are not fully democratical.

What Powers shd. be granted to the Govt. so constructed is a Question which deserves much thought — I think the more, the better — the States retaining only so much as may be necessary for Domestic purposes & all their principal officers civil & military being commissioned & removable by the national Govt.

These are short Hints. Details would exceed the limits of a Letter and to you be superfluous.

A Convention is in contemplation, and I am glad to find your name among those of its intended Members.

To me the policy of such a convention* appears questionable. Their authority is to be derived from acts of the State Legislatures. Are the State Legislatures authorized, either by themselves or others, to alter constitutions. I think not. They who hold commissions can by virtue of them neither retrench nor extend the Powers conveyed to them.

Perhaps it is intended that this Convention shall not ordain, but only recommend. If so there is Danger that their Recommendations will produce endless Discussions perhaps Jealousies and party Heats.

Would it not be better for Congress plainly & in strong Terms to declare that the present federal Governmt. is inadequate to the purposes for wh. it was instituted, that they forbear to point out its particular Defects or to ask for an Extension of any particular powers, lest improper Jealousies should then arise; but that in their opinion it would be expedient for the people of the States without Delay to appoint State Conventions (in the way they chuse their general assemblies) with the sole and express power of appointing Deputies to a general Convention who or the majority of whom should take into consideration the Articles of Confederation, and make such alterations amendments and additions thereto, as to them should appear necessary and

**A note with this letter explains that Jay questioned the legality of the Annapolis Convention's call for a Federal Convention. Washington excerpted this letter and took it with him to Philadelphia.*

proper and which being by them ordained & published should have the same force and obligation which all or any of the present articles now have

No alterations in the Government should I think be made, nor if attempted will easily take place, unless deduceable from the only source of just authority The People.

Accept my Dear Sir my warmest & most cordial wishes for your Health and Happiness and believe me to be

with the greatest Respect and Esteem
Your most obt. Servt.

Despite his immersion in the political scene, John Jay's thoughts turned again and again to his retirement: to building a house where he and Sarah could live peacefully. Eventually they decided to enlarge the farmhouse on land in Bedford that John had inherited from his mother, but fourteen more years would pass before the Jays moved in.

(JJ to SLJ) Bedford Sunday 20 May 1787

Dear Sally

Hitherto my jaunt has been pleasant. We passed Thursday evening at Rye with Peter & Nancy, who made many friendly Inquiries about you and the Children, and wished it could be convenient for us both to pass some part of this charming Season with them.

On Thursday we came here, and the next Day completed the Business which induced the Doctor to come with me. He left us Yesterday too early to admit of my writing by him.

I passed yesterday at the Farm, where altho much has been done, much yet remains to be done. The Farm House I am building tho but small goes on slowly. It is more easy to build many Houses in a City than a few in the Interior of the Country for to collect Materials & workmen is in the latter Case difficult.

I was in hopes to have extended my Excursion beyond this Place, but Business of some Kind or other must it seems pursue me. I find I have further Security to require & if possible obtain from two persons who owe me some money, & whose ability to pay it now appears too doubtful to merit sanguine confidence.

As yet I find but little Alteration in my Health, if any, it is for the better. You shall hear from me by every opportunity. Kiss our little girls for me & believe me to be

very affy. Yours

Since returning from Europe, Sarah Jay and the family had enjoyed many extended visits with the Livingstons in Elizabethtown. Although there had been concerns about her health early in her marriage, Sarah seems to have been quite well throughout her stay in Europe and upon returning to New York. To judge from the lists of *Invitations to Supper & Dinner 1787 & 1788* that Sarah kept, the Jays frequently hosted large parties. They were clearly the early practitioners of networking: getting people of different points of view to talk with each other over a good dinner. However, in August 1787, Sarah became extremely ill and went to Liberty Hall, where her mother and sister Susan could take care of her. She was sufficiently recovered by September 10, 1787, to be entertaining once more.

(SLJ to JJ at New York) Elizabeth Town Monday, Augst. 1787

My dr. Mr. Jay,

I've this inst. return'd from riding; & while out was amusing myself with tracing in idea, & following you in your journey homeward from Rye. As I supose you [are] at present at Duyckinck's I presume you are at leisure to tell me how your sister & brother have their health, & whether they do not impute to negligence that delay in visiting them which I have so much regretted. But joking apart, I long to hear from you and wish to know whether Peter has had a return of his fever or not.

As to my little Prattlers, I had rather hear the music of their tender voices than the united melody of all the birds in the Country. I begin to feel a little stronger, & to-day for the first, have had a little color, perhaps I am indebted to the bath for it. Mama continues chearful & in good health. She desires to be remembered to you.

Remember me to Peggy & our Neighbors, & believe me my dr. Mr. Jay (with the full expectation of seeing you here next Saturday, or friday if convenient)

Your very sincerely affectionate wife
S. Jay

(SLJ to her sister Susan at New York) Elizabeth Town Thursday morning, 1787
[late August or early September]

I cannot express the gratitude I owe you my dr. Susan for yr. kind letters & affectionate attention to my health & family. To your care & that of my dr. Mother I owe under providence a reprieve from the silent Tomb. Indeed my dr. sister you hardly imagined how ill I was when I left you, several complaints of which you was ignorant sounded the alarm to my feelings & when I embraced my little ones in the boat, it was with difficulty I supported myself, but enough! my health is mending & I hope to see you all again.

Remind Mr. Jay that I am still living & that a line from him would be of more avail than ten Phiscicians. Adieu! my dr. sister. I have often attempted to write both to you & him, but am always prevented by tears. Papa & Mama expected Mr. Jay last Saturday & still expect him the next; should he come, be so good as to send me 2½ yds of that book-muslin we bought together, & if you have leisure copy a square or two of the apron you work'd for me & buy an ounce of Cotton fit to work it & send them by him. I have leisure here & no work & it would amuse me if Mr. Jay complies with Mama's request & indeed my own of bringing Maria with him it would greatly oblige me. She can bring all her frocks except her finest even her old blue would do to run about with.

Give my love to Mr. Jay & all the Children &

believe me to be dear Susan
yrs. affectionately,

Page from *Invitations to Supper & Dinner* by Sarah and John Jay, 10 January 1788.

Charles Thomson, secretary of the Continental Congress 1774–1789.

Bishop Samuel Provoost, 1st Episcopal bishop of New York 1786–1801.

Don Diego Maria de Gardoqui, Spanish chargé d'affaires.

Daniel Huger, member from South Carolina to Continental Congress.

John Armstrong, member from Pennsylvania to Continental Congress.

Nicholas Gilman, member from New Hampshire to Continental Congress.

James Madison, member from Virginia to Continental Congress; co-author with Jay and Hamilton of *The Federalist*.

Cyrus Griffin, member from Virginia to Continental Congress.

Pieter Johan van Berckel, minister from the United Netherlands.

Alexander Hamilton, member of New York State Assembly; co-author of *The Federalist*.

Baron Friederich Wilhelm von Steuben, Prussian military officer who reorganized the American troops during the Revolution.

Robert R. Livingston, 1st Chancellor of New York; former secretary for foreign affairs.

William Duer, financier; secretary of the Board of the Treasury 1786–1789.

General Henry Knox, secretary of war 1785–1794.

Walter Livingston, member of the Board of the Treasury.

[James?] Barclay, New York City merchant.

Col. Aaron Burr, American political leader; member of New York State Assembly.

General [Walter?] Stewart, American military officer; merchant in Philadelphia.

On September 17, 1787, the Convention at Philadelphia had agreed to a constitution that required ratification by the states. Alexander Hamilton and James Madison joined John Jay in the writing of a series of newspaper articles under the title The Federalist, to explain to the public how ratification of the proposed Constitution would benefit the nation. Jay wrote five of these essays and might have written more had he not become gravely ill. Sarah, still not totally recovered from her own illness, nursed him back to health. In February 1788, he wrote that, though better, there was "a constant pain in my left side."

(SLJ to her Mother at Elizabeth Town) [New York after 27 March, 1788?]
Thursday night . . o'clock

My dr. Mama,

Nothing could have been more acceptable to Susan & myself than the appearance of mr. Woodruff with your letter this evening. As the roads improve I flatter myself you will gain health, for you know it is a long time since exercise has been absolutely essential to it. I could almost say that nothing can equal my impatience to see you, but that would be injustice to your tenderness for me, for I am well assur'd that the wish is mutual, & I sincerely hope will soon be gratifyed. Dr. Charlton presses for my departure, & I think that if nothing unexpected happens to prevent our intention we shall see you next Saturday se'ennight. I am not anxious for Bells' coming before I return from Eliz. Town, unless you find it troublesome to keep her so long, for I think polly will do best alone in my absence.

Mr. Jay went to Bedford 8 or 10 days ago & took Peter with him in the Chais as far as Rye where he has been ever since & I do not expect them home until saturday. In their absence we have had the house cleaned from the Garret to the Cellar & on Monday a Woman has engaged to come & wash. Susan sends you 2 Lb. shashong tea which aunt Clarkson bought & recommends & 1 Lb. of excellent Hyson; she keeps the two small baskets in case we should want them to bring anything.

Mr. [Gouverneur] Morris has paid Susan & me a sociable visit since I began to write. He has received a letter from Ridley dated the 27th of March, mentioning that he & Kitty were in good health & just going to Baltimore. Adieu! my dr. Mama. God bless you & reward you for all your kindness to your affectionate

daughter
S. Jay

Susan intends writing on saturday by Miss de Hart. The Children are well. Nanny [Nancy] says when Grandmama comes to Town she'll go & stay with Aunt Susan & then she will not distress Grandmama.

My Love to papa

> On April 13, 1788, incited by rumors that medical students were performing autopsies on cadavers stolen from cemeteries, rioters ransacked New York Hospital. A group of the students were held in the jail for their safety. When the rioters threatened to break into the jail, the authorities fired into the crowd, killing three people.

(SLJ to her Mother near Elizabeth Town) New York April 17, 1788

My dr. Mama,

Last Sunday Evening Mr. Ricketts let me know that he should breakfast with you the next morning, I therefore sat down & wrote you a letter immediately; as it contain'd an invitation for Papa to dine with us on Tuesday & Thursday, & we received no answer I feel anxious least either him or you should be unwell.

How just is yr. observation that 'in the midst of life we are in death.' On Monday, the evening preceeding the day on which we expected a large company to dine, just as we were going to tea, Genl. Clarkson call'd in to know if we could lend him a sword, for says he the rioters are proceeding to the Jail & are determined to open the doors & liberate the prisoners as well as to tear in pieces the Doctors who are confin'd there, & if they effect their plan confusion, murder &c. may be the result. Mr. Jay ran up the stairs & handing Clarkson one sword, to my great concern arm'd himself with another, & went towards the Jail which the Citizens determin'd to defend.

Just as he was going up the steps of the jail, a stone thrown by one of the Mob (for it was too dark to discern which) took him in the forehead & stunn'd him so that he fell. Clarkson & Rutherford who were near, carried him into the Poor-house & fetch'd Charlton & then brought them both home together in the Carriage. The stone must have been large as it had made two large holes in his forehead. Judge Mama of my feelings when I saw him hurried from the Carriage to the Chamber by the Dr. & other gentlemen.

The Dr. immediately examined his wounds, & to my unspeakable relief pronounced that there was no fracture. After dressing the wound he bled him & gave him some drops that he said wd. compose him; it did not however make him sleep, but still his head felt better the next day tho' his eyes were much swell'd & discolor'd, & indeed remain so yet. He is quite out of danger, but suffers vast pain from his neck & shoulders which we think must proceed from a cold he may have taken that rainy evening that he receiv'd his blow.

Just after the gentlemen left to go on their expedition that fatal eveng., a young woman of the name of Ludlum came to inquire if I wanted to hire a person. My spirits were agitated about what might be the issue of the riot & I hardly knew what to tell her. She told me she had liv'd a twelve-month with Mrs. Chandler & desir'd me to write a few lines to her for her Character; I did so, & she said she would give my letter to a boatman: not having recd. an answer I think it has probably miscarried & should be glad if it is convenient that you could inquire whether she is honest & industrious.

I cannot quit the Chamber except to wait upon Mr. Jay & therefore beg that my dr. Mama will excuse my not having purchased the things for her. Judy is much better & thanks you kindly for your disposition to relieve her, but having now Mrs. Aims to assist her finds it unnecessary to trouble you with the children. It distresses me exceedingly to find you are troubled with that sad cholical complaint & I long excessively for Susan's return. Yr. parting with Mrs. Aims I continue to regret.

Remember us all to Papa & believe me my [dear] Mama to be sincerely

Yr. dutiful Daughter
Sa. Jay

Mrs. Taylor has just now handed me another letter from my dr. Mama. This week has indeed been a busy one! but in a very different manner from that which we expected. Altho' every thing was prepared for a great deal of company yet none have I been able to receive.

On Tuesday my dr. Mr. Jay's situation was extremely critical, as it was difficult to decide whether his brain was injur'd or not; many sy[m]ptoms seem'd to favor the apprehension; at present thank God! my fears are vanished but he is very low.

Before he was injured in the Doctor's Riot, John Jay had written "An Address to the People of the State of New-York" which was published on April 15, 1788. In this persuasive document, Jay cogently laid out the weaknesses of the Articles of Confederation and the strengths of the proposed Constitution. Under the Articles, for example, Congress "may make war, but are not empowered to raise men or money to carry it on. They may make peace, but without power to see the terms of it observed." Jay urged New Yorkers to ratify the Constitution even though he personally did not agree with all its terms. He did think it imperative "to give the proposed Constitution a fair trial, and to mend it as time, occasion and experience may dictate." During the ensuing weeks, Jay would be in Poughkeepsie where the delegates to the New York State Ratification Convention were meeting, using all his diplomatic skills to urge approval of the proposed Constitution. As William Jay later noted:

> The final question on the ratification of the constitution was taken on the 26th of July, and the State of New-York became a member of the new confederation by a majority of three votes. This happy result, so little anticipated a few weeks before, was no doubt owing in part to the accession of New-Hampshire and Virginia during the session of the Convention.

(SLJ to JJ at Poughkeepsie) Eliz. Town 19th June 1788

My dr. Mr. Jay,

The morning we left you, we arriv'd at Eliz. Town after a pleasant passage and found our Parents in good health. The Children continue very well and I am myself much better than when I left N. York. By this time I suppose you have arrived at Poughkeepsie & arranged your affairs so as to be tollerably settled. The ride I flatter myself has been beneficial to you & hope to find from your letters that I am not mistaken.

Our children behave admirably well; Maria is now spelling & Nan pratling beside me; Peter is with his Grand-Papa shooting robbins.

The Pamphlet entitled an address to the inhabitants of New York &c. has been received in this State with great approbation, nor has the tribute of applause been with-held from the author, that usually accompanies his writings; for tho' thro' modesty his name was conceal'd it seems the well-known style discovered him.

Agreeably to your request I have written to Ridley, & to oblige Mama have done the same to Susan, & my fingers now feel a little crampt, I will therefore bid you Adieu! Wishing you the blessings of health & success in yr. business,

I am my dr. Mr. Jay

Your affectionate &
dutiful wife
Sa: Jay

(JJ to SLJ at Elizabeth Town) Poughkeepsie, 21 June 1788

My Dear Sally:

A gentleman now in town, and who will set out for New York in about an hour, gives me an opportunity of writing you a few lines. The convention assembled with unusual punctuality. There are not more than two members that I recollect absent, and the house has entered on the business with great assiduity and regularity. As yet, these proceedings and debates have been temperate and inoffensive to either party. The opposition to the proposed Constitution appears formidable, though more so from numbers than other considerations. What the event will be is uncertain. For my part I do not despair on the one hand, although I see much room for apprehension on the other.

It would give me great pleasure to hear that your health has been mended by the leisure, air, and exercise which your present situation affords. Mine continues in the state it was when we parted. As Peter omitted to take leave of me, I hope he will think it but right to make amends by the number of his letters.

Remember me affectionately to all the family. Adieu, my dear Sally.

Yours very sincerely,
John Jay

(SLJ to JJ at Poughkeepsie) Elizabeth Town June 25, 1788

My dear Mr. Jay,

How happy did your letter of the 21st inst. make me this day. Altho' I was convinced that you had wrote me, yet I could not altogether silence my apprehensions least the journey had proved too fatiguing for you. I hope to find from your next letter that your health is better than it was when we parted, for as your Colleagues are Men of Abilities, I hope you will not have a greater share of business imposed upon you than your just proportion; & of course flatter myself you will have more leisure to unbend your mind & to devote to exercise.

Our dear Children are well, & as gay as youth, health & innocence can make them. Last Evening as I was sitting in my Chamber rather pensively disposed, I was thinking of you, & regretting that the time just previous to our seperation had been so occupied that little leisure had been left for conversation &c. I was roused by a Call from my Father, & hastening down found himself & my good mother enjoying the spirits & activity of the little ones, nay mingling in their sports; & I thought I perceived an unusual degree of tenderness in their Countenances when stealing a glance from the Children their eyes caught mine. It was difficult for me to suppress the tear of sensibility. It was impossible! for both Peter & Maria felt my wish. Oh Mama says they how delighted! Papa would be were he here.

Our little son had been writing to you this morng. & when I mentioned to him what you had written he was affected, & said that he had been sent down to the boat to see the things disposed of properly, & Mr. Lee telling him that he only waited for us, he came up to tell us, but meeting us by the way, without farther thought he joined our Company & went on. He behaves admirably well.

When I first came here I candidly inform'd Mama of the state of my health, & was sorry to find her so much alarm'd; she assur'd me that the Continuance of those Complaints but a little longer must have brought on a Dropsy or Consumption, & I sincerely believe that the former would soon have been my unhappy fate, for to what else can I impute the unaccountable swelling of my feet? The dread of that dreadful lingering Disorder has made me very obedient to her directions & prescriptions. I take some simples as well as bark, & moderate exercise. When I first came here, my paleness I may rather say sallowness was observed by every body. At present I am still yellow but not quite so pale & I think my Complaints abate.

Excuse my making myself the subject of so large a part of my letter. Your own often repeated injunctions to be particular on what relates to my health have induced me to be thus tedious.... Mr. Watkins tells Judy that he often calls at our house & that our servants keep Saturday all the week or in other words are always cleaning.

You have sometimes told me that I am too lazy & too careless to write well. Never was any thing more true, now ever more so than in the present instance but I'm inclin'd to think you had reference only to letters of form, for I am persuaded that the mere effusions of a heart chiefly possessed by yourself & Children will not be unwelcome & that even this scrawl will be acceptable from

your devoted & dutiful Wife
Sa. Jay

Papa & Mama give their love to you

I have just heard that New Hampshire has adopted the proposed Constitution & Congratulate you upon it. I wish it may prove a stimulous to your Convention & should rejoice still more were they to anticipate Virginia. Please to present my Compts. to Judge Hobart, & let me know how you like your accomodations.

(JJ to SLJ) Poughkeepsie, July 5, 1788

My Dear Sally:

Col. W. S. Livingston, who brought us the news of the adoption of the Constitution by Virginia, is about setting out, and I will not let him go without a few lines for you. Yesterday was a day of festivity, and both the parties united in celebrating it. Two tables, but in different houses, were spread for the convention, and the two parties mingled at each table, and the toasts (of which each had copies) were communicated by the sound of drum and accompanied by the discharge of cannon.

We shall probably be here another week. The weather has not yet become settled, and I have had but little exercise. My health, however, continues as usual, and I shall be well content if it remains as it is. I wrote to you a few days ago.

Adieu.

Yours very affectionately,
John Jay

(SLJ to JJ at Poughkeepsie) Eliz. Town July 7th, 1788

My dr. Mr. Jay,

Yr. letter in answer to mine of the 19th ult., I've recd. & thank you for. By the last Post I hope another of mine & one from our son has reached you. I am happy to find that I had acted agreeably to yr. Judgment in having made the same requisition of Peter before I recd. your letter, that in it you desire; he studies & draws & shoots & fishes &c. I cannot say I have seen him idle. As yet Mr. Wright has not been well enough to attend his school, & I think the Vacancy has been more usefully spent here than it would have been at New York had we remained there. Last Monday I went over & found the servants properly employed. Mary is recovering, & Chresia tells me Abram behaves well. Mr. Collis will not have the paper ready for hanging before you return.

My Father is happier than you can imagine in the Company of our little ones. They behave charmingly. Altho' he readily admits a great deal of merit in Maria yet the vivacity of Nan steals upon him. At breakfast, observing that her Grand-father did not take cream with his tea, she ask'd why he did not? He reply'd because he did not like it. Oh Governor (said the little gipsie with an arch look) you must learn to like every thing. Thus without the least constraint she prattles to him daily, but at the same time softens every seeming pertness with such sweetness, & an air so fine that it [is] impossible to check her. I think I see you smile at the Consequence I give these trifles by relating them. Content My Love! to cheat you of a single care or of more numerous ones but for a single moment would recompence me for more trouble than folio's of such letters would cost me.

Mama & myself are going to take a ride, the object of which is to inquire if there is a letter at the Post-Office for me, & to drop this one there. Every one is anxious to hear the effect which the accession of Virginia has had upon your Convention, & the expectation of having my own Curiosity gratifyed on that subject, as well as my solicitude about your health encreases my impatience to hear from you.

My Mother lets me know she is waiting for me & desires her love to you. My Father is impatient to see you. I hope you know too well your influence upon my heart to require me to tell you how very happy your return will make

Your affectionate Wife
S. Jay

(JJ to SLJ) Poughkeepsie, 16th July, 1788

My Dear Sally:

I was yesterday favoured with your kind letter of the 7th instant. You mention having written me a letter by the preceding post, enclosing one from Peter; as yet I have received but one letter from Peter.

Our business here goes on heavily. The issue is yet uncertain. Nor can I tell you how long we may yet remain here. The season of the year makes many of the members impatient to return. Before the end of the week it is probable that some important question will be decided.

Last night my sorrel mare was taken out of the stable, and I think it very doubtful whether I shall see her again. I am much obliged to the thief for leaving the horse. You see, it might have been worse....

I must go and employ some persons to look for my mare; and therefore must, though unwillingly, conclude this letter.

Adieu, my love.

Yours affectionately,
John Jay

The family was reunited. Sarah was busy not only with her household but also entertaining the socially and politically prominent people in New York. Family and friends such as Alexander Hamilton were invited to dine and possibly to taste the wines Thomas Jefferson had so kindly sent from France. Travelers from out of town received an equally warm welcome at the Jays'. Abigail Adams was a sympathetic guest for Sarah, who was suffering from morning sickness.

(Abigail Adams to SLJ at New York) Braintree Febry 20th 1789

My dear Madam,

When I left your Hospitable mansion, I did not design So many days should have elapsed, before I had express'd to you the pleasing Sense I entertain'd of your kindness and Friendship. They had left a durable impression upon my mind, and an ardent desire to cultivate them in future.

I reachd Home Ten days after I left Newyork. We had an agreeable journey, good roads fine weather and tolerable accommodations. Our mush and Lemon Brandy were of great Service to us, and we never faild to Toast the donor, whilst our Hearts were warmed by the Recollection. I hope my dear Madam that your Health is better than when I left you, and this not for your own Sake only, but for that of your worthy partner, who I am sure Sympathized so much with you, that he never really Breakfasted the whole Time I was with you; my best Regards attend him. I hope both he and you will one day do me the Honour of visiting Braintree, where I would do all within my power to render the fireside as social and as pleasing as I found Broadway.

If Miss Livingston is still with you pray present my Regards to her. My love to Master Peter, the Grave Maria & the sprightly little French Girl [Nancy]. Compliments to Mrs. Knox to Lady Kitty, and to all the other Ladies from whom I received particular attentions whilst at New York, and do me the Favour to let me hear from you by the first opportunity.

This letter will be deliverd to you by Mr. Ames, the Suffolk Representative, a young Gentleman of an amiable Character and very good abilities. He was so good as to offer to take charge of any letters I might have for New York. I have embraced this opportunity to present my little Friend Maria with a Brooch which I hope may be pleasing & usefull to her.

Mr. Adams joins me in affectionate Regards to Mr. Jay & best wishes for your

Health and happiness. Be assured I am my dear Madam with Sentiments of esteem and regard, Your

Friend & Humble Servant
Abigail Adams

(JJ to George Washington) [Draft]
NYork 14 Ap 1789

Dr. Sr.

On my return last Evg. from a fortnights absence in the country, I was informed that proper arrangements for your immediate accommodation were not yet made. Permit me therefore to take the Liberty of requesting the favor of you to be with me in the mean Time, & if Mrs Washington shd. accompany you we should be still more happy. As the measures that were in Contemplation on this Subject, would have given an earlier Invitation the appearance of a mere Comp[limen]t it was omitted; considering all circumstances I really think you would experience at least as few Inconveniences with me as in any other situation here. Your reluctance to give Trouble, will doubtless suggest Objections. Apprized of this we shall be particularly careful, to preserve such a Degree of Simplicity in our domestic management as will render you easy on that Head. In a word you shall be recd. and entertained exactly in the way which if in your place, I should prefer vizt. with plain & friendly Hospitality.

You will soon want a Secy, & it would be convenient to have him near you. Let me therefore add that I have a Room very much at his Service, and which may as well be occupied by him as remain as it now is empty.

I cannot conclude this Letter without thanking you as an american for generously complying with the wishes of our Country at this interesting Period. Personal considerations strongly recommend Retirement & none but public & national ones could draw you from it. The people at large seem sensible of this & do you Justice, and I am glad of it, for their sake as well as yours, for the more Justice they do you the more good you will be able to do them.

With the most perfect Esteem & Regard, I am

Dr. Sr.
your affte & obt. Servt.

(Thomas Jefferson to JJ at New York) Paris, Sept. 17, 1789

Dear Sir,

I have sent from this place, together with my own baggage, two hampers & two boxes, which when arrived at Havre I have taken the liberty to order to be separated from my baggage and sent by the first vessel to New York to your address. The marks & contents are as follows.

T.J. No. 30 } These are hampers containing samples of the best wines of this country,
T.J. No. 31 } which I beg leave to present to the President and yourself, in order that you may decide whether you would wish to have any, & which of them for your own

tables hereafter, and to offer my service in procuring them for you. The kinds are, 1. Monraché (the best kind of white Burgundy.) 2. Champagne non mousseux (i.e. still) much preferred here to the sparkling, which goes to all foreign countries. 3. Sauterne (a white Bordeaux). 4. Rochegude (from the neighborhood of Avignon, somewhat of the Madeira quality). 5. Frontignan. I have bought all of these from the Vignerons who made them, the 1st, 2d & 5th when on the spots myself, the 3d & 4th by writing to them. The Vigneron never adulterates his wine, but on the contrary gives it them most perfect & pure possible. But when once a wine has been into a merchant's hands, it never comes out unmixed. This being the basis of their trade, no degree of honesty, or personal friendship, or of kindred prevents it. I must beg the favor of you to deliver one hamper to the President with my offer of service, and the preceding explanation....

Hoping they may come safely to hand, I beg leave to assure you of the sentiments of sincere esteem and respect with which I am, Dear Sir,

Your most obedient & most humble servant
Thos. Jefferson

P.S. Every bottle is marked (with a diamond) with the initial letter of the wine it contains.

In response to President George Washington's offer of a position in the new government, John Jay indicated he would like to be chief justice of the Supreme Court. Washington's nomination on September 24, 1789, was based on Jay's capabilities and preferences rather than just their friendship. Establishing the groundwork for the judicial system of the new nation was a daunting task. Jay had the credentials for this post: he was a lawyer with judicial experience, having been chief justice in New York State, and thus eminently suited to undertake the challenge.

(JJ to George Washington) New York 6 October 1789

Sir

When distinguished Discernment & Patriotism unite in selecting men for Stations of Trust & Dignity, they derive Honor not only from their offices, but from the Hand which confers them.

With a mind and a Heart impressed with these Reflections, and their correspondent Sensations, I assure You that the Sentiments expressed in your Letter of Yesterday, and implied by the Commission it enclosed, will never cease to excite my best Endeavours to fulfill the Duties imposed by the latter, and as far as may be in my power, to realize the Expectations which your nominations, especially to important Places, must naturally create.

With the most perfect Respect Esteem & Attachment I have the Honor to be

Sir
Your most obedt. and h'ble Servt.
John Jay

(George Washington to JJ at New York) New York, Monday November 30, 1789

The President of the United States presents his best compliments to the Chief Justice of the United States and his lady, and encloses them tickets for the theatre this evening.

As this is the last night the President proposes visiting the theatre for the season, he cannot deny himself the gratification of requesting the company of the Chief Justice and his Lady; altho' he begs at the same time that they will consider this invitation in such a point of view as not to feel themselves embarrassed, in the smallest degree, upon the occasion, if they have any reluctance to visiting the theatre; for the President presents the tickets as to his friends who will act as most agreeable to their feelings, knowing thereby that they will meet the wishes of the person who invites them.

(JJ to George Washington at New York) November 30, 1789

The Chief Justice of the United States and Mrs. Jay esteem themselves honoured and obliged by the President's invitation, which they accept with pleasure, and by his delicate attention to their embarrassment, which he had reason to think probable, but which ceased with all questions between government and the theatre.

(George Washington to JJ at New York) [New York 1789]

The President of the United States presents his Compliments to Mr. Jay, and informs him that the Harness of the President's Carriage was so much injured in coming from Jersey that he will not be able to use it today. If Mr. Jay should propose going to Church this Morng. the President would be obliged to him for a Seat in his Carriage Sunday morng.

Life for the Jays was extremely hectic in this period. Though John Jay had been confirmed as chief justice, he continued as secretary for foreign affairs until the new appointee, Thomas Jefferson, returned from Paris on March 22, 1790.

On July 17, 1789, Susannah French Livingston died. She had been a secure haven to her children and grandchildren and an unwavering support to her husband. Her death was a blow to them all, but especially to William. He did not long survive her though lovingly attended by his daughter Susan. Sarah, sustained by her strong faith, put aside her own grief to bolster other members of the family: her husband, her children, her sister Judith.

(SLJ to her sister Susan at Elizabeth Town) New York 7th Febry 1790

My dr. Susan,

Last friday evening I recd. yr. favor of the 2d. inst. I am sorry to find your spirits continue so much depress'd. That we have for some months past had great cause for affliction is most true, & that to be insensible of it wd. be impossible & very wrong. But whom my dear Susan is exempt from tryals or indeed dares wish to be so, since, short-sighted [as] we are, we are incapable of judging what is best for us. Let us not confine our view to the melancholy events we regret, but reflect with gratitude on the many blessings Providence has kindly continued to us. Remember my dr. Susan that it is your duty & will afford you great satisfaction to administer consolation to your declining father. The day cannot be very distant when he too will be taken from us & then how will it mitigate your grief to consider that you have been enabled to chear his solitary hours & smooth his descent to the silent tomb! May kind Heaven postpone the Aweful hour!

Judy has been extremely ill & is yet very low. She will gratefully embrace Papa's offer & send William [her son] as soon as the weather will admit & I sincerely hope Papa may find amusement in the society & instruction of his little Grandson. It will amuse Papa & give him pleasure to hear that his former pupil (Peter) receiv'd a premium last friday, & that he continues to behave himself as well as his Grand-papa can wish. He is certainly an excellent child & as I cannot but impute a great deal of his worth to the early impressions he acquired at Eliz. Town under the care of his Affectionate Grand-Parents & yourself I am led by duty not vanity to mention it to you.

I should be very happy could I accept your friendly invitation & pass a few days with you, but I must do violence to my inclinations & postpone a little longer that pleasure. At present the federal court is sitting [with] Mr. Jay much engaged. It is expected that it will not be long before it will adjourn & then shd. Mr. Jefferson arrive Mr. Jay wd. be at leisure to attend me on a visit to Papa & yourself; a circumstance he has much at heart.

I wish you wd. request Woodruff to call for your things. I have put your spangled gown & book muslin petticoat in the little trunk I shall send by him. As I had worn your petticoat before I made my apron I've had it wash'd. Yesterday I paid Mrs. Simson, she says the cost of the spangles she mentioned to you was with reference to the Throat you first proposed to the silk sprigg. The work appears to me to be well done & I think you'll not repent the price of it when you see it; but shd. you not be reconciled to it perhaps I may take it of you. You say you know very little that passes in the City, indeed there is very little that is new. This week the President will become our neighbour by removing into Mr. McComb's large house. It is a circumstance that gives general satisfaction as any thing that can render his situation more convenient must do; for it was known that the house he at present occupies was not sufficiently commodious....

I am my dr.

The highest federal court consisted of the chief justice and five associate justices. Each year the court met in early February and again at the beginning of August. In between, the justices, protesting loudly, rode circuit in prescribed geographical areas, often for weeks at a time.

In April 1790, John Jay began his first judicial circuit through New England, traveling as far afield as Portsmouth, New Hampshire. In Boston, Harvard University conferred upon him the diploma of Doctor of Laws, an honor of which Jay was very proud.

Sarah, with a new baby, William, remained at home but kept a busy schedule by visiting prominent dignitaries, offering hospitality to friends, overseeing her children's education, keeping in touch with relatives, and managing her household. Her energy seemed boundless; she faltered only when in ill health or when depressed by thoughts of her beloved husband's prolonged absence.

(SLJ to JJ at Boston) Friday 23d April 1790

My dear Mr. Jay,

As you have had some disagreeable weather I am impatient to hear whether it has affected your health or not. Peter Munro tells me, that in a letter to him you mention having written to me. I have not received your letter. Col: Wadsworth inform'd me last evening that the influenza was again very prevalent at Hartford: I dread the effects of that disorder more than ever, & sincerely hope you will guard against it as much as possible.

Our little folks are very well. The distance they suppose you to be at present, the still greater distance you are to travel, the impediments likely to interrupt yr. journey & the pleasing idea of your return are the interesting subjects of our domestic conversation. A week has elapsed since your departure & the servants have not yet given one occasion for the smallest dissatisfaction. Tomorrow or monday I shall pay my father the long intended visit.

Last Monday the President went to Long Island to pass a week there. On Wednesday Mrs. Washington call'd upon me to go with her to wait upon Miss Van Berckel & on thursday morning agreeable to invitation myself and the little girls took an early breakfast with her & then went with her & her little grand Children to Breakfast at Genl. Morris's Morissania. We pass'd together a very agreeable day & on our return dined with her as she wd. not take a refusal, after which I came home to dress & she was so polite as to take Coffee with me in the evening....

Adieu! my best beloved! May Blessings ever attend you!

Sa. Jay

(SLJ to JJ at Portsmouth) New York May 13th 1790

My dear Mr. Jay,

Your kind letters of the 3d & 6th insts. came to hand to day. Accept my beloved! my sincere thanks for them. The instant I was closing my last to you I was seized with a Giddiness in my head which was succeeded by violent pain & fever & pain in my Limbs. The little Babe has been likewise very ill. Thank God! he is better & I apprehend no danger. The Doctr. thinks he is again teething & that he is affected with the influenza likewise.

Yesterday being the day that Lady Temple sees company I had ordered a Carriage, but before the time for dressing, was too ill to keep off the bed. This morning Mr. & Mrs. Dalton were here. Mr. Dalton has offered to Frank any letters for you that come to my hand, & I intend to accept his offer for several that are lying here which I shall inclose in other Covers for him to direct. Among them you'll find that one has been opened; it being mark'd Baltimore & not having heard from Kitty, I fear'd she might be ill & had desir'd a friend to inform you of it.

Mary has taken it in her head to go to Nova Scotia with Mrs. Wright, & as William is a stranger to his new Nurse, it is rare that he will quit me. Mrs. Hamilton had gone to N. Ark to visit her Mother who is ill, before we were taken sick. When I write again which shall be by the next Post I hope to write you better accounts. Sick or Well, Living or Dying

I shall remain my dearest husband!

ever yours!
S. Jay

(SLJ Jay to JJ at Portsmouth) New York, May 15th, 1790

My dr. Mr. Jay,

When I wrote you last, William & myself were very poorly, so was likewise Peggy Jay. Thank God! we are all three much better, & will I hope soon be well. The rest of the Children are well. Mr. Lewis has recollected that the price Peter [Munro] offer'd him was in fact the one he had agreed to take, & consequently he has recd. the payment; & that business is settled. A person that has hir'd a farm adjoining the one of yours at Havrestraw on which old Theele liv'd, wishes to make a purchase of yours and wants to know the terms. He can pay down 200£ & the rest as you may agree. The President is ill & has been so some days. The family think his illness serious. Dr. Jones has been sent for from Philadelphia & is here now & attends with Bard, Charlton & McKnight....

Yesterday I recd. 50£ from a Mr. Ball on acct. of Rutherford for your sister Nancy, & I have just been paying it to Peter Munro for her, which is apropos as he is going to Rye on Monday.

The little girls are gone to drink tea with their Cousin Munro, who dines with me to-morrow. We make out very well, no difficulties have yet occur'd. Ain't you a little fearful of the consequences of leaving me so long sole mistress. Peter Munro paid me 65£ for you which I've been spending at a great rate. Adieu my dear Mr. Jay. Believe me to be

sincerely & affectionately Yours
Sa. Jay

Not a single person of Mr. Adams's family have call'd upon me in your absence.

(SLJ to JJ at Boston) New York, 3rd Novbr, 1790

My dr. Mr. Jay,

I was sorry to find by your letter from Springfield that you had left Hartford the very day that my letter must have arrived there, & that in consequence of that you must have remained longer in suspense about our healths & the causes of my silence than otherwise you would have done. By this time however I hope your solicitude is removed by the rect. of my two last letters.

I shall continue to write by every post, relying upon the directions you will give the Post-master. The Children still remain in good health, not excepting William, who is as playful as a Kitten. I am not quite as well myself as when I wrote last, but hope I shall be better soon. Our son Peter is this inst. returned from Rye. He left the family well yesterday, & came to Town by water, having been all day yesterday & all last night upon the river. His arrival is very providential as the weather is now quite stormy & it would have been unsafe to be on the water longer. He looks extremely well, & intends writing to you this afternoon....

On Monday last I was at a Ball at Mrs. Knox's. There were several Ladies from Boston there who were much admired: Miss Brick & Miss Storer were of the number. Be so good as to remember me to Judge & Mrs. [William] Cushing & any other acquaintances of mine that you may meet with in your travels. Susan & the Children desire to be remembered to you. If it will give you pleasure to invite the Judge & his Lady to stay with us in their way to Philadelphia, it will give me pleasure to entertain them.

Adieu my dr. Mr. Jay. When I look forward to 5 or 6 weeks longer of absence my spirits almost shrink. Endeavor to raise my spirits when you write me again. I acknowledge that it is weakness in me to find any thing insupportable that is unavoidable but you know we (females) are but weaker vessels. Adieu my best beloved!

Yours affectionately
S. Jay

(JJ to SLJ) Boston, 10th November, 1790

My Dear Sally:

I hope this evening to be favoured with assurances under your hand that you and the children continue well. My cold and consequently the cough occasioned by it have left me. I am happy in being rid of such disagreeable companions.

Governor Bowdoin is to be interred this afternoon. His funeral will strongly mark the estimation in which he was held. Various societies will attend it, etc. To him these attentions will be vain, but to his family pleasing. Posthumous fame is in no other respect valuable than as it may be instrumental to the good of survivors.

I dined two days ago with Mr. [Elbridge] Gerry; they have a pretty seat. He will go on to Congress the last of this month; she will remain at home, and both will experience from absence what you and I have often done. Her situation at six miles' distance from Boston will be but solitary, but she has children and domestic employments to amuse and occupy her attention.

I have dined but once at my lodgings, viz., the day I arrived, and am engaged for every day previous to the one on which I shall set out for Exeter—that is, until Monday next. The hospitality and sociability of this place are singular. I remark another circumstance that is pleasing. Almost at every table you find a clergyman. Instead of being a check to the cheerfulness of company, they partake in and promote it. Their characters are in general amiable, and they are respected accordingly....

I am, my dear Sally,

Yours very affectionately,
John Jay

(SLJ to JJ at Providence) New York, Nov 28, 1790
Sunday Morng. near 6 o'clock

My dear Mr. Jay,

Our dear little girl [Nancy] being now in a sweet slumber, & the house all quiet, I will endeavor to employ some of my lonely sleepless moments in continuing an account of her situation. You know I wrote you by the last Post, which was on Wednesday evening; on thursday the Doctr. gave her more mercury, & finding her on friday considerably salivated desisted, and, tho' her throat still continues ulcered, he told me the salivation was a favorable circumstance & he flattered me wh. hopes that she wd. recover. I then regretted sincerely having inform'd you of her illness, & wish'd I had suffered alone the anxiety occasioned by it.

Yesterday morning however I was more reconciled to the conduct I had pursued; for when the Dr. upon examining her throat found the complaint still the same, he confess'd his apprehension of a mortification (for the situation of the dear little lamb from salivation was such as evinced the danger of administering more mercury) and requested me to call in another Physician lest you might be dissatisfyed shd. he prove unsuccesful. I told him, that I knew the confidence you reposed in his skill, attention & friendship was such, that should that be the case, tho' it wd. give You infinite concern, yet I was sure that he wd. remain perfectly free from censure; but that nevertheless, I was ready to acquiesce in any thing he proposed. He then told me that it wd. be agreeable to him to have further advice, & mentioned Bard. To him therefore Peter went immediately, & after a consultation, it was agreed that Bark shd. be immediately given in substance & by injection to prevent putressence. It has therefore been administered according to direction & I hope good effects will result from it. She has rested better this last night than heretofore, tho' she has frequently awaked with tooth-ach & pain in her gums. A little while ago I put Laudanum on cotton & put it in her tooth, since which she has been easier. I long for 8 o'clock to hear the Doctor's opinion.

Altho' there are many persons confin'd with colds & sore throats, yet Nancy's is the only instance we have heard of the putrid kind. The rest of the Children are well. As to myself, I am as well as can be expected. I have not left the child an hour since she has been known to have the putrid sore throat which was last Monday, nor do I mean to leave her. The effluvia from her breath is so offensive that it creates a great nausea at my stomach.

2 o'Clock The Doctors have been, and direct a continuance of the Bark as yesterday. They think her throat looks rather better. I forgot to mention that Susan is

very ill with a fever, severe cough & pain in her side. Peggy Munro has had a miscarriage & is a-bed, but not uncommonly ill. I sent a note to church for Nancy.

7 o'Clock Doctr. Charlton has this inst. left us. He says I may assure you our dear little girl is out of danger. I flatter myself that you will receive this & my last letter at the same time & that therefore your suspense will be lessened. As it will be impossible for me to tell where to direct to you in future, you must not be uneasy if you do not hear from me, tho' I imagine next thursday's post may find you at Providence & shall accordingly write by that.

Adieu my dear Mr. Jay! May you be preserv'd from every danger & restored to your expecting family &

affectionate Wife
Sa. Jay

Peggy Munro is quite bravely, & P[eter]. M[unro]. likewise who has had a severe sore throat.

(SLJ to JJ at New York) (originally sent to Providence) New York Decbr. 1st 1790

My dear Mr. Jay,

Just before I closed my last letter to you I was so happy as to have the Dr's opinion in favor of our dr. little girl's recovery, since which her throat has been gradually mending, & her health rapidly returning. Her fever is quite broke, & her appetite restored. Could I have flatter'd myself with hopes of her recovery, I wd. with pleasure have spared you the anxiety which reluctantly I was obliged to excite. As I have not heard from you by the last two Posts, I hope this evening to receive a line & shall not close this until I have sent to the Office.

With what pleasure do I recollect that the last Court you are to hold will be this week; & that from next Monday you will be every day approaching home. I wrote Mrs. Peter Jay, informing her of your health & Nancy's illness; I shall this evening write her the alteration that has taken place in her health. P. Munro & his little Wife are both bravely. So are Fady & Peggy. Sister susan remains very ill. She has for 4 days taken James's powders without success. The Dr. calls her fever a bilious inflammatory one.

Uncle R[obert]. Livingston Dyed in his Chair last monday. He had been declining some time. Oh my dr. Mr. Jay! how many of our friends have been called home this last twelve month. Oh! may they not have dyed for us in vain. Nancy says I must tell Papa she is impatient to see him. She is standing by my side shaking me. She says sick persons must be indulged.

The Post has arrived & Yaff has return'd without a letter. The Doctr. try'd to make mischief, I'll tell you one these days what he says prevents you from writing.

Adieu my dr.

yours affectionately
Sa. Jay

(JJ to SLJ at New York) Wallingford Conn 12 Dec 1790

My dear Sally,

This is Sunday. On Wednesday last I set out from Providence. The weather very cold, and the Roads rendered bad by Snow and Ice. I was strongly tempted to wait untill Saturday for your Letter, but considering that to be relieved from Suspence respecting Nancy was less interesting to us all than to be at Home speedily, I concluded it would be best to return without Delay, & direct the post master to send the Letter after me. By rising early and travelling late, I reached Hartford on Friday night. Yesterday it rained. I am nevertheless come to this place, with Intention to go on early this morning to New Haven. The distance being only 13 miles. This morning the weather is so bad that it would be very imprudent to turn out. It rained constantly during the night, and the Roads are in a sad Plight. I have had so much to do with cold and wet, that I really wish for a Respite, and shall be very happy to enjoy the comforts of Leisure and my own fireside with You and the Children. I did flatter myself with the Pleasure of being with you on Wednesday next, but that cannot now be the Case. I hope however that in the Course of the Week I may be able to reach New York. Altho your Letter assures me that in Doctor Charltons opinion Nancy was out of Danger, yet it would give me great Satisfaction to learn that he was not mistaken. I do not expect to have Information of this before I get to Rye. God grant that I may there receive good Tidings of you all. As passing thro' Bedford would detain me at least a Day, I shall postpone visiting it to another opportunity.

I write this letter with Intention to send it to the post office at New Haven; for there is now no Reason to doubt that you will recieve it before you will see me. Had the weather continued fair I should have been in New York as soon as the next post. Unless it should again freeze the Roads will be deep & heavy, and if it should freeze they will be very rough and bad for the Horses at least for four or five Days. To these circumstances we must accommodate ourselves and be content.

Adieu my dear Sally. My Love to the children &c.

Your affecty.
John Jay

New Haven Sunday Evg.

The weather clearing this afternoon I came to this place. The Roads are now so bad by Reason of the Rain that I cannot promise myself the pleasure of seeing you before Friday; especially as the greater part of Tomorrow morning will be spent in having my Horses shod. They had had hard service, and must be drawn with Patience and Care. I learn tonight that Slidells House has been on fire. My Informer was at it. He could not tell me how you and the children did. He said he had not heard anything to the contrary of their being well, which I think it not unprobable he wd. have done, had Nancy not have recovered. I think of her constantly, and tho' not with gloomy apprehensions, yet with a mind not wholly free from apprehensions. I expect to set out about Noon Tomorrow. The Brooks and Rivers are exceedingly swelled. The Country and Roads are full of water. I have a ferry (not very well attended to pass) and much bad Road. I will make what haste I can. On Friday or Saturday at furthest, if the weather continues good you may expect me. With fresh Horses I might see you sooner.

John was home for a short interval before setting off again, this time to Philadelphia. John Adams, now Vice-President, invited Jay to stay at his home, an offer Jay probably accepted at least once. On other visits to Philadelphia, he stayed in lodgings.

In the spring of 1791, Sarah and Peter Augustus accompanied John Jay on the circuit tour. Maria, Nancy and William stayed behind with their Aunt Susan. After an enjoyable visit with brother Peter and his wife Polly at Rye, the Jays went on to Bedford to inspect their retirement farm. At they wended their way toward New Haven, Sarah particularly enjoyed the inn in Norwalk, Connecticut. The trip ended in Newport, Rhode Island, when Peter became ill. Mother and son returned to New York City while John continued on his circuit.

(SLJ to her daughter Maria at New York) New Haven Apl. 23d. 1791

My dear Maria,

We arrived here last evening after a very agreeable ride, having had a great deal of pleasant weather. I sent immediately to the Post-office hoping to receive a letter from your Aunt Susan, but as there was none, I flatter myself I shall receive one by the next Post, & another by the 12th of May at Boston. If your Aunt shd. hear when Mrs. Dalton passes thro' New York, I'm sure she wd. take charge of a letter [for] me with pleasure.

I hope my dear, that you & your sister behave well and attend to your Aunt's directions; if you do (and I should be very sorry to think otherwise) you may both begin to learn to dance of Mrs. Graham as soon as she is ready to teach in our neighbourhood, & if when I return I find your progress in dancing & in those studies you are to pursue under the direction of yr. Aunt equal my expectation, you shall then learn some other branch of Mrs. G. In the mean time take great pains with what you are now learning, practise your dancing & don't forget St. Aivres' directions for I have a great opinion of his skill in his way. It will give me particular pleasure if I find on my return that you and yr. sister stand high in Mrs. Graham's favor on account of your polite & very attentive behaviour. As I expect great pleasure from the conduct of yourself & sister when I return, I will endeavor to amuse you both by a short detail of occurrences since I left you.

After passing a week at Rye we went to Bedford where we stayed until last wednesday, when we set out for this place, & as the weather was fine, & we were not hurried, we travel'd leisurely, and have been very fortunate in putting up at good houses, where we found civil people, clean beds, & good-fare. At Norwalk we lodged at a good Inn, situated near a mill dam which is on a pretty stream, & the fall of the water from thence, together with the view renders the place very rural: but what I fancy wd. have delighted you & Nan is a very pretty spring which the Land-lord has stoned round & put trout in, whom he keeps tame by feeding & you may at any time see them by throwing some crumbs into the spring which they immediately catch at. The Country in genl. thro' which we have pass'd abounds wh. pretty towns & fine views. The most beautiful View however is at the brow of an Hill about two miles & a half from this place....

May I my dear flatter myself with the hopes of receiving a letter from [you]. If you cannot write well enough yet, I hope you will soon. Embrace Nancy & William for yr. Papa, Peter & myself & they must return the embrace on our part to you. Believe me my dear daughter to be

your affectionate mother
Sa. Jay

(JJ to his son PAJ at New York) Newport, R. I. 17 June 1791

My dear Son

I was very agreably surprized to Day at dinner to receive a Letter from your Mama, acquainting me with her & your safe arrival. I did not expect to have heard from her so soon. It will give me pleasure to hear that your Health is entirely re-established.

Peet has written a Letter to Mr. King, which it seems is the name of a black man (Servant belonging to old Mr. Lewis, but who lives with his wife a free woman in Nassau Street). He requests me to enclose this Letter to you. He requests also that you will be so kind as to send it to King immediately by Yaff, or by Clarindas Husband Pompey, both of whom know where King lives. Direct the one whom you may send to tell King that Peet has written two Letters to him, but recd. no answer. If neither Yaff nor Pompey can go, it would be good natured in you to leave this Letter at Mr. Lewis' House. Providence has placed these Persons in Stations below us. They are Servants, but they are Men; and Kindness to Inferiors more strongly indicates Magnanimity than Meanness. Inform me of what you may do respecting this Matter. Peet wishes the Letter to be delivered without Delay, that King may answer it by the Packet & he have a chance of recieving it before I set out for Vermont.

Farewell my dear Peter. Continue attentive to the Health both of your Mind & Body, and be assured that I desire nothing more ardently than that you may be happy here and hereafter.

I am your affectionate father
John Jay

On October 11, 1791, John Jay again began to ride the Eastern circuit. Accompanied by his son Peter, he made stops at Rye and Bedford. In his Circuit Diary John wrote:

> The crib is finished — gave Directions for a Hay House 50 by 28 near the Meadows. Place for Potatoes in ye Bank near the House begun. Well 20 feet & as yet no water — the last 20 feet thro' a rotten Rock. A Bridge over the Brook in the intended Lane nearly finished.

Father and son went their separate ways, John on to Hartford, Peter back to Rye. During her husband's prolonged absence, Sarah had to contend with the illnesses of children and the death of Frederick Jay's wife.

(SLJ to JJ at Hartford) New York Octbr 29th 1791

My Dr. Mr. Jay,

Yr. Letter of the 25th did not come to hand 'till yesterday & the Post for Hartford left N.Y. the day before, when, supposing a letter by it wd. not find you there I omitted writing by it. Your letter written at Bedford & committed to Peter's care arrived this inst. The moment Essex comes in I shall send to Captn. Post. Maria is recovered. William for this week past has been ill with boils & worms, & I have, in consequence of the fatigue attending his sickness been much indisposed. It is with difficulty I shall [take] these few moments to write, for he will not quit me.

Thus much I have endeavored to collect my thoughts enough to relate, thinking it important you shd. be made acquainted with the state of the family. But the unfortunate catastrophe in yr. brother's family has distress'd my mind & shock'd my nerves so that I scarcely know what I write. Yesterday morning Dr. Charlton as usual call'd to see Wm. He asked me if I had heard that Mrs. F. Jay was ill. He then proceeded to tell me that at 5 o'Clock that morning he had been sent for to her & that he had found her in an appoplectic fit from which he apprehended much danger. After a little more preparation he told me that she had expired at half past eight that morning. Judge my dr. Mr. Jay! how awful such an unexpected summons appeared to me! & how sincerely I felt for your brother. I immediately sent Saunders to him to know if he could be useful. P. Munro at his request wrote to your brother Peter & Mr. Courtlandt & Saunders went with the letters. I likewise wrote one to Polly & am in hourly expectation of their arrival. Sir James unfortunately was in Jersey, whither an express was sent in the night, but he did not arrive until she was past relief.

I have not been down to Fady's. I am unable. Last night Susan took Wm. in her bed; but finding I could not rest & that my nerves were much agitated, I sent for Elixer Paragoric which composed me tho' it did not procure me much sleep.

....Adieu my best beloved! when I write again I hope to be in better health & spirits. Excuse this unconnected scrawl. William shakes & interrupts me so often that had I felt more at ease I could not have written with satisfaction. It was a great consolation to me to find you had reached Hartford without suffering in yr. health for I had much feared the bad weather would have impaired it. Once more Adieu! blame me not for not writing oftener but think with the tenderness of

your affectionate Wife
Sa. Jay

Sunday morng. Yesterday brother P. & Polly arrived here.... Fady is tolerable. This evening poor sister Jay is to be interred. William & myself are better.

(SLJ to JJ) New York Monday 31st Octbr 1791

My dear Mr. Jay,

To-days post carries a letter from me to you.... To-day for the first I visited yr. unfortunate brother, it was a painful task. He is however tolerable. I told him it wd. give me pleasure if he wd. relinquish the cares of house-keeping & stay with us 'till spring, that it wd. make yr. absence seem more tolerable & I hoped conduce to his health as he could attend to his business then without the additional care of Domestic concerns. He reply'd that I was very good, but that having that little Girl & Tommy* it wd. be necessary for him to hire some discreet woman to take charge of the family. Peter & Polly are gone there this evening & they have promised Fady to stay there to-night.

Our son came with your brother to Town, he still continues well. William is yet very sore, but his fever has left him. I have been so much engaged the whole day that I have not had a moments leisure to write before, & it is now so late that I can only repeat that I am with the greatest sincerity

yours most affectionately
Sa. Jay

(SLJ to JJ at Providence) New York Novbr [1791]

My dear mr. Jay

Your favors ... have all reached me & infused pleasure into my bosom! I thank you my dearest best of friends for your very kind attention in writing so frequently. The last Post had not any letter from me as I imagined you wd. be on the Road from Exeter to Providence. Your absence renders me insensible to the value of time, for instead of prizing it, I wish & wish the hours away longing for your return.

I this moment came from your brother's, I was happy to find him up, he begins to recover. Mr. Watson he told me had applied for his house for the branch of the National bank that is to be established at N.Y. & he did not doubt that he could obtain 500£ per Annum for it, but added he I cannot turn myself out of doors at this season of the Year. I told him that he was undoubtedly the best judge what step was best to be taken, that he knew our house & that if he could make it servicable to himself or to dispose his things while making arrangements, it would be giving us pleasure. He said he had a family & could not spare his house; hard to be saddled with other People's children as to be unable to act for oneself.

The Family are well. Susan desires her Love: I am interrupted by company & fear to detain my letter until they leave me but the mail shd. be closed.

Yours affectionately
Sa. Jay

**Fady's wife's niece and nephew.*

(SLJ to JJ at Boston) New York 13th Novbr 1791

My dear Mr. Jay

I am afraid you'll think it a long time since I've written, but I flatter myself you know me better than to impute my silence either to inattention or to indolence. The truth is that Mrs. Hamilton did not return 'till after the Post left N.Y., & tho' you was not an hour absent from my mind I could not snatch a moment to tell you so.

From the time you left Rye 'till this day, one or other has been indisposed, which of course increased my cares, & Mrs. Hamilton's visit of 3 weeks prov'd tedious to me. Essex, Maria, & Yaff have taken their turns to be confin'd with sore throats, fever &c. and at present our son Peter is confined with it, which has prevented him from visiting his Uncle Fady as he would otherwise have done. They have none of them had the malignant sore throat nor is it true that a putrid complaint prevails. Nevertheless the Doctor has attended the children. Your brother is bravely. He & Tommy & sister Munro & her son & his wife dine with me to-day, your friends at Rye are well. I am myself likewise as well as usual & so are the Children except Peter, who is recovering.

Oh! my dr. Mr. Jay shd. you too be unwell & be absent from me, & I deprived of the satisfaction & consolation of attending you how wretched shd. I be! but away disquieting apprehensions! An over-ruling providence guards my husband & protects his family. Oh my dr. Mr. Jay how I long to see you.

Our friends are just entering the door & I must bid my dearest best of friends Adieu. The Children & their Aunt Susan all desire to be affectionately remembred to you.

I am my dear
your sincerely wife
Sa. Jay

(SLJ to JJ at Exeter) New York Novbr 23d 1791

My dear Mr. Jay,

I had the pleasure of writing to you by the last post, since which yr. favor of the 13th pr. post came safe to hand. I am very happy to find you continue to enjoy yr. health, may providence still preserve it to you & restore you again to a family who loves you tenderly. Myself & children are bless'd with health likewise. Your brother still remains indisposed. I visited him this morning & found he was yet confined to his bed. The gathering in his knee has been lanced which has procured him relief from pain, but the loss of appetite & of sleep render his situation uncomfortable & makes me uneasy. It will be charitable in you to write to him.

A few evenings ago Judge Hobart favor'd me with a friendly visit. He told me that Mrs. Hobart had been these six months talking of waiting upon me. I told him that I should be much flatter'd by her company, but to convince him that I was in earnest, I intend to-morrow to send for them to eat Wafles. Yesterday I waited upon Lady Temple & from her heard of you.

Captn. Post has secur'd the drain. There is one Hogshead of Paynes red-streak arrived for you. It costs £5.10s. Susan accidentally mentioning it at Dr. Jones's he said he shd. be happy to have 1 Barrel if we had more than we wished. I have not given him an ansr. yet as I wished first to know whether it would be agreeable to you. I offered P. M. a barrel, but he does not wish for any.

This morning I walked out with the children the weather being very inviting, & on my return call'd upon Mrs. Barrett. She told me that in the same house a gentleman lodged who was going to Salem & would have opportunities of forwarding letters to you; the Children will write by him, but I could not defer 'till then the pleasure of assuring you of the unceasing affection of

yr. faithful Wife
S. Jay

(JJ to his son PAJ at New York) Boston 29th Novr. 1791

My dear Son

I returned yesterday in the afternoon from Exeter. This morning I recd. and read with Pleasure your Letter of the 23d. Instant. The Inaccuracies in it scarcely required an appology. Some Errors are observable in the Stile, very few in the matter. I regard the attempt as a mark of attention to my wishes, and shall not forget it. Having many Letters to answer and many Visits to pay, I can devote only a few moments this Evening to you. Early on Thursday morning I expect to set out for Scituate, and from thence proceed with Judge Cushing to Providence on the ensuing Saturday.

The Letter which Essex [Ridley] mentions to have written to me has arrived, and shall be answered as soon as I can find Leisure for the Purpose.

Few books, if properly read, afford more useful Lessons than the Lives of great Men, and among Biographers Plutarch is certainly entitled to the first Place. To enjoy the Experience of others without paying the Price which it often cost them, is pleasant as well as profitable. Mankind is the same in all ages, however diversified by colour manners or customs. To regulate our conduct wisely relative to Men, is the most difficult Task we have to perform in the course of our Lives. To know them is necessary but not easy. History will teach us much, but unremitted observation more. Both assist each other. Habituate yourself to trace actions up to their motives. Let me again repeat that we have two worlds to exist in, and that you may be happy in both, is not only the wish but the Prayer of

Your affte. Father
John Jay

(John Adams to JJ at New York) Philadelphia January the fourth 1792

Dear Sir

As the week is approaching when you are to be expected at Philadelphia, I take this opportunity to present to you and your Lady the Compliments of the Season, and request the honour and pleasure of your Company, at our House during your visit to this City. We live in Arch Street at the Corner of fourth Street where your old bed is ready for you in as good a Chamber and much more conveniently situated for your attendance on your Court and intercourse with your Friends. Mrs. Jay we hope will bear you company and in this request Mrs. Adams joins with me. The winter is very mild: Politicks dull. Speculation brisk. As we have little Interest in these Things we shall have a freer Scope for Friendship. I am, dear Sir

with Sincere Esteem,
yours
John Adams

(JJ to John Adams) [Draft]

NYork 10 Jan 1792

Dear Sir

I cannot easily tell you how much I am pleased & obliged by your friendly Letter of the 4th Instant. Were I to pursue my Inclinations I shd. without Hesitation accept your kind Invitation but our Inclinations even in things innocent must not always be gratified. My Visits to Philadelphia have ceased to be occasional, or I shd. certainly avail myself of those opportunities wh. your Hospitality would afford, for that free and social Intercourse which I shall always be happy to enjoy & indulge. The Courts call me regularly & periodically to Philadelphia, and they will continue to call me as long as I remain in office, or the present order of Things continues unchanged. This circumstance produces considerations which press me on those occasions to be in Lodgings; and the more so, as your living in Town obviates Impediments to our seeing each other frequently, and passing as many pleasant Hours together as our official affairs may permit.

Mrs. Jays situation will not admit of her being from Home next Term. We expect an Increase of our family abt. that Time. A severe cold and croup have confined her to her chamber for ten Days past. She is much indisposed, and as yet I do not percieve that her Complaints abate. Indeed the present state of her Health added to the Situation she will soon be in, strongly oppose my leaving her. She requests the favor of you to present her best compts. & acknowledgements to Mrs. Adams. Be pleased to add mine....

With sincere Esteem & Regard I am
Dr Sr yr obliged & obt Servt.

Though it may have seemed to John, as he set off for Philadelphia in early 1792, that this year would be a repeat of the last, there were two differences. There was a new baby, Sarah Louisa, at home and John had been nominated for governor of New York State. The adherents of the incumbent George Clinton lost no time in mounting an attack, not on Jay's integrity, which was unimpeachable, but on his support for a strong federal government and his advocacy of the abolition of slavery. Opponents claimed that it was Jay's particular wish "to rob every Dutchman of the property he possesses most dear to his heart, his slaves ... [and] to oblige their masters to educate the children of those slaves." Scurrilous pieces purported to have been written by Jay appeared in the newspapers but he denied any knowledge of them. In fact, Jay did not campaign and showed very little interest in the outcome. On April 15, he left New York for Rye and New Haven, his mind more on trees and his family than on ballots.

> [P]lanted 2 willow Trees—one in the Row between ye wash House & orchard Wall—ye other nearly opposite to the first between the Locust & Walnut Trees ... Also planted some plumb Trees along ye board house in ye Garden & a pear Tree in ye patch [Rye, 15 April 1792].

(SLJ to JJ at New Haven) New York April 22d, 1792

My dear Mr. Jay,

As this letter will arrive at New Haven about the time the Court meet there, you will have the satisfaction of hearing that the family continue well. Peter & Nancy are quite recovered from the mumps: and the rest of the children remain well. Frank you know was indisposed when you left us, & he still keeps his bed. The Docter has discovered that his disorder proceeds from stomach worms.

Last tuesday Mr. Watts call'd to look at your horse, & afterwards sent for it to ride. I've not heard from him since, but he afterwards met Peter in the street & told him that the horse would not suffer him to mount. Carver has since rode it out, & says he must repeat his rides several times before he can offer it for sale, as it is very unmanagable. He advises sending it to [the] Coffee-house to be sold at Vendue, but of that you are the best Judge. The trees you left for your brother have been sent to Rye. The Cattle you expected are not yet come.

Peter Munro will I suppose give you any political information that may occur. Your friends at Philadelphia seem to relinquish the expectation of seeing you there again, at least in your official capacity, as Mrs. Morris has sent your Robe to you, which Mr. Soderstrom was so obliging as to leave here this morning. Susan desires her best respects to you. The Children desire me to assure you of their love & of their endeavors to merit yours.

We have not heard from Mrs. Ridley or from Charles-town since you left us. Essex & Susy are well. I feel such a depression of spirits that I cannot even hope to amuse you; when I write to you again, I hope I shall have received a letter from you, & that I know will dispel the vapours that make me dull & gloomy.

Adieu! my dear Mr. Jay. May that serenity in which you delight be ever yours & Oh! may it be reflected from your bosom on that of yr. at present dejected

S. Jay

(JJ to his son PAJ at New York) New Haven 25th April 1792

My dear Son

I had flattered myself that a letter from you would have accompanied the one I received from your mama. She will recieve two letters from me by the packet which is to carry this; in one of them is enclosed a little white mulberry seed, and I shall also enclose some in this for your Uncle Peter. Plant a few in our garden; the trees will be but small by the Fall, and we may then carry them to Bedford, where in time they will become ornamental, and perhaps useful. When you visit your uncle you may propose planting some of them in his nursery, or in any other place that he may think more eligible. It always gives me pleasure to see trees which I have reared and planted, and therefore I recommend it to you to do the same. Planting is an innocent and a rational amusement. My Father planted many trees, and I never walk in their shade without deriving additional pleasure from that circumstance; the time will come when you will probably experience similar emotions.

On my way here I dined yesterday at Lewis's Inn, about three miles west of Stratford on the post road. He told me that several years ago he was grafting apple-trees, and that near them had grown a young walnut-tree. A fancy took him to graft it; he did so, and with an apple graft, it took and flourished, is now alive, and above three inches in diameter. This is singular, and contrary to our modern ideas. If I am not mistaken Columilla* mentions something like it. I think he says that any tree may be grafted on any tree; a little experience is worth much theory. If I had leisure I would try many experiments.

I am, my dear Peter,
Your affectionate Father,
John Jay

(SLJ to JJ at Boston) New York April 29th 1792

My dear Mr. Jay,

Yesterday morning the Vice President call'd upon me, & after he took leave of me I waited upon Mrs. Adams, & invited her to dine with me to-day, which she declined, being indisposed. She just now returned my visit, and offered to take a letter for you. Nothing new has happened since my last. P[eter] M[unro] has returned & is going to write to you this evening. Carver has this instant left the parlour. He says there is no demand for horses, but thinks it most expedient to send the sorrel in the Country to be kept in the cheapest manner.

As you are no longer in danger of inconvenience from your southern friend, would it not be best to resume your plan of building? I just hint this, because I am inform'd materials for that purpose are cheaper in this city at present than they have been since the peace.

I have had our dear little babe innoculated three times without effect, which has kept my mind a long time in suspense.... The Child is perfectly healthy & good humor'd. As Mrs. Hamilton wish'd to stay here a little longer, & Mrs. Low was desirous of paying a visit to her daughter at Brunswick, it was perfectly convenient to me to gratify them both. I have no idea of going to Rye at present, & doubt my doing it before you return.

**Lucius Junius Moderatus, Latin writer on agriculture and care of domestic animals.*

When Mrs. Ridley wrote me she had not received your letter. Susan & the little folks beg to be remembred to you. I have been witness to some scenes between William and his little sister that were so interesting that I would have given a great deal you could have shar'd the pleasure with me.

I am my dear Mr. Jay
very affectionately yours
Sa. Jay

(SLJ to JJ at Boston) New York 6th May 1792

My dear Mr. Jay,

Since yours of the 30th of April came to hand, I flatter myself you've recd. mine of the 28th & 29th Ult. It gives me great pleasure to find that your health has been improved by travelling, & I hope it will be preserved during the rest of your journey, myself and family likewise continue well; and I had the satisfaction to find from sister Jay's letter of yesterday (in answer to mine) that she & your brother remain so too. The man who drove your Marlborough Cattle to Rye, return'd yesterday, & brought me a letter from Polly in which she mentions their arriving in good order, which has relieved me from anxiety on that subject.

Yesterday our son went to Rye. A day or two ago I received a letter for you from London, & as I imagined it was from Mr. Johnson I opened it, & found he had ship'd for you 24 Doz. of Porter: I gave the letter to Peter to take to the custom-house, where, after paying the duties he obtained a permit, which he left with the Captn., who promised to send up the porter as soon as he conveniently could.

I believe I wrote you that our little girl had been three time[s] innoculated ineffectually. I was then discouraged but the Doctor advising me to repeat the attempt, I consented to his performing the operation the fourth time on monday last; he thinks she has taken the infection, but I confess I have my doubts. She still enjoys perfect health & is as complacent as an Angel. Will is all vivacity. You are the prevailing subject of his prattle. I believe he dreamt the other night that you had returned, for when he awoke he insisted upon your being at home, nor would he be convinced to the contrary until I carryed him in your room. My little name-sake, contrary to your opinion, is likely to remain unrival'd.

My Compts. to inquiring friends & believe me my dearest Mr. Jay

to be affectionately yours
Sa. Jay

(JJ to his daughter Maria at New York) Brookfield 7th may 1792

My dear Maria

The Day before I left New Haven, I had the Pleasure of recieving from Mrs. Adams, your Letter of the 28th of last month, enclosed in one from your mama. I think your Handwriting still continues to improve, and I hope you will remember how much you are indebted for it to your Aunt Susan's kind Attention.

By this Time I presume the Garden is in order. Request your Brother to assign a place for You and Nancy to plant your Flower Seeds. Whatever part you have, I daresay you will be mindful to weed and keep it in order. Mama will shew you how to plant them so, that they may be most ornamental. You should make it a Rule to do every Thing in the best manner, and take pains to learn what the best manner is.

Give little Wm. a kiss for me. I know you love him dearly, but take care not to humour him in any Thing improper. The sooner he learns to bear being denied, what he ought not to have, the better. While he has no Discretion of his own, the Want of it must be supplied by that of others; and when he shall be of Age to judge for himself, he will not be pleased with any, whose indiscreet Indulgencies may have led him into mistakes, and into a Habit of expecting that all his Caprices and Passions are to be indulged.

I make these Remarks not because I have observed or suspect any Thing amiss; but merely because I think them worthy of Attention. What I mean is, that you should, as I dare say you do, endeavour to improve as well as to please him. May you all love and improve each other. Adieu my dear Maria, I am your very affectionate Father

John Jay

(SLJ to JJ at Boston or Portsmouth) New York, 13th May 1792

My dear Mr. Jay,

Your favor of the 5th of May as well as the others you mention came safe to hand. The family still continue well. Our dear little babe remains proof against the small-pox. It is a fortnight since she was innoculated the fourth time, & there is not the least appearance of the disorder, not even about the incision....

Susan desires me to remind you of her lottery ticket.* Your friends at Rye & New York are well. Mr. Munro, his wife & mother dine with me to-day. I sent likewise for your brother & his wards, but as he was going to Rye he could not come. He has twice call'd in upon business, but had not leisure to set down. Our Son & Essex are both at your brother's. Your directions about the sorrel horse shall be attended to; the other, Peter rode to Rye.

Frank, & indeed all the servants behave very well. Our domestic concerns have never been conducted with so much facility as at present. Indeed it is incredible how much our tranquility depends upon our servants. There is a total stagnation of news. The papers no longer contain the price of stock, the publication of it being prohibited by the Legislature to impede the progress of speculation; but that had already recd. such a check that I doubt the Act being necessary. Mr. Duer & [Mr.] Mc Comb still are in confinement.

It being time to prepare for Church, I must bid you adieu. Many of our friends flatter me with a probability of your return next month. For more reasons than one

**Lotteries were commonly used to raise money both before and after the Revolution. They provided funds for education, public works, the relief of Loyalist refugees, and the Revolutionary War itself. They were also influential in the growth of New York City's banking and financial markets.*

I wish their calculations may be justifyed by the event. Once more my dear Mr. Jay let me repeat that I am with the most tender attachment

yours affectionately
Sarah Jay

(SLJ to JJ at Boston) New York, May 23d. 1792

My dear Mr. Jay,

By an accident I miss'd writing pr. the last post, which I regret as I fear it has occasioned your feeling anxious about us. The letter inclosed in mine for Mr. Pintard was delivered to a young gentleman at his house, he himself not being in town.

I wrote you in my last by Mr. Dalton that your brother Fredk. was married, but believe I did not mention that it was to Miss Dunscomb. It seems he was already married when you left town, his wedding being on the 10th of April. Mr. Jay's relations resent the want of [respect] to her memory so much that none of them visit either him or his wife. Last saturday just as P. Munro & myself were deliberating what was to be done on our part, Fady came in. I suppose said he advancing towards me you have heard that I am married again. I have Mr. Jay, but not being authorised from you to believe it, did not credit it. It's true said he, I am. Will you take a chair Mr. Jay? No, I must be going, good bye. Good by Mr. Jay, that is all that has passed between us. Peter presently after went to Mrs. Dunscombs; she came herself to the door. He inquired if his Uncle Jay was at home, upon her replying in the negative he left a Card which he desired her to be good enough to give to his Uncle & then return'd & told me the result of his visit. He said he wd. carry Peggy to Rye on Monday & send our son the next day in your brothers chair for me, so that we might take Peter's sentiments respecting Peggy's conduct & mine towards the present Mrs. Jay. Fortunately Fady & his wife went to Brunswick the same day he, in that laconic manner, communicated his marriage to me. I feel the mortification his conduct must give you, who really love him; but we have both felt so much for those who feel not for themselves that we must both become less susceptible.

If I go to Rye I shall only stay a day or two. Susan is still here. By a letter from Kitty she learns that she cannot [put] the Tenant out of her house, & consequently cannot get [it for her] self, so that the Baltimore plan is not to be executed. The 29th inst. they begin publishing their votes, so that I shall soon know whether I am to have the pleasure of seeing you next month or attend that satisfaction still longer....

The family are well & desire to be remembred to you. Adieu my ever dear Mr. Jay, believe me with the sincerest affection

Unalterably yours
S. J.

(JJ to his daughters Maria and Nancy) Boston 1st June 1792

My dear little Girls

How happened it Maria! that your second Letter has not been finished. I was pleased with the first, & answered it. Your Mama in one of her Letters, says handsome Things of you; and I am happy to find that you merit her commendation. Go on my dear child! The more Progress you make in acquiring useful accomplishments, and amiable Manners, the more you will do Honor to yourself & to your Parents. You know that the Merit of my children is the only Rule by which my affection for them will ever be measured; and I please myself in the Expectation that I shall have Reason to love them all exceedingly.

And now for a few Lines to you Miss Nan! I have recd. your second Letter. It is a clever one, but was it all of your own composing? If it was, so much the better. Some of the words are written in a fine hand. The occurrence you mention is a pleasant one. Strange Things often come to pass from the want of seasonable consideration. I have not seen the Tales of the Castle, but from Lady Temple's recommending it, I presume it is a useful Book. Besides, if I mistake not, your Mama in one of her Letters to me, speakes well of it; and her opinion in its favor has much Weight with me.

I hope on my Return to find you both my dear children! much improved. Now is the Time for you to lay the Foundations of your future characters. Virtue and Religion must be the corner Stones; & if with these you connect useful Knowledge, mildness of Temper, & Prudence and good Manners, you will not only have great Reason to expect Happiness here, but what is of more Importance, be certain of it hereafter. After a few Years we must all quit this world, but in the next we are to abide forever. God bless and preserve you my dear children!

I am your very affectionate Father
John Jay

You must each give little Wilm. and Sally a Kiss for me
Maria is to keep this Letter, and Nancy the next that I may write to both.

The gubernatorial election took a month and a half to be decided because ballots from each county had to be properly forwarded to the office of the secretary of the state. The pro–Jay ballots from Otsego County were termed invalid on a technicality and burned. As a result Clinton was declared the winner. Jay, unruffled by his loss, refused to participate in any protest or action for redress. However, the next gubernatorial election would have a very different outcome.

(SLJ to JJ) New York, June 2d, 1792

My dear Mr. Jay,

I have had the pleasure of receiving your favor by Mr. Alden & the one of the 23d Ult. and thank you for them as well as for the kind allowance you make for the apparent silence on my part. I say apparent because in reallity I had written; but the letter which Mr. Dalton took charge of, I requested might be left with Mr. Gore, least it might share the fate of one sent you at Exeter last year; & another letter you will find at Rhode-Island. This I shall like wise send by the packet. The Children as well as myself still enjoy health; the little miniature piece continues good humor'd, healthy

& sprightly. Clarinda & her Child are also bravely. I am surprised that no one has yet presented your order for the Naraganset horse.

I believe I inform'd you that Mrs. Low immediately succeeded Mrs. Hamilton. Yesterday Mrs. Hamilton's brother call'd here to let me know that she was willing to return here at the expiration of the month that Mrs. Low had engaged to serve me, for you may recollect that she was fearful of engaging for a longer time. I mentioned the proposition I had received to Mrs. Low, observing to her that it was necessary she should make up her mind fully at present, as it would put me to great inconvenience should she find herself unequal to the fatigue unavoidable in her station when you are at home & we in the way of entertaining a great deal of company. As I did not endeavor to lessen her idea of the activity & health necessary to the performance of the tasks required, she concluded she had better cede the place to Mrs. Hamilton, who doubtless excedes her in those requisites. I have managed the affair in a manner that suits myself & satisfies them. So much for the home Department.

Now for the elections. How my Love will you bear the mortification of embarking on board a Rhode-Island Packet to return to New York, leaving to Judge Cushing the superlative pleasure of traversing the green woods, & attending learned disquisi[ti]ons at Bennington? Yet that I believe must be our deplorable fate unless something very unexpected should occur. I shall send you a news-paper from which you will perceive how the election stands, & this evening I will obtain an account of the examination of the votes this day. Judge Hobart is so sanguine, that he is sure of a majority for you, even tho' the Otsego votes shd. be lost. You will doubtless be pleased at having a majority in the City of New York & County of West-Chester, as being the places in which you are most known....

To morrow the packet is to sail & if any thing new takes place I shall have the pleasure of communicating it to you. It is expected that Votes will all be canvass'd by this day se'en night. If earlier you shall have immediate intelligence pr. post, Judge Hobart told me that he wd. write you if he did not depend upon me, but that it was unnecessary to make you pay double postage.

[incomplete]

(SLJ to JJ) New York 10th June 1792

My dear Mr. Jay,

On friday myself & the Children had the pleasure of receiving your kind letters of the last of May & first of June, since which I hope you have recd. two packets from me sent to Judge Marchant's care by Captn. Peterson & Captn. Cahoon. I intended to send this by to-morrow's post, but I have just heard that Captn. Peterson is again to sail on tuesday, so that I think it best to postpone it 'till then, as I can then send you the papers & give you decisive accounts relative to the election.

At present the issue of it is doubtful, rendered so by a Quibble. If the suffrages of the people are admitted, they give you a majority of 400 Votes, but if the County of Otsego are to lose their's, Clinton will have the majority of a small number. Yesterday was published in Childs's paper the opinion of 8 of the principal Lawyers of the City in favor of the legality of the return of the votes. I will send you the Gazettes that contain the discussions on that question. To-morrow I am inform'd are to be published the opinions of 8 or 9 on the other side & to be signed by them. Oh how is the name of Livingston to be disgraced! Brockholst, Edward, William S. Maturin &c. are to be of the number: those shameless men, blinded by Malice Ambition & interest have conducted themselves with such indecency during the election & daily since the Canvassing of the votes, as to open the eyes of every one respecting their views in their opposition to you. It is said, & I believe it, that Brockholst & Ned first suggested the doubts on that subject.

The Canvassers of the votes are eleven, eight of whom are partizans of Clinton, & three are in favor of you. In order, as is supposed, to Cloak themselves, they Officially asked the Opinion of Burr & King. Their Opinions have not yet been printed, but I'm inform'd by good Authority that King's is decidedly in favor of the Old Sheriff's being intitled to act, until a new Sheriff was commissioned to succeed. Mr. Burr (as was suppos'd) was too sore to be unbiassed, he has therefore delivered in an Opinion which like a two edged sword cuts both ways, for he declares that there was no Sheriff: which, if admitted destroys the legality of the votes & casts an Odium on the Governor for suffering so important an Office to be vacant. Should the Canvassers be hardy enough to decide against the privileges of the People, & instead of suffering them to <u>choose</u> a Governor, take upon <u>themselves</u> to <u>give</u> them one, it will occasion great agitation throughout the State. I am satisfyed that the sentiments of the people are with you, whether you are, or are not Governor, it appears that you are the choice of the people.

Munro & his Wife return'd from Rye last evening; they left your brother & his wife & our son & Essex well.

I was pleased to find that, prior to the receipt of your letter, I had exactly pursued the line of conduct you suppose to be the most proper on a late unpleasant occasion. I find from Munro that your brother will readily concur with you, as both himself & Mrs. Jay disapprove the Union. I wrote you that I had visited Mrs. Jay; she has not returned the visit, but I shall not complain of it.

Monday evening.

Well! my dear Mr. Jay, the Canvassers have taken upon them to give the people a Governor of <u>their</u> election not the one the people preferred. When Governor Clinton was 108 votes a head, it was thought dangerous to examine the votes of Tioga County, it being reduced to a certainty that that County alone wd. give you a Majority independant of the Votes of Otsego. Another quibble was therefore invented, & they were likewise set aside. I am inform'd that the Recorder, Isaac Roosevelt, & Mr. Ganzevort are determined to enter their protest, & likewise to publish the votes of those Counties which they think illegally thrown aside; & which if admitted would have given you a majority of a thousand votes.

The dejection, uneasiness & dissatisfaction that prevails, casts the darkest Odium upon our shameless Governor, while it makes your light shine still brighter than ever. One of the Clintonians told a gentleman of our acquaintance that he too was now convinced of the necessity of a change. Judge Hobart came last evening to Congratulate me on your triumph; I told him I really conceived it such. Peter Munro is writing to you, & has promised to collect those papers which are most interesting. The handbill inclosed is Duer's, but I think it best to conceal the Author's name. Those Lawyers who had boasted their design of publishing their opinions against the votes, have taken care not to perform their promise.

Since you have so honorably lost your election, I could acquiesce in it with pleasure, did it not deprive me of the pleasure of seeing you soon & of enjoying your company for a great part of the year, but I will not dwell upon one disagreeable circumstance when so many agreeable ones concur to make me happy. Oh my dear Mr. Jay! What transport does it give me to hear the praises that are daily bestowed upon you. Much rather would I lose a Crown as you have lost the Office contended for, than gain an empire upon the terms Governor Clinton steals into his.

Tuesday Morng.

I find they have not yet announced in the paper the appointment of Governor. I am told that it is intended that it shd. be accompanied with the protests of Jones &c. There is such an ferment in the City that it is difficult to say what will be the consequence. I shall leave my letter unseal'd until evening shd. any thing occur in the interval that is interesting you shall be apprised of it. I am sitting in your room to write & at your table & have almost persuaded myself that I am making my communications verbally.

People are running in continually to vent their vexation. Poor Jacob Morris looks quite disconsolate. King says he thinks Clinton as lawfully Governor of Connecticut as of New York, but he knows of no redress.

Captn. Peterson is ready to sail as soon as the wind changes, I think it best therefore to close this letter & send it; I can again write to-morrow as that is Post-day if there is any thing worth writing. We are all well, & had been delighting ourselves with the prospect of seeing you soon. The Children therefore when they heard of the decision of the Canvassers exclaimed Oh! Mama then we shall not see Papa this great while. My only consolation is, that time has wings, & tho' they will appear to me to be clogg'd, yet they will finally waft you back to us.

Till then my best beloved farewell!

S. Jay

(JJ to SLJ) East Hartford, 18th June, 1792

My Dear Sally:

About an hour ago I arrived here from Newport, which place I left on Friday last. The last letters which I have received from you are dated the 2d and 4th of this month. The expectations they intimate have not, it seems, been realized. A Hartford paper, which I have just read, mentions the result of the canvass; after hearing how the Otsego votes were circumstanced, I perceived clearly what the event would be. The reflection that the majority of the Electors were for me is a pleasing one; that injustice has taken place does not surprise me, and I hope will not affect you very sensibly. The intelligence found me perfectly prepared for it. Having nothing to reproach myself with in relation to this event, it shall neither discompose my temper, nor postpone my sleep. A few years more will put us all in the dust; and it will then be of more importance to me to have governed myself than to have governed the State. The weather is very warm; towards evening I shall go to Hartford, where I hope to find a letter from you. In a letter from Newport I requested you to direct a letter for me there.

Hartford, Monday evening. Peet has returned from the office without letters. I fear you did not receive mine from Newport in season.

Tuesday Morning. I am waiting to have my horses shod, and in expectation that Judge Cushing, who is behind, will be here this morning I have concluded to cross from Bennington to Albany and return from thence by water. A letter directed to me there, if seasonably written will probably meet me.

My love to all the family.

Yours very affectionately,
John Jay

From mid–July to mid–September, John was at home. En route to Philadelphia, he contracted such a severe inflammation of the eyes that he was forced to retrace his steps. Sicker than he had realized, he took to his bed for six weeks, nursed by the ever-faithful Sarah.

(JJ to Alexander Hamilton) [Draft]

New York 28th Septr. 1792

Dr. Sir,

On Monday the 17th. inst. I set out for Sussex in New Jersey with design after dispatching some private business I had there to proceed from thence on my Circuit. On the 19th. I found myself with a slight inflamation in one eye & some flying rheumatic pains, to which not suspecting any thing serious I paid little attention. By the 25th. my Eyes were so much inflamed that it was with difficulty I read your letter which I reciev'd that morning. Throughout the course of the day those symptoms attended with a little fever increased & convinced me that I was not to be well in a few days & under these circumstances it appeared to me best if possible to return home. I set out the next day, the weather was favorable, I arrived with much pain the day before yesterday.

Notwithstanding bleeding & physick, both inflamation & rheumatism continue obstinate. As my eyes would not permit me to answer your letter I've sent it to Mr. King. Judge Cushing does not appear yet. It wd. be a sad thing if he also shd. be laid up. Respecting the duration of my confinement I can as yet form no conjectures. The moment I regain sufficient health for the purpose I shall again proceed on my circuit.

Yours sincerely

(SLJ to her sister Susan at Queen Anne's County, Eastern Shore, Maryland) New York, 12th Novbr. 1792

My dr. Susan,

I have just been writing to sister Ridley & Mr. Jay: to Catharine I have written chiefly on business which she will doubtless communicate to you as it equally concerns you both.

At the time I receiv'd your agreeable letter, Mr. Jay was so extremely ill that I was wholly confin'd to his chamber. He is at present much better tho' very weak, & has by the advice of his Physician gone to Rye to enjoy retirement, change of air & exercise. I suppose Caty wrote you of his being taken ill after he had set out on the Circuit, & being obliged to return. It was a most fortunate resolution that he took of returning when he did, for had he postponed it one day longer, it would not have been in his power, & perhaps I never should have had the pleasure of seeing him again. The charge I have taken upon me of my little girls render'd it inconvenient for me to accompany him, tho' it would have been more agreeable to me to have done so, but sister Jay and his brother you know are both very kind & attentive.

....The little girls had lost their writing so much while at Rye that they have been ashamed to write to you, but as they have resum'd their studies, they flatter themselves they will soon be in capacity to avail themselves of your kind permission & give you the news that circulates from time to time.

The fatigue & anxiety I underwent during Mr. Jay's illness which continued 6 weeks impaired my health a good deal, but it is already restored & I am now quite well. I suppose Caty has inform'd you how near we were losing Peggy Munro. That danger is now over, tho' she is still confin'd to her room, & a great part of the day to her bed, being too weak to set up long at a time....

Our little folks are pretty much as when you left them, they still have the hooping cough. Clarinda has lost her youngest child [David] with it, & nurse tells me that Phillis, fearful least want of music should make the kitchin dull means to supply David's place in the spring. So much for the Home Department.

Adieu my dear Susan. Let me hear from you by the Post. [As] Catharine will be occupied in making her arrangements for the winter, I depend upon hearing of her from you & you may rest assured your welfare will ever be interesting to your

affectionate sister
Sa. Jay

I wish you could get me some worm-seed for Frank.

(SLJ to JJ) Rye Saturday 13th July 1793

My dear Mr. Jay

It is three weeks since I left home & but once have I heard from you & that by a letter from you a few days after we parted. I have no doubt but there are letters for me at New York and anxiously hope that there will be one for me at the post-office at New Rochelle (where we are just going) or that Cousin Peter will bring me one this evening.

The day after my arrival at New York, I had the pleasure of writing to you & since I've been here have sent for you two letters to the White-plains. Last tuesday your son & daughter, Effy & myself went in the waggon to Bedford. We dined at Holly's & arrived early in the afternoon at the Farm. The Major & his wife made us very welcome & after setting with them a little while we began our rambles. The place looks much prettier than when I was there before. The Cellar for the new house is dug & the bricks are there, but the stone is not yet drawn. The Major says he means to have them on the spot as soon as the harvest is over, which he means to begin in a day or two. Mrs. Lyon seems much pleased with the idea of a change in the situation of her house which she flatters herself will be more convenient still than where she at present is. Ann was as much pleased as I expected she would be & we felt no other wish than that we were peaceably settled there.

The next morning after breakfast we went in the waggon to see the Mill where we found John who performs the part of Miller himself, having dismissed the one he used to employ. He was very civil & explained the use of the different parts, & attended us up-stairs & down stairs. Notwithstanding what I had heard of it, the size & apparent strength of it surprised me. After our Curiosity was gratified we took leave of the Major & Mrs. Lyon, & declining their pressing invitation to prolong our stay, returned and dined at Rye at 4 o'Clock. I am so excessively anxious to see you & the Children that if Brother would have consented to my leaving him I should have set out for that purpose next monday but neither he nor Polly will hear of it.

I shall write you again by Cousin Peter next monday. Our friends here are all well & desire their love to you & Maria. Ann joins me in love to you & the Children.

With the greatest desire to see you, I am my dearest, best beloved!

most affectionately yours
S. Jay

PART IV

Separated, Reunited, Parted

April 9–10, 1794–
January 20, 1803

In the years following the signing of the Treaty of Paris of 1783, relations between the United States and Great Britain had been delicate, indeed often difficult. Britain had never vacated its forts and outposts in the Northwest Territory. The British navy never ceased interfering with American shipping on the high seas, in particular with ships bound for France. Many of these ships were not only turned back, but American seamen were also often pressed into service aboard British ships. However, the Americans had not lived up to their agreements either. They had not honored their commitments with regard to the treatment of former Tories or to the payment of debts owed to British merchants.

In the spring of 1794, relations between the two countries reached such a low point that war seemed imminent. Clearly, President Washington needed to act and act quickly in order to prevent a conflict that America could not afford and was not prepared to fight.

(JJ to SLJ at New York) Philadelphia, 9th April, 1794

....I arrived here on Monday evening; and yesterday dined with the President. The question of war or peace seems to be as much in suspense here as in New York when I left you. I am rather inclined to think that peace will continue, but should not be surprised if war should take place. In the present state of things, it will be best to be ready for the latter event in every respect.

10th April, 1794

....The aspect of the times is such, that prudential arrangements calculated on the prospect of war should not be neglected, nor too long postponed. Peace or war appears to me a question which cannot be solved. Unless things should take a turn in the meantime, I think it will be best on my return to push our affairs at Bedford briskly. There is such irritation and agitation in this town, and in Congress. Great Britain has acted unwisely and unjustly; and there is some danger of our acting intemperately....

In April 1794, Sarah Jay bids a fond farewell to her sister Susan who, currently in Baltimore visiting their widowed sister Kitty, has agreed to marry Judge John Cleves Symmes. Judge Symmes plans to take Susan to Cincinnati in the Northwest Territory, where he owns a large tract of land on which they intend to build a house.

(SLJ to her sister Susan at Baltimore) New York April 11th 1794

My dr. Susan,

I feel much pain'd at the idea of yr. leaving this part of the world without my first seeing you. The Country to which you are going is I am informed a very delightful one & the gentleman that is to conduct you thither is (as I've heard) a man of sense & of an amiable disposition. May my dr. Susan be happy!....

By the next spring we expect likewise to emigrate as far as Bedford. Last Autumn Mr. Jay had laid the foundation for 2 houses in Broad-Street, but a variety of circumstances have concur'd to prevent his carrying up the buildings; he has therefore relinquish'd that object & we have adopted the idea of building at Bedford, which we shall pursue immediately upon Mr. Jays return from the Circuit. There I would willingly stay until Maria is 16 & then I wd. return to finish her education & that of her sisters. This spring Peter leaves College & enters Munro's office. There is a very good Accademy at Salem a New England Town 6 miles from Bedford where we think of placing William, so that we can send for him every Saturday & he can return early on Monday. As our retirement will afford more leisure to Mr. Jay, he will be enabled to aid me in the instruction of our daughters....

I suppose you will inform Catherine what you wd. wish with respect to any thing of yours that may be here. With my best love to Catherine, I remain my dr. Susan

your[s] affectionately
S. J.

George Washington, realizing the seriousness of the critical relations with Great Britain, asked John Jay whether he would consider going to England to effect a treaty between the two countries. Jay had not sought this new position but considered the effort at reconciliation so important that he agreed, if nominated, to accept it. Although there is speculation that he had his eye ultimately on the presidency, on this occasion he put personal ambition aside. After three days of debate, the Senate confirmed him as envoy extraordinary for the negotiation of the treaty.

Even though the Jays wrote to each other daily, the postal service was so slow that Sarah learned of her husband's nomination by way of the newspaper.

(JJ to SLJ) Philadelphia, 15th April, 1794

My Dear Sally:

I was this evening favoured with yours of the 14th. It is now between eight and nine o'clock, and I am just returned from court. I expect, my dear Sally, to see you sooner than we expected. There is here a serious determination to send me to England, if possible to avert a war. The object is so interesting to our country, and the combination of circumstances such, that I find myself in a dilemma between personal considerations and public ones. Nothing can be much more distant from every wish on my own account. I feel the impulse of duty strongly, and it is probable that if, on the investigation I am now making, my mind should be convinced that it is my duty to go, you will join with me in thinking that, on an occasion so important, I ought to follow its dictates, and commit myself to the care and kindness of that Providence in which we have both the highest reason to repose the most absolute confidence. This is not of my seeking; on the contrary, I regard it as a measure not to be desired, but to be submitted to.

A thousand reflections crowd into my mind, and a thousand emotions into my heart. I must remember my motto, *Deo duce perseverandum* [with God leading, one must persevere]. The knowledge I have of your sentiments on these subjects affords me consolation.

If the nomination should take place, it will be in the course of a few days, and then it will appear in the papers; in the meantime say nothing on the subject, for it is not impossible that the business may take another turn, though I confess I do not expect it will.

My dear, dear Sally, this letter will make you as grave as I am myself; but when we consider how many reasons we have for resignation and acquiescence, I flatter myself that we both shall become composed.

If it should please God to make me instrumental to the continuance of peace, and in preventing the effusion of blood, and other evils and miseries incident to war, we shall both have reason to rejoice. Whatever may be the event, the endeavour will be virtuous, and consequently consolatory. Let us repose unlimited trust in our Maker; it is our business to adore and to obey.

My love to the children. With very sincere and tender affection,

I am, my dear Sally, ever yours,
John Jay

P.S. It is supposed that the object of my mission may be completed in time to return in the fall.

(JJ to SLJ at New York) wednesday Pha. 16 ap.1794

My dear Sally

I wrote to you a few Lines last night. They were written in Haste. This Day the nomination alluded to in that Letter was made. The Decision will be made Tomorrow. I will then write to you again.

The letters by the Miss Allens reached me this morning. I am pleased with them, and with those who wrote them. It is not in my power now to write to the Children, having scarce a moment unoccupied. The court did not adjourn untill between 8 and 9 oc[loc]k last night....

How little do we percieve of Things to come. There is a Providence that over rules all our Plans, and I may add Resolutions.

I have much to say & to do, and am very impatient to be with you. My Love to the Children. God bless & preserve you & them.

I am my Dr Sally
your very affecte. Husband
John Jay

(SLJ to JJ at Philadelphia) New York 18th April 1794

My dr. Mr. Jay,

Your letter of yesterday gave me reason to think that one from me wd. hardly reach you before you left Philadelphia. From the one I've this inst. received you think I may write; how my dr. Mr. Jay is it possible! The Utmost exertion I can make is to be silent. Excuse me if I have not philosophy or patriotism to do more. I heard of the nomination yesterday, so did the Children. The paper of to-day mentions it as a report that deserves credit. Before this reaches you the event will be determined. Had any one predicted that dread wd. be mingled with my desire to see you could I have believed it? Never! Yet so it is. Should you leave us I must intreat you to permit your son to acompany you. It would give him infinite pleasure & me great consolation. Continue my dr. Mr. Jay to let me daily hear from you & if possible inform me when I may expect to see you.

Your brother Peter came to Town on tuesday & left us on thursday. He & Polly were well. The Children are well. I have had a most acute head-ach & my eyes are very sore....

Genl. Schuyler this inst. left me. He goes to-morrow to Philadelphia & will deliver this to you.

Adieu my best beloved! Absent or present I am wholly yours

Sa. Jay

(JJ to SLJ, Broadway, New York) Saturday morng 19 Ap. 1794

My dear Sally

I refer you to the two last Letters which I wrote to you this Week. It was expected that the Senate would Yesterday have decided on the nomination of an *Envoy* to the Court of London; but measures respecting the Embargo occupied them thro' the Day. To Day *that* Business is to be resumed; and you shall have the earliest notice of the Result. So far as I am personally concerned, my feelings are very very far from exciting wishes for its taking place. No appointmt ever operated more unpleasantly upon me; but the public Considerations which were urged and the Manner in which it was pressed, strongly impressed me with a conviction that to refuse it would be, to desert my Duty for the Sake of my Ease and Domestic concerns & comforts. I derive some Consolation from the Prospect that my absence will not be of long Continuance, and that the same providence which has hitherto preserved me, will still be pleased to accompany and restore me to you and our dear little Family.

Your Letter by the Miss Allens is the last that I have recd. I ought to have seen those Ladies, but the Court has unceasingly engrossed my Time. We did not adjourn until 9 last night. I feel fatigued in body and mind; but Reflections of this kind are not to be indulged. I must endeavour to sustain with propriety the part assigned me; and meet with composure and fortitude whatever disagreable Events may occur to counteract my wishes or increase my Task. I shall have *Rest* in Time; and for *that* Rest I will not cease to prepare. I am very anxious to be with you, and the moment the preparatory Measures here will permit, I shall set out.

....~~It will be best to apprize our friends at Rye of the nomination~~. My Love to the Children, and believe me to be unalterably and affy

Yours
John Jay

(President Washington to JJ at Philadelphia)

TO JOHN JAY, GREETINGS:

Reposing especial trust and confidence in your integrity, prudence, and ability, I have nominated, and, by and with the advice and consent of the Senate, do appoint, you, the said John Jay, Envoy Extraordinary from the United States of America to the Court of His Britannic Majesty, authorizing you hereby to do and perform all such matters and things as to the said place or office doth appertain, or as may be duly given you in charge thereafter, and the said office to hold and exercise during the pleasure of the President of the United States for the time being.

In testimony whereof, I have caused the seal of the United States to be hereunto affixed. Given under my hand, at the city of Philadelphia, the nineteenth day of April in the year of our Lord one thousand seven hundred and ninety-four and of the independence of the United States of America, the eighteenth.

Go. Washington

By the President:
Edm. Randolph, Secretary of State

(JJ to SLJ at New York) [Draft]

Sunday Eveng 20 Ap 1794

My dear Sally

I this moment recd. yours by Gen. Schuyler. As yet I have not seen him. It found me alone and not a little pensive. Your own Feelings will best suggest an Idea of mine. God's will be done; to him I resign; in him I confide. Do the like. Any other Philosophy applicable to this occasion is delusive. Away with it.

Your Indisposition affects me; resist Despondency; hope for the best.

~~When we meet we will talk of Peter's going with me. The Expediency of it does not strike me forceably. What real Advantage will it afford him? Many objections present themselves to my mind which merit Attention and ought to be well considered. They will readily occur to you.~~

Yesterday the Senate approved of the nomination by a great Majority. Mr. Burr was among the few who opposed it. I have hopes that our Friend Mr. Trumbull will consent to go as Secy. ~~Mr. S. Bayard was recommended to me. I think well of him but Mr. Trumbull's long Residence and Connections in London will enable him to be more useful~~. To morrow the Preparations for dispatching me will begin. When they will be completed so as to admit of my leaving this place I cannot yet decide. I am exceedingly impatient to set out for New York. ~~Tell our dear sweet little Boy that I have got a Picture for him, and that there is a Puss in it.~~ God bless and preserve you all. Be assured that I shall never cease to be

My dear Sally
your very affectionate Husband
John Jay

~~Continue to write. You shall have timely notice of my leaving this place.~~

Sarah Jay, the devoted mother of five children, knew that she could not accompany her husband to London while he negotiated a treaty there. However, since their son Peter Augustus, age 18, had just graduated from Columbia and had not yet begun his apprenticeship in a law office, she persuaded her husband to take him along for company and the educational experience. The four children who remained at home with her were Maria, age 12, Nancy, 11, William, 5, and Sarah Louisa, 2.

Sailing for London on May 12th aboard the *Ohio* were John Jay, Peter Augustus Jay, John Trumbull as secretary, and a Jay slave named Peter (or Peet) Williams.

(SLJ to JJ at Philadelphia) New York 22d April 1794

My dear Mr. Jay,

Yesterday I received yr. two kind letters of Saturday & Sunday. I do indeed judge of your feelings by my own & for that reason forebore writing while under the first impression of surprize & grief.

Your superiority in fortitude as well as every other virtue I am aware of, yet I know too well your tenderness for your family to doubt the pangs of seperation. Your own conflicts are sufficient; they need not be augmented by the addition of mine. Never was I more sensible of the absolute ascendancy you have over my heart. When almost in dispair I threw myself on my bed and renounced the hope of Domestic bliss. Your image in my breast seem'd to upbraid me with adding to your trials, that idea alone roused me from my Despondency. I resum'd the charge of my family & even dare hope that by our example I shall be enabled to look up to that Divine Protector from whom we have indeed experienced the most merciful Guardianship.

I cannot say I perceive your objections to taking with you our son. Having just finished his college studies & not yet commenced his Law studies, it seems a favorable period to indulge under your auspicies a laudable curiosity with respect to a Country that was once so intimately connected with this. His Cousin has not a doubt of your taking him, indeed it appears to be the opinion of every one that has convers'd with me on the subject. Those conjectures have I'm sure excited powerful inclinations in him, which without serious objections it wd. be a pity to controul. I am convinced too that his tenderness for you has a great share in his desire of accompanying you. I hope you do not sail from Philadelphia. You may recollect our being 8 days in the Delaware.

The Court being held here at present Col. & Mrs. Lewis are in Town, & have brought with them Pete's wife, which will give Pete an opportunity of taking leave of her. The Children continue well. They were exceedingly affected when they received the tidings & intreated me to endeavor to dissuade you from accepting an appointment that subject us to so painful a seperation.

Farewell my best beloved! Your wife 'till Death & after that a ministring spirit

---

(JJ to SLJ at New York) On board the *Ohio*, 13 May 1794

My dear Sally

It is now ten o'Ck. at night. We are under way and sailing with a fair Breeze. The

Pilot who is conducting the vessel will be the Bearer of this. I wrote to you this morning and was soon afterwards facd. with yours, which Peter immediately answered. I thank you for it, and you will oblige me exceedingly, by embracing every opportunity of writing to me during my absence. You may rely on my attention and Punctuality. Peet does not recollect, and does not believe that I owe for shoeing Horses to any Person except that I owe 2/ to Mr. Bell, the Blacksmith. I know that I settled with the Smith at the North River, whose name I do not recollect, shortly before I went to Ph[iladelphi]a and yet I suspect that after that ... he shod a Horse or two for me. Peet says not. I have heard him spoken of as an Honest Man; and should his account be only for once or twice shoeing I should incline to pay it. By the Time this reaches you Peter & Polly I suppose will have left you. However when next you write to them let them know when I sailed... Remember me to Fady & P. Munro and Families. Appologize to Mr. Cortlandt &c. for my omitting to Take Leave of Them. You know how much I was pressed for Time.

I have seen this Days news paper & the Ph[iladelphi]a Democratic Resolutions published in them. They give me no Concern and I hope they will be equally indifferent to You. The less you say on such Subjects, the less you will flatter the Importance of those who may not wish me well. I find Mr. Scattergood an agreable Man, and am pleased with his being a passenger with us. A Party went on Shore on Staten Island this afternoon and brought on board a clever parcel of Fish and 2 Sheep. We have the prospect of a good voyage, but it would be infinitely less disagreable if it was towards, instead of being from, you and our children and Friends. I look forward to that pleasure, and sincerely hope and Pray that a kind Providence will so order Events as that my Return be not protracted beyond the Time we contemplate. Tell Fady I shall write to him directly after my arrival. When we left New York I expected he was on Board, having understood that he purposed to go part of the way with us. I suppose he was hindred.

Kiss our little ones for me. Once more farewell and that the author & giver of all consolation may be and remain with you and them forever, will not cease to be the Prayer of

your very affectionate Husband,
John Jay

(PAJ to SLJ at New York) [On the *Ohio*] May 13th 1794
10 oClock at night

Dr. Mama

We lay still at the same place where mr. Munro left us last night. We made an attempt this morning to get out but the wind obliged us to return. A Boat which has just come along side & brought letters for Mr. Scattergood gives us this opportunity of writing to you.

I was sick for an hour or two yesterday, but since that I have been perfectly well. Papa too has not been incommoded he is now writing to you. Be so good as to give my love & bid good bye again to my Sisters & Uncle & Aunt Jay & Mrs. Munro. We feared Mr. Munro would have had a long disagreeable passage up, but were very agreeably disappointed to find that he had returned to town with pleasure & expedition. We live very well on board at least as yet. Our ducks lay, & the goat gives a large quantity of milk & tho' our Cook is none of the cleanest yet Pete make up the deficiency & together with the steward dresses our victuals.

My dear Mama I again bid you adieu; may that all merciful being upon whom we depend for preservation give you every blessing & happiness

I am
Your very affectionate son
Peter Augustus Jay

(SLJ to JJ) New York 29th May 1794

My dear Mr. Jay,

I did myself the pleasure of writing to you on the 26th by the *Belvidere* Captn. Depeyster which Vessel still remains in Port. The *Factor* tis said will soon sail, & your brother takes charge of my letters. I would wish not to omit a single opportunity of letting you know we are all well. It was with inexpressible pleasure I heard the *Ohio* had been met on the 18th inst. & that all was well. How rejoiced should I be to hear similar intelligence after the storm which now prevails. Oh! my dear Mr. Jay how greatly does circumstances alter our ideas of things. I've known the time when in your company I have enjoyed a storm like this, perhaps because it seem'd to secure to me the sole enjoyment of that pleasure. At present I cannot, nor would I wish to describe the painful fancies it gives birth to. I know you disapprove the anticipation of evils, but indeed my best of husbands such a storm as this is enough to prostrate ones Reason. At this season of the year it is so un[u]sual. The Poplars this morning were on the ground & the cherries tho' still unripe were blown from the tree before the dining-room window into the stable-yard. Frank has raised the Poplars. When I droop who shall raise me if the wide ocean should swallow up my husband & my child. Don't chide me, I'll recover myself instantly, it was a slip of my pen. When one has their all at stake a little solicitude demands pity rather than censure.

The Children are ignorant of my anxiety & undesignedly increase my sensibility. They are washing the little prints that ornament their Chimney, & in taking them down for that purpose, a tender contest ensued about which should have the pleasure of improving the appearance of yours. Maria had first taken it down & nothing from Nan could persuade her to relinquish her charge. I was silent but the affection it discovered for the Original, in the present state of my mind, affected me. They call me to take Coffee. I hope to recover my spirits before I resume my pen....

Our Connections and intimate friends are well. The Children join in Love to their Papa & brother.

I am my dear Mr. Jay

Your very affectionate wife
Sa. Jay

(JJ to SLJ) London, Pall-Mall, Royal Hotel 21st June 1794

My Dear Sally:

I wrote you a letter while yet at sea, and on my arrival at Falmouth added to it a few lines. That letter was left in the care of our consul there, who promised to forward it by the *Active*, Captain Blair, who expected soon to sail from thence for Philadelphia.

On Sunday morning, the 15th of this month, we reached this place. Excellent roads, good inns, and a variety of interesting objects and scenes rendered the journey agreeable, perhaps the more so from our having just left the sea. Our way led us through Glastonbury, famous among other things for a thorn said to have been introduced by Joseph of Arimathea, which ancient legends say blossoms at Christmas. On our arrival at the next town (Wells) we visited the cathedral, a Gothic structure worth seeing. The sexton who showed and explained to us its history, peculiarities, and curiosities, and who seemed an intelligent man, assured us very seriously that there really was such a thorn at Glastonbury, that some of the same kind was then growing at Wells, and that he himself had seen it blossom at Christmas. Had it been Christmas, I should have desired him to show it to me....

We dined yesterday with Mr. and Mrs. Constable, who made very friendly inquiries about you and the children in the evening. I took tea with Mrs. Low, who looks very well and spoke much of America and her friends in it. Mr. and Mrs. Pinckney seem very amiable and much disposed to do everything that is proper and friendly. As to my political objects, I can as yet say nothing; more time being necessary to acquire information and form a judgment.

....I am this moment informed that a vessel bound for New York will sail on Tuesday next; I shall endeavour to write by her also, but I am so pressed for want of time by business and circumstances which, though not important, consume time that it will not be in my power to write either so many or such long letters as I otherwise should.

God bless and preserve you, my dear Sally. My love to the children. Remember me to our friends.

Yours affectionately,
John Jay

In John Jay's absence, Sarah Jay continued to monitor the progress of the building going on in Bedford: the enlargement of the farm manager's house as well as the construction of several mills. Major Samuel Lyon, the farm manager, was assisted in his work by his son Johnny.

(SLJ to JJ at London New York 7th July 1794

My dr. Mr. Jay

Mr. LeRoy tells me that a Ship will sail for Amsterdam tomorrow, & as I cannot hear of any destined for England, I have determined to write you a few lines, being sensible how grateful it will be to you to hear of the continued health & Welfare of your family & friends. Maria Ann & William have been ten days at Rye with their Uncle & Aunt. Little Sarah & myself are alone, sister Ridley not being yet arrived.

Johnny Lyon came to Town to-day. He has not told me yet what sum he'll want tho' I believe it will be pretty considerable. The Mill is raised & almost under cover. The freshets which have been the last month excessive have not injured it in the least. He is very sanguine about the importance of your Mill & thinks that when it is compleated it will be very beneficial to the Country & lucrative to you. Your opinion of Mrs. Lyon's death I believe was but too well founded. Her loss to her husband & the farm will not be soon or easily repaired. J[ohnny] seems to think his Father too much Abroad & domestic concerns too much neglected....

Remember me most affectionately to Peter & be assured the best wishes & most ardent prayers for your health, happiness, & success & for your safe & speedy return to your Country family & friends shall be unceasingly offered by

your affectionate wife
Sa. Jay

(PAJ to SLJ at New York) London 1st August 1794

Dear Mama

We have for some time past been in daily expectation of hearing from you, by the numerous vessels from America which constantly arrive. We hope however that it will be but a short time before we experience that pleasure. Maria & Nancy wish me to give them a description of London; they will perceive perhaps how impossible it is for me to comply with the request when I tell them that such a description fills five octavo volumns which they may find in the city Library. I have been in this place near two months & have seen but a very small part of it indeed. The house in which we lodge is 5 miles from the place where the American Ships lye at Anchor, & the town extends considerably beyond each of those places.

A fire broke out some days ago which destroyed 630 houses, many of the Inhabitants who are of the poorer class are reduced to very great distress. They now live in tents pitched in the church yards by order of Government. A Subscription is opened for their relief which will probably amount to a very considerable sum. The Salt-petre warehouses of the East India Company first fell a sacrifice to the flames & the explosions & torrents of fire produced from this drug were the principle means of spreading the conflagration. Those who were spectators of this dreadful scene, say that a stream of melted nitre almost resembling the Volcanic Lava flowed down into the Thames and continued burning even amid the water.

An Eruption of Mount Vesuvius too has lately happened which has destroyed the Town of Porto Greco containing about 18,000 inhabitants together with several adjoining villages. But it is said that a very small proportion of lives were lost. This eruption has had the effect of lowering the mountain several hundred feet; the conic summit has fallen in & a new crater opened on the side.

Your Chairs are in the hands of a workman: he says that from the shape of the work he will not be able to make them so fashionable as he would wish, & he equally laments your prohibition of gilding. Aunt Jay's bracelets are doing, they are to cost twelve guineas. Papa has not yet had leisure to sit for his picture but I shall not cease to remind him of it, & as soon as it is finished I will have it set & a companion made to it according to your directions.

Be so good as to give my love to Maria & Nancy. Tell little Wig not to forget me, & to kiss Sally for me.

I am my dear mama
Your Affectte. Son
Peter Augustus Jay

In this letter and those that follow, Sarah Jay shows her aptitude for managing the family's finances and properties. She often mentions that she would be grateful for the assistance of her nephew, Peter Jay Munro, or the advice of her husband, but with both absent, she seems perfectly capable of handling matters herself.

She was also anxious to receive the portrait of John Jay by Gilbert Stuart (the Jays always write "Stewart") that the painter was slow to deliver. The portrait depicts Mr. Jay in black judicial robes trimmed in crimson.

(SLJ to JJ at London) N. York Augst 2d 1794

My dr. Mr. Jay

This morng. Genl. Clarkson inform'd me that a Vessel wd. sail for Liverpool to-morrow, & as a long time has elaps'd since an opportunity has offered by which I could write I recd. the intelligence with pleasure. As I am well convinced that you are more interested in the health & comfort of myself & children than any other circumstance, it heightens the satisfaction I feel in having it in my power to asure you we still enjoy those blessings. All our near connections are well. The three children pass'd a fortnight at yr. brother's, & it is now a fortnight since they return'd. I've not had the pleasure of seeing either Peter or Polly since you left me.

At present Peggy Munro & her little son are at Rye & to-day Mr. Munro is gone there & leaves it on Monday for Albany. I suppose he writes you as he tells me he does, of the business he transacts for you. Messrs. W. & B. have each pd. him 100£ on their respective notes & he has delivered it to me. Since you went away I have advanced to John Lyon 156£ for the Mill & besides that have paid 62£ for a pr. of Mill-stones which Mr. Greene bought here at N York. He thinks that in about 6 weeks he shall be able to begin to grind. I have recd. from Mr. A. Van Horne on Acct. one thousand three hundred & eighty pounds for you, & other sums which added to that makes upwards of 200£ not a farthing of which can Mr. Munro or myself improve. Mr. Grant delayed the payment so long that stock of every kind is too high to purchase nor indeed is it for sale.

The situation of affairs in Europe & discontents in Canada lead people here with full confidence to anticipate peace & indeed the extreme prosperity of the Country is such that your mission is much more popular & I have heard from good authority that many who wish'd for war & were disaffected to the public measures are now as desirous of Peace & success to your mission is become an Universal toast. Money is so plenty that a friend of ours told me he had taken it up on Long-Island at 6 pr. cent & could have as much as he wanted at that rate. A friend of ours has not been able to put out any upon good security. The Waggon you engaged has not yet arrived....

Mr. Smith's Lot next to us was sold at Auction for 4450£ & the Auctioneer by Mr. Smith's order inform'd the bidders that your house extended 2 feet on his ground & that for those 2 feet you had offered 200£ which had been refused. Mr. Henderson who purchased it said he would not be hard with you but that he would not say he would accept the 200£ for the 2 feet. Cousin Peter who was alarm'd at that assertion came here to examine your Deed & thinking their claim groundless wrote Mr. Henderson that he believ'd it so, & that he never had heard you express an apprehension of the kind. Mr. Henderson still thinks you have made some mistake as it is indorsed in the hand-writing of the late Chief Justice on his Deed. At first I did not intend to trouble you with a relation of this malicious transaction as I am sure your mind must be sufficient[ly] employed with public business to require an exemption from private vexations, but Mr. M[unro] thought it best you shd. be inform'd of it. I think it was best Mr. Munro pursued the measure he did least the silence of your friends should be misconstrued into an acknowledgement of the claim....

Would you believe that Stewart has not yet sent me yr. picture? I call upon him often, I have not hesitated to tell him it was in his power to contribute infinitely to my gratification by indulging me with yr. portrait. He has at length resum'd the pencil & Munro has been sitting with your robe for him. It is your very self, it is an inimitable picture & I am all impatience to have it to myself. There is an excellent engraver here & Stewart has been solicited by a respectable number of Citizens to permit an Engraving to be taken of that picture for which he has asked & obtained my consent. He begs me to remind you of the promise you made him the day he breakfasted with you....

Genl. Clarkson call'd for my letter before I had finished copying it; a great deal of it is therefore from memory & copied to preserve facts only. [incomplete]

(JJ to SLJ at New York) London 16 augt 1794

My dear Sally

....This is intended to go by the *Belvedere* Capt. Depeyster.... Mrs. Johnson has sent me two Bracelets and two pins which Peter by Polly's Desire requested her to have made. I think them neat, and am at a Loss whether to send them now, or bring them with me. For the present I believe I will keep them, and wait her orders, which shall be punctually executed....

Peet begins at times to wish himself Home again. The novelty is a good deal over. I wish we were all entering the Street Door and you and the Children and Servants running to meet us. God grant that this wish may be realized, and in the mean Time preserve and bless us all

Adieu my Dear Sally, my Love to the Children

Your's Sincerely and affecy
John Jay

(SLJ to JJ at London) New York 27th Sepbr 1794

My Dear Mr. Jay

In my last to you of the 27th Ult. I mentioned that yr. brother intended waiting upon Mrs. Dunscomb to town. He did so, & finding me with very sore eyes insisted upon my accompanying him & spending a fortnight at Rye. Susan being here & the family well I acquiesced in his proposition & recd. vast benefit from the ride & change of air &c....

On my return from Rye I found yr. letters by the *Francis* & *Mary* of the 4th & 6th of July, & in the course of the same week had the pleasure of receiving those of the 17th & 18th by the *Ohio*. You can judge, & only you, my dr. Mr. Jay of the effect of so many letters upon my spirits. On my first perusal of them, my eyes pass'd over the lines with rapidity to seek for the supposed time of your return, but not finding that & a sigh & a tear relieved me from the oppression occasioned by the disappointment & reperused your letters, reproaching myself for having too much expected, & recollecting the early dates, found it impossible you could at that period have even guess'd the time. I write to you my dr. Mr. Jay without disguise. An absence already of five months! A Distance of 3000 miles! Those are no trifles. Yet should the Almighty smile upon yr. mission and once more restore you to a grateful Country We shall not regret the present circumstances. I will exert myself & hope the best....

The tierce* of spirits you sent for has arrived and is in our Cellar, and your Waggon was brought here a few days ago & paid for. I shall write to Lyon abt. it. Inclose[d] is the amount of money I've advanced for the Mill. Munro is at Court & a Vessel sails tomorrow, so that I cannot learn whether or not he has settled with Post. There is great plenty in the Country yet every thing is immensely high; new hay has been sold all summer at 5/6 & is now at 6/. Oats at 3/3. Money as well as provisions being plenty yr. Nephew has not been able to put out any. I have ventured by the Advice of Dr. Charlton to purchase 5 shares in the Bank of the U. States at 24 PCent Advance; he has purchased at the same advance, thinking it preferable to the NYork Bank, which tho' at 30/ does not yield more than 6 PC. If I had been sure of yr. approbation I wd. have doubled the purchase, as it is believed it will be ere long at 60 PC. And the Dr. advised me to lose no time. A share is only 400 Dollars.

....With the most ardent wishes for the success of your Mission, Your happiness & the re-union of our family

I am my best best beloved!
yours very Affectely
Sa. Jay

**42 gallons.*

Have you set yet for yr. picture. Stewart has not yet gratifyed me by sending me the one he has taken of you.

(JJ to SLJ at New York) London 2d October 1794

My dear Sally

I was last week favd. with yours of the 2d. Augt. by Mr. McEvers. Had you not heretofore been in Europe and often experienced anxiety to hear from our Friends in America, you could not easily conceive how sollicitous I am to recieve Letters from you, and how much pleasure I derive from being assured under your Hand, that you and our little ones and Friends are well.

From the monies you have advanced to Johnny Lyon, I suppose the mills were nearly finished. The Stones purchased by Mr. Green, I presume were Bur Stones, and intended to make the best Flour. Those Mills ought to be proffitable. They will cost a considerable Sum before they are completed. I take it for granted that the Saw Mill still remains to be done. Mr. Munro I suspect was too much employed in preparing for his Albany Journey to write to me. I have recd. one Letter from him since my arrival here.

I am glad Mr. Grant has paid you more money than you know what to do with. As to Stocks I should prefer Bank Stock. However I am not anxious, for on my Return I shall be able to employ usefully the little that will remain after paying what I owe.

I begin to fear that the Termination of my Business will be protracted until so late in the Season, as to render it adviseable for me rather to stay here until Spring, than expose myself to the Severities of a winter passage. How my mission will end is not yet ascertained. I have Hopes but there still are Doubts. This entre nous.

I have never suspected that our House encroached on Mr. Smith's Lott. I never expressed such apprehensions to any body, nor did I ever make any such offer as is pretended. I did once offer Mr. Tom Smith to buy 20 or 25 feet next to us, but mentioned no Price, nor had I any other Inducemt. than because I then thought it might be had cheap, and might either be so used or so sold, as to save our windows on that side and thereby avoid the Trouble & Expense of making a Sky Light.

I am much obliged to Mr. Stewart's attention to your Request, and am persuaded that his work will meet with your approbation. Make my Compts to him.... This Letter will go by the *Molly*, Capt. Morgan, to Ph[iladelphi]a. You might write to me a little Letter once a month by the Packet. I hope you have taken care to fill the Stable with Hay and that you will drive your young Hermosos on before Spring; but by no means before. They are perfectly well broke and gentle. No Risques ought to be run. Young Horses, on first coming to Town, are not to be incautiously trusted.

Remember [me] to Susan and Mrs. Ridley and our other Friends. How do the girls go on, and little Will and little Sall. God bless and preserve you all....

Yours very sincerely & affectionately
John Jay

Maria Jay, age 12, had a great desire to continue her education at the Moravian Academy in Bethlehem, Pennsylvania, a very fine boarding school for young ladies. When the opportunity arose for her to consider enrolling, and she was not able to ask permission of her father because he was in England, her mother took it upon herself to see that Maria's wishes were granted. John Adams wrote this description of the school to his daughter (17 March 1777):

> I have seen a remarkable institution for the education of young ladies, at Bethlehem. About one hundred and twenty of them live together under the same roof; they sleep all together, in the same garret; I saw one hundred and twenty beds, in two long rows, in the same room; the beds and bedclothes were all of excellent quality, and extremely neat. How would you like to live in such a nunnery?

(SLJ to JJ at London) New York 11th Octbr 1794

My dr. Mr. Jay

Since my last to you of the 27th Ult. I've had the pleasure of receiving yr. obliging letters of the 30th July & the 6th & 13th of Augst.... The repugnance I have to writing ... ceases when you are absent, at least so far as relates to a Correspondance with you, which is always a source of pleasure. The disappointment you felt at not hearing from me could not possibly have given you more painful sensations than the relation of it has given <u>me</u>, to which is added the regret for having been tho' innocent the cause. Too long has incertitude been an inmate of my own bosom not to wish to preserve from its anguish the bosom of my beloved husband. Perhaps in ordinary Life few persons have experienced oftener the disagreeableness of suspense than you & I have even at the instant I'm writing; I am uncertain whether you'll be in Europe to peruse this letter when it reaches that Country. I do not even wish nay on the contrary I wish sincerely you may be a thousand miles nearer America before this letter reaches the place of it's destination. Yet I've fears as well as hopes, were patience & resignation commodities for sale, I think I should turn monopolizer; methinks I see you shake your head, & in thought observe that I write as I frequently speak, without due reflection or that I would consider that though they are not to be purchased, yet they are by proper means to be obtained. You always [have] the advantage of me: I know whats right & you do it.

The Children, myself & servants continue well. Our friends too enjoy health. In my last I gave you an account of my visit to Rye & indeed of a great many other things which I don't now recollect, only I know it was very long but I hope not tiresome. Since I've been writing, your brother Augustus has come in, he is delighted with your attention, tho' he has not yet seen your letter, as it was sent this morning to Mr. Schuyler for him. Indeed since I've began to write I've been interrupted at least a dozen times, not to mention the interruptions from little Sally who always takes her seat at table & pretends she is likewise writing to you. She does not connect her words, but those she attempts to use she speaks plain. When I desire her to say any thing she is conscious she is unable to say, she replies Sally can't & don't attempt it. William asked if I did not think I might venture to tell you that he is a very good boy. I told him I really could, & can with sincerity assure you that every favorable indication in his countenance &c. becomes more & more reallized, he is a lovely child that interests ones feelings & promises much. I flatter myself he will resemble his amiable brother. His little sister is I confess too much of a pett. I cannot resist the fascination of her beauty & caresses, & you would be diverted tho' perhaps you would blame me could you see them follow me from place to place & hang at my side as tho' they were necessary appendages. Apropos, have you yet set for your picture? You and Peter are silent about it, but I hope you do not repent your promise. Stewart still keeps your portrait.

It will give you pleasure to be assured that our eldest daughters grow more & more amiable. Maria has a long time had a great inclination to go to Bethlehem & has solicited me to write for admission for her. I told her that I had been inform'd the school was full & that they had the names of 60 Children who wished admission when vacancies occurred. When Judge Symmes was here, Bethlehem being mentioned in conversation Maria express'd her regret for the impossibility of gaining admission into the school there. The Judge told her that her Aunt, his daughter, & himself were to pass thro' that place in their way to Cincinati & that if she would permit him to have the pleasure of introducing her to the directress of the society, he did not doubt being able to procure admission for her as the society were indebted to him for acts of friendship during the war, for which they had often express'd their gratitude & a desire of evincing it. Upon this Maria renewed her intreaties, telling me she wished to make a greater proficiency in her studies than in her present situation she was able, & that she hoped by answering your expectations, to justify me to you for consenting.

As you my dear Mr. Jay, the guardian & Protector of our little flock, was too distant to be consulted in time for this only prospect of admission, I enquired of those most able to inform me what was best & was almost unanimously advised to embrace the proposal. I have done so, & sincerely hope it will meet your approbation. She is discreet, has a great desire to improve, & there I am told they have every opportunity. Mr. & Mrs. Arden have two daughters there to whom they mean to pay a visit about the time Maria is to go, & they have promised to take her under their protection in case they refuse to admit her. Had Mrs. Ridley been here I shd. have gone myself with Maria, but as she is not, I cannot leave my family. Nelly was married the 6th of Sepbr. & her place has not been supplied; while you are absent I do not require a person to take care of the Children as they are my own most pleasing companions....

Last tuesday J. Lyon came to town upon business with the Court & brought the Carriage horses. They are lean & intirely unbroke, even to a waggon. I was advised to send for Swan, a man who teaches riding & understands breaking horses very well. He has undertaken it, & if he succeeds is to receive 6£ but not to be paid any thing if he does not. Frank attends him with the horses, for Swan say the Coachmen of this City require breaking as much as the horses....

Please to remember &c., &c.

(SLJ to her daughter Maria at Morris-Town) New York Octbr 21st 1794

My dr. Maria,

Just after you left us I discovered that you had left your pen-knife & thread-case & I recollected that I had not fulfilled my promise of a Bible for you. I could not have been at ease while you was deprived of that best of Books. My dearest Daughter! do not omit reading in it daily; in it you will find the best rules for your Conduct in this life & the most elevated hopes for futurity. Give my best Love to yr. Aunt. It was my fullest intention to have written her by to-morrow's post but my eyes are so weak it is with difficulty I can write or read what is written. Tell her that I felicitate her upon having so amiable a Companion as Miss Symmes. Altho' I have so short an acquaintance with her I already love her, & you may tell her that I do. Present my best respects to the Judge & do my dear endeavor to render yourself worthy [of] the attentions of yr. friends....

Sally says you've been da da a long time & that Aunt Coty gave lally her plums. Nancy & William both join in Love to you & their Aunt.... Adieu my dear Maria! May Providence guard! protect & bless you.

Yours affectionately
Sa. Jay

Nancy desires you will ask yr. Aunt if she has taken by mistake an hand-kerchief of hers. Don't forget the Question relative to the grate. In the bundle is the Bible, yr. thread-case, a pen knife & half a dollar in change. I found in yr. drawer in a green purse half a Crown, but Nancy claims the half.

(SLJ to JJ at London) New York 25th Octbr 1794

My dr. Mr. Jay,

Your favor of the 16th of Augst was handed me by Captn Depeyster, who arrived here the 22d inst. How I long for a letter announcing the rect. of those I have written to you. The season is already advanced & I am yet ignorant whether you have embarked, or whether you will be detained 'till spring. Much as I wish to see you, I could not advise you to venture a winters passage.

By this time I hope you have recd. my letters informing you that your Jamaica business is satisfactorily settled. The Money which I have received for you on that Debt, not being able to loan, I have embarked in the National Bank: the first sum of near 1000£ procured 5 shares of 400 dollars each at 24 pr. Cent advance as I wrote you formerly, & I then intended awaiting your orders respecting the disposition of the rest; but finding it improbable that it could be placed to any advantage at all (a friend of yours having for a long time had 2000£ to put out without having any applications for it) & the funds continuing to rise, I resolved last week to purchase 5 shares more at 29 pr. Cent advance; I shall however take care not to be so sanguine as to risque it after having by its rise cleared the interest that sum ought to make. Had I not been diffident of acting without yr. advice I shd. already have cleared 12 pr. Cent. but I shd. not now have done what you when here, disapproved, had I not been of opinion that were you here at present, you would have altered your sentiments with the times. I shall however respect yr. sentiments more than my own, & will therefore probably sell out again in a month's time, perhaps less. At the rate I've purchased for you it yields 6 pr. Cent, & even at fifty advance (which 'tis thought it will soon be) better than 5 pr. Cent. It is in higher repute than the N.Y.B[ank] which is at 28/. But Mr. Bleecker advised me by all means to give the preference as I have, because he said the interest was payable at option in Europe or America, which was a circumstance that would enhance its value with foreigners. I sincerely hope that what I've done will receive yr. approbation, as my Conduct has not been the effect of a Gambling disposition, but the result of mature reflection aided by the Advice of those in whose judgement I had reason to confide.

The day before yesterday I rode out with our little folks, & call'd upon Mrs. Watkins; in the course of conversation she mentioned that Mr. Watkins had purchased the whole of Mr. Rutherfurd's right in the Lands he held with you in Greens Town at 2 dollars pr. Acre. As Mr. W. has been on that Ground & is acquainted with the Value of Lands in that part of the Country, I have not a doubt but that he is convinced it may command 20/.

Last Saturday our dear little Maria went with Judge Symmes & his daughter to Morris-Town where Mrs. Symmes is, to go from thence with them in their Cochee as far as Bethlehem. In my last I inform'd you how very desirous she was of residing there 12 or 18 months as the means of promoting her Education. As we were inform'd that the school was full & that numbers had applied for admittance without obtaining it; I did not expect that she would be gratifyed; but Judge Symmes was of a different opinion; and as he was not ready for his journey when Mr. & Mrs. Arden went upon a visit to their daughters; he requested them to take charge of a letter from him to the Clergy-man there, which they did, & they have return'd; & Mrs. Arden call'd upon me to inform me that Mr. Van Vleck, the principal of the Society told her that the Clergyman told him that they could not hesitate about the reply, for that the Society were under obligations to Judge Symmes for past favors which ought never to be obliterated, & to the chief Justice of the U. States for past & present exertions for the Welfare of the Union; & that therefore his family merited the Assistance of those who were capable of being useful to them.

As Mrs. A[rden] was very desirous of Maria's being there, she was kind enough to impress them with a favorable opinion of her understanding, representing her as a young Lady that was willing to forego the indulgences her situation in Life afforded, merely to derive advantage from retirement & application. She has acquired great éclat among her friends here likewise who know it to be her own choice. May a kind Providence be propitious to her laudable endeavors to excel. Little Ann is very industrious at home. I did not wish her to accompany her sister, but if I had, she could not have been prevail'd upon to quit me. She is setting by me studying her french. The Children all behave well, enjoy perfect health & are very chearful. Yourself & Peter are the constant theme of our conversation.

In my last I inclosed a letter from Major Lyon for you. His Son has not yet performed his promise of writing to you, but punctuality is not the greatest merit of either of them. I told you that the Major had sent me yr. young horses lean & unbroke, but they are become gentle & tractable under the tuition of Mr. Swan & yr. man Frank.

I have rode out with them, & last evening paid some visits in Town, they stood very quietly, & what to me was of equal consequence, they did not like a former pair stand longer than I wish'd.

The News-papers have doubtless inform'd you that a malignant fever has prevail'd at Baltimore & New Haven. From the same medium of intelligence We learn that it no longer exists in either place. Indeed a dreadfully putrid fever has curtail'd the lives of many of our own Citizens; but the police, while it has been vigilant & careful has likewise been very silent & it has therefore made little Noise....

Just before Mr. Depeyster gave me your letters, & the bracelets &c., Mr. Deal had call'd upon me & inform'd me that Peter & Polly were very well; he was good enough to be the bearer of a letter from me to them. I sent yr. sister her pins; she, as well as Peggy & the Children are well. Munro is at Albany. He wrote when I did, by a vessel for Hull, about a fortnight ago.

Adieu my dearest, best of friends! Wherever you are may you ever be sensible of the divine protection & favor. Uncertain whether you are still in England, or at present tossing on the waves, you can have no idea of my sensations. If you have not left England when this reaches it, I think I should prefer your remaining there, shelter'd from the wintry storms, to your hazarding a passage in so tempestuous a Season. There is at present a strong Easterly wind that sounds so hollow & dreary that it inspires the most gloomy ideas, but I will endeavor to banish them, by recollecting that a beneficent Providence had already wafted you beyond their reach at a period that I once before dared to feel anxious, & that shd. you now be on the Ocean that same Providence may make this dreary Wind to facilitate yr. return to yr. Country, your family & friends.

Once more, my dearest Mr. Jay receive the Adieus of

your ever affecte. Wife
Sa. Jay

P.S.

If you remain of the same opinion still of selling out of the 6 pr. Cents when they are at 20/, it would be best to let Cousin Peter know, for they are now at 19/8 & it is expected will soon be at 22/ or 24/. I fear you'll think my mind wholly occupied with pecuniary matters. The fact is, that your being removed at such a distance from your family & affairs, I think it my duty to turn my attention more to those subjects than would otherwise be either proper or necessary.

27th I have just sent to Captn. Kemp to ask the favor of him to Deliver this letter into your own hands if you are in England when he arrives there, & if not, to return it to me. He returns for answer that it will give him pleasure to comply with my request & that he will call for it to-morrow. I have just thought it might be agreeable to you to know exactly what I have receiv'd for you & what expended. I will therefore inclose the acct. of both, for your satisfaction. Mr. Remsen when he pd. me your Sallery to-day inform'd me that he has written to you to request you to join in the purchase of some Lands in this State; I wish the proposition may be such as to merit yr. approbation, for if those Lands which you & Mr. Rutherford purchased command 2 dollars how much more may those he proposes to buy sell for in a few years. In short it is the only way of making a provision for a family & the sum I have laid out will speedily be re-converted into Cash & will be very convenient for you. Adieu.

(SLJ to her son PAJ at London) New York Octbr. 26th 1794

My dr. son,

Your favor of the 17th Augst. was handed me by Captn Depeyster the 22d. inst. I think Aunt Jay's bracelets very handsome. Your Aunt Munro's pins I've sent her, & she is much obliged to you for your attention to her request. I long to have my pin with your hair & to hear that your Papa is setting for his Picture. That your dear Papa shd. be uneasy & even dissatisfyed at not hearing from me is natural, but still I plead not guilty. If Vessels have left this Port without letters from me it has been owing to my ignorance of their going, for I am intirely out of the line of being acquainted with those things. Several of our friends have promised to let me know of opportunities when they offered, but I believe before the occasion arrived, other matters had taken place of the promise & it has been forgot. It was but accidentally that I heard the *Ohio* was to sail tomorrow.... It is sometime since I've seen our friends at Rye, for as sister Ridley is not yet come I think it unsafe to leave the Children alone; and your Uncle [Peter] is so much dissatisfyed with his man Pete's behavior when in Town, that he seldom visits me. It is near three weeks since I've seen Fady or any of his family. Your sister Maria before she left me, beg'd to be affectionately remembered to you & yr. papa.

Your Aunt Susan, who is at Morris-Town, writes me that Maria arrived there, in good health & spirits, & that they propose pursuing their Journey this week. Your sister will thank you, if you'll cut an exact pattern of the back arms & seat of one of those work'd Chairs, as she wishes to work some to suit them in size, & if any of your acquaintances will assist you in choosing the kind of silk that will be proper to work them, she'll thank you to send her some.

Your Papa in one of his letters asks if little Sal had found her tongue, but could he hear her incessant Prattle he would probably think she had monopolized those of her little friends. Wig often ex[c]laims 'why Ba! will you never be tired'! There prattle often amuses, & rarely tires me except when I am writing & then it often dissipates every idea. At present Van Hagen is tuning Ann's Piano forte, Martel is hearing her french lesson & William & Sally are engaged at my elbow in a very interesting conversation about some sugar plumbs & almonds that Mr. Martel has given them. I am just interrupted by a letter from Mrs. Ridley. She is well. Have you received a letter from Essex since you have been in L[ondon]?

I am again interrupted & must bid you adieu.

Your affectionate Mother
Sa. Jay

(SLJ to JJ at London) New York lst Novbr. 1794

My dear Mr. Jay,

After writing to you on the 27th Ult., I sent to Captn. Kemp & requested the favor of him to take charge of my letter himself, & he was kind enough to call upon me & promise that he would deliver it to you or in case of your return previous to his arrival to restore it to me. Since which I've learnt that two ships by wh[ic]h I have lately written to you have been captured by the french, & I therefore think it best to send you duplicates of them as they will serve to throw light upon some passages of my last letter that might otherwise appear obscure. I have not time to copy the letters I have written to Peter, nor indeed have I preserv'd them all, or even those to you, but if I had, my eyes are too weak to admit of more writing at present, for I find they suffer very much from it. His sisters in their letters to him requested him to bring each of them a box of paints, & silks to tambour & embroider with: and Maria wrote to him to bring out a Couple of skreen-frames like those Cousin Munro brought out with her, as she proposes to embroider or paint them for the sattin-wood stands we already have. They wished likewise for some filligree paper & frost like that on the skreens we have & cement to put it on with. I am sorry Munro is still absent, as he wd. probably send duplicates of his last to you, which wd. have inform'd you that the Grant business was settled &c....

Please to present my Compts. to Mr. Trumbull. Congress will meet next monday. The President has return'd to Philadelphia. I inclose last evening's paper which contains the President's Farewell to the Army. Yr. friend [Rufus] King promised to send me a letter to inclose for you but he has not done it. My most affecte. Regards to our dear son.

Once more my dearest Mr. Jay Farewell

Yours most sincerely
Sa. Jay

Maria wishes the skreen frames to be made so as to admit of a glass being set in to preserve the work. Little Sally has just given me a kiss & a Curtesy for you.

(PAJ to his sister Nancy) London Novm. 8th 1794

Dear Sister

Your entertaining letter of the 27th Sept. arrived about a week ago. I think you are a little severe upon poor Pete about his adventure upon the river. He would be mortified if he knew what you said of him & still more so if he supposed you were acquainted with a circumstance that happened some time since. He had expressed a great desire to see the Lions & complained exceedingly of his having too little time to visit them at the Tower. At length a white servant of ours told him that he might satisfy his curiosity without taking so long a walk, for that on the first day of every month the Lions were regularly brought to London bridge & there washed in order to preserve their health. This was told with so grave a countenance that Pete believed every word & set out on the appointed day to see the Lions washed. But being sadly laughed at by a person he met & to whom he imported the object of his journey, he returned so much displeased & mortified & he is still so tormented by the other Servants of the house, that I suspect it will be long before he forgives William who first sent him on that fools errand.

When you write to Aunt Susan, wish her joy in my name

Your Affectionate Brother,
Peter Augustus Jay

> It is likely that the unseemly behavior of the farm manager Samuel Lyon, now a widower, is the reason for Mrs. Smith's mention of "things sadly neglected at the house upon the hill."

(SLJ to JJ at London) New Y. 11th Novbr. 1794

My dr. Mr. Jay,

I was mortified by seeing in this morning's Paper that Mr. Bayard had sailed the 8th for London. Had I been informed of his going, with what pleasure wd. I have written to you by him ....

A few days ago Mrs. Smith from B[edford] call'd here to pay me a visit, I found her sociably disposed & listen'd to her information. She told me things were sadly neglected at the house upon the hill. The tenant of it being in an very improper manner with a young woman in the Neighbourhood, spending some times 2 or 3 days with her at her house & receiving visits from her as unsuitable at his own. The young woman (she told me) had kept one of the farm-horses all summer at her father's for her use & that the neighbours censure them both very much. With a great number of Cows, some of which are excellent he makes no butter but for his own use; & a number of annecdotes which I think discover inattention to business which I cannot but regret. I wrote to the old Woman's Son-in-law lately about flour &c., & in my letter dropt a hint that I fear'd in the hurry of business he had forgot his promise of writing to you, suggesting that it was not yet too late. Munro has not yet return'd from Albany, as he means to take B[edfor]d in his way home, he will be able to tell you how your affairs there are conducted.

Your brother Fady is I believe offended with me. About a month ago he sent his Clerk here to ask me for the money for the tierce of spirits; I told the young man I would with pleasure pay for it, and asked for the Order. He told me he had none, but wd. give me his rect. I declined paying without the Order. Half an hour after Moncrieffe call'd upon me & in like manner offer'd his rect. for the money. I told Tommy that in his Uncle's letter from Mr. Hilton he was requested by that gentleman to pay the money to Mrs. Hilton his mother, & I sd. I was ready to pay it to her Order. A few days after Fady call'd here for his wife, his Countenance indicated displeasure. So you refused to pay for the spirits, says he. By no means sir I replyed, I only requested to have Mrs. Hilton's order as an indemnification. Very well said yr. brother, I've pd. for it & shall charge my brother interest on the sum. I asked if that would not be rather hard as I had both money & inclination to pay & only wished to do yr. business regularly. From that time I've not seen him. I sent for yr. Nephew & acquainting him with what had pass'd, he approv'd my conduct & advised that I should let it rest 'till he sent me Mrs. Hilton's rect. or 'till you return'd.

I received a beautiful letter to-day from Maria, written just before she left Morris-Town. I long for her next letter which will be from Bethlehem.... An advertisment in to-days paper relative to Mr. Bayard's business in England, seems to suggest an Expectation of the President's that Mr. Bayard will find you in Europe. If that should be the case, for Heaven's sake my dr. Mr. Jay don't risque a winter's passage. At least don't let any considerations about me & the family induce you to hazard what you do not approve but do that only which you think best after consulting able Mariners. You must be convinced that it will give me infinite pleasure to re-embrace you & your son; but you may be assured that should your business demand your still longer detention, no exertion shall be omitted on my part to bear with fortitude the seperation, nor any thing neglected in my power to perform to lessen the injury your family & affairs might sustain from yr. absence.

The 2d. of Novbr. I wrote you by Captn. Kemp & likewise sent you duplicates of 2 other letters. I sincerely hope he'll arrive safe, & that letters from my dear son & yourself will e'er long inspire with new fortitude

your ever affectionate wife

(SLJ to JJ at London) [Draft]

[New York] 12th Novbr. 1794

My dr. Mr. Jay

....A few hours ago I had the pleasure of receiving yours & Peter's favors by the *Sansom*, & take this early opportunity of returning you both my thanks. In a former letter you promised to tell me when you might probably leave England; you do not however mention the subject, or drop the most distant intimation of the state of your business. You know best. The letters you sent to my care I immediately forwarded agreeable to their respective addresses.

By the *Ohio* I have written you long letters & sent you duplicates of others. Should any accident happen to that Vessel, it will be a relief to your mind to be inform'd again that the Grant business is settled, that I've recd. the money & placed it in the U.S.B[ank]. The 1st of Janry. it will draw half an years interest, after which if you think proper I can sell out. Be so good as to inform me what you wd. wish me to do. What I've already done has been in the absence of Mr. Munro, who however has always declin'd his advice about the funds. As to loaning it, 'tis out of the question, he can't do it. The funds continue to rise, & if I sell out to-morrow you will be a gainer by what I've done.

I understood [from] Mrs. Smith that the Mill-house, & every thing but the Dam was compleat, but that they were still at work upon the Dam. To-day I've recd. a letter from Maria from Bethlehem, I'll inclose it for your satisfaction. We have as much reason as ever Parents had to be grateful on account of our Children. I ask'd your dr. little son what I should tell you of his little sister. He said I should tell you she talk'd enough to employ three tongues to repeat. In short, if it was not for your little Counter-parts, I should want chearfulness & vigour to enable me to perform a variety of extra duties that devolve upon me in consequence of your absence. To-morrow I shall resume my pen.

At present I will only request you to give my love to our dear son, & wish you my best beloved a very good night.

....I have not been able yet to get yr. picture from Stewart. Have you set for a Miniature? Would it not be worth while for Peter likewise to set?

(SLJ to her son PAJ) New York, Novbr 15th 1794

My dr. Son,

....It was a great disappointment to me that neither your Papa or yourself hinted in your letters any thing of your return. There is such magic in the word that I intreat you never to write me in future without mentioning it, even if it is to say you cannot tell when it is to take place....

I see by the Papers the Prince of Wales was to be married, & I suppose by this time is & probably the wedding gave occasion to fêtes &c. that were novel to you. You are silent about the effect the variety of objects & scenes make upon your mind, but I flatter myself they entertain & instruct you. No young gentleman from this Country had ever equal advantages on going to Europe & as your mind was always disposed to draw improvement from objects capable of affording it, it gives me infinite pleasure to reflect upon the many Opportunities you must have to indulge a judicious taste. Indeed my dear Son the hope that you will be highly gratifyed, is after all, the greatest Consolation I have in yours & your dear Father's absence. As to my patriotism, having been worn in all seasons for twenty years past, by Sea & Land, at home & abroad, it is become so thin that it will not much longer even serve to veil my disquiet at being so often obliged to be seperated from a beloved husband....

I depend upon your perseverence for obtaining your Papa's miniature. I believe it is to my own [meri]t I owe his Portrait, for Stewart has been [persuaded] at last to yield it to my importunities. Remember me to those of your acquaintances to whom I am known....

Adieu my dr. son, 'tis very late

Yours affectionately
S. Jay

(SLJ to JJ at London) New York 18 Novbr 1794

My dear Mr. Jay,

The letter I wrote you on the 15th & intended for the *Rosana*, I sent yesterday by the *Hope* & will send this by the *Rosana* which sails to-morrow. Tho' the Contents of yr. dispatches remain a secret to the Public, yet I have been inform'd that your business was nerely compleated, & that nothing but the hazard of a Winter's Passage would detain you, & that all your friends think Ought to detain you. If what I've heard be true, I most sincerely felicitate you, & the consideration that a few months of repose will succeed to your anxieties & labour shall greatly aleviate the tediousness of absence. No opportunity shall be omitted of giving you intelligence of myself & family, & the idea that our dear son will enjoy his situation, shall be to me instead of the pleasure of his Company....

This being the 5th time I've written in this month, you won't be surprised that nothing material has occurr'd. I'll thank our son if he will bring out 4 pair of shoes for me like those he sent out to Cousin Munro; hers fit me exactly. I do not wish them till you come yourself. Remember me Affectionately to him & tell him if you please I wrote him last week.

Your friends here are well & in good Spirits, many of them desire to be remembred to you. May the Olive entwine your Brow & the sweet chearer which it denotes never desert your breast! Oh may you be as happy as you deserve to be! & May affectionate friends & a grateful Country once more hail you to your native Shores. But if I attempt to express the wishes my heart entertains for I shall not have room to assure you that I still remain

Your sincerely affectionate
Wife
Sarah Jay

(SLJ to her daughter Maria at Bethlehem) New York, Novbr: 19th 1794

My dr. Maria,

On the 12th inst. I had the very great satisfaction of receiving your affectionate letter.... Mr. Stewart has at length sent home your Papa's picture which I have placed at the side of the Alcove where your brother's Canary-birds used to hang. It gives me pleasure to see William & Sally's attention to it; they are delighted with it.

....When you write me again tell me particularly what studies engage your attention at present, & which of the Ladies you are indebted to for instruction. Read as much history as you conveniently can, & let me know what it relates to. Without Geography history will be but a blind study, you will therefore I am sure be attentive to that....

Adieu my dearest Child!
S. Jay

(John Sloss Hobart to JJ at London) New York 20th Novr. 1794

My dear Sir

....I drank a glass of porter and smoaked a pipe with Mrs. Jay on Saturday evening. Master William took a Segar and attempted to play Papa, but his stomach was too weak. He sunk under the operation and was as sick as if he had been 500 leagues at sea. You will naturally conclude what was the subject of our conversation.

Haveing just seen an Account that Mr. Bayard was appointed to go to London with power to pledge the U.S. for certain expenditures under your direction induced us to dispair of seeing you before the next Summer. Indeed I am scarce ever in company but the most interesting, if not the first, questions are when will Mr. Jay return? Will he be in season for the next election? &c. We are amused with various accounts respecting the situation of your negotiations, all of which concur in the prospect of a fortunate termination tho' they vary as to the progress made; it is expected the speach will aford some light on the subject in the course of a day or two....

Mrs. Hobart desires to be respectfully remembered to you. I am with great sincerity

Your most affect hble. servt.
Jno. Sloss Hobart

On November 19th, John Jay signed the treaty that he had negotiated with Great Britain. The major objective of avoiding another war was accomplished.

The British agreed to give up the forts and outposts in the Northwest Territory, the navigation of the Mississippi became unrestricted, and trade was to be free between territories of both countries. But severe restrictions were placed upon American vessels trading with the British West Indies, and British vessels were to be permitted at American ports. In addition, there was to be no indemnity for those Americans whose slaves had been carried off and no guarantee of protection for American seamen against impressment.

John Jay anticipated the controversy that the treaty would generate at home. In a letter to George Washington (13 September 1794) he wrote:

> I learn that Virg[ini]a is escheating british property, and I hear of other occurrences that I regret, but they shall not abate my perseverance in endeavouring to prosecute peace and bring the Negociation to such a conclusion, as will either ensure peace with this country or produce union among ourselves in prosecuting War agt. it. Whatever may be the Issue, I am determined not to lose the only Satisfaction that I can be sure of vizt. the satisfaction resulting from a consciousness of having done my Duty.
>
> That attempts will be made in America to frustrate this Negociation, I have not the most distant Shadow of a Doubt. I brought this Belief and opinion with me, and my Dependence then was and still is, on the wisdom firmness and Integrity of the governmt. on the general good sense of our people and on those enlightened and virtuous characters among them, who regard the peace honor and welfare of their country as primary objects. These men regret the Differences wh. subsist between this Country and their own, and sincerely desire to see mutual animosities give way to mutual good will. As to a political connection with any country, I hope it will never be judged necessary for I very much doubt, whether it wd. ultimately be found useful. It wd. in my opinion introduce foreign Influence, wh. I consider as the worst of political plagues.

The treaty, known as "Jay's Treaty," was very unpopular. In March 1795, after it reached Philadelphia and its terms were made known, John Jay was hung and burned in effigy. A crowd stoned Alexander Hamilton as he spoke in its defense. With the exception of the clause about American vessels trading with the West Indies, Congress, after lengthy debate, eventually ratified it on June 24th.

(JJ to SLJ at New York) London 21 novr 1794

My dear Sally

I have within a few weeks past written to you by the *Eagle*, by the Packet, and by Capt. Burril bound to new York. This Letter will go by the way of Virginia, under cover to the Secretary of State.

It will give you Pleasure to be informed that my mission has been successful. A Treaty was yesterday signed, and will be transmitted under the same cover with this Letter. I hope it will give Satisfaction to our Country in general.

My further stay here not being very necessary, I exceedingly regret that I cannot immediately return to you, but the Season is too far advanced. I have not Health enough for a winters Voyage. I have been for some time past troubled with the Rheumatism. Having been advised to wear vests of fleecy Hosiery under my Shirt, I have had some made, and think them useful. For some Days past I find myself better, and I ascribe it to that circumstance....

Peter is well, and has written to you by the NYork Vessel. He is now attending the Tryal of mr. [John H.] Tooke. He has many advantages here, and is not a little indebted to you for them. My Love to the children &c.

yours Sincerely
John Jay

(SLJ to JJ) [New York] Decbr. 5th 1794

My dr. Mr. Jay,

Since Monday I've recd. both your favors, the one by the *Pigou* & the other by the *Brigg Molly*; for which I return you my sincere thanks....

Mr. Phill: Livingston who took tea with me last evening told me that a Gentleman of the Law in this City, told him that within a few weeks he had received one thousand dollars as a fee, & several times within a short time two & three hundred pounds. Surely that is sufficient encouragement to induce a young man to be eminent in that profession.

One of your friends who has read our dispatches, tells me there is not a doubt but that your business is satisfactorily concluded 'ere this. Let me then my dearest Mr. Jay felicitate you on the success of your efforts. Oh may this Country once more secur'd in the blessings of Peace, require no more from you such arduous endeavors. Both you & myself have great reason for regret, & both are free from blame, on the subject of our Correspondence. The solicitude you express at not hearing from me, is at the same time kind & painful. To me 'tis inexpressibly mortifying that my endeavors to promote your tranquility should have been so unsuccessful, still I flatter myself that my fugitive letters will be recd. (as formerly has been the case) & be my best Apologists.

The Children continue to enjoy health & to behave well. Maria remains satisfyed with Bethlehem & Ann is very attentive to me at home; William & Sally are as engaging as it is possible for Children of their age to be. Plato I send to school, but I fear Nature will prevail. Your brother & Polly are well, so are Fady's & Munro's families.

Peter & Polly often express their affectionate regard for you & your son & desire me to present their love & best wishes to you both. I've written to Polly this evening, & inform'd her of the rect. of your letters & the improbability of your taking your Christmas dinner with her. She & your brother have a long time been prevented from visiting me by the illness of their man Pete; & as Col: Budd's servant told Yaff he lay at the point of Death when he left Rye, I thought it proper to renew the Offer of Yaff.

Your conjectures that the saw-mill was not begun & that the Mill-stones I wrote about were burr-stones were just; as Johnny promised to send me flour &c. as soon as the Mill was in condition to grind, & as he has as yet sent me only one barrel of flour, & that of very inferior quality, I fancy the Mill is not yet finished. He is very sparing of intelligence. In two of my letters I have stated an account of the sums I've advanced him....

Decbr. 9th. Since I wrote the above I find that the *Sansom* does not sail in less than 8 or 10 days & I've sent Yaff to inquire if Captn Smith knows of any other Vessel which will soon leave this for England. On the 7th Inst. Mr. Robt. Morris paid me 732 dollars for your share of some Lands sold in Orange County. The purchasers would have been glad of a Deed, but Mr. Munro's powers were not adequate to a Guarantee Deed & such an one they wanted.

Since I began this letter Plato has been guilty of such misconduct that it rendered it highly improper to permit him to stay in the house. Indeed Aunt Cortlandt advised me rather to give him away than to suffer him to remain here. I have this morning promised to bind him for 6 years to a Gentleman in this City of the name of Hartshorne on Condition that he pays you annually 5£ during the 6 years, & if he wishes to part with him before the expiration of that term you are to have the refusal of him. Plato has been with that gentleman before, about 6 weeks & is much pleased wh. the treatment he received there. The gentleman has a wife, an infant Child, a Nurse & a Cook. Plato was constantly employed in waiting in the house. When Mr. Munro returns, he will draw the writings of agreement.

I had just now an application for money on security in this City, I have referred the person to Mr. Munro & if he finds the property safe & sufficient I can in January put out 500£ including the sum recd. of Mr. Morris.

Decbr. 15th. Yesterday Mr. & Mrs. Munro left Rye & our friends there well. Their Man Pete is recovering & of course they will not want Yaff for which I'm very glad, as parting with Plato would have obliged me to hire another in the place of Yaff. Mr. Munro tells me that an Ox from Lyon for me will be here to-day. I've already agreed with a Butcher to kill it & to-morrow Frank will carry it to the Slaughter house. I've been disappointed in the Potatoes Mr. S. was to supply us with as he says they are too bad to send. Lyon is to send me 40 Bushells.

The Season is remarkably mild altho' advanced to the middle of Decbr I've not yet seen any ice. The rivers continue open & the weather delightful; notwithstanding which Nut-wood is 20/ a load & every thing proportionably high. The day before yesterday Post sent to Bedford at John Lyon's request 100£ of those nails from our closet, some rope, tarr & sheet-iron, without which articles Johnny writes him he cannot set the mill a going. It has been extemely fortunate for your affairs here, that we have such a delightful season for I am in hopes that they will compleat the Mill, tho' had we had the usual weather of the time of the year it undoubtedly would not have been finished. I am glad Munro has returned before the *Sansom* sails as he has settled accounts with Lyon for the last year.

My most affectionate regards attend you my dr. Mr. Jay & our beloved son. May a kind Providence ever be with you both & restore you in health & spirits to a family who loves you beyond expression.

Yours sincerely
S. Jay

(JJ to his daughter Maria at Bethlehem) London 9th Decr. 1794

My dear Maria

Your Letter of the 27th of Septr. gave me Pleasure. Had I not been constantly employed in public Business, I should have written to you more frequently and less concisely than I have done. To write familiar elegant Letters, and in a good Hand, are accomplishments which recommend those who possess them. They can be acquired only by attention and Practice and by always endeavouring to write neatly, and express your Sentiments in the best Language, that is, in a free and easy manner; avoiding not only vulgar Expressions, but also what some call Dictionary words. Be cautious never to write what it would give you uneasiness to see published.

Mama informs me that you had sollicited, and obtained her consent, to pass some months at Bethlehem, from an Expectation that you would there have better means of Improvement than at New York. Your motive certainly was laudable, and I sincerely wish your Expectations may be realized. As much will depend on yourself, as well as on your Teachers, I flatter myself that they will derive Credit, and your Friends Pleasure, from the Progress you will make. I do not mean by this remark, to urge you to unceasing application. Exercise and Relaxation are essential to Health; and Health is a Blessing without which no other temporal ones can be enjoyed. Apply diligently, and play heartily. I need not add properly, of that I am sure you will be mindful.

Your Brother is well, and assures you of his affection. We hope by the Blessing of Providence to be home next Spring. I shall be happy then to take the earliest opportunity of seeing you; and of assuring you that, by being, what I am persuaded you will be, prudent, amiable and accomplished, and ever mindful of your Creator, you may rely on the Esteem, Love and attachment of

My dear Maria
Your very affectionate Father
John Jay

Peter Augustus Jay made a year-end visit to Scotland to see his uncle, the Rev. Harry Munro. Mr. Munro, a Tory, had fled America in 1777, leaving his wife of 11 years, Eve Jay Munro, and his son, Peter Jay Munro, to be cared for by the Jay family. The task of Peter Augustus was to have Mr. Munro execute three quitclaims, releasing property in America to his son. Peter Augustus was successful in his mission.

(JJ to SLJ, Broadway, New York City) London 2 Jany. 1795

My dear Sally

The *Aurora*, by whom I wrote you several Letters has at last sailed. There are several vessels here from New York, but as none of them are yet ready to return, and I know your anxiety to hear from me and Peter, I write these few lines by the Packet.

Peter went about three weeks ago to Scotland with Doctr. Adair who was our fellow Passenger on the *Ohio*. He returned the Day before Yesterday in good Health, and much pleased with the Jaunt. It has given him an opportunity of doing a friendly office to his Cousin Munro, and of seeing many things that have gratified his curiosity. P. Munro will explain this to You. I expect that Peter will write to you and to him by the Packet.

It is now three o'Clock and I am writing by candle Light, in a Chamber with three windows in it. When the Smoke of the Town unites with Fog, which is frequently the Case here, at this Season of the Year there is not sufficient Light from the Sun to read by. They speake of this winter as a severe one, there being more Frost and Snow than usual. As yet I have not experienced any weather so cold as is common at New York in January; but there is almost Constant Chilliness in the air, which to me is more disagreable than hard Frost.

My Rheumatic complaints have much abated. Clear weather and Sunshine would be no less useful than acceptable to me, but in this northern Latitude the Sun shines but feebly in winter. May the new Year be a happy one to us all! If we use it properly it will be. My Love to the children, and to you.

Yours very affecty
John Jay

(PAJ to SLJ at New York) London 2d January 1795

Dear Mama

I had yesterday the pleasure of recg. your letter of the 15 Novr. upon my return to town from a very pleasant journey to Edinburgh, where I have been for the purpose of becoming a witness to a deed to Cousin P. Munro from his Father. As I went in the Mail Coach which travels without ceasing even in the night, I stopped a day at York to recover from the fatigue & see the curiosities of the place. Another day was spent in the same manner between Durham and Newcastle, & yet I reached Edinburgh (400 miles distant from London) in 4½ days. While there I was introduced to most of the remarkable people, & heard a sermon from Dr. Blair. Dr. Adair our fellow passenger to England, who had been some days in London, returned with me to Edinburgh & was exceedingly useful to me indeed; he means to return with us in the spring in order to settle in America.

You will perhaps expect me to give you a description of Edinburgh, but this I assure you is utterly impossible, as it is entirely different from any thing of it's kind. One part however which has been lately built is an exception. It is called the New Town & far exceeds in beauty any Thing I have seen. I remained there about ten days.

A Circumstance which you mention in one of your letters affords us very great pleasure: you say that you have not had occasion for the Doctor since our departure. We have been equally favored. Papa has indeed been several times indisposed but never seriously & excepting a little Rheumatism is now perfectly well. As for myself I have not experienced a single hour of sickness even of the slightest kind since I landed at Falmouth.

As our letters are to go by the Packet & it is now high time to put them in the Post office, I shall not be able to write to my Uncles or to sisters, I must therefore beg you to wish them all in my name a merry Christmas & Happy New Year.

With my earnest prayers that you may enjoy very, very, many of both

I remain
Your affectionte. Son
Peter Augustus Jay

(PAJ to Peter Jay Munro at New York) London 2d January 1795

Dear Cousin

I have just returned from a journey which has afforded me much pleasure & for which I owe you many thanks. I left your father five days ago at Edinburgh much better than could be expected; he was afflicted by the Palsy but said that he now experienced from it no other inconvenience than the continual trembling which it occasioned. He executed in my presence triplicates of all the three quitclaims which you sent him, for the estates at Munro's field, at Albany & at Princeton. The other witnesses were his Attorney Mr. McFarlane a Clerk to the signer, & one Thomas Forsyth his Gardiner. One of each of these copies he had kept to be sent by himself, & the others he has committed to me, with instructions to send one set by the first safe opportunity, & to deliver the others along with all his papers relating to his lands in America with my own hands to you upon my return. He expressed the greatest anxiety for your welfare & the most ardent wishes for the health & prosperity of yourself & of his daughter-in-law.

As this letter is to go by the packet, papa concurs with me in thinking it best not to send the papers along with it, but to wait for some American Vessel, & it cannot be long before such an opportunity offers. Before this jaunt I had in my hands remaining of your money £17.15.10. The journey cost £31.8.4. It has consequently brought you in debt £13.12.6. By the next opportunity I will send you a statement of your Account with me. In some instances you will find it less than the bills I have sent you in consequence of the discount for prompt payment which I have been allowed on every purchase of any magnitude.

The French have gained another victory in Spain, & as the cold is now intense, it is not improbable, that the ice will soon enable them to cross the Waal & put a finishing stroke to the disasters of the Campaign. Yet notwithstanding all these disasters the people of this country really do not appear (as Mr. Jay asserts) universally desirous of peace. From all the misfortunes of the war, the minority in Parliament has only gained an addition of 7 or 8 it now amounts in the Commons to 73 & in the House of Lords to 12. The armed Force now in Great Britain only & of which the regular Troops form a very small part, cannot be less than 100,000 men. Yorkshire alone has raised 5 regiments of Militia. And a short time ago Mr. Pitt's Loan for 24,000,000 was filled in three days. All these facts seem to militate strongly against a general wish for peace. Everything which I saw in Scotland led also to the same conclusion. A printer who had ventured to insert in his paper some paragraphs against the ministry lost all his subscribers, & several Merchants who had been members of the popular Societies were obliged to make public apologies in order to preserve their customers. Not a single Anti-Ministerial paper is published in Edinburgh & I believe but one or two in Scotland. It is in the great manufacturing towns such as Sheffield & Glasgow where the Spirit of disaffection principally resides.

From what I have heard from New York, I expect that we shall return in the midst of a contested election and this makes me a little surprized that a certain match (which I should suppose a very unpopular one) was not put off 'till after April. It is said too that your old master* is about to offer himself as a candidate. If he means this in earnest, I should like to know what side our worthy family of the Turncoats will take in the contest.

Wishing very many & very happy New Years to you & Mrs. Munro, I am my dr cousin

Yours sincerely
Peter Augustus Jay

(JJ to SLJ) London 3 Feb. 1795

My dear Sally

My last to you was of the 2 Jany. by the Packet — since which I have not had the pleasure of recg any Letters from you; nor have any opportunities of writing to you since offered, that I know of.

This has hitherto been one of the most severe winters known in this country for many Years. There has been so much Snow and Frost that for a Fortnight Sleighs might have been used. The weather has nevertheless been gloomy. The clouds of Smoke wh. constantly hover over the city will not permit us to enjoy much Sunshine, even when the Sky is free from other clouds. You know how much I enjoy Sunshine, and consequently how much I must regret this unceasing Gloom. I shall nevertheless enjoy the Day, whether dark or otherwise, that I shall set sail for NYork, for altho' I have every Reason to be satisfied, which a stranger can well have, yet like "a Bird that wanders from its nest" I am anxious to return to mine. The first of March you will suspend writing to me, but I shall continue writing to you by every opportunity during my stay here.

On Monday next Peter and I purpose to go out of town to pass some Days at a gentleman's Country Seat. I hope to return before Capn. Kemp will sail. If so, he will bring you a Letter from me....

**Aaron Burr.*

My love to all the Children.

Yours very affectionately
John Jay

(JJ to George Washington) [Draft]
Private London 6th. March 1795

Dear Sir

My last to you was written on the 25 ult: and is gone in the *Ohio* Capt. Kemp, who sailed last week for New York. It was not untill after my dispatches were sent to him, that I had the pleasure of recieving your's of the 18th Decr. last....

I have great reason to believe that the King the Cabinet and the Nation, were never more unanimous in any system than in that of conciliation with us. Even Lord Hawksbury does not oppose it. If it should not succeed, they will naturally pass like a Pendulum to the other extreme.

This system rests principally on their Confidence in the Uprightness Independence and Wisdom of your Conduct. No other man whatever enjoys so completely the Esteem and Confidence of this Nation as you do; nor except the King is any one so popular. The Idea which every where prevails is that the Quarrel between Britain and America was a family Quarrel, and that it is time it should be made up. For my part I am for making it up, and for cherishing this disposition on their part; by Justice Benevolence and good manners on ours. To cast ourselves into the arms of this, or of any other nation, would be degrading, injurious and puerile. Nor in my opinion ought we to have any political connection with any foreign power.

Before I came here, I had no idea that the King was so popular as he is, his Reign having been marked by national Calamities produced by reprehensible measures.

But his Popularity is owing to his private rather than his official character. As a man there is much in him to commend; and I have not heard any vice imputed to him. As a domestick man, affectionate and attentive to his Queen and Children, and affable to all about him, he is universally esteemed. Few men are so punctual in all things. He patronizes the Arts and Sciences. He pays uncommon attention to Agriculture and delights in his farms. He lays out about Ten Thousand Pounds a year in improving and embellishing the Royal Estates. He is industrious, sober and temperate; and has acquired much various Knowledge and Information. He converses with ease & often with Adroitness, and has an uncommon memory. They who ought to know him concur in these accounts. That he is a great and a wise king I have not heard asserted. That he does (to use a vulgar expression) as well as he knows how seems not to be doubted; but yet some say, that he occasionally is cunning instead of being wise. I have heard him described as being a great man in little things; and as being generally well intentioned, pertinacious and persevering....

I am your obliged & affectte. friend & Servant

(JJ to SLJ at New York) London 13th. March 1795

My dear Sally

On the 22d. Feby. I wrote to you by Capt. Kemp, who will also bring you a few lines enclosing a bill of Lading and Invoice of some Ale & Porter, which I have sent you by him. Capt. Hervoy of the *Ellice* went away last Saturday; he also had a letter for you. Since the *Ohio* sailed, no letters from you have come to hand, as you will have ceased writing the first of this month. I cannot expect the pleasure of recieving many more letters from you, but in exchange for it, I shall have that of being with you in the course of a few months. By the 1st. of April I hope my final orders respecting the Treaty will arrive, I shall then take the earliest opportunity of embarking, so that before the first of July I shall be at home, indeed at present I think it will be sooner, but as the sailing of vessels is uncertain, it is impossible to calculate exactly.

You will find herewith enclosed Duplicates of the Bill of Lading and Invoice of the Porter and Ale, sent you by Capt. Kemp. I think it best to send them, though I do not apprehend, they will be necessary. I hope to find those articles safe in our cellar, and yet to have the satisfaction of partaking of them with you and our friends. I suppose Judge Hobart will be so occupied in the improvement of his farm, that you will see him but seldom, and as Benson delights in Poughkeepsie, he will not be frequently in New York, so we separate and scatter. But our little family are growing up around us. Let us resign, to what we cannot alter, and enjoy, whatever Good Providence may bless us with.

In one of your letters, you mention, having written to me, and enclosed a letter from Major Lyon, it never came to hand. I think I heard that the vessel, by which it was sent, sprung a leak, and put back. What finally became of her, I do not know. I mention this, that, if the Major should say anything of my not having answered that letter, he may know the reason. As the time of my return approaches, I think more of our concerns at Bedford so, unless I should be assigned to the Fall circuit I hope before next winter to put more affairs in train, and take measures for doing, what remains to be done. Much of our lives is spent. A few years of leisure and tranquility are very desirable. Whether they will fall to our lot, cannot be known, as they are the objects of my wishes and desire, so shall they be of my endeavours. If they come, let us enjoy them, if not, let us be resigned. Content is in our power, let it also be in our inclination.

Col Trumbull is gone to France on his way to Stuttgard, where he has some plates engraving. He cannot ascertain the time of his return precisely. In the mean time Peter will act as his Deputy Secretary, and I believe, very well. I think he has deserved advantages from being here, and that your expectations on the Head, will not be disappointed. He is nevertheless desirous to return, and will carry with him no acquisitions, which you would wish him to leave behind. Remember however, that the best way to avoid disappointment, is not to expect too much.

Remember me to Mrs. Ridley. I shall not write to the children by this vessel, having written to them by Capt Kemp. A much longer absence from you all, would give my patience a very severe trial. I often think of those french emigrants, who left their families in France, and who have reason to think my situation, compared with theirs, very desirable, so things figure by comparison. Peet prefers New York to London, & is anxious to be at home again.

Adieu my dear Sally,
yours very affectionately.
John Jay

Waiting in London for a safer spring passage, John Jay and his son entertained and were entertained by American and British friends for breakfast and dinner, at dances, at musical evenings, and for weekends in the country.

(JJ to Lady Sarah Amherst) [Draft]
Royal Hotel, Pall Mall 20 March 1795

Mr Jay presents his best compts. to Lady Amherst. He has recd. the note wh. her Ladyship did him the honor to write this morning, and wh. accompanied her obliging present of Mrs Montagu's Essay on Shakespear. He recieves with gratitude and sensibility this token of her Ladyships Esteem. The Sentiments with which he is impressed of the amiable giver, and those wh. he entertains of the ingenious author unite in rendering this Token particularly agreable to him. The Party on Saturday, and the vocal music on Monday Evg, promise pleasing hours; and Mr Jay returns many thanks to Lady Amherst for honoring him & his son with an Invitation to participate in them....

On April 13th, John Jay and Peter Augustus sailed aboard the *Severn* from Bristol for New York. Mr. Jay had no idea that in his absence his friends and supporters had entered his name in the election for governor of New York State. When he arrived in America on May 28 he discovered that he had won the contest. Once again, pursuing what he perceived as his duty, he resigned from the Supreme Court, and took the oath of office on July 1st.

The Jays settled back into their life in New York, surrounded by friends and family. They continued with their plans for building a retirement home in Bedford and for making the property surrounding it into gardens, orchards, and crop-bearing fields.

(SLJ to Margaret Munro) [Draft]
[New York] Novbr. 30th 1795

Mrs. Jay presents her Compts. to Mrs. M. Munro. As Nancy does not purpose to attend any longer to Music in wh. it is not probable she would acquire much Proficiency, Mrs. Jay means to dispose of the instrument she purchased for her. But Mrs. M. Munro having reason to expect the first offer, Mrs. Jay now makes it & requests to be favored with her answer.

(JJ to Edmund Burke) New York 12 Decr. 1795

Sir

The last time I had the pleasure of seeing you I promised to send you some apple Trees. Fifty Trees of five different sorts are now on board the *Rosanna* Capt. John Pollard, whose Rect. for them you will find herewith enclosed. Ten of these Trees are the Newtown Pippin you know what they are. Ten are what we call Spitzenberghs, from the name of the man in whose orchard the first Tree of the kind was found. The apple is red, large and fair, it keeps untill in January, and we esteem it next to the Newtown Pippin. Ten are of a kind called Rhode Island Greening, from being of very green [color] when ripe, and from having been first produced in Rhode Island. It is a very good apple, tho' in my opinion inferior to the two first. Ten are Summer Pippins, a very large & fair yellow apple, ~~& in perfection late in autumn but seldom sound and good beyond December — a mild tart agreable apple.~~ Ten which bear large and sweet apples, which are ripe soon after Harvest. As these Trees are from a nursery man in whose care I have confidence I presume no mistakes have been committed.

The great majority of our orchards consisting of Trees wh. have never been engrafted, afford a variety of apples so great as not to be enumerated, among them are many that are excellent, and a great many that are worth but little....

With great Respect and Esteem and with the best wishes for your Health and Happiness I have the honor to be

Sir
yr most obt. & hble. Servt.

Ann (Nancy) Jay, age 14, followed her sister to the boarding school in Bethlehem, Pennsylvania. Both girls enjoyed and benefited from their education there.

(JJ to his daughter Nancy at Bethlehem) New York 8 June 1796

My dear Nancy

I had this moment the Pleasure of recieving your Letter of the 5th. of this month. Your Mama and Brother have lately written to you, and a little Bundle was sent at the same Time. You will probably recieve them before this Letter will come to your Hands.

Your apprehensions relative to a Fever prevailing here are not well founded. I have no Information nor Reason to believe, that any credit is due to the Reports which you have heard on that Subject.

When you return you will find the grounds within our Enclosure here much altered. They have been levelled, and excepting a little part reserved for a garden, the Rest is laid out for grass; and I hope the next Spring to surround the whole with Trees. A well is now digging near the Kitchen door; so that the Inconveniences we have experienced in that Respect will soon be at an end. Your Brothers & Sisters are well, and your Mama is recovering from the Effects of the accident she met with, much faster than was expected; for she again walks with Ease, tho' I think rather more than is adviseable, considering that her foot is not yet quite restored to its former state.

If nothing should occur to detain me, I expect to go to Rye tomorrow, and on my Return shall flatter myself that further Letters from you to some of us, will by that time have arrived.

I am my Dear Nancy
Your affte. Father
John Jay

The Jays and their friends believed that visiting mineral springs was a cure for many ailments. In the summer, Lebanon Springs, Saratoga Springs, and Ballston Springs in New York State and Warm Springs in Virginia were popular watering places.

This description of Lebanon Springs comes from the diary of William Strickland of Welburn in Yorkshire, who toured the United States in 1794–1795:

> The mineral spring here is much resorted to, but for what diseases in particular I could not learn; Some who come here drink great quantities of the water, and bath also in it, for which purpose there are two baths and a shower bath, and suppose themselves better for it, though I am told afflicted with quite opposite diseases; There has not yet been sufficient time to ascertain the properties of this or the other mineral waters in America. The spring issues out of a rock about half way up a high and steep hill in a streem sufficiently copious, with the assistance of another much smaller one to turn an overshot grist-mill within an 100 Yards of its source. It is sensibly warm to the hand, perfectly limpid, and extricates a considerable quantity of air at the spring head but does not part with any when taken into a glass. It is perfectly devoid of smell and taste, but drinks flat and spiritless and much liked boiled water that has took some time to cool.

(SLJ to her sister Kitty) Lebanon [Springs], New York 29th July 1796

My dear Catharine,

Peter has I suppose given you an account of our Perigrinations from the time we left NYork until the time he left us, the same day that Peter went from here....

Whether I shall be benefited by coming here or not is yet uncertain. Not the least irruption has appear'd since I left home, tho' I frequently feel those sensations which used to precede the irruption. I shall at any rate rejoice on Maria's account, for the sore upon her nose which had made its appearance before we left home puts on an appearance so like poor Mamma's, & proves so obstinate that I believe nothing less than these Springs would have cur'd it. Yesterday I thought it better, but today the scale was washed off in the Bath & I percieve a humor from it which threatens to be tedious. Another sore of the same nature has appeared upon her finger. I long very much to hear from Sally, I am more than ever uneasy about that humor in her little face. Kiss her & Matilda for me. Little Wig I suppose is at Rye.

Depend upon my writing by every opportunity either to you or Mr. Jay. Give my love to my dr. Peter, & tell him I shall remember with pleasure his polite & engaging attentions to us. When you write to Susan remember me to her & little Susy. Mrs. Cortlandt & Maria join in regards to you, Mr. J. & Peter. Adieu my dr. sister, believe me sincerely

yours
Sa. Jay

(SLJ to her sister Kitty) Lebanon 29th July [17]96

My dr. Catharine,

I did myself the pleasure of writing to you yesterday by Mr. Francis Huger, since which Hetty, who is dissatisfied with our Land-Lady has determined to go to New-York. She will on Monday set out for Albany in the stage that runs from this place to that, & from thence will take the stages to New York.

As there would be an impropriety in my remaining without a Maid, I wish Peter to engage a birth for Eliza either in an Albany stage or Sloop as he thinks best; if in a Sloop he can recommend her to the Captain's care, & request him to procure a seat for her in the stage from Albany here.

Except the propriety there is in my having a Maid there is very little use for one until we take our passage; so that Eliza will be quite equal to any thing I want with one; the sooner however she can come the better, & if that little box should have arrived from Baltimore I should be glad (if) she would bring it with her. If Peter can find the travelling back-gammon table Mrs. Cortlandt wd. be very glad she could bring that with her likewise.

Give my love to Mr. Jay & Peter & remember me to inquiring friends. Adieu!

yours sincerely
S. Jay

(JJ to his daughter Nancy at Bethlehem) New York 3d. Augt. 1796

My dear Nancy

I was this moment favored with yours of the 31st of last month, and am happy to be assured that your Health continues to improve. A Letter from me to you written within three or four Days is going to you by the Post. Before this can come to hand, you will probably have recd. it. I have since, vizt. the Day before Yesterday recd. a Letter from your Mama, from which it appears that she was then in good spirits, and therefore already the better for her Excursion. We have Reason to hope and expect that change of air, Exercise and Leisure together with the water of the Spring will restore her to Health.

The city is more healthy than it usually is at this Season of the Year and no

Reports to the contrary deserve credit. There are no cases of the yellow fever among us, of this I am assured by Doctr. Bayley the Health officer, and others who have the best opportunities of information.

As your festival is to be on the 17th. of this month, you may be disappointed if you should rely on having a frock from hence by that Time. Have one made without Delay. I enclose a Bill to pay for it.

I can deny myself the satisfaction of having you with me while your absence is conducive to your Health & Improvement. Both those objects are highly important to you, and therefor exceedingly interesting to me. As your complaints abate even in this warm relaxing weather, I flatter myself that the cool air of the autumn will remove them entirely; especially if you guard against colds, and constantly attend to what promotes or injures your Health. That a kind Providence may always guide and bless you is the sincere wish and Prayer of

my Dear Nancy
your very affectionate Father
John Jay

P.S. Our cousin Mr. Augustus van Horne was buried yesterday. How uncertain is Life!

(JJ to SLJ at New Lebanon Springs) New York 4 Augt. 1796

My dear Sally

....It gives me pleasure to assure you that the Town is perfectly free from the Yellow Fever, so that no Credit is due to any Reports to the contrary. Indeed I understand from those who have the best opportunities of being informed, that the city is more than commonly healthy at this Season of the Year. Little Sallys Face is again as smooth as ever, and altho she is I think somewhat leaner than she was, yet is in very good spirits.

William and Peter are well, and often talk of you. I had a Letter two Days ago from Nancy, assuring me that her complaints continue to abate and her Health to improve. She expresses a strong Desire to be frequently informed respecting you & Maria....

I wish I could join with you in listening to the murmuring Brook you mention; but my busy Life allows me few of the pleasures which Leisure and Retirement afford. Adieu my Dear Sally

Yours very affectionately
JOHN JAY

The Jay family moved into Government House in lower Manhattan during John Jay's first three-year term as Governor. When the capitol moved to Albany during his second term, he first rented rooms for himself and then a house on State Street for his family, so that they could all be together.

(JJ to SLJ at Government House, New York City) Albany 1 Jany 1797

My Dr. Sally

Many happy Years to you and the children. We arrived here Yesterday, after a pleasant Journey, from the high Lands to this Place we travelled in a Sleigh; and I should have taken the Road by your Sisters [Kitty], tho circuitous, had I been alone, and had not the apprehension of a change in the weather induced me to come on as expeditiously as we could do conveniently; especially as the convening of a Council of Revision Tomorrow was not to be dispensed with.

The Lodgings taken for me at Mr. RoseBooms by Mr. Ten Broeck appear to be very good ones; so that I have at present no Reason to doubt of my being as comfortably circumstanced here during the winter as could reasonably be expected. For tho I shall not, and cannot forget that I am not at Home; yet I flatter myself that my Stay here will not be in other Respects disagreable....

I have heard of nothing new or interesting to communicate to You. In passing thro' Kinderhook we saw Mr. Van Schaack & his Family, and recd. from them very friendly and hospitable Invitations; which our Haste to reach Albany, would not permit us to accept. They made very friendly Inquiries respecting you and Peter.

Let me request the favor of you to write frequently, and by the Post. I hope the Incendiaries have caused no new alarms; and that a kind Providence will continue to protect and bless us. My love to you & to the children

I am Dr. Sally
Yours affy
John Jay

(JJ to SLJ at Government House, New York City) Albany 12 Feb. 1797

My Dr. Sally

I was this morning favd. with your's of the 7th Inst: — and thank you for the pleasure I have in hearing frequently from you. In my opinion I shall be left to reside in New York, but I believe the future Sessions of the Legislature will be at this place, and that some of the public officers will be removed from New York.

I am glad Mrs. Ludlow has been and continues to be satisfied with the Rent. Her doing us Justice on that Head, entitles her to moderation on our part. The Person you mention may have the Lott another Year on the Terms you state, with this additional one that a way must be left open from the Gate to the back building in which are several Things which I wish to have access to, and which I was prevented taking an account of last Fall, by Reason of the coal heaped up in the way to and against that Building. Let this Business be settled in the presence of Peter, and let him make a note of it at the Time.

This morning a Report ran thro' the Town of a serious affray having happened at New York between some officers of the Govt, and a vessel said to be arming for the french Service, and that some Lives were lost. Whether this Report be well or ill founded, we cannot as yet ascertain. Tomorrow we shall probably be relieved from Suspence, I hope by being assured that the Report was groundless.

13th This Day having passed without our Recieving any Intelligence to confirm the above Report; and not being able to trace it, we begin to presume that it is unfounded. Mr. Macomb sets out for New York in the morning, and I purpose to send this Letter by him. Remember me to the Children. It has snowed the greater part of the Day, so that Mr. Watkins will probably be able to go on.

I am my Dear Sally yours very affecly
John Jay

Sarah Jay had intended to go to a ball celebrating the 65th birthday of President George Washington, but on hearing the news of the death of Peter Augustus' friend and cousin by marriage, Essex Ridley, she changed her plans.

(SLJ to her sister Susan at Cincinnati,
North Western Territory) New York 22d. Febry. 1797

My dr. Susan,

I did myself the pleasure of writing to you last Novbr. soon after the marriage of Catharine, & with impatience have I expected a line from you since....

Your friends are very solicitous for your return. Mrs. Jones particularly & kindly inquires for you. Mr. Watkins & Judy are about removing from Albany to Seneca with their family; our sister anticipates much happiness in their seclusion. William [Livingston, Jr.] & his family are settled at Flatbush. You'll observe by the date that this is the birthday of our illustrious President & as there is to be a grand Ball in commemoration of the day & as my son & myself are to participate in the general joy, I must now leave you to dress for the Occasion as the hair-dresser has just enter'd. To-morrow I'll give you an account of the Ball.

Wednesday evening.

Altho' the interval since I left my pen to the present time has been short, it has been eventful. Upon returning to the parlor after being dress'd, I found Peter reading a letter. As he had long been expecting one from Essex I asked him with some animation if it was from his friend. With a Countenance over-spread with grief & a voice scarce audible he replied he wish'd it was. At the same time handing it to me I percieved, what from his manner I but too justly dreaded that all was not right with Essex. It was a letter from Mr. Dorsey of Baltimore informing him of the Death of that amiable youth. As the gentleman mentioned no particulars respecting the melancholy event & as Peter had recently receiv'd a letter from Essex dated at St. Domingo where he had lately arrived & where the yellow fever was prevalent we conjecture that he has fallen a victim to that baleful disease. I have just sent to Mr. Farquar to apologize for our absence from the Ball to night & to request him to apologize to the other managers by informing them of the occasion.

Thursday noon.

Peter continues pensive & sad, Maria & Nancy look ill; they neither eat nor sleep. I had no idea says Maria that I was so very much interested in the fate of Essex. Poor Aunt Ridley! Peter's grief afflicts me, yet I would not wish it less; the extreme sensibility he discovers but endears him to me the more. Indeed in many respects Essex was a counterpart to Peter. The more I dwell upon the merits of each the more I lament the interruption of their early & well placed friendship. My letter has proved very different from what I intended writing.

Mary (who has been with me since the 16th. Ult:) desires to be remembred to you. Present Maria's & Ann's Compts. as well as my own to Mrs. Harrison & believe me my dr. sister to be

Sincerely affectionately
& Unalterably Yours
Sa. Jay

(JJ to SLJ at Government House, New York City) Albany 10 March 1797

My dear Sally

....For two Days past we have had severe cold weather. No water to be seen in Streets— all hard frozen — so that unless much Rain should speedily fall, the River will probably continue in its present State longer than was expected.

I am not certain that I gave Peter Directions to send nails to Bedford for John Nichol's House. If not, let him ask our Carpenter how many nails 3000 Shingles require. Some will be wanted for the Sides and Floors of the House. A Quantity for these purposes should be seasonably sent. Perhaps some person going from New York to Bedford would take charge of them.

The Bill fixing the Seat of Govt. here has become a Law. It provides that the Legislature shall convene here, and that the Treasury, Secretary's and other offices shall be removed to this place as soon as the arrangemts. necessary for the Purpose shall be made. With Respect to the Govr, the Law is silent. There are opinions however that he ought to reside here. What difference these opinions may have on the next Legislature cannot be foreseen.

It gives me pleasure that Peter and Polly consented to stay with You as long as they did, and that they were in such good Health & Spirits. Of your attentions to them I am well persuaded, and so I am convinced they are. Another month will I hope put an End to our Separation and that I shall then have the satisfaction of finding you and the children well. My Love to them.

I am my dear Sally
yours very affectionately—
John Jay

Saturday morng.— It snows very fast. This letter arriving at the Post office after the mail was closed I have opened it to acknowledge the Rect. of yours by Mr. Glen, who delivered it to me this morning. As it informed me that you and the children were well it is interesting and I thank you for it. This is a fine warm Day, and the Snow which fell yesterday is melting very fast. I find there is much Conversation about providing a House here for the Governor; but I rather doubt its being done this Session. When next you write to our Friends at Rye remember me to them. Remember me also to Mr. & Mrs. Munro. I hope her Health is re-established and the little one doing well.

(SLJ to her sister Kitty at Baltimore) [New York July 2/3, 1797]

My dr. sister,

The inclosed letter was brought here a day or two ago by the post, as it is from Baltimore I presume it is from you.... As we are preparing for our removal you may suppose I am not unoccupied & the great number of strangers that frequent this City in the summer season engage a great deal of my attention. This last week has been a melancholy one & I have been much indisposed in Consequence of the Accident that made it such. Last Sunday Afternoon little Peter Munro* went with his Grand-Mama [Eve Jay Munro] to Church and after service went with her to take tea at Mrs. Titford's. After he had drank his tea he went to play but his Grand-mama not being easy in his absence soon went out to look for him, but in vain. Mrs. Dunscomb seeing the lid of the well up was startled, & upon examination the dear little fellow we found at the Bottom of it intirely lifeless. A Number of Physicians were call'd in & every measure pursued that offer'd a gleam of success, but every effort prov'd fruitless. You may easily Judge of Peggy's affliction & of our sympathy. Poor Munro was absent, but Mr. Jay sending an express for him he arrived at 6 o'Clock on Monday morning. The poignancy of their grief is somewhat abated. The old Lady's grief affected her son so much that he endeavored to suppress his own & to aleviate hers. Witnessing so much distress & lamenting the cause of it affected the health & spirits of the whol[e] family. We have none of us been quite well ever since. I was recovering when a Cold I took by setting in too much air brought on a Cholic which has left me weak & low.

I've had the satisfaction of receiving two letters from Judy expressive of her intire satisfaction where she is, but I lament the emotions she will experience when she hears that her husband who came to New York on business of moment to his family, & intended returning in 8 or 10 da[y]s has been arrested & thrown into prison [for debt], there in all probability to remain during the rest of the season. She is never out of my mind & I don't doubt the regret I feel for her & her family increased the extreme depression of my spirits this last week. I wish you could make time to write to Susan by the post, you must observe by her letter the World is very full of Trouble!

Little Wm. says he does not know why any one is desirous of living since if they do they must surely expect trouble. Present my best Compts. to Mr. Livingston Mrs. Rutgers & Mary, embrace the Children, burn this scrawl & believe [me] to be

sincerely yours
S. Jay

**Peter Munro was the 5-year-old son of Peter Jay Munro and his wife Margaret White. He was the first-born of their twelve children.*

....If you should not come to town this summer I doubt my seeing you till Autumn as it will not be possible to stop when moving.

(JJ to Benjamin Vaughan) NYork 31 Augt. 1797

Dr Sir

I had this afternoon the pleasure of recg. your favor of the 10th Instant. Mrs. Jay joins me in sincerely congratulating you & your amiable family on your arrival in this country. May your Expectations of Happiness in it be perfectly realized.

The reasons which have determined you to settle on the Kennebeck, I can easily concieve are cogent; but I flatter myself, you will sometimes find Leisure for Excursions this way.

I presume that our political Sentiments do not differ essentially. To me it appears important that the american governmt. be preserved as it is, untill mature Experience shall plainly point out very useful amendments to our Constitution, that we steadily repel all foreign Influence and Interference, and with good Faith and Liberality treat all nations as Friends in Peace and as Enemies in War, neither meddling with their affairs, nor permitting them to meddle with ours. These are the primary objects of my Policy. The secondary ones are more numerous such as to be always prepared for War & to cultivate Peace, to promote Religion, Industry, Tranquility and useful Knowledge; and to secure to all the quiet Enjoyment of their Rights, by wise & equal Laws irresistably executed. I do not expect that mankind will before the Millennium be what they ought to be, and therefore in my opinion every political theory wh. does not regard them as being what they are, will probably prove delusive.

It will give me pleasure to receive the publication you mention. Being from your Pen it will I am persuaded be interesting. Be pleased to present our best Compts. to Mrs. Vaughan and yr Sister. I am

Dr Sr
your affte. & hble Servt

(JJ to Sir John Sinclair) Albany 7 Novbr. 1797

Dr Sir

I was yesterday honored with yours of the 15 July together with the papers mentioned in it, and for which accept my thanks....

You will teach us useful Lessons, in agriculture, & they will cost us nothing; which is more than we can say for some of the other Lessons we are learning.

It is asked, how long the same Root or plant may be cultivated to advantage in the same Field or spot? I well remember that (excepting from 1776 to 1783) Potatoes have been annually planted for at least forty years in the same spot of ground on a farm at Rye, which formerly belonged to my Father, & now to my Brother. And that spot yields, on an average one year with another, as much now as ever it did. The land is rich, being a black mould, on a strong loam, with clay under it & manured every year with Dung from the barn yard. It was the common practice first to put

Dung in the Furrows or Trenches, and then lay the seed Potatoes upon it. For some years past, it has been said that the seed Potatoes should be first placed in the Furrows, and long Dung put upon them, and then covered as usual with Earth.

Last year I planted a small piece of ground (not rich, stiff & inclined to bake) alternately in those methods, and the fact was, that the Rows where the Dung was placed over & upon the seed Potatoes yielded more than the Rows where the Dung was placed under them. This is the only Experiment of this kind which I have made and therefore do not regard it as conclusive. I frequently hear it asserted that long Dung is better than rotten Dung in the Furrows for Potatoes and several Reasons are assigned why it should be so. But why it shd. be so? is less interesting than how it actually is; to this latter Question I cannot yet give a decisive answer.

You have so many Letters to read as well to write, that unnecessary Prolixity can neither be proper for me, nor pleasant to you. With the most cordial & best wishes ....

I am Dr. Sir
your faithful & obt. Servt.

(JJ to SLJ at Albany) NYork 28 June 1798

My dear Sally

You have doubtless by this Time recd. a Letter from me and I thank you for your's of the 21 Instant. I am happy to learn that nothing had occurred to give you uneasiness. You have my best wishes that nothing of that kind may occur.

Maria's Picture is nearly finished. I saw it yesterday, but being unfinished, can only say there was a Likeness, tho' not a very exact one.

Peter thinks the floor cloth* you mention is rolled round the other larger one that was sent us sometime ago—we shall nevertheless search for it. The other matters mentioned in your Letter shall also be attended to. Mrs. Munro and her little one continue well.

....My Journey has not taken away my Rheumatism but it is not worse. Remember me to the children.

I am my Dr Sally
yours very affecty
John Jay

(SLJ to JJ) Albany 31st May 1799

My dear Mr. Jay

I have not had the pleasure of hearing from you since yours of the 19th inst.... The Children are in very good health & desire to be affectionately remembered to you.

**A floor cloth was the precursor of linoleum. A design, often intended to represent marble, was painted on a piece of canvas, to which several coats of varnish were applied. Such a floor covering had several advantages: it resisted wear, was easily cleaned, and could be rolled up and transported to another room or dwelling.*

Ann recd. a letter from her brother by the last post, & is now engaged in answering it. Give my Love to him & his sister & to Peter & Peggy. Thank our Cousins in my name for their very kind attentions to Maria. Let me know what arrangements are likely to be made at Bedford & how you left our friends at Rye. Adieu My dearest!

Believe me with the tenderest regard

your ever affectionate Wife
S. Jay

A little circumstance that has just occurred induces me to resume my pen. Wig & his little sister were at play; she took offence & told him he did not love her. Upon which he stole silently into the garden & robbing his own little spot of two peach-trees transplanted them into her little garden. She was on the back-stoop & seeing him near her flowers ran precipatantly into the Garden, but when she perceived what he had been doing she threw her little arms around him acknowledging his generosity & reproached herself for having doubted his tenderness. She then came to inform me how delicately he had removed her suspicions & what a sweet little brother he was. I returned with her & found him employed as related, his Countenance glowing with benevolence. I did not know which most to admire his generosity, or her grateful sensibility & Candid humility which led her to confess her error & acknowledge his superiority.

I have not yet had an application for either of the Cows. Fr[ank] took the Calf yesterday. I was just call'd down to I. Duer, by whom I've recd. a letter from Maria. Give my love to her if you please & thank her. Tell her not to puzzle herself about hats for Ann & my self; if she meets with those she likes well, if not she need not purchase any. Once more Adieu.

While visiting Peter and Polly Jay in Rye, Sarah and daughter Nancy are recovering their health. The Governor is in Albany with Maria, William, and Sarah Louisa. Peter Augustus is practicing law in New York.

(JJ to SLJ at Rye) Albany 12 July 1799

My dear Sally

Your Letter of the 1st Instant is the last which I have recd. from you. I wrote to you by the last post. Nothing interesting has occurred, and I now write again more because I have a good opportunity of sending you a Letter, than because I have any thing of Importance to communicate.

Yesterday Sally went very chearfully to Mrs. Wilson's School, and will this Day begin to learn to write. I shall take care that she be not detained too many hours in School. That practice which arises too often from a Desire of having children out of the way as it is called, is certainly improper. It is useful that they should attend regularly at stated Times, for by that means Habits of Punctuality are formed — and valuable Habits they are.

The weather for a few Days past has been remarkably cool, and at this moment

Above left: Peter Augustus Jay, 1797. Engraving by Charles B.J.F. de Saint-Mémin (1770–1852). With the use of a physionotrace, the artist was able to draw accurate profiles, which he then engraved. John Jay Homestead State Historic Site. New York State Office of Parks, Recreation and Historic Preservation (JJ.1982.68). *Above right:* Maria Jay, 1798. Engraving by Charles B.J.F. de Saint-Mémin (1770–1852). On 23 August 1798, John Jay noted in his account book: "Pd. St. Memin for Profile of Miss M. Jay 30." John Jay Homestead State Historic Site. New York State Office of Parks, Recreation and Historic Preservation (JJ.1982.69). *Lower right:* Ann "Nancy" Jay, c. 1801. Miniature, watercolor on ivory by Gideon Fairman (1774–1827). The portrait may have been done in Albany, New York. John Jay Homestead State Historic Site. New York State Office of Parks, Recreation and Historic Preservation (JJ.1970.9).

is far from being too warm. The pastures and meadows in this neighbourhood look well. Showers have been frequent; and this morning there is much appearance of Rain.

We are all well. Maria will probably write few Lines to you this morning. I know she intends it, but it is possible she may not find Leisure to do it in Season. Remember me to Nancy and our friends at Rye & Mamaroneck

I am my Dear Sally
yours affy
John Jay

(SLJ to JJ) Rye 15th July 1799

My dear Mr. Jay

How shall I express the pleasure I've this evening recd. from perusing the three affectionate letters you have been so kind as to write me of the 26th. 6th. & 10th....

Sarah Livingston Jay with her children, William and Sarah Louisa, c. 1796. Detail of a pastel by James Sharples (c. 1751–1811). This informal and charming portrait is unusual in the artist's work for its size. John Jay Homestead State Historic Site. New York State Office of Parks, Recreation and Historic Preservation (JJ.1987.9).

Our friends here are all well & desire to be remembred to you & Maria. We drank tea this afternoon with Old Mrs. Purdy who mentioned you with great esteem. I participate the pleasure little Wig enjoys in the possession of his poney. I hope my best beloved! that you will be induced to ride out with him, as that would be beneficial to your own health as well as gratifying to him; nor can I omit to hint to you the use of the bath. Do my dear Mr. Jay attend more to your own health; that of others always shares your attention. I fear you will think I pay you a very ill compliment in writing you always in such haste that my letters are scarce legible, but it has happened unavoidably. They are now bolting the doors & I must stop & give this to Sylvia* before she goes to bed. Embrace the Children for me & believe me most

affectionately yours
S. Jay

I thank you for the key.

(SLJ to JJ at Albany) Rye July 21st 1799

My dear Mr. Jay,

I had the pleasure of writing to you a few days ago acknowledging the receipt of several of yours up to the 10th July which are the last that have come to hand. I did expect to have left Rye before this, but Peter & Polly will not listen to it. They say I must remain here 'till I recover strength & that Ann's health requires our stay as much as my own. I really think she is much better than when we arrived, her appetite emproves, but her hands are much too warm still. They are very kind & seem very much gratifyed by our being with them.

Cousin Peter came up yesterday, he left our Son well but did not bring me a line from him. I am sorry Sally is so thin but as she continues lively I hope it is not caused by any indisposition. Cousin Munro's little Margaret is likewise very thin indeed more so I think than I've ever seen Sally. Kiss the dear little poppet for me. I have regretted leaving her at home ever since I did so. It gives me great pleasure to find that William goes chearfully to school. May our fond hopes in him be realized! If you could some-times ride out with Maria early in the morning, & with your son of an evening, it would be useful to you & gratifying to them. You omitted informing me how your health was, don't my dr. do so again.

When we were at Bedford, the Major & Mrs. Lyon both solicited us to make a longer stay. We thanked them for their civility & I told the Major it wd. give me very great pleasure indeed to be able, with my family to pass the next summer there if he would endeavor to expedite the building. He assured me he would & that he believed it might be ready in time to have my wish accomplished. Indeed my Love I more than ever wish for the time that will put a period to your public cares & permit the indulgence of retirement, rural quiet &c. Our Jaunt to Bedford has furnished your daughter & myself with a great many pleasing hopes & fanciful ideas. The ideas that

**A servant who will watch for the stage.*

amuse us chiefly respect the little embellishments of the place, & the hopes that elevate our minds, arise from the expectation of our own emprovements in the social virtues & intellectual bliss. In the Country I feel ever sensible of an ever-present deity-dispensing Light & life & chearfulness around & my heart is animated with Confidence & joy & love.

Your brother & Polly & Ann desire to be remembred to you, Maria & the Children. That I do most ardently long to see you & the Children is as true as that I am

your most affectionate Wife
Sa. Jay

(JJ to his son PAJ at New York) Albany 7th Decr. 1799

Dear Peter

On the 30th Ult. I recd. and answered your Letter of the 25th. On the 3d. Inst. the silk muslin and mustard, sent by one of the sloops arrived but without any Letter from you. Your mama and sisters are pleased with the silk & muslins, & with your having sent them so speedily....

When you was here you could not give me particular Information how far the Preparations for the House had advanced. In your Letter of the 26th. Ult: you inform me that, on your Return from this place to Bedford, you found things in status quo. What this status quo precisely is, I am yet to learn. Are all or how many of the floors ready for laying, are the Boards for all or any of the partitions ready to be put up, are all the sashes Shutters and Doors, or how many of them made, is all the Timber collected and ready for its proper places and uses? &c. &c. Without particular answers to these and similar questions, no definite Ideas of the actual State of Things, can be formed. Minute Inquiry and some Trouble and attention are necessary to the doing of such Business well. You will endeavour to contract for the Lime and for the Delivery of it, before you leave Bedford—it may be prudent to engage 1000 Bushels. You know how sollicitous I am not only that what I desire to be done should be done, but also to be informed that it is done....

Your Mama's Health continues much the same.

I am your affectionate Father
John Jay

(JJ to his son PAJ) Albany 2d Jany 1800

Dear Peter

On Monday morning last, (being post Day), I recieved from the post office some news papers, but no Letters....

Of your affection & attachmt. I have no Doubt, and I believe that few fathers have more valuable or numerous Reasons to be pleased with a Son, than I have to be pleased with you. There is nevertheless a Tendency in your Disposition to musing & consequently to Procrastination; wh. sometimes leads you to postpone even necessary attentions for the sake of indulging Disinclinations & Gratifications, wh. if they do not moderate will gradually produce a relaxed & absent State of Mind. I tell you this my dear Son from the best motives. And for the best purposes....

Uncle Fady had in his Possession as Exr. to your grand father, three silver hilted Swords. One of them was given by my grandfather to your uncle Augs. and which he told me shd. be for you. One other of them was my great grand father's, and the third I believe was purchased by my father. He also had the seal with the family arms, wh. belonged to my great grand father. These articles shd. remain in the Family. There may perhaps be Books or papers or other articles belonging to the Estate. Consult with your cousin Munro as to the best Manner of applying to the widow, and whether by <u>him</u> or <u>you</u>, for that may depend on circumstances better known to him than to me.

I am your affectionte. Father
John Jay

At the turn of the century, the electoral college, whose delegates were chosen by each state's legislature, actually elected the President and the Vice President of the United States. In the New York State election of 1 May 1800 to choose a new state legislature, the Antifederalist candidates won, almost guaranteeing the election of Thomas Jefferson as President.

In the following letter, Alexander Hamilton suggests that John Jay, as Governor, had the power to change the rules of the game by calling a special session of the sitting state legislature, which would remain in office until the newly elected candidates took over. This body could then pass an act for redistricting the state, which would enable presidential electors to be chosen by popular ballot, in the hope that the Federalists would triumph.

Governor Jay, a reasonable, fair, and honest man, decided that the voters had already spoken by their ballots. On the back of the letter, he wrote: "Proposing a measure for party purposes, wh. I think wd. not become me to adopt." He did not respond to Hamilton's letter.

(Alexander Hamilton to JJ at Albany) New York May 7. 1800

Dear Sir

You have been informed of the loss of our Election in this City. It is also known that we have been unfortunate throughout Long Island & in West Chester. According to the Returns hitherto, it is too probable that we lose our Senators for this District.

The moral certainty therefore is that there will be an Antifoederal Majority in the ensuing Legislature, and the very high probability is that this will bring <u>Jefferson</u> into the Chief Magistracy; unless it be prevented by the measure which I shall now submit to your consideration, namely the immediate calling together of the existing Legislature.

I am aware that there are weighty objections to the measure; but the reasons for it appear to me to outweigh the objections. And in times like those in which we live, it will not do to be overscrupulous. It is easy to sacrifice the substantial interests of Society by a strict adherence to ordinary rules.

In observing this, I shall not be supposed to mean that any thing ought to be done which integrity will forbid, but merely that the scruples of delicacy and propriety, as relative to a common course of things, ought to yield to the extraordinary nature of the crisis. They ought not to hinder the taking of a legal and constitutional step, to prevent an Atheist in Religion and a Fanatic in politics from getting possession of the helm of State.

You Sir know in a great degree the Antifoederal party, but I fear that you do not know them as well as I do. Tis a composition indeed of very incongruous materials but all tending to mischief—some of them to the overthrow of the Government by stripping it of its due energies others of them to a Revolution after the manner of Buonaparte. I speak from indubitable facts, not from conjectures & inferences.

In proportion as the true character of the party is understood is the force of the considerations which urge to every effort to disappoint it. And it seems to me that there is a very solemn obligation to employ the means in our power.

The calling of the Legislature will for object the choosing of Electors by the people in Districts. This (as Pensylvania will do nothing) will insure a Majority of votes in the UStates for a Foederal Candidate.

The measure will not fail to be approved by all the Foederal Party; while it will no doubt be condemned by the opposite. As to its intrinsic nature it is justified by unequivocal reason of public safety.

The reasonable part of the world will I believe approve it. They will see it as a proceeding out of the common course but warranted by the particular nature of the Crisis and the great cause of social order.

If done the motive ought to be frankly avowed. In your communication to the Legislature they ought to be told that temporary circumstances had rendered it probable that without their interposition the executive authority of the General Government would be transferred to hands hostile to the System heretofore pursued with so much Success and dangerous to the peace happiness and order of the country; that under this impression from facts convincing to your own mind you had thought it your duty to give the existing Legislature an opportunity of deliberating whether it would not be proper to interpose and endeavour to prevent so great an evil by referring the choice of electors to the people distributed into Districts.

In weighing this Suggestion you will doubtless bear in mind that Popular Governments must certainly be overturned & while they endure prove engines of mischief, if one party will call to its aid all the resources which vice can give and if the other, however pressing the emergency, confines itself within all the ordinary forms of delicacy and decorum.

The legislature can be brought together in three weeks. So that there will be full time for the object; but none ought to be lost.

Think well my Dear Sir of this proposition. Appreciate the extreme danger of the Crisis; and I am unusually mistaken in my view of the matter, if you do not see it right and expedient to adopt the measure.

Respectfully & Affecly
Yrs
A Hamilton

(JJ to SLJ at Albany) New York 6 June 1800

My dear Sally

My Letter to you by the last post informed you, that the Doctr's. Medicine was producing its Effect, and that part of the little Tumor [on my face] had separate[d] and come out. The remaining part, which the Doctr. thinks the most important, still continues; but he expects it will be discharged in the course of a few Days more. All the symptoms he says are favorable.

Not long after sending that Letter to the post office, I recd. from thence yours of the 2d. Instant.

The account it gives of your Indisposition was very unexpected, and not a little distressing. You nevertheless did well in communicating to me a candid State of the matter; and in my opinion that kind of Tenderness which leads persons to keep such unpleasant Circumstances from the Knowledge of their absent Friends, is not to be commended.

I am very anxious to have further accounts of your Health; and beg that nothing material respecting that interesting Subject may be withheld. I very much wish again to find myself with you and the children; tho' I have every Reason to be satisfied and pleased with the attentions I recieve from this part of our Family. Peggy is suffering from a severe swelled Face. All the Rest of the family are well, and with our Son desire to be remembered to You and the Children.

Tell Wm. that I am much disposed to take his word for his being a fine and a good Boy; and that I hope to find on my Return that he has not formed that opinion too hastily. My love to them all.

I am my dear Sally
Yours very affecty
John Jay

(SLJ to JJ at Albany) Lebanon Monday 28th July [1800]

My dr. Mr. Jay,

The only circumstance that has induced me to remain so long at a distance from you & from home has been the evident progress of my health. The air of this place no less than the Bath has had a wonderful effect upon it. The Mayor & Mrs. Van Ranselear, myself &c. last evening climbed one of the highest mountains here & I was not at all fatigued; the view from it was superb. Bathing now has the same effect upon me it formerly had that is to say it gives me a charming glow & occasions a quick circulation. Remember me if you please to our friend the D[octor]. He will be gratifyed to hear that I am so much recovered. I long very much to see you & the Children & can hardly believe that a fortnight has not quite elapsed since we parted.

To-day Judge Lowel will call upon you as he passes thro' Albany on his way to Ballstown. Our quills are cut up & the family not having risen yet I am writing with the stump of a pen that is as stiff as my knife. Maria is very well & still sleeping. Sammy & horses are very well. Hannah has answered our purposes as well as an elder person wd. have done. Give my love to Ann, tell her there is not any body here that she is acquainted with except the Mayor & his party. Kiss Sally & Wm. for me. I hope to hear from home this evening by Mr. & Mrs. Perkins who are expected here. I hope they meet with no impediments at Bedford for I am more than ever desirous of being there, then we may roam together & together inhale the salubrious breeze. Now a cruel regret that my beloved husband & children do not with me partake of the Rural pleasures in which they so much delight diminishes the satisfaction these wild scenes are calculated to inspire.

Adieu my dr. Mr. Jay!

believe me ever yours
S. J.

John Jay declined to become a candidate in the next election. In a letter to Richard Hatfield (8 November 1800), he wrote:

> The Period is now nearly arrived at which I have for many years intended to retire from the cares of public Life, and for which I have been for more than two years preparing. Not percieving, after mature consideration that any Duties require me to postpone it, I shall retire accordingly, but I shall retain and cherish the warmest affection for my country, as well as the Esteem wh. I entertain for many, and the good will wh. I bear to all my fellow Citizens.

Sarah Jay had been ailing for some time. She fell ill in December with symptoms indicative of a slight stroke. In May of 1801, she went to her sister's home, Oak Hill, to recuperate and thereafter to Rye before settling at Bedford in early December of that year.

(JJ to his son PAJ at New York City) Albany Monday 8 Decr 1800

Dr Peter

Last Friday night your Mother was taken very ill, and was in some Degree delirious. Dr Stringer was immediately sent for. He considered her Complaint as being a strong nervous affliction, caused by the Debility & exhausted Spirits which care and too little Leisure sometimes produce — and he treated it accordingly by giving her spiced wine &c. &c. Her Speech being affected, and the use of her right hand and arm being diminished, I was apprehensive that there was some Thing of the paralytic kind in the case. But he was not of this opinion, saying that all the Symptoms were explicable on the former Principles, that there was no appearance of Danger, tho' he thought her Recovery would require some time.

She continued much indisposed thro' Saturday, and at Intervals a little delirious. She passed Saturday night better than was expected, was very composed and had some good and quiet Sleep. Yesterday morning she was much better. There has since been no appearance of Delirium. She has nearly recovered her speech, and the use of her right Hand, so that at present her Prospects of Recovery are fair.

I shall write to you again by the next post. I leave the enclosed open for your perusal.

I am Dr Peter
Your affte. Father
John Jay

(JJ to SLJ at Oak Hill
to the Care of the Post Master at Hudson)

Bedford 17 May 1801

My dear Sally

The morning after we left you, we arrived at Sinsing, & having sent on some of the most necessary articles of Furniture &a. we came here last Evening. We found the House has been white washed and well cleaned, wood ready at the Door, and every thing to accommodate us on such an occasion.

My Health and that of our Daughter has, to say the least, not diminished. We have been favored in the weather and other circumstances. Five waggon Loads with our Effects have been brought, with but little Injury. Tomorrow a number of Teams will set out for more. So that as yet we have not met with more Difficulties, nor indeed with near so many as might have been expected. A place for a Kitchen Garden has been fenced and ploughed, so that we shall not be so destitute of Vegetables as we apprehended.

Good Tidings respecting your Health would render us as comfortable, as during your absence we could be. I flatter myself that you will gradually derive great Benefit from your being at Oak Hill, and the attentions of our kind Friends there. I suspect the daily Fever you have, is a slight attack of an Intermittent, caused perhaps by the damp weather during your Passage; I hope it has ceased. Bark you know is useful in such periodical Complaints. If you have a good Physician near you, I think you shd. consult him.

This is the first Letter wh. I have had Time to write, since I landed, to anybody. The Servants are all well and satisfied. I imagine they all found things better than they expected. Remember me to our Friends. With the most sincere and ardent wishes that you may have and enjoy Health and every other Blessing I am my

Dear Sally
[signature cut away]

(SLJ to JJ at Bedford)

Oak-Hill May 27th 1801

My dear Mr. Jay,

Your kind letter of the 17th as well as those from our dear daughter communicated to me a considerable share of the pleasure you must both of you have experienced upon your arrival at Bedford & the agreeable circumstances that occur'd. The Major & Mrs. Lyon's friendly attentions merit a suitable return. Please to remember me to them. It is some time since I had the pleasure of writing to you, not my love from indifference but from tenderness did my silence proceed.

The fever sister hinted to you she thought I had, harressed me every night with an excessive heat in my back & extreme restlessness notwithstanding increased doses of opium. At length sister sent to Catskill for a Physcisian of whom she entertains a good opinion who upon being consulted directed bark in decoction to be taken in small quantities, & advised me to use moderate exercise in the open air. I have taken his advice, & if my fever is not quite broke it is nearly so, for I did not experience that restlessness above an hour last night & the heat in my back not at all. It is about 4 nights that I have intirely quitted the use of laudanum & I have now rather more natural sleep than I had then of artificial & it is much more refreshing. The most serious simptom that I now think I have is in the extreme expectoration which the Dr. imputes to extreme relaxation, the lungs he says partaking of the general debility. The feeble & fluctuating state of the pulse continues the same. I rode about 3 miles to day in a Waggon & was not in the least fatigued with the exercise. I have a good appetite & digest what I eat. If there is any alteration in the Rheumatism it is for the better.

Yesterday I wrote to our dear little Wig. Peter I fear has not rec. the letter I wrote him a fortnight ago as I have not heard from him since, tho' it is not improbable there may be a letter from him at the post-office at Hudson.... As Maria in her last letter mentioned her intention of being here this week & as this is the 4th day of it, & the weather extremely delightful, we are not without hopes of seeing her this evening. Say every thing to our dearest daughter that a fond & delighted Mother could express, thank her for her charming letters & tell her nothing but the stiffness of wrists shd. prevent my writing to her. No cordial could have had so salutary an effect upon my spirits as the dear letters I recd. from you both. I have perused & re-perused them twenty times at least. Little Sal is very hearty, she is out upon the green. Nothing can exceed the Care and attention of sister Livingston who desires to be remembred to you & Ann.

May you my dearest Mr. Jay long very long enjoy Health, tranquility & every other blessing that Providence ever permits its favor'd servants to enjoy here below is the fervant prayer of

your sincerely affectionate
wife
Sa. Jay

(JJ to SLJ at Oak Hill) Bedford Tuesday 16 June 1801

My dear Sally

It [is] not easy to describe to you the Pleasure which your last Letter to Nancy, gave to us both. The account which it gives of your Health is indeed a pleasing one. May that Blessing be speedily restored to You, and You to us. I forbear however to press your returning, while your Recovery proceeds so prosperously at Oak Hill—

especially as Fatigue, and other unpleasant Circumstances which sometimes attend travelling by Land and water, may endanger a Relapse.

My brother Peter and Polly left us last Saturday, and were surprized to find us so far settled. They expressed much Sollicitude about you, and wish you to pass some time with them, on your way here. At present sick persons would not be comfortable in our House. The Noise and Hurry of carpenters masons & Labourers in and about the house, are Inconveniences to be submitted to, but not to be chosen by Convalescents or Invalids.

The additions to the House (the Piazzas excepted) were raised last week; and Yesterday the Foundations for the Stable were begun. Nancy continues in good Health & Spirits, and is much pleased with living here. Nobody could manage better than she does, & she accommodates herself admirably to the unavoidable Inconveniences of our Situation. When our Buildings are finished, and Things about us put in order, there will be an end of many disagreable Embarrassmts.

I am glad that Mr. Banyer & Maria and Wm. have paid you a visit. Their company I am persuaded had a happy Effect on your Spirits. I hope that before the Conclusion of the Year we shall all be again together.

Except going to meeting on Sundays, I have not been even once from home since I came here. For altho' I have every Reason to be satisfied with the Majors attention [to] the Business now going on, yet I find myself engaged by it, and in it from morning to night.

The Post goes from hence every Thursday, and comes in every Saturday—so that we can send Letters only once a week. Either Nancy or myself will write to you by every Post, and you will gratify us Exceedingly by favoring one or the other of us with a few Lines every Saturday to inform us how you do.

This is only my third Letter to You. In future I shall have Leisure to write more frequently. I am this moment called upon to go and give Directions &a.

God bless and preserve you, my Dear Sally

I am ever your affte. Husband
John Jay

Wednesday—Having postponed sending this Letter to the post office by Saml who is gone to Rye for Boards, I have an opportunity of adding that I had this morning the pleasure of recieving yours of the 12 Instant, mentioning that your Health continues to mend. Peter will probably be here next week, for then the Court sits at the White Plains. Whether he will come before or after the Court is uncertain. I hope your next Letter will give us further agreable Tidings of your Health. Kiss little Sal: for me. Remember us affecy to our Friends with you.

(SLJ to JJ at Bedford) Oak Hill June 17th 1801

My dear Mr. Jay,

Agreeably to your request I continue to write tho' I have very little to write about. I flatter myself that to-morrow when sister L[ivingston] goes to Hudson she'll pick up a letter from Ann for me. Maria writes me that she & William are well. Last Saturday Brockholst came here & went with Mr. Livingston to Scott's Patent from whence they expect to return the next saturday.

My health is very tolerable. The Rheumatism continues to diminish, tho' very gradually; were it not for a swelling upon my right heel which continues very obstinate I should not be in the least lame. Thus much for my health. Let Ann whenever she writes to me inform me of your health. Sally is writing & chatting at the side of me. She desires her love to you & her sister.

Give my love to my dr. Ann & Remember me to the Major & Mrs. Lyon. I am

my dear Mr. Jay
yours affectely
Sarah Jay

(SLJ to JJ at Bedford) Oak-Hill June 27th 1801

My dear Mr. Jay,

Last tuesday I had the pleasure of recg. your kind letter of the 16th inst. as well as my dear Ann's of the 7th & 14th & likewise one from Maria. Thank God my dear friends were all well.

The tender interest you take in my health is most grateful to my feelings, & redoubles the satisfaction I have of assuring you that it still continues to mend. When Brockholst was here he mentioned to Mr. Livingston that he had had an iron oven fix'd in the Jam of his Kitchin fire-place so constructed as that the smoak & heat from the Kitchin Chimney kept it perpetually hot & that all the meet, puddings, Cakes & Custards used in his family were cooked in it, so that it had superseded the use of spits & tart pans &c. There is but one that fixes them & he has thirty dollars for the Oven & fixing it in the Jam. I thought best to mention it before you shd. have built yours. If you think it worthy yr. attention you can let Peter examine his Uncle's, & inquire of him the person's name who makes them. Brockholst says his Cook says it saves half the work of Cooking, a great deal of fuel & being in constant readiness is inconceivably convenient. Mr. L. says the person's name is Batchelor, a white smith. I am happy to hear that the frame is raised, & wish you joy on the success of Lyons experiment for drawing water.

Mr. Livingston insists upon my proposing to you to purchase Phill: Hoffman's place at Johnstown which can be had for 2500£. He says there is an house on the farm (which consists of 200 acres) nearly as large as the one he lives in, & built on the same plan, a fine Orchard, excellent Garden & good fruit. That you will be near Maria & near his family. He has written to the person who has the selling of it to engage it for himself, but he says it is with a view to your having it. It was in vain that I told him it was needless for me to propose it to you. He insisted upon it, so you must excuse me.

It was kind in Peter & Polly to visit you, & I am much obliged to them for their Civilities to me. Mr. L. & Caty declare I shall not leave this [place] before Sepbr.

....Remember me most affectionately to my dearest Ann. Give her a thousand thanks for her charming letters. Little Sal is very hearty & full of spirits. She desires her love to you & her sister. Mr. Livingston & Catharine give their love to both of you. If our son is with you when you receive this Give my love to him & accept my best beloved the assurances of gratitude & affection from

yours sincerely
Sa. Jay

(SLJ to JJ at Bedford) Oak-Hill 13th July 1801

My dearest Mr. Jay,

I've lately had the pleasure of receiving a letter from our dear Ann of the 25th: Ult:, & the last I've been favor'd with from you was of the 16th since which I've written to you both. Although my residence here has been much longer than I expected it wd. have been, yet both sister & Mr. Livingston wish me to prolong it: but several reasons induce me to prefer going to Rye as soon as I conveniently can. Whether it is owing to the unusual warmth of the weather or to any other cause I cannot tell, but the restlessness of nights, of which I used to complain, has return'd, attended with those debilitating sweats and my distance from home, occasions, together with those circumstances, a depression of spirits. I cannot but think that change of air, a sail upon the river & some exercise wd. remove it, if it is again to be removed, & if it is not, I may better be nearer home.

Mr. Livingston is at present at NYork & he writes Mrs. L. that Mr. & Mrs. Rutgers & their Children are to come up with him, so that were I even to wait until Sepbr., I cannot promise myself the pleasure of her Company to New York. Last night as I scarcely closed my eyes, my West Chester friends engross'd my whole thoughts, & this morning, finding sister had recd. the above information, I beg'd to be indulged in my wish to go to NY. After a good deal of persuasion I've prevailed upon her to promise to send to Catskill to inquire whether there is any sloop to sail from thence & when; and she has likewise been good enough to promise to let a white woman who lives with her go down with me, and as I am now able to dress & undress myself without assistance I think I shall do very well.

The permission I've obtain'd has already relieved my spirits. Yesterday sister sent to the Post-office at Hudson to inquire if there were any letters for me & sadly disappointed was I to find that he return'd without any. God grant that you may both be well. The day after tomorrow a servt. will go again to Hudson who will take this there & inquire for others. Oh my dear Mr. Jay! the distance that seperates us is too, too great. Catharine & Sarah join me in love to our dear Ann & yourself.

14th. Yesterday we sent to Catskill, but it was with regret I learnt that there was not any Sloop to sail this week. A little after midnight Mr. L. & Mr. Rutgers & his family arrived. To-day I mentioned my wish to Mr. L., he tryed to dissuade me from going, but finding my spirits depress'd, he kindly consented.

After you receive this, If you are so kind as to write to me, please to address to me at Munro's at NYork. Don't mention to Ann either the dejection of my spirits or my restless nights. I do not mean to quit Rye for Bedford until you think it best for me to do so. Once more my dear, dear Mr. Jay Adieu!

Believe me ever Yours
S. Jay

Mr. L. has brought up with him two scotch men that he hir'd at NY. Perhaps Peter might meet with some that might do for you for this season as laborers.

Wednesday 15th. Last Night I rested much better & did not sweat at all. I take the bark.

(SLJ to JJ at Bedford) Rye Octbr 6th 1801

My dr. Mr. Jay,

Cousin Peter delivered to me your kind favor of the 3d. inst. for which I beg you will accept my thanks. Most sincerely do I regret the impediments that have seperated us these five or six months past, as well as the disappointment of not returning with Maria to Bedford, occasioned by your brother having taken a most severe cold.

I have been rendered very happy by the company of our dear children but could we have been All together it would have heightened the satisfaction. Every word & every look of our dear little boy I regretted your losing. Your brother himself frequently exclaimed 'you are a dear little dog.' Banyar & his Little wife are an amiable couple & I often, I shd. say daily, bless God for giving us such amiable Children. May they long be pre[served] a blessing to us & to the community.

Kiss our dear girls for me & believe me my dear Mr. Jay

your affecte Wife
Sarah Jay

(SLJ to her daughter Maria) Bedford 2d. Decbr. 1801

My dear Maria,

Your sister & myself are obliged by your kind favors. We were very happy to learn from them that you still retain your health. May it long very long be continued to you. Our Masons were interrupted by frost before the second coat of plaister was began on the dining-room, tho' the kitchin & the small chambers adjoining it were finished. And it is most probable that the masons will not be able to prosecute their business before next April. As that was the case your Papa directed the Carpenters to attempt inclosing the Coach-House & they have been so expeditious & the season so favorable that they will this day compleat it, & they can now proceed to finishing that & the house during the winter.

We have had a very delightful autumn & even now I can hardly persuade myself it is winter; the weather is so much milder than we have of late years been accustomed to at this season. Ann is at this moment in the garden planting peach-stones. You I imagine have already been visited by snow, so indeed have we, but it was only a visit of Ceremony & soon retir'd. Your brother left us about a fortnight ago. Your Uncle & Aunt have been ever since intending us a visit, but the completion of it we are still to expect. Your Papa & sisters continue to enjoy their health & desire to be affectionately remembred to your good husband & yourself & brother with Compts. to the old gentleman in all which I beg you to believe my heart unites. Present my Compts. to Mr. & Mrs. Ellison & other friends whom you know I esteem.

Tell William I long to peruse a journal of his travels from Bedford to Albany &c. How sincerely do I lament Mrs. Hamilton's fate in the untimely death of her son.* Adieu my ever dear Maria.

Believe me affectly yours
Sa. Jay

I must not omit mentioning that my health continues to improve

---

(SLJ to JJ at New York) Bedford March 2d, 1802

My dear Mr. Jay,

I think it will give you pleasure to hear from us, even tho' nothing new has occur'd. To tell you that the storm began here on sunday evening the 21st & that it has continued ever since with the intermission of only a single day would I am sure be to tell you what you already know to your own disappointment.

As Jose expected to have gone to Rye the monday after you left home, he engaged Baker to come here on sunday evening, where he has been till yesterday morning, the weather having been too inclement for him to go home; but he was unwell the whole time. Nancy & I prescribed for him as well as we could but he thought it best to go home & consult his Physician. The Rain, snow & frost hindered Joe not a little, for the wood was almost buried under the snow & Henry was unable to cut it or bring it in. He had likewise to cut wood & fetch water every day for Mrs. Clarke. We have regretted the long continuance of the bad weather the more as it will delay your return. It is however a great blessing that we have none of us taken cold, but retain our usual share of health.

There are several letters here for you, among them is one from Munro, your son & Augustus V Cortlandt. A week ago I recd. another letter from Mrs. Hamilton [a servant] letting me know she should remain where she was & was ready to wait upon me whenever I shd. point out the mode for her coming, & offered to serve us at 7 dollrs. pr. month, to which I defer'd an answer until I shd. hear from our daughter. Last eveng. I had the pleasure of receiving a letter from her. She as well as Banyer & Wm. were well & desir'd their love to you. The Patroon had gone to Washington, but Westerlo upon being applied to by Banyer, call'd upon Maria & told her Mrs. H would not suit us by any means. He added that she had taken up her wages of the Overseer & left the Patroon without ever apprising any of the family of it. I have therefore this morning written a few lines to her in answer to her last letter, letting her know that I should not have occasion for her.

**Philip Hamilton, son of Alexander Hamilton, was killed in a duel on November 23, 1801.*

Nancy & I think it would be worth while to advertise for one that would come to us the 1st of May, if you think proper, perhaps one might apply while you are in town. From the woman Sam mentioned we have not heard any thing. Sam's Wife & Children are well. Barbary sleeps there every night. Ann tells me to remind you of tobacco for she says it is nearly out. I just now sent for Jose & told him I was writing to you, & wish'd to know if he wanted any directions from you about any thing. He told me he did, for that he had plained all the pales & did not know what further to do with them. I told him, I had understood that you intended to get Tracy or Luther to cut a pattern for him, & to give him directions about them; & that I had heard you say they were to be like those at Rye. He said he had seen those, & would tell the Carpenters how they were cut. I asked him if he had cut the tree you had mentioned to him for rails, he said he had, & that this morning he had been trying to draw up a log for more pales but that the team he then had was too weak.

The Major has call'd here several times. Give our united love to Peter & Peggy & your son & accept the same from your Children & myself. I am my dr. Mr. Jay

sincerely & affectionately yours
Sa. Jay

Jose just brt. me a pattern to look at which James had cut, I thought it very handsome, but I advised him to wait for Tracy or Luther (who were gone to Cantito) as you had probably given them some directions. Joe is delighted with the work.

Tuesday evening.

Sam has just sent Joe in with yr. Letter. When Henry first told me of his arrival I was exceedingly alarmed. I am sorry you have been indisposed & am glad to find you are better & coming home. Do you think it worth while to send Sam to New York to carry Hannah when the stage passes your brother's door, & she might be put in with a letter to Munro.

I suppose Sam was uneasy because he left his wife without a stick cut at the Door, but the same day he went Joe went to cut wood & carry water for her & has done it ever since he went away. Remember us affectately. to Peter Polly & Effy. Ann wrote a letter to her Aunt 8 or 9 days ago when she expected Joe was going.

Altho' I shd. be very happy to see you, yet as Joe will have sufficient employ, & you are already half way on your Journey & besides will be still more wanted at home the latter end of this month & the beginning of the next I shd. not know what to advise but if you could borrow the sley, It might be as well to proceed. No servts. could have behaved better than ours have done.

Tell Peter if you please that we long very much to see him & Polly. A boy has just brt. in 5 quails which with a Couple of partridges I send to Polly.

Maria Jay, who had married Goldsborough Banyer, Jr. and lived in Albany, wrote this note on the back of the following letter: "From my dear Mother — The last letter she ever wrote me. She departed this life on the 18th [actually the 28th] of the same month." Amazingly, news of Sarah Jay's death did not reach Albany until

View of the Jay homestead at Bedford. Nineteenth century lithograph. John Jay Homestead State Historic Site. New York State Office Parks, Recreation and Historic Preservation (JJ.1980.206).

about a week after the event. At the time of their mother's death, Peter Augustus was 26, Maria was 20, Nancy 19, William 13, and Sarah Louisa 10.

Sarah Jay was interred in a vault at Saint Mark's in the Bowery, but later her remains were moved along with those of other family members to the Jay Family Cemetery in Rye.

(SLJ to her daughter Maria at New York) Bedford Wednesday 5th May 1802

My dear Maria,

The short time I've injoy'd the pleasure of your company seems but like a pleasant dream. Happy shd. I have been could your stay have been longer. In Augst. or Sepbr. I flatter myself we shall see you for a longer time, in the mean time finish all the business at New York so that if you shd. think proper you may only stay with us & not be obliged to go there again. I must beg, my Love, that you will not omit consulting a Physician about your side, & I request that you or your sister write me by the post, & let me know whether you continue to take the bark, & what effect it has, & whether your sister's tooth is cut & how she is. Tell her I shd. be sorry she shd. hurry herself, for she has left every thing in such good order that Sally keeps house without difficulty, & she behaves delightfully, so does William.

Your Papa's health is better to-day than usual. And I can with the greatest sincerity assure you that my health & appetite increases daily & that I really & truly feel very well indeed. Tell our dear Nancy so & tell her for her Comfort that Mrs. Johnson came here pretty early yesterday morning & that she & Mrs. H. began & finished the wash that same day & that Mrs. H. is ironing & Mrs. J. has cleaned the stairs & entry & is now cleaning the Piazza. Clarinda's health & spirits gradually improve & I do really believe in a few [days] she will be quite well. Notwithstanding she is better, I still wish you both to endeavor to procure another serv't for us.

Your Papa & the Children join me in affecte. remembrance to your Amiable husband, yourself, your sister, & Peter.... I am my dearest Children

your ever affectionate Mother
S. Jay

I wish Ann would buy a couple of small looking-glasses & put them in her trunk & likewise that she wd. inquire about the box that contained the lamps.

Obituary of Sarah Livingston Jay
From the *New York Herald*, Wednesday June 2, 1802

Died

At Bedford yesterday morning, after a short & severe illness, in the 45th year of her age, Mrs. Sarah Jay, the amiable & much respected wife of his Excellency John Jay, later Governor of this State, & one of the daughters of the late Governor Livingston deceased.

The language of eulogium on the dead is too common & too indiscriminate to entitle it always to respect. The writer of this feeble tribute to the memory of departed worth, cannot, however, but indulge the hope that when it meets the eye of living recollection, it will be allowed to be neither feigned nor exaggerated. All who had the happiness of an intimate acquaintance with Mrs. Jay, will bear testimony to the uncommon merits of the woman — the amiableness of the friend — the cheerful placid temper of the wife — the tenderness of the mother — the elegant accomplishments of the Lady — the unaffected piety of the Christian.

From an admiring world she chose to fly:
With nature there retir'd and nature's God,
The silent paths of wisdom trod,
And banish'd every passion from her breast,
But those the gentlest and the best,
Whose holy flames with energy divine
The virtuous heart enliven & improve,
The conjugal and the maternal love.

(Goldsborough Banyer Jr. to JJ at Bedford) Albany June 4th 1802

My dear Sir

On Tuesday Evening was presented to me by a Friend a New York Paper containing the truly distressing and afflicting Account of Mrs. Jay's death. I immediately after received Mr. Munro's Letter confirming the melancholly Event. How to impart this distressing news to my dear Maria added fresh Grief to my feelings; I however prepared her for the Shock in the best manner I could and at 11 oclock unfolded to her the truth. She has not yet left her Room but is more calm and composed and last Evening slept tolerably well. Most sincerely my good Sir do I condole with you all on this most distressing Event and God grant you may support the Calamity with fortitude and composure. Oh! that I could add a word of Comfort to your wounded Breasts, Judge of our feelings from your own. Be good enough to present our best wishes to Nancy Sally and William for whose feelings on this occasion do we also most sincerely Sympathize do let us hear from you soon and frequently a line now will be doubly welcome.

I am Dear Sir

Your affectionate
& humble Servt
Goldsbh Banyer Junr

(JJ to Rufus King at London) [Draft]

Bedford 20 Jany 1803

Dear Sir

I ought to have written to you long ago, but a Series of occurrences have for two years past, left me little Leisure for epistolary Correspondence. I allude to Mrs. Jay's long and painful Illness, and (when she appeared to be fast recovering) her unexpected Death. The Vicissitudes in my own Health, the Removal of my Family to this place, and the many Things to be done for their accommodation, the gradually increasing Indisposition of my son who is now on the Ocean going to Italy to avoid the winter here, &c. These are afflicting Circumstances; but considering where and what we are, Troubles of one kind or other, are to be expected and to be borne with Patience and Resignation.

My Expectations from Retiremt. have not been disappointed, and had Mrs. Jay continued with me, I should deem this the most agreable part of my Life. Many Blessings yet remain and I enjoy them.

The Post once a week brings me our news papers, which with those you are so kind as to send me, furnish a History of the Times. By this History as well as with those of former Times, we are taught the Vanity of expecting that from the Perfectibility of human nature & the Lights of Philosophy the multitude will become virtuous and wise, or their Demagogues candid and honest.

As G. Morris says "what is, is" and we must make the best of it. For the present they probably reason so in France. It would not however surprize me if future Irruptions from that Volcano, should again desolate some of the neighbouring Countries. Viewing the french Revolution as a Tragedy, I am inclined to think that we have only seen the <u>first</u> act concluded. You may live to see the <u>next</u>, but I shall doubtless by that Time be removed to a Theatre of a different kind.

Remember me to mrs. King to mr. & mrs. Gore, and to mr. Trumbull. With great Esteem and Regard I am

Dr. Sr.
Your most obt. Servt.

Not having had Leisure to visit New York since my Removal from Albany to this place I cannot give you any particular Information relative to our mutual Friends there. Judge Benson is again at the Bar, and I regret it. If these are not upside down Times, they certainly are up and down Times, but Athens the City of Philosophers, and Rome the City of every thing saw and felt much worse.

Epilogue

The family motto—*Deo Duce Perseverandum* "God leading we must persevere"—encapsulates the strong Christian faith so essential to the Jays. William Jay in later years recalled that, on the day his mother unexpectedly died, his father gathered the children together and "with a firm voice but glistening eye" read them the fifteenth chapter of First Corinthians, which deals with the resurrection. John's firm faith was a great solace to him. Still, Sarah's death left a great void. They had looked forward to life together at their Bedford farm: "had Mrs. Jay continued with me, I should deem this the most agreeable part of my life."

The work on the farm had only just begun, and John delighted in directing the improvements: planting trees, building the ha-ha (a landscaped stone wall), growing various crops, overseeing the cider-, grist- and saw-mills, and learning animal husbandry. The Bedford farm came to have many of the park-like qualities of an English country estate. John rose at daybreak, often going for a horseback ride before breakfast. Upon his return, everyone—family, visitors, servants, slaves—would join together for prayers; a similar gathering was held at nine in the evening. Always an avid reader, John's main study now was the Bible. Other tasks that engaged his energies were the support of St. Matthew's Episcopal Church in nearby Bedford and the American Bible Society.

As the years passed, he withdrew from the political scene, turning down offers of new duties by claiming ill health. Still, when the United States declared war on Great Britain in 1812, John felt that "the declaration of war was neither necessary, nor expedient, nor seasonable." He joined Gouverneur Morris and other political friends to explore the possibility of nominating peace candidates to a state convention. In his correspondence, religion, politics, and agriculture engaged his attention. Though he preferred to stay at home, John was delighted to have visitors, and many came to spend time with him. Morris "always came with his valet, was shown straight to his room without seeing any one, dressed himself with scrupulous nicety—being very particular about his powdered hair—and then came down to see his host" (Roosevelt 341). On one such occasion, while reviewing the events of the Revolution, Morris exclaimed: "Jay, what a Set of damned Scoundrels was had in the Second Congress."

And what of the Jay children? Peter Augustus Jay, on his doctor's advice, traveled to Europe in November 1802. While he was in Paris, Robert R. Livingston and

James Monroe entrusted him with bringing the Louisiana Purchase Treaty back to Congress. After living with his father for two years, his health restored, Peter resumed his law practice. On July 29, 1807, he married Mary R. Clarkson; they had eight children. In 1816, he was elected to the New York State Assembly and supported legislation for building the Erie Canal and for the abolition of slavery in New York. In 1821, Peter was a member of the convention to rewrite New York's Constitution. He and his family used the property at Rye (deeded to him by his father in 1822) as their summer home until 1838, when Peter tore down his grandfather's old homestead and constructed a large Greek Revival mansion. A trip to Madeira in the fall of 1838 failed to restore his wife Mary's health; she succumbed to her illness in December of that year. Peter died on February 22, 1843.

On the day of her mother's death, Maria Jay was not at Bedford. She had married Goldsborough Banyer, Jr., on April 22, 1801, and was living in Albany at her father-in-law's house. Two children were born to the young couple: Goldsborough and Sarah. Tragically, Maria lost her husband and both children within a three-year span. A devout woman though frequently in poor health, Maria spent her life taking care of others.

Nancy served as John Jay's hostess and housekeeper. An enthusiastic gardener, she also helped her father with the improvements on the property. After his death, she moved in with Maria. They traveled together, visited friends and relations, gave liberally to worthy causes, and died within nine days of each other in November 1856.

William began his law studies in the office of John B. Henry in Albany, but was forced to abandon them because of weak eyes. On September 4, 1812, he married Augusta McVickar; they had eight children, six of whom survived to adulthood. They lived with John Jay on the Bedford farm. William was named a judge of the court in Westchester County in 1818, a post he held until 1843, when he was removed by proslavery Democrats. He became a prolific writer on a variety of subjects: dueling, temperance, Sunday Schools, commentary on the Old and New Testaments. His biography of his father is disappointingly dry (as he himself admitted). William's voice was most passionate calling for the immediate abolition of slavery; he supported the establishment of the New York City Anti-Slavery Society. In the early 1840s, he was nominated for several political offices by the abolitionists but was defeated, in part by his own unwillingness to compromise on a party platform. His paper urging arbitration to settle international disputes moved his friend James Fenimore Cooper to call him "Thou most pugnacious man of peace." Augusta Jay died on April 26, 1857, and William on October 15, 1858. Frederick Douglass delivered his eulogy the following spring.

Kind-hearted, friendly, and helpful, Sarah Louisa was a great solace to her sister Maria. She attended the school of a Mr. Andrews in Albany and would "try & be an *ex-tra-or-di-nary* good girl" (1812). She seems to have had several suitors but did not marry. When visiting Bedford, she took pleasure in teaching her young nieces. After a short illness, she passed away in New York City on April 22, 1818.

Mention should be made of Peter Jay Munro. Though a nephew, he was treated like a son by John and Sarah Jay. After his return from France in 1784, he studied law in the office of Aaron Burr and became a highly regarded lawyer. In 1790, he married his cousin Margaret White. In 1821, Munro was elected to represent Westchester County at the New York Constitutional Convention and was appointed chairman of the judiciary committee. Ill health forced his retirement from active practice in 1826. He died at his home in Mamaroneck, New York, on September 23, 1833.

Upon John Jay's death on May 17, 1829, the Bedford farm was inherited by William. His son, John Jay II (1817–1894), a lawyer and active abolitionist as well as a diplomat, continued his father's work, improving the farm and making changes to the house. The property subsequently devolved upon William II (1841–1915), who saw service during the Civil War and became a lawyer. He was an accomplished horseman and a prominent member of New York society. His only surviving child, Eleanor Jay Iselin (1882–1953), was the last Jay family member to reside at the Bedford farm. Among the additions she made to the property were a prefabricated house for the workers and a new wing on the main house after part of it was destroyed by fire. After her death, the house, with some of the property, was purchased by Westchester County; in 1958, it became a New York State Historic Site. Now called The John Jay Homestead, it has been restored to what it might have been like during Jay's residence and is open to the public.

Appendix: Issues of Daily Life

The following short essays are intended to provide the reader with information concerning commonly held attitudes and practices with regard to several important topics of the time, as well as illustrations of how these figure specifically in the lives of the Jays as reflected in their correspondence.

Health and Medicine

One aspect of almost every letter written by Jay family members is the mention of health and health-related issues. John and Sarah Jay were constantly concerned about each other's health and that of their parents, children, friends and neighbors. Because they were so interested in this topic, readers may be curious to learn about health and medicine in the latter half of the eighteenth century: the training of medical doctors, diseases and health problems that were prevalent, and the kinds of treatment patients received.

Until the late eighteenth century, only a few doctors were graduates of medical schools, the most famous being the University of Edinburgh; more often they were men who had been apprenticed to a doctor for a minimum of seven years. One indenture agreement, for example, promised to teach the "art and mystery of physic, surgery, and pharmacy" (Ford 1). Doctors might also be pharmacists or apothecaries, making and dispensing their own medications; barbers often doubled as surgeons or dentists. Older women frequently served as midwives.

In fact, medical customs had not changed much since the time of Galen, a Greek physician (circa 200 B.C.), who taught that the four elements of earth, air, fire, and water made up the humors of the human body: blood, phlegm, yellow bile, and black bile. Blood was moist and warm, phlegm was moist and cool, yellow bile dry and warm, and black bile dry and cold. Sickness was thought to be caused by one or more of these humors being either impure or out of balance. Bleeding, purging or sweating was prescribed to relieve an excess or imbalance, while rest, diet, and medicine were believed to assist the patient in regaining health. Doctors dispensed drugs according to their qualities of being warm, cold, moist, or dry. Patent medicines abounded.

New York's doctors were highly regarded. By 1790, they had formed a Medical Society that agreed to a table of fees which included charges: "...for a visit with a single dose of medicine, $1.25; ... $1.00 to $5.00 for bleedings; ... $15 to $25 for an ordinary case of midwifery and $25 to $40 for a difficult or tedious case..." (as quoted in Monaghan and Lowenthal 86).

Dentists, unlike doctors, appear to have had little if any formal training. "They undertook to preserve the teeth and gums, make them adhere, remove tartar, cure 'scurvy in the gums,' destroy bad breath ...

and insert 'artificial teeth in so neat a manner as not to be perceived from the natural,'..." (as quoted in Monaghan and Lowenthal 88).

As doctors were beginning to understand the human body, they were also learning more about illness and disease. However, they were still mystified by the causes of disease and clung to age-old theories. The entire Jay family came down with "influenza" en route from Madrid to Paris. Sarah Jay wrote to sister Kitty (16 November 1782): "Mr. Jay has but tolerable health, a continual pain in his breast, the consequence of the influenza and too much application...." John Jay continued to suffer a pain in his chest almost the entire time he was in Europe. Did he have indigestion? pleurisy? pneumonia? consumption? He never knew for certain. In women, pregnancy was described as an "illness." Sarah Jay had a friend in Paris who was "ill" for only an hour and a half before a baby arrived! Children were particularly prone to sickness, often being victims of unexplained colds, sore throats and fever, whooping cough, chicken pox, measles, mumps, etc.

Time-honored methods of treatment included home remedies as well as doctor's prescriptions. Bleeding was the preferred method of treatment for a lengthy list of disorders. When John Jay was caught in the Doctors' Riot of 1788 and received two severe gashes in his head, his doctor bled him. One method of bleeding was simply cutting into a vein and allowing the blood to flow into a bowl. Another method of bleeding was "cupping," the practice of drawing blood to the surface of the body by using a heated glass cup or vessel.

Native herbs were popular remedies for many ailments. Quinine, known as "the bark," was given for fevers in general and was very successful in treating malaria. Another cure for a fever was blistering: mixing and mashing together irritants—for instance, mustard or another caustic — which was then spread on a cloth and applied to the skin in order to raise blisters. Opium and laudanum (a preparation of opium) were the only anesthetics in use.

Like many at that time, the Jays believed that they could obtain relief from various ailments by visiting mineral springs. Indeed, John Jay in 1783 "took the waters" in Bath, England, for the pain in his chest. Lebanon Springs, Saratoga Springs, and Ballston Springs in New York State were popular destinations where visitors drank the mineral water as well as bathed in it. Sarah often sought relief at Lebanon Springs.

Epidemics were the bane of the century: smallpox, dysentery, yellow fever, and malaria. With no antiseptics and little appreciation for proper sanitation, authorities instituted quarantines to control epidemics, keeping people out of cities or restricting their movement within an area. In the 1790s, doctors understood only that yellow fever occurred in summer, disappeared in cold weather, and could be partially controlled by limiting people's travel.

Although a vaccination for smallpox had been available in the early eighteenth century in Boston, a safer procedure was developed in England by the Drs. Sutton fifty years later. While in Paris, Sarah Jay took advantage of this new method by having her two little girls inoculated.

Despite the progress of medical science and the Jays' access to the very best medical care available, Sarah Jay became desperately ill in her early forties. She wrote to her daughter Maria (27 May 1801) of

> excessive heat in [her] back, extreme restlessness at night, notwithstanding increased doses of opium and decoction of small quantities of bark. The most serious simptom is extreme expectoration which the Dr. imputes to extreme relaxation, the lungs he says partaking of the general debility with a continuing feeble and fluctuating pulse.

What was Sarah's affliction? Was there one or several? Did the treatment she received improve her condition or make it worse? It is difficult to tell. Although she was visited by a number of doctors, she did not recover. According to her obituary, she died "after a short and severe illness in the 45th year of her age."

John Jay, who had fairly good health in

his retirement, lived to the ripe old age of 83. Perhaps his longevity was due to luck, perhaps it was genetic. It is not likely to have been due to his medical care.

Education

In the eighteenth century, American children received their earliest formal instruction in the three Rs—reading, 'riting and religion—at home. Education was viewed as important in all the colonies but especially in New England, perhaps due to the Puritan belief that literacy was essential to understanding the Word of God (Westerkamp 18). A literate person would not only expand the faith but would be a more responsible Christian member of society. In New York City, education was promoted by various denominations, among them the Dutch Reformed Church and the Anglican Church. Charity schools were organized to provide the rudiments of reading, writing and accounting that lower class children would need for their livelihoods. Formal schooling was of short duration—several months a year for three years at the most. Apprenticeship indentures were the norm after that. Less than one-quarter of all school-age children in New York City attended school during the 1770s; attendance was higher in rural areas (Klein 173). In general, Americans were more literate than their western European counterparts (Larkin 36). Beyond the essentials, it was left to mothers to instruct daughters in the household arts, to fathers to introduce sons to their trades.

Acquiring an education depended on social status and wealth. Only the elite could afford to "enlarge the Mind, improve the Understanding, polish the whole Man" as the Trustees of King's College proposed to do in 1754 (Columbia University Fact Book 9). A close look at the educational paths of John and Sarah Jay and their children offers insight into how upper class Americans attained these goals.

John Jay's first teacher was his mother, Mary Van Cortlandt; from her he learned reading and writing, in Latin as well as English. The Bible was essential reading, and the family worshipped together daily. At age seven, John was sent to a Huguenot school; after three years there, he was privately tutored at home to prepare for college. Peter Jay, pleased that John showed a predilection for books, hoped he would go into the ministry. When he opted for the law, John's father agreed as long as he would apply himself "very close to it, and if possible ... take a delight in it."

Having passed an oral exam, which included selections from Caesar's *Gallic Wars* in Latin, the Gospels in Greek, and some arithmetic, John Jay, aged 14, entered King's College. Latin, Greek, mathematics, and the study of "the Art of Reading and Speaking English with propriety and elegance" made up his course of study that first year. Later the works of authors such as John Locke, Plutarch, and Hugo Grotius would be added to his required reading. John also had to overcome a speech impediment; he seems to have had faulty diction and mispronounced the letter 'l'. With diligent practice, his elocution must have improved, for when he graduated in May 1764, he was much praised for his commencement address "On the Happiness & Advantages arising from a State of Peace" (Johnson 51).

Sarah was also educated at home, but she did not go to college. Her instruction was rigorous nonetheless, for her parents believed that an educated girl was an asset in a family and in a marriage. Her father, William Livingston, described the ideal: home life was to be cherished and women should be industrious, economical, and virtuous—in short "a crown to their husbands." Sarah was taught not only the three Rs, but also proper etiquette, dancing, and the domestic arts of sewing, knitting, and managing a household. As members of a political family, she and her sisters, Susan and Kitty, were deeply interested in the issues of the day. Kitty wrote of herself in a slightly mocking tone, "what a rage this girl has for politics." Such would not have been the case for most girls; they were expected to be amiable, gracious, frugal, and subservient to their husbands.

When it came time for John and Sarah

Jay to educate their own children, they followed the tenets of their parents. Peter Augustus Jay, born in January 1776, spent most of his early years with his maternal grandparents. He was less than two years old when his father wrote: "I wish to see him possess a sound mind in a sound Body, and to grow up free from those unreasonable Humors & Impertinencies by which favourite Children are too often distinguished" (21 December 1777). After John and Sarah sailed for Europe, they relied on William Livingston and his daughter Susan to guide Peter's schooling. As soon as he was old enough to hold a quill pen, his aunt would move his fingers across the page: "You must not have so bad an opinion of little P as to think he loves money better than his book, no, no, Grandpapa, I have learnt three or four lessons in my primmer that you sent & I know a great deal of my catechism already" (30 January 1781).

From abroad, the Jays occasionally suggested the course of study their son should follow: academics were important, but so was exercise. John wrote to Kitty: "remember that he is not a Girl, and that an untanned Face is one of the last Things which will recommend him to me or to others.... Idleness is too agreeable to human nature to be indulged without Risque, and Habits of application are best acquired in Youth. Let him at least rise with the Sun" (November 1780). He wrote Peter: "Study in earnest when you study, and play in earnest when you play. Do nothing by Halves" (8 April 1784).

At this time, John and Sarah had a more immediate influence on the education of her 23-year-old brother, Brockholst, and on John's 13-year-old nephew, Peter Jay Munro. John felt that while in Europe his brother-in-law "might perfect himself in two useful languages, gain a knowledge of mankind, form useful connections, and at the same time make such a proficiency in the study of the Law as might ennable him with a little practice on our return to make himself master of it" (24 June 1781). Brockholst had tutors for Spanish and French, with the result that he became fluent in both languages. Sarah also had a Spanish tutor. Once in France, young Munro was sent to a boarding school in Passy; his best friend there was John Quincy Adams. John Jay, while acknowledging the importance of studying foreign languages, came to feel that an American education was preferable to a European one. "I think the Youth of every free, civilized Country should if possible be educated in it, and not permitted to travel out of it till age has made them so cool and firm as to retain their national and moral Impressions" (13 October 1782).

Upon John and Sarah's return to New York, the education of their three children was of primary concern. William Livingston kept his hand in, writing his grandson a letter in Latin, expecting one in return. John wrote him: "Peter has begun his Latin Letter but the apprehension of not being able to write one that you wd. approve seems to make him procrastinate more than I think he would otherwise do" (11 February 1788). Moreover, another course of study had been added: "A drawing master attends him every Day, and he appears to have Taste & Talent for that art." Peter's young sisters were not neglected. Sarah taught them to read and write.

The children were praised for good penmanship — an essential accomplishment — and for punctuality in answering letters. Sarah wrote her daughters: "The punctuality, & attention to the manner of writing & spelling which you have discovered, evince your grateful obedience. Continue my dear Children to observe the directions of your Parents & your own satisfaction will equal that of ours" (22 May 1793). Monsieur Martel was their French tutor. Nancy took piano lessons but showed little interest in it, and Maria had a drawing master. Dancing lessons rounded out their instruction.

Maria was so intent on her education that in October 1794 she asked permission to attend the Moravian Young Ladies Seminary (founded in 1742) in Bethlehem, Pennsylvania. Her course of study there included not only languages, history, geography, arithmetic, and religious studies but also sewing, knitting and music. Maria was happy at the school and stayed two years. Nancy also attended the school for a year.

Peter graduated from Columbia College (formerly King's College) in 1794, traveled with his father to London that same year to broaden his education, and, once home again, began his legal studies in his cousin Munro's law office. Maria and Nancy finished at the school in Pennsylvania. But there were still two young children at home: William and Sarah Louisa. "Little Wig" was a "vigorous, sturdy boy, full of health & animation, with laughing eyes, cheeks glowing and dimpled ... with a strong will." His little sister was his close companion; they shared their mother's time, love, and precepts. Now that Sarah's health was less robust, it is likely that Maria and Nancy assisted her in their siblings' education.

When William was eight, he was placed in the school of the Reverend Thomas Ellison, rector of St. Peter's Church in Albany. A schoolmate, James Fenimore Cooper, described their education as "an old-fashioned training." William complained, "I learn nothing but Latin" (1799), but later boasted: "Mr. Ellison put me in Virgil, and I can now say the first two eclogues by heart, and construe and parse and scan them" (1801). After being privately tutored, William entered Yale College in January 1804, receiving his degree in September 1807. He returned to Albany to work in a law firm, but weak eyes forced him to give it up.

Sarah's death in May 1802 was not only a shattering blow to the family but also drastically altered the course of Sarah Louisa's education. Her father, settling in at his Bedford farm, turned to his older daughters: Nancy took on her mother's role as hostess and housekeeper, and Maria, Sarah Louisa's education. John clearly had confidence in Maria's oversight but did inquire of his youngest daughter about her course of study: "What Progress have you made in History, Geography and Arithmetic? Drawing Dancing and music I presume are not neglected. All these things deserve a Degree of attention proportionate to their Importance — air and Exercise being essential to health, and Health being the most valuable of temporal Blessings, are not to be disregarded" (8 February 1807). Sarah Louisa increasingly occupied herself with domestic tasks and doing good works within her church community. She seems to have become a kind and virtuous young woman: Grandfather Livingston would have been proud of her!

John Jay strongly believed that the new nation would be better served if its people were educated: a proper education should be available to all and at a reasonable cost. From Paris, he wrote the Reverend John Witherspoon, president of the College of New Jersey (later Princeton University): "The public with us, are in my opinion so deeply interested in the Education of our Citizens, that universities &c ought no longer to be regarded in the Light of mere private Corporations. The Governmt. should extend to them their constant Care, and the State Treasuries afford them necessary Supplies" (6 April 1784).

There is no doubt that John and Sarah Jay, like their parents, took the education of children very seriously. John wrote (22 December 1788):

> Whether Children will prove Comforts or Thorns to their parents, cannot be foreseen, nature certainly has much Influence, and so have Education and Example. The first is not under our Controul, but the two latter depend greatly on our Cares and if mine disappoint my Hopes, it shall not be for want of that Care.

Religion

Approaching by ship, a visitor's first glimpse of New York City in the 1730s would have been of a skyline dotted with church spires: Trinity Church, the Lutheran Church, the New Dutch Church, the Eglise du St.Esprit, the Old Dutch Church, and the church in Fort George on the Battery. Once ashore, he would have been able to worship with other congregations as well: Baptist, Congregational, Jewish, Quaker, to name but a few.

Immigration and economic growth had contributed to this religious pluralism (Bonomi 1986,132). New arrivals brought not only their cultural traditions from their homelands but also their religious teachings. By and large, these were rooted in dissenting Protestantism, key elements of which were the acceptance of the Bible as the Word of God, the belief that a Christian could live by faith alone, and the emphasis on the "priesthood of all believers." Not only did Protestants reject Roman Catholic dogma, they also continued to be suspicious of priestly control of the laity (Schouler 242). The Reformation had seen the emergence of the state as the institution overseeing the teachings and doctrines of Christian worship. In England, the government had established the Church of England; in Scandinavia, the Netherlands, and parts of Germany, state churches had also dictated the rituals and beliefs of Christian worship (Butler 1990, 10–11). Even in France, the Edict of Nantes (1598) had defined the rights of Protestants, though these privileges were short-lived.

In the colonies, diversity of belief was tolerated in varying degrees, not from principle but from practicality. William Penn encouraged "religion of all sorts" in Pennsylvania so that political and religious freedom could flourish. In the other colonies, however, Catholicism was suspect, the papacy being viewed as foreign and tyrannical.

The Anglican Church was particularly eager to proselytize, setting up the Society for Promoting Christian Knowledge (1699), which provided books and religious tracts, and the Society for the Propagation of the Gospel in Foreign Parts (1701), for the purpose of promoting Christianity in the New World (Butler 1990, 34). In New York, Anglicanism prospered; its first church, Trinity, was chartered in 1697. Within 50 years, the Anglican Church had expanded sufficiently to propose building a college on farmland it would donate for that purpose. A public lottery to raise the necessary funds was authorized in 1746 but drew protests from leaders of other denominations, who opposed a strictly Anglican school. The trustees of the new King's College agreed that, though the president would be an Anglican and services at the college would be conducted in the liturgy of the Church of England, "diversity would not be denied" (Gaustad and Schmidt 81).

By the 1760s, the power of the Anglican Church was such as to alarm many colonists. The appointment of Anglicans to provincial councils and judicial offices aroused their ire as well. When it was suggested that an Anglican bishop be sent from England to instill the principles of submission and loyalty, other denominations mounted furious protests (Bonomi 1986, 203). For over a year (1768–July 1769), newspapers fulminated against the Anglican desire to crush the rights of dissenters. Episcopacy and unquestioning obedience to the government came under attack by no less a public figure than the lawyer William Livingston, a Presbyterian. The Stamp Act had attempted to curtail the rights of the colonists, and now the Anglican Church was encroaching on their religious liberties. The worst fears of the colonists were realized when the English government recognized the Catholic Church in the French territories of Canada (Quebec Act of 1774), an action widely perceived as a threat, both to American Protestantism and to American political freedoms (Butler 1990, 199).

As tensions between England and the colonies escalated on the political front, clergymen of all denominations took to their pulpits. The Presbyterian minister John Rodgers called on his listeners to "put on the honor of your country and the cities of our God" and to show "the spirit of Englishmen" to defend "your inestimable privileges" (14 January 1776). The conservative Presbyterian clergyman John Witherspoon was elected to the Continental Congress and was a signer of the Declaration of Independence. Patriot Samuel Adams, a Congregationalist, denounced popery and the monarchy as the foes of popular freedom (Schouler 243).

However, the tradition of acquiescence to authority and obedience to the church silenced others. Fear of discrimination was widespread. Many colonists had come to America fleeing repression, and its perils had not been forgotten. Moreover, people of various faiths in the colonies had been harassed for doctrines of neutrality or pacifism.

Although the colonists viewed the domination of the Anglican Church and the English government as usurping their rights, the Declaration of Independence does not cite a single religious issue in the list of grievances against the British Crown (Butler 1990, 196). Nor do the Articles of Confederation include any express mention of the religious rights of citizens. It was clearly expected that the doctrinal diversity that existed would be maintained.

What was John Jay's view? Certainly he believed that liberty of conscience was not to be jeopardized. It was the great diversity of faiths represented by the members of the first Continental Congress that moved him to object on September 5, 1774, when it was proposed that the sessions open with a prayer. Congregationalist Samuel Adams spoke up, maintaining that he would have no objection to hearing an Episcopalian clergyman; in consequence, Congress did indeed appoint a chaplain.

Though his forebears were French Huguenots, Jay was brought up in the Church of England. His grandfather, Auguste Jay, had fled France to escape persecution and settled in New York City ca.1688. Like so many other Huguenots in the colonies, he was quickly assimilated into New York society (Butler 1983, 193). Following a clerical dispute at the French Church where he was an elder, in 1725, Auguste left and joined Trinity Church. John was baptized there. His older sister Eve, however, had been baptized in the Dutch Reformed Church, the church of her maternal grandparents, the Van Cortlandts. John's family life thus mirrors in a small way the religious diversity of New York. He was truly a product of his time.

Most likely John Jay's antagonism to Roman Catholicism stemmed from his Protestant roots; that his ancestors had been driven from their home in La Rochelle, France, for their religious beliefs may have played a part as well. Announcing the imminent birth of his daughter Ann in Paris, Jay wrote wryly to his friend Robert R. Livingston: "If People in Heaven see what is going on here below, my ancestors must derive Pleasure from comparing the Circumstances attending the Expulsion of some of them from this Country, with those under which my Family will be encreased in it" (19 July 1783).

His hostility to Roman Catholicism motivated Jay to introduce two amendments to the New York Constitutional Convention on March 20 and 21, 1777, that would have denied the property and civil rights of Catholics unless they took an oath renouncing the authority of the papacy. When he did not prevail, Jay introduced a third amendment proposing that "the liberty of conscience hereby granted, shall not be construed to encourage licentiousness, or be used in such manner as to disturb or endanger the safety of the State." This, modified by the Convention, was adopted. Furthermore, he was successful in having a stipulation inserted that "all Persons holding Offices under the Government should swear allegiance to it, and renounce all allegiance and Subjection to foreign Kings Princes and States in all matters ecclesiastical as well as civil" (29 April 1777).

Jay's belief in an omniscient Providence was shared by his wife Sarah. Her letters reflect a calm acceptance of God's plan and the certainty of His care and protection. During the gale that battered the ship *Confederacy* in late December 1779, she admitted: "I gave fear to the winds & chearfully resign'd myself to the dispensations of the Almighty." Sarah educated her children to be moral and caring Christians. Living in America, it is likely that she attended church regularly but, in Paris, she lamented that there was no public worship — other than Catholicism —for Americans. "Besides there are likewise some young Americans here for their Education and it really distresses me that they should be brought up without any idea of religion. Being unprejudiced they see the absurdity of many things taught in their school, but they have none to direct them right" was her astute comment to her sister Kitty (14 December 1782).

Sarah was perhaps more accepting of different points of view than was her husband. Her close friend in Paris was Adrienne de Nouailles, Marquise de la Fayette, a

Catholic. At home in New York, she entertained people of many faiths: the Dutch Reformed clergyman John Henry Livingston; Episcopalian Benjamin Moore; Presbyterians John Mason, Hugh Williamson, and John Rodgers; Quaker Samuel Franklin; and Samuel Provoost, rector of Trinity Church and the chaplain of the United States Senate in 1789. The Spanish minister, Don Diego de Gardoqui (who laid the cornerstone of the first Roman Catholic Church in New York, St. Peter's, in 1785) was a frequent guest as well.

John Jay's deep faith was based on a life-long study of the Bible. He advised his son Peter (8 April 1784) "to read it, and to regulate your Life by its precepts." He himself had done so, and was guided by "acquiescence in and resignation to the will of God." As he matured from a cautious New York lawyer into a national figure, Jay would do his duty to his country with God's help.

Slavery

On December 28, 1779, Captain Joseph Hardy, in command of the marines on board the *Confederacy*, sat at a table, writing in a neat hand about his canoe trip into St. Pierre's, Martinique. The canoes, he wrote:

> are rowed by five or six Negroes whose Lives appear to be as wretched as any part of the Human race. some of them are chained by one leg to the Boat and others shew the stripes of cruelty on their Body's in this manner these unhappy Mortals row in these Boats for Weeks without 10 hours intermission and as Naked as the moment of their Birth not even the Galley Slave in Barbary is more miserable.

Others on shore, he continues, have to drag 50 or 60 pounds of chain while performing their duties. Hardy's fellow traveler, John Jay, perhaps moved by these sights, purchased a young man of 15 named Benoit, who was to serve him faithfully during his stay in Europe. On March 21, 1784, Jay drew up a conditional manumission document: "whereas the Children of Men are by Nature equally free, and cannot without Injustice be either reduced to, or held in Slavery," he promises that Benoit will be "a Free Man" once he has served Jay "until the Value of his Services amount to a moderate Compensation for the money expended for him." This purchase of a slave and his promised manumission clearly demonstrate how inconsistent the Jays and other Americans were in dealing with slavery.

During the eighteenth century, Great Britain was the leading slave-trading nation, and New York City was a major slave-trading port — second only to Charleston, South Carolina. Slave ownership in New York was widespread among the general population: wealthy merchants as well as bakers, wheelwrights, artisans, and many others often owned at least one slave. Slavery was not just a Southern phenomenon.

In the 1760s, John Jay's father, Peter, owned 10 to12 slaves who worked as field hands and household servants. In 1742, one of his slaves, named Brash, had been committed to jail for his part in the "Negro Plot Conspiracy." Brash, unlike many other accused slaves who were executed, was transported to Madeira. Peter Jay's ownership of slaves was small when compared to the Livingston or Philipse families, whose slaves numbered in the hundreds.

John Jay therefore grew up in a society that tolerated owning slaves; slavery was thought an economic necessity. Other prevalent forms of servitude were apprenticeships and indentures, but these usually had a time limit. Slavery was for life. It is probable that Peter Jay took care of his slaves. In 1764, he arranged for a young slave girl, Mercy, to be inoculated against the smallpox. Having had two of his children blinded by that disease, he was only too well aware of what could happen if he did not tend to his servants as well as his family: a sick or disabled slave was of little use. One of John Jay's friends, the theologian and teacher Timothy Dwight, might have been describing the plight of the Jay slaves in his anti-slavery poem "Greenfield Hill," published in 1794:

> He never, dragg'd, with groans, the galling chain; ...

But kindly fed, and clad, and treated, ...
Lost liberty his sole, peculiar ill,
And fix'd submission to another's will [Basker 468].

It was in this atmosphere that John Jay's views on slavery slowly evolved from tacit acceptance to Christian denial. Just as John's commitment to the rebel cause took shape gradually, so did his ideas on human bondage. Viewing themselves as slaves deprived of liberty by the Mother Country, the rebels were faced with the dichotomy of being enslaved and enslaving at the same time. How to reconcile this contradiction? The Declaration of Independence initially called for the immediate discontinuation of the slave trade, but political pressures by slave owners made sure that this article did not survive the first draft. The principles of the Enlightenment were stimulating ideas for a more humane society. Individuals such as the Quaker Anthony Benezet and the Methodist John Wesley joined others agitating for the abolition not only of the slave trade but also of slave labor. Petitions for manumission increased sharply after 1774. The slow-boiling ferment of anti-slavery thought certainly had an impact on John Jay and his wife. Pamphlets, poems, plays, tracts, and sermons would have been read by the couple, their families, and their friends.

Once hostilities broke out between the colonists and the British, slaves in New York gained some bargaining power. They could demand freedom for loyal service or, if denied, flee to the British army for asylum. The British general, Lord Dunmore, had enlisted runaway slaves in Virginia by promising them freedom. The Continental Army, at first loath to use black soldiers, eventually followed suit — except in South Carolina and Georgia — allowing them to serve in the rank and file. By the end of the war, more than 4,000 black soldiers had served in the Continental Army and many more in local militia. It is estimated that the British evacuated 14,000 former slaves.

From letters and other documents, we know many of the names of the slaves owned by the Jays over the years. In 1775, John's personal servant, Claas, is important enough for mention in a letter to Sarah. Claas travels everywhere with John, but in September 1779 he is no longer with Jay but is at a parson's home, and in April 1781 he is with Sir Henry Clinton's family. What happened? Had Claas been enticed by promises of freedom? From Europe, John wrote to his brother Frederick (3 October 1782), "If New York should be evacuated and Claas remain there, treat him kindly for his Mothers Sake." A year earlier, he had written to his brother: "As to old servants, who have expended their strength and youth for the family, they ought and must be taken good care of, while we have the means of doing it; common justice, and I may say gratitude, demands it." Here we see John Jay as slave owner.

But then comes John Jay as abolitionist, working on the New York State constitution in April 1777, voicing support for "a Clause against the Continuation of domestic Slavery." Unable to remain for deliberations due to his mother's final illness, Jay left it to his friend Gouverneur Morris to introduce a motion to abolish slavery in New York "consistent with the public safety, and the private property of individuals." The motion's defeat bothered Jay. Later, from abroad he wrote his good friend and fellow lawyer, Egbert Benson:

> An excellent Law might be made out of the Pennsylvanian one [passed March 1, 1780] for the gradual Abolition of Slavery. Till America comes into this measure her Prayers to Heaven for Liberty will be impious. This is a strong Expression but it is just. Were I in your Legislature I would prepare a Bill for the Purpose with great Care, and I would never cease moving it till it became a Law or I ceased to be a member.

That an intelligent man like Jay could react with such passionless caution to the cruel and degrading evil of slavery may seem strange to the modern reader. He was a right-thinking man who had to overcome his patrician heritage. Slowly he moved ahead, founding with others the "Society for Promoting the Manumission of Slaves, and Protecting such of them as have been or may be Liberated" in 1785. Jay served as its first president. Two years later, he helped found the African Free School, which he supported financially for many years. As governor of New York State, John Jay was able to enact a law for the gradual abolition of slavery, though it would not end until 1827. The terms of the law were that, from July 4, 1799, all children born to slave parents would be freed after serving the mother's owner until age 28 (for men) or 25 (for women). Jay saw the horrors of slavery and could write in 1786 that the "Condition of Slaves in this State is far more tolerable and easy than in many other Countries." He recognized the inconsistency, excusing slavery on the grounds that "the great body of our people had been so long accustomed" to it. Surely he was speaking for himself.

John Jay saw offenses to humanity elsewhere as well. He wrote to Thomas Jefferson (14 December 1786): "In my Opinion our Indian Affairs have been ill managed.... Indians have been murdered by our People in cold Blood and no Satisfaction given, nor are they pleased with the Avidity with which we seek to acquire their Lands." On an intellectual level, he acknowledged the existence of injustice. As a devout Christian, he regarded one man holding another in servitude as a sin. As an astute politician, he grappled with the hypocrisy of demanding liberty for one segment of the American people while denying it to another, solely on the basis of skin color. On a personal level, however, he and his extended family were dependent on their servants.

Abbe, a slave belonging to William Livingston, went to Europe with the Jays. She left a husband at home. While in Spain, Sarah Jay wrote home, praising Abbe: "The attention & proofs of fidelity which we have receiv'd from Abbe, demand, & ever shall have my acknowledgements" (28 August 1780). She was irreplaceable. Apparently always a bit spirited, Abbe left the Jay household while in Paris in early November 1783, possibly lured away by an offer of pay from a washerwoman. At the suggestion of Benjamin Franklin, Abbe was incarcerated, in the hope of bringing her to a more acquiescent state of mind. Although Jay urged his wife to "suspend all attention" to Abbe, Sarah sent Peter Jay Munro several times to the jail to persuade her to come home — to no avail. On December 7, Sarah wrote William Temple Franklin requesting that he arrange for Abbe's release, as she was "very ill and extremely anxious to return." Once Sarah paid the jail expenses of 60 livres, Abbe came back to the Jay household. However, she did not recover from her illness and died in mid–December. John wrote Sarah: "I lament Abbe's Death ... I am persuaded of your attention to her, and think with you, that her being at Home, and well taken Care of, are Circumstances of Consolation" (26 December 1783). He had planned to manumit Abbe once they were back in America. Perhaps the manumission document for Benoit, Abbe's colleague and friend, was a substitute for what might have been. Interestingly, it is unknown what happened to Benoit when the Jays left Paris.

On returning to New York City, the Jay family found they had inherited slaves from Peter Jay. At least one slave, Peter Robertson, belonging to Frederick Jay, had left him in 1779 and had gone behind British lines. The "Book of Negroes" lists him on 31 October 1783 evacuated from New York, bound for Nova Scotia. But there had also been economic changes: servants now could be hired for a wage, without the costs of clothing, board, and medical care that slaves incurred. A frazzled Frederick Jay had informed John that Old and Young Platt, a boy (possibly named Lewis), and Kingston (Sir James Jay's slave) were working in Fishkill. Zilpha and Old Plato had been freed but elected to stay on as paid servants. Susan and Moll were boarded elsewhere. Younger Mary had been hired out; another Mary could choose with which Jay family member she wished to live; another slave named Plato had been willed to John, and Clarinda was sold.

The statement "Clarinda is sold" is a bald one, and shocking. At this time, slaves were "rented" to other owners for a limited period, after which the slave returned to the original family. Such seems to be the case for

Clarinda; she came back to the Jay household, married a man named Pompey, and had two children, David (who died young) and Zilpah. In the early 1790s, John acquired a slave named Peter Williams from Morgan Lewis; finding Peet "handy and attentive," John took him along on his circuits and to London in 1794. Jay wrote (24 May 1798), "Peter shall be free, if he serves faithfully seven years, as a compensation for Principal, Interest, and Risque, & those Expenses which hired Servants defray themselves." By then Peet was married and had a child.

In 1791, John Jay wrote to his son, Peter A. Jay, "They are Servants, but they are Men, and Kindness to Inferiors more strongly indicates Magnanimity than Meanness." It seems that the Jays treated their slaves well; that they bought and sold or placed slaves with other owners is also true. The New York Census of 1790 indicates that Frederick Jay owned four slaves, John owned five, and Peter in Rye owned nine. In 1810, John owned one slave (Clarinda), and in 1820, there were two black females in his household, who we know were Clarinda and her daughter Zilpah. They lived out their lives at the Jay farm. Zilpah, however, was not with the Jays from birth; in 1809, John, displeased with her behavior, had sold her to a relative. Her mother Clarinda was so adamant for her return that Jay hired her back by the month. Zilpah was manumitted in 1817. She outlived John as well as his son William. Her grave in St. Matthew's churchyard, Bedford, New York, is marked with a headstone provided for in William's will.

In 1813, John Jay's ledger book shows that he gave 47 dollars to a free black employee, Chester Tillitson, to enable him to purchase his nine-year-old son, also named Chester, from his owner. Did John expect or receive repayment? We do not know. On March 3, 1815, John hired as an indentured servant "Jack ... a free black Boy bound to me ... with the consent of his Father Caesar Pine ... I am to give him one Quarters Schooling in each Year, and at the Expiration of the said Term I am to give him Twenty Five Dollars."

Throughout their married life, John and Sarah Jay had white servants as well as black. Mary Brown, hired in Cadiz, worked for them during their stay in Spain. The nanny Louisson joined the family in Paris and traveled with the Jays to America. Mrs. Hamilton was a long-time housekeeper. Major Samuel Lyon was the manager of the Jay farm at Bedford. While her husband was in England in 1794, Sarah had occasion to chastise Major Lyon for not properly breaking some horses he had sent to New York City for her use. In an extraordinary diatribe, the Major, his pride hurt, asserted that he was ill-used, and closed the letter with "Madam altho I am Your Servant I am Not your Slave I was free born and as Such remain."

On October 1, 1798, John Jay, in Albany, submitted the following list of slaves between the ages of 12 and 50 in his possession: "I have three male and three female slaves—five of them are with me in this City; and one of them is in the City of New York. I purchase slaves and manumit them at proper ages, and when their faithful services shall have afforded a reasonable Retribution; but while the Property remains vested in me, I consider them as being within the Intent of the act of obedience to which this list is given." It would be left to William Jay to forge the path — not genteelly like his father but passionately — toward an immediate end of slavery.

Bibliography

A word about the letters selected for this volume: these are only the tip of an iceberg. The Jay family correspondence is extensive, broad in scope, and of long duration, as can be ascertained by reading the essential two-volume work (unfortunately unfinished) by Richard B. Morris or viewing the Papers of John Jay online at www.columbia.edu/cu/lweb/eresources/archives/jay. Moreover, not all of the letters written by John and Sarah arrived at their destinations, many being lost or stolen in transit. John Jay, like other Founding Fathers, carefully preserved his papers, but, ever prudent, at some point began to destroy letters he considered confidential or too personal. He states in his will: "I have greatly but not yet Sufficiently reduced their number." After his death, Jay's sons, Peter and William, also weeded out letters they did not deem worthy of preservation. Later family descendants gave Jay letters and books away as gifts. However, in 1957, Columbia University acquired about two thousand papers of John Jay from the estate of his great-great-granddaughter Eleanor Jay Iselin, and this collection has been augmented by other gifts and purchases.

All of the letters or quotations from letters in this volume belong to the John Jay Papers, Rare Book and Manuscript Library, Columbia University, with the following exceptions:

The Gilder Lehrman Collection, courtesy of the Gilder Lehrman Institute of American History, New York: GLC3107.04189. John Jay. ALS: to Robert R. Livingston, 26 Jan. 1776; and GLC 1220. John Jay. ALS: to Sarah Jay, 4 March 1776.

The Huntington Library, San Marino, California: HM 9963. Sarah Jay to Mary W. Morris, 25 Nov. 1782.

Formerly Collection Richard Maass: John Jay to Sarah Jay, 29 July 1776.

William Livingston Papers, Massachusetts Historical Society: William Livingston to Peter A. Jay, 13 Feb. 1783; John Jay to Catharine Livingston, 26 Aug. 1783; Peter A. Jay to William Livingston, 7 Apr. 1786.

William Livingston Papers II, Massachusetts Historical Society: John Jay and Sarah Jay to Susan Livingston, 16 March 1778; Henry Brockholst Livingston to Catharine Livingston, 4 June 1780; Henry Brockholst Livingston to Susannah French Livingston, 30 Apr. 1780; Sarah Jay to Catharine Livingston, 22 Nov. 1783; Sarah Jay to Susannah French Livingston, after 27 March 1788.

Matthew Ridley Papers, Massachusetts Historical Society: Gouverneur Morris to Catharine Livingston, 11 Jan. 1773; John Jay to Catharine Livingston, 8 Nov 1776; John Jay to Catharine Livingston, 17 Dec. 1780; M. Ridley to Catharine Livingston, 26 March 1783.

Matthew Ridley Papers II, Massachusetts Historical Society: John Jay and Sarah Jay to Catharine Livingston, 20 Jan. 1777; John Jay to Catharine Livingston, 21 Dec. 1777; John Jay to Catharine Livingston, 23 Nov. 1780.

Sedgwick Family Papers II, Massachusetts Historical Society: John Jay to Sarah Jay, 21 July 1776.

Museum of the City of New York: John Jay to Peter Jay, 29 Jan. 1781. Gift of Pierre Jay Wurtz, 32.421.1; John Quincy Adams to Peter Jay Munro, 4 Nov. 1783. Purchased with Funds from the Mrs. Elon Huntington Hooker Acquisition Fund, 42.315.225; Peter Jay Munro to John Jay, 12 Nov. 1783. Purchased with Funds from the Mrs. Elon Huntington Hooker Acquisition Fund, 42.315.127; Peter A. Jay to Peter Jay Munro, 2 Jan. 1795. Purchased with Funds from the Mrs. Elon Huntington Hooker Acquisition Fund, 42.315.195.

The New-York Historical Society: John Jay to Margaret C. Meredith, 12 May 1780, B. V. Croaker; John Jay to Robert R. Livingston, 23 May 1780 and 14 June 1782, Robert R. Livingston Papers; John Jay to Sarah Jay, 13 March 1795, B.V. Ide, John Jay; Strickland Diary quotation, B. V. Strickland, William, Vol. 15, p. 344–345.

The New York Public Library, William Livingston Papers, Manuscript and Archives Division, The New York Public Library, Astor, Lenox and Tilden Foundations: Henry Brockholst Livingston to William Livingston, 5 May 1780 and 12 July 1780; Peter A. Jay to William Livingston, 30 Jan. 1781.

New York State Library/Manuscripts and Special Collections: 23 Dec. 1775. Single Accession 13684; 18 Jan. 1779. Single Accession 13685.

New York State Office of Parks, Recreation, and Historic Preservation. John Jay Homestead State Historic Site: Page from Invitations to Supper & Dinner, 10 Jan. 1788 (JJ.2002.1); Peter A. Jay to Ann Jay, 8 Nov. 1794.

Kenneth W. Rendell Inc.: John Jay to Samuel Shaw, 30 Jan. 1786; John Jay to Sarah Jay, 12 Dec. 1790; 13 May 1794; 2 Oct. 1794.

Westchester County Historical Society: John Jay to Sarah Jay, 21 Nov. 1794.

Wisconsin Historical Society: John Jay to Sarah Jay, 3 July 1777.

The following letters were found in published works (see Books section following) by:

Giunta, Mary A., editor-in-chief National Historical Publications and Records Commission: 28 Feb. 1786; 3 March 1786.

Jay, William, vol. II: 6 July 1777.

Johnston, Henry P.: 21 June 1788; 5 July 1788; 16 July 1788; 10 Nov. 1790; 18 June 1792; 9–10 April 1794; 15 April 1794; 19 April 1794 (George Washington to John Jay); 21 June 1794.

Livingston, William: 14 Dec. 1778.

Monaghan, Frank, p. 55: 29 June 1774.

Pellew, George, pp. 105–6: 5 March 1779; 17 March 1779.

Books

Bard, Samuel, M.D. *A Discourse on the Duties of a Physician*. New York: A. & J. Robertson, 1769. Reprint Bedford, MA: Applewood Books, 1996.

Basker, James G., ed. *Amazing Grace: An Anthology of Poems about Slavery, 1660–1810*. New Haven: Yale University Press, 2002.

Bayard, Martha Pintard. *Journal of Martha Pintard Bayard, London 1794–1797*, Dod, S. Bayard, ed. New York: Dodd, Mead, 1894.

Behrman, Howard T., M.D. "John Jay's 'Pimple', A Medical Puzzle." *Journal for Dermatologic Surgery and Oncology* 4:2 February (1978): 150–152.

Bonomi, Patricia U. "John Jay, Religion, and the State." *New York History* 81 (2000): 9–18.

_____. *Under the Cope of Heaven: Religion, Society, and Politics in Colonial America*. New York: Oxford University Press, 1986.

Brecher, Frank W. *Securing American Independence: John Jay and the French Alliance*. Westport, Conn.: Greenwood Press, 2003.

_____. *Losing a Continent: France's North American Policy 1753–1763*. Westport, Conn.: Greenwood Press, 1998.

Bushman, Richard L. *The Refinement of America: Persons, Houses, Cities*. New York: Alfred A. Knopf, 1992.

Butler, Jon. *Awash in a Sea of Faith: Christianizing the American People*. Cambridge, Mass.: Harvard University Press, 1990.

_____. *The Huguenots in America: A Refugee People in New World Society*. Cambridge, Mass.: Harvard University Press, 1983.

Carmichael, Ann G., and Richard M. Rastzan, eds. *Medicine: A Treasury of Art and Literature*. New York: Beaux Arts Editions, Hugh Lauter Levin Associates, 1991.

Clinton, George. *Public Papers of George Clinton, First Governor of New York*. Published by the State of New York. Albany: Wynkoop Hallenbeck Crawford, 1899.

Columbia University Fact Book 1997–1998. Office of University Development and Alumni Relations, 1997.

Cousins, Norman, ed. *"In God We Trust": The Religious Beliefs and Ideas of the American Founding Fathers*. New York: Harper & Brothers, 1958.

Davis, Curtis C. *The King's Cavalier: A Biography of Lewis Littlepage*. New York: Bobbs-Merrill, 1961.

De Pauw, Linda Grant. *Founding Mothers: Women of America in the Revolutionary Era*. Boston: Houghton Mifflin, 1975.

Drinker, Elizabeth. *The Diary of Elizabeth Drinker*, Crane, Elaine F., ed. Boston: Northeastern University Press, 1994.

Duncombe, Frances. R. *Katonah: The History of a New York Village and Its People*. Katonah, N.Y.: Katonah Village Improvement Society (Centennial Edition), 1996.

Duyckinck, Evert A. *Portrait Gallery of Eminent Men and Women*. New York: Johnson, Fry, 1872–1874.

Ellet, Mrs. Elizabeth Fries. *The Queens of American Society*. Philadelphia: Porter & Coats, 1867 (the chapter on Sarah Jay is purportedly written by John Jay II).

Estes, J. Worth, M.D. "Medical Care in the New Republic: The Example of John Jay and His Family." Paper delivered at the John Jay Homestead, Katonah, N.Y. Oct. 30, 1983.

Fenn, Elizabeth A. *Pox Americana*. New York: Hill and Wang, 2001.

Flick, Alexander C., ed. *The American Revolution in New York: Its Political, Social and Economic Significance*. Port Washington, N.Y.: Ira J. Friedman, 1967.

Ford, Thomas K. "The Apothecary in Eighteenth-Century Williamsburg." Williamsburg, VA: Colonial Williamsburg Publications, 1997 (based on *The Apothecary in Colonial Virginia* by Harold B. Gill, Jr., 1972).

Fuller, Wayne E. *The American Mail— Enlarger of the Common Life*. Chicago: University of Chicago Press, 1972.

Gaustad, Edwin S., and Leigh E. Schmidt. *The Religious History of America*. San Francisco: Harper, 2002.

Gellman, David N. "John and William Jay as Abolitionists." Lecture delivered at the John Jay Homestead, Fall, 2000.

_____. "John Jay, William Jay, and the Problem of American Slavery." SHEAR 25th Annual Meeting, Columbus, Ohio, July 18, 2003.

Giunta, Mary A., editor-in-chief. *Emerging Nation: A Documentary History of the Foreign Relations of the United States Under the Articles of Confederation 1780–1789*. Vols. I–III. [Washington, D.C.] National Historical Publications and Records Commission, 1996.

Hoffman, Ronald, and Peter J. Albert, eds. *Peacemakers: The Treaty of 1783*. Charlottesville: University Press of Virginia, 1986.

Horsmanden, Daniel. *The New York Conspiracy or a History of the Negro Plot of 1741*. Originally printed by James Parker, N.Y. in 1744. Reprint, Boston: Beacon Press, 1971.

Horton, Jan. "Listening for Clarinda." Research paper. The John Jay Homestead, Katonah, N.Y., 2000.

Howard, James L. *Seth Harding Mariner, a Naval Picture of the Revolution*. New Haven: Yale University Press, 1930.

Jackson, Kenneth T., ed. *The Encyclopedia of New York City*. New Haven: Yale University Press, 1995.

Jay, John. *Memorials of Peter A. Jay Compiled for His Descendants by His Great-Grandson John Jay*. ©1905. Printed for Private Circulation, 1929.

Jay, William. *The Life of John Jay*. 2 vols. New York: J. & J. Harper, 1833.

Johnson, Herbert A. "John Jay and the Supreme Court." *New York History* 81 (2000): 59–90.

_____. *John Jay 1745–1829*. University of the State of New York, revised edition, 1995.

_____. "When John Jay Was Jack." *Columbia College Today*. Spring & Summer (1963), 48–51.

Johnston, Henry P., ed. *Correspondence and Public Papers of John Jay 1763–1826*. 4 vols. New York: G. P. Putnam, 1890–1893.

Kaminski, John P. *George Clinton, Yeoman Politician of the New Republic*. Madison, Wisc.: Madison House Publications, 1993.

_____. "Honor and Interest, John Jay's Diplomacy During the Confederation." *New York History* (2002): 293–327.

_____. "Shall We Have a King? John Jay and the Politics of Union." *New York History* 81 (2000): 31–58.

Kaplan, Sidney. *The Black Presence in the Era of the American Revolution 1770–1800*. New York: New York Graphic Society, 1973.

Kerber, Linda K. *Women of the Republic, Intellect and Ideology in Revolutionary America*. Chapel Hill: University of North Carolina, 1980.

Kierner, Cynthia A. "From Entrepeneurs to Ornaments, the Livingston Women, 1679–1790." In *The Livingston Legacy: Three Centuries of American History,* edited by Richard C. Wiles. Bard College Office of Publications 1987.

Klein, Milton M. *The American Whig: William Livingston of New York*. New York: Garland, 1990.

_____, ed. *The Empire State A History of New York*. Ithaca: Cornell University Press, 2001.

_____. "John Jay and the Revolution." *New York History* 81 (2000): 19–30.

Klingelhofer, Herbert E. "Matthew Ridley's Diary During the Peace Negotiations of 1782." *William & Mary Quarterly* XX (1963): 95–133.

Langstaff, John B. *Dr. Bard of Hyde Park*. New York: E.P. Dutton, 1942.

Larkin, John. *The Reshaping of Everyday Life 1790–1840*. New York: Harper & Row, 1988.

Levy, Leonard W., and Dennis J. Mahoney, eds. *The Framing and Ratification of the Constitution*. New York: Macmillan, 1987.

Littlefield, Daniel C. "John Jay, the Revolutionary Generation, and Slavery." *New York History* 81 (2000): 91–132.

Livingston, William. *The Papers of William Livingston*, Prince, Carl E., ed. 5 vols. Trenton: New Jersey Historical Commission, 1979; Rutgers University Press, 1987.

McManus, Edgar J. *A History of Negro Slavery in New York*. Syracuse: Syracuse University Press, 1966 & 2001.

Monaghan, Frank. *John Jay, Defender of Liberty*. New York: Bobbs-Merrill, 1935.

_____, and Marvin Lowenthal. *This Was New York: The Nation's Capital in 1789*. Garden City, N.Y.: Doubleday, Doran, 1943.

Morris, Richard B. "The American Revolution Comes to John Jay." *Aspects of Early New York Society and Politics*, Tarrytown, N.Y. (1974): 96–117.

_____. "John Jay and the New England Connection." *Proceedings of the Massachusetts Historical Society* LXXX (1968): 16–37.

_____. *John Jay: The Making of a Revolutionary, Unpublished Papers 1745–1780*. New York: Harper & Row, 1975.

_____. *John Jay: The Winning of the Peace, Unpublished Papers 1780–1784*. New York: Harper & Row, 1980.

_____. *The Peacemakers: The Great Powers and American Independence*. New York: Harper & Row, 1965.

_____. *Seven Who Shaped Our Destiny*. New York: Harper & Row, 1973.

_____. *Witnesses at the Creation: Hamilton, Madison, Jay, and the Constitution*. New York: Holt, Rinehart & Winston, 1985.

National Maritime Museum, Greenwich, London, England. *1776: The British Story of the American Revolution*. April 14–Oct. 2, 1976.

Onuf, Peter S. *Jefferson's Empire: The Language of American Nationhood*. Charlottesville: University Press of Virginia, 2000.

Palmer, Gregory. *Biographical Sketches of Loyalists of the American Revolution*. Westport, Conn.: Meckler Press, 1984.

Pellew, George. *John Jay*. Boston: Houghton, Mifflin, 1890.

Piwonka, Ruth. *Portrait of Livingston Manor 1685–1850*. New York: Friends of Clermont, 1986.

Pomerantz, Sidney I. *New York, An American City 1783–1803: A Study of Urban Life*. New York: Columbia University Press, 1938.

Powell, Nowland Van. *The American Navies of the Revolutionary War.* New York: G.P. Putnam's Sons, 1974 (Introduction by Richard B. Morris.).

Reardon, John J. *Edmund Randolph: A Biography.* New York: Macmillan, 1975.

Roosevelt, Theodore. *Gouverneur Morris.* 1888. Reprint, New York: Haskell House, 1968.

Rousselot, Jean, ed. *Medicine in Art: A Cultural History.* New York: McGraw-Hill, 1967.

Scheele, Carl H. *A Short History of the Mail Service.* Washington, D.C.: Smithsonian Institute Press, 1970.

Schouler, James. *Americans of 1776: Daily Life in Revolutionary America.* Williamstown, Mass.: Corner House, 1984.

Smith, Paige. *John Adams.* 2 vols. New York: Doubleday, 1962.

Staff, Frank. *The Transatlantic Mail.* London: Harrap, 1956.

Stahr, Walter B. MS. copy *John Jay: Founding Father.* London: Hambeldon Press, 2005.

Strickland, William. *Journal of a Tour in the United States of America 1794–1795.* New York: The New-York Historical Society, 1971.

Swiggett, Howard. *The Extraordinary Mr. Morris.* New York: Doubleday, 1952.

Thornton, Tamara Platkin. *Handwriting in America, A Cultural History.* New Haven: Yale University Press, 1996.

Ward, Harry M. *The War for Independence and the Transformation of American Society.* London: University College London Press, 1999.

Wecter, Dixon. *The Saga of American Society: A Record of Social Aspiration 1607–1937.* New York: Charles Scribner's Sons, 1970.

Westerkamp, Marilyn J. *Women and Religion in Early America 1600–1850: The Puritan and Evangelical Traditions.* London & New York: Routledge, 1999.

Whalley, Joyce Irene. *Writing Implements and Accessories.* Detroit: Gale Research Company, 1975.

Wiencek, Henry. *An Imperfect God: George Washington, His slaves and the Creation of America.* New York: Farrar, Straus and Giroux, 2003.

Wilbur, C. Keith, M.D. *Revolutionary Medicine, 1700–1800.* Chester, Conn.: Globe Pequot Press, 1980.

Wiles, Richard C., ed. *The Livingston Legacy: Three Centuries of American History.* Symposium sponsored by the Friends of Clermont, Bard College/Hudson Valley Studies Program and the New York State Office of Parks, Recreations and Historic Preservation, Taconic Region June 6 & 7, 1986. Bard College Office of Publications, 1987.

Index

Numbers in *italics* refer to illustrations.

www.ingramcontent.com/pod-product-compliance
Lightning Source LLC
Chambersburg PA
CBHW081331090726
47907CB00011B/2448

* 9 7 8 0 7 8 6 4 4 5 0 4 2 *